POETRY: SIGHT AND INSIGHT

POETRY: SIGHT AND INSIGHT

JAMES W. KIRKLAND
East Carolina University

F. DAVID SANDERS
East Carolina University

Consulting Editor
Peter McCook

Random House　New York

First Edition
987654321

Copyright © 1982 by Random House, Inc.

All rights reserved under International and Pan-American Copyright Conventions. No part of this book may be reproduced in any form or by any means, electronic or mechanical, including photocopying, without permission in writing from the publisher. All inquiries should be addressed to Random House, Inc., 201 East 50th Street, New York, N.Y. 10022. Published in the United States by Random House, Inc., and simultaneously in Canada by Random House of Canada Limited, Toronto.

Library of Congress Cataloging in Publication Data

Kirkland, James W.
  Poetry, sight and insight.

  Includes index.
  1. Poetics. 2. English poetry. 3. American poetry. I. Sanders, F. David. II. Title.
PN1042.K53   808.1   81-11915
Student edition ISBN 0-394-32353-X   AACR2
Teacher's edition ISBN 0-394-32920-1

Manufactured in the United States of America.
Composed by American–Stratford Graphic Services, Inc., Brattleboro, Vt.
Printed and bound by R.R. Donnelly & Sons, Co., Harrisonburg, Va.
Production: Suzanne Loeb

Cover photograph: © Erich Hartmann/Magnum Photos

Cover design: Karin Gerdes-Kincheloe
Text design: Karin Gerdes-Kincheloe

Since this page cannot legibly accommodate all the copyright notices, pages 445–456 constitute an extension of the copyright page.

*To the memory of
Edwin Craig
and
Catherine Lillian Sanders*

PREFACE

Poetry: Sight and Insight is more than the usual encyclopedia of terms using poems as examples. Its emphasis is on the poems themselves; its purpose is to initiate students into the ways of reading poems.

The text has a three-part structure, which gives instructors a choice of method in using the book. With the exception of the first chapter, which deals with the relationship between the poet, the poem, and the reader, each of the chapters in Part I treats a different aspect of poetic technique. Each of these chapters begins with a headnote, which discusses five or six poems employing the technique and which aims at helping students enjoy the poems by understanding the concept and its supporting terms. Next comes a group of poems with questions that take the students through the works and focus on the concept of the chapter, followed by a selection of poems, without comment, for further reading and study. Because these concepts vary in complexity, some require fuller treatment than others. Chapter 9, *Formal Patterns,* for example, is especially long because it deals with three interrelated techniques that, in our view, cannot be fully understood in isolation from one another. In Parts II and III, on the other hand, poems are presented without editorial comments or chapter divisions. The number of poems in these two parts is substantial, but neither section is intended to be comprehensive. Many of the poems that would enrich the content of Part II or Part III appear elsewhere in the text, where they serve an equally important function; and others—including some of the best and most representative works of the Old and Middle English periods and those of the Restoration and of the Eighteenth Century—are too long for inclusion.

Many instructors will choose to organize the discussion of poetry in the order followed in the book; others may wish to emphasize variations on a theme or historical development, using the early chapters for reference. Obviously, the first of these methods of organization seems to us the most natural for an introductory class, but—particularly with the help of the separate resource manual—instructors may work the complete book using any of these patterns.

In each headnote of Part I, we introduce students to a poem they should be able to respond to. We reinforce what they should already understand and then ask them to consider the kinds of questions they should learn to ask about a poem. Next, we interpret the poem, providing answers to the questions and building a model of the type of analysis the students should learn to perform. The discussion at this level leads students inductively to an understanding of a concept, for which a term and its definition are given. We hope that students, recognizing the need for the term, will understand the role of critical vocabulary in analyzing the poem. Our aim is to develop an informed reader of poetry not just a master of technical terms. Thus we have included a large number of very recent poems with experience and language familiar to the student. Overall, however, we have tried to attain a balanced selection of traditional and modern poems. Poems in the "Further Study" sections are arranged not so much for order of difficulty as for interesting couplings and subgroupings.

Since the headnotes are developed in the way instructors usually discuss material in class, students will have a good grasp on the concepts after reading their out-of-class assignments. Instructors can use class time to answer questions about the headnotes and then proceed to a discussion of the poems in the readings sections to reinforce the knowledge acquired from the headnote. The poems in Part II and Part III can be integrated with these readings, assigned for independent study and writing, or discussed as separate units after the students have completed the chapters in Part I.

Throughout the text, we have emphasized the value of diversified, comparative reading and in-depth analysis of individual poems. Indirectly, we have also sought to provide students with an opportunity to learn, through their own inquiries and discoveries and the guidance of the headnotes, the qualities by which literary excellence is usually measured. We decided to treat the matter of evaluation in this unobtrusive and usually positive way rather than devoting a separate chapter to the subject of how to distinguish good poems from bad. It is our conviction that judgments about quality are more reliable and more meaningful when they evolve naturally from a discussion of how and why a poet uses a particular technique in a given poem rather than being handed down as arbitrary editorial pronouncements about what readers should or should not admire and enjoy.

Some poems *are* better than others, of course—more precise and vivid in language, more tightly organized and coherent, more penetrating and profound in insights—but the ability to make such evaluative judgments is one of the most difficult and demanding of critical skills. For it requires a firm grasp of poetic conventions, a knowledge of literary history, and a sensitivity to language and form. Even then, evaluation is an inexact and unpredictable endeavor, influenced by personal taste, the preferences of a particular age, the reader's frame of mind, and a host of other subjective factors. For these reasons, we believe that for the beginning reader, at least, interpretation is more important than value judgment; that understanding poems—how they work, what they mean, what they can add to our knowledge of the universe without and the world within—is more rewarding than trying to rank them on a scale of relative value.

Before beginning our exploration of the poems in this book, we would like to pause long enough to thank all those who helped make it possible. We are grateful to our students in English 1200, who allowed us to test early drafts of these chapters on them. We are also indebted to the editors at Random House, especially Richard Garretson and Christine Pellicano, for doing what needed to be done to turn an abstract idea into a book; to our reviewers, particularly our colleagues McKay Sundwall and Susan Donaldson, for many helpful comments; to East Carolina University reference librarian Artemis Kares; to graduate students Robin Cox, Helena Woodard, and Warren Cobb, who did much of the early footwork; to Mary Koonce and Jane Adams, who typed the final draft; and to Paula Kirkland, who did the initial typing and otherwise entertained the book as an uninvited guest in her home.

CONTENTS

PART I

Chapter One: THE POEM, THE POET, THE READER — 3

    Mark Strand, *Eating Poetry* — 3
    Dorothy Parker, *Résumé* — 5
    Robert Frost, *Acquainted with the Night* — 10
    Robert Wallace, *The Double Play* — 14
    A. E. Housman, *When I Was One-and-Twenty* — 15
    Countee Cullen, *Incident* — 15
    Emily Dickinson, *After Great Pain, A Formal Feeling Comes* — 16

Chapter Two: THE SPEAKER, THE AUDIENCE, THE SITUATION — 17

    Janis Ian, *At Seventeen* — 17
    Randall Jarrell, *The Death of the Ball Turret Gunner* — 20
    Robert Browning, *My Last Duchess* — 22
    Edwin Arlington Robinson, *How Annandale Went Out* — 25
    Anthony Hecht, *The End of the Weekend* — 26
    E. E. Cummings, *Spring is like a perhaps hand* — 28
    Ted Hughes, *Hawk Roosting* — 31
    Robinson Jeffers, *Hurt Hawks* — 32

    W. H. Auden, *The Unknown Citizen* — 33
    Henry Reed, *Naming of Parts* — 34
    John Donne, *The Sun Rising* — 35
    William Shakespeare, *Sonnet 48: How Careful Was I, When I Took My Way* — 37
    William Shakespeare, *Sonnet 65: Since Brass, Nor Stone, Nor Earth, Nor Boundless Sea* — 37
    Matthew Arnold, *Dover Beach* — 38
    Anthony Hecht, *The Dover Bitch* — 40

    George MacBeth, *Bedtime Story* — 41
    Linda Pastan, *Notes From The Delivery Room* — 42
    Terry Stokes, *Crimes of Passion: The Slasher* — 43
    Adrienne Rich, *Rape* — 44
    D. C. Berry, *On Reading Poems To A Senior Class At South High* — 45
    John Donne, *Batter My Heart, Three-Personed God* — 45

Chapter Three: THEMATIC STRUCTURES — 47

William Carlos Williams, *This Is Just to Say* — 47
Anonymous, *Sir Patrick Spence* — 50
Genevieve Taggard, *The Enamel Girl* — 53
Andrew Marvell, *To His Coy Mistress* — 56
Gary Snyder, *Marin-An* — 61
Adrienne Rich, *Living in Sin* — 64

W. H. Auden, *That Night When Joy Began* — 65
John Donne, *A Lecture Upon The Shadow* — 66
James Wright, *Gambling in Stateline, Nevada* — 67
William Shakespeare, *Sonnet 73: That Time Of Year Thou Mayst In Me Behold* — 68
Robert Frost, *Fire and Ice* — 69
George Herbert, *Easter Wings* — 70

Robert Herrick, *Upon Julia's Clothes* — 71
George Herbert, *Prayer (I)* — 71
Roger McGough, *40—Love* — 72
Grace Butcher, *On Driving Behind A School Bus For Mentally Retarded Children* — 72
Alan Dugan, *Love Song: I and Thou* — 73
Robert Frost, *Stopping By Woods On a Snowy Evening* — 73

Chapter Four: TONE — 75

Samuel Hazo, *My Roosevelt Coupé* — 75
William Cowper, *Light Shining Out of Darkness* — 79
Reed Whittemore, *Psalm* — 80
William Blake, *The Clod And The Pebble* — 82
Robert Frost, *Design* — 83
Michael Dennis Browne, *Paranoia* — 86

Anonymous, *The Three Ravens* — 87
Anonymous, *The Twa Corbies* — 88
Oliver Goldsmith, *An Elegy On That Glory Of Her Sex, Mrs. Mary Blaize* — 89
Theodore Roethke, *Elegy For Jane* — 91
Stephen Spender, *An Elementary School Classroom in a Slum* — 92
Philip Larkin, *A Study of Reading Habits* — 93

Dylan Thomas, *Fern Hill* — 94
Edna St. Vincent Millay, *Spring* — 95
Gwendolyn Brooks, *of De Witt Williams on his way to Lincoln Cemetery* — 96
Louis Simpson, *Vandergast and the Girl* — 97

William Blake, *The Tyger*	99
Sir John Suckling, *Song: Why So Pale and Wan?*	99
Kathleen Fraser, *Poem In Which My Legs Are Accepted*	100

Chapter Five: INCONGRUITY — 102

Arthur Guiterman, *On the Vanity of Earthly Greatness*	102
Kenneth Koch, *Variations on a Theme by William Carlos Williams*	104
Richard Lovelace, *To Althea From Prison*	106
William Wordsworth, *She Dwelt Among The Untrodden Ways*	108
Donald Baker, *Formal Application*	110
Percy Bysshe Shelley, *Ozymandias*	114
Karl Shapiro, *Buick*	115
Ron Ellis, *Alas, Poor Buick*	115
Emily Dickinson, *Success Is Counted Sweetest*	116
William Shakespeare, *Sonnet 94: They That Have Power To Hurt And Will Do None*	117
George Herbert, *The Collar*	118
Richard Wilbur, *Playboy*	119
John Frederick Nims, *Love Poem*	120
John Crowe Ransom, *Bells for John Whiteside's Daughter*	121
Robert Frost, *"Out, Out—"*	121
William Blake, *The Garden Of Love*	122
Wilfred Owen, *Arms and the Boy*	123
Stephen Crane, *War Is Kind*	123

Chapter Six: IMAGE AND ABSTRACTION — 125

Matsuo Bashō, *On a Withered Branch*	125
Ralph Waldo Emerson, *Sacrifice*	125
Gary Snyder, *Drinking Hot Sake*	127
Theodore Roethke, *Night Journey*	128
Wilfred Owen, *Dulce et Decorum Est*	129
Thomas Lux, *The Midnight Tennis Match*	132
D. H. Lawrence, *Piano*	136
Robert Hayden, *Figure*	137
William Carlos Williams, *The Red Wheelbarrow*	138
Amy Lowell, *The Taxi*	139
Alfred, Lord Tennyson, *The Kraken*	139
John Keats, *To Autumn*	140
William Butler Yeats, *A Deep-Sworn Vow*	141
Etheridge Knight, *As You Leave Me*	142
William Blake, *The Divine Image*	142
William Blake, *The Human Abstract*	143

Marianne Moore, *The Fish*	144
T. S. Eliot, *Preludes*	145

Chapter Seven: FIGURATIVE LANGUAGE   147

Emily Dickinson, *It Dropped So Low—In my Regard*	147
Langston Hughes, *Dream Deferred*	149
Sylvia Plath, *Metaphors*	151
Robert Francis, *Swimmer*	155
Dylan Thomas, *The Hand That Signed The Paper*	158
May Swenson, *The Watch*	161
Gary Soto, *The Creature*	162
John Updike, *Ex-Basketball Player*	164
William Shakespeare, *Sonnet 130: My Mistress' Eyes Are Nothing Like The Sun*	165
Diane Wakoski, *Overweight Poem*	166
Anne Sexton, *For My Lover, Returning To His Wife*	167
John Donne, *The Canonization*	169
Robert Graves, *Ulysses*	171
Alfred, Lord Tennyson, *Ulysses*	172
Richard Wilbur, *A Simile For Her Smile*	174
Charles Simic, *Bestiary For The Fingers Of My Right Hand*	174
George Herbert, *Love (III)*	175
Emily Dickinson, *I Taste A Liquor Never Brewed*	176
Robert Frost, *Departmental*	176

Chapter Eight: SYMBOL   178

William Wordsworth, *Strange Fits Of Passion*	178
Edgar Allan Poe, *Eldorado*	183
A. E. Housman, *To An Athlete Dying Young*	186
James Dickey, *Fence Wire*	190
John Ciardi, *On Flunking a Nice Boy Out of School*	194
Robert Frost, *Desert Places*	197
William Butler Yeats, *The Magi*	198
T. S. Eliot, *Journey Of The Magi*	199
George Herbert, *The Pilgrimage*	201
Charles Baudelaire, *The Albatross*	202
William Blake, *Ah Sun-Flower*	203
W. S. Merwin, *Green Water Tower*	204
Delmore Schwartz, *The Heavy Bear Who Goes With Me*	205
Walt Whitman, *I Saw In Louisiana A Live-Oak Growing*	206
Wallace Stevens, *The Snow Man*	206

CONTENTS xv

John Donne, *Hymn to God My God, in My Sickness* 207
William Blake, *The Sick Rose* 208

Chapter Nine: FORMAL PATTERNS 209

Gerard Manley Hopkins, *Spring And Fall:* to a young child 209
William Butler Yeats, *The Song Of Wandering Aengus* 213
Robert Penn Warren, *The Faring* 219
William Shakespeare, *Sonnet 60: Like As The Waves Make Towards The Pebbled Shore* 224
Theodore Roethke, *The Waking* 227
Lawrence Ferlinghetti, *The Pennycandystore Beyond The El* 230
Emily Dickinson, *The Soul Selects Her Own Society* 235
Walt Whitman, *Me Imperturbe* 236

Anonymous, *A Pretty Young Thing From St. Paul* 236
John Keats, *On First Looking Into Chapman's Homer* 237
Percy Bysshe Shelley, *Ode to the West Wind* 238
Robert Frost, *Mending Wall* 241
Elizabeth Bishop, *Sestina* 242
Wallace Stevens, *Peter Quince At The Clavier* 244

Gwendolyn Brooks, *We Real Cool* 246
Ben Jonson, *Song: Drink To Me Only With Thine Eyes* 246
Michael Drayton, *Since There's No Help* 247
Wilfred Owen, *Anthem for Doomed Youth* 247
E. E. Cummings, *O sweet spontaneous* 248
Dylan Thomas, *Do Not Go Gentle Into That Good Night* 248

PART II

STUDENTS AND TEACHERS 253

Lyn Lifshin, *You Understand The Requirements* 253
William Butler Yeats, *The Scholars* 254
Langston Hughes, *Theme for English B* 254
Paul Zimmer, *Zimmer's Head Thudding Against the Blackboard* 255
A. Poulin, Jr., *To My Students* 255
Reed Whittemore, *A Teacher* 256
Thomas Gray, *Ode on a Distant Prospect of Eton College* 256

SPORTS AND GAMES 259

Gary Gildner, *First Practice* 259
Margaret Avison, *Tennis* 260

Robert Penn Warren, *Skiers*   260
Grace Butcher, *Young Wrestlers*   260
Peter Makuck, *Running*   261
Samuel Allen, *To Satch*   261
Paul Goodman, *Surfers At Santa Cruz*   262

YOUTH AND AGE   262

William Shakespeare, *Sonnet 2: When Forty Winters Shall Besiege Thy Brow*   262
William Butler Yeats, *Among School Children*   263
John Berryman, *The Ball Poem*   265
Theodore Roethke, *My Papa's Waltz*   265
Sylvia Plath, *Daddy*   266
Robert Hayden, *Those Winter Sundays*   268
William Meredith, *Parents*   268

FAILURE TO COMMUNICATE   269

Naomi Lazard, *Re Accepting You*   269
George Herbert, *Denial*   270
Adrienne Rich, *Trying to Talk with a Man*   271
David Ignatow, *Lunchtime*   272
Bob Dylan, *Ballad of a Thin Man*   272
Mari Evans, *When in Rome*   274
Pablo Neruda, *Fable of the Mermaid and the Drunks* (tr. by Alastair Reid)   275

LOVE, SEX, AND FRIENDSHIP   276

Anonymous, *Western Wind*   276
Thomas Wyatt, *The Flee from Me*   276
Robert Herrick, *To the Virgins, to Make Much of Time*   277
Richard Wilbur, *A Late Aubade*   277
William Shakespeare, *Sonnet 57: Being Your Slave, What Should I Do But Tend*   278
Edna St. Vincent Millay, *Passer Mortuus Est*   278
Nikki Giovanni, *Seduction*   279
John Donne, *A Valediction Forbidding Mourning*   279

A SENSE OF PLACE   281

William Wordsworth, *Composed Upon Westminster Bridge*   281
Andrew Marvell, *The Garden*   281
Nikki Giovanni, *Nikki-Rosa*   283

Hart Crane, *To Brooklyn Bridge* — 284
James Wright, *Lying In A Hammock At William Duffy's Farm In Pine Island, Minnesota* — 285
Adrien Stoutenburg, *Subdivider* — 285
Robert Lowell, *The Mouth of the Hudson* — 286

DEATH — 287

Dudley Randall, *Ballad of Birmingham* — 287
Richard Eberhart, *The Fury of Aerial Bombardment* — 288
John Donne, *A Nocturnal Upon St. Lucy's Day* — 288
Sylvia Plath, *Lady Lazarus* — 289
Ben Jonson, *On My First Daughter* — 291
A. E. Housman, *With Rue My Heart Is Laden* — 292
Emily Dickinson, *I Heard A Fly Buzz* — 292

PERSPECTIVES ON RELIGION — 293

Philip Larkin, *Church Going* — 293
John Donne, *Hymn To God The Father* — 294
Maxine Kumin, *The Jesus Infection* — 295
George Herbert, *Redemption* — 296
Henry Vaughn, *The World* — 297
Gerard Manley Hopkins, *God's Grandeur* — 298

POETRY AND OTHER ARTS — 298

Dylan Thomas, *In My Craft Or Sullen Art* — 298
Lawrence Ferlinghetti, *Constantly Risking Absurdity* — 299
John Keats, *Ode On A Grecian Urn* — 300
W. H. Auden, *Musée des Beaux Arts* — 301
William Carlos Williams, *Landscape With The Fall Of Icarus* — 302
Randall Jarrell, *The Knight, Death, and the Devil* — 302

PART III

OLD AND MIDDLE ENGLISH — 307

Anonymous, *The Seafarer* (tr. by Charles W. Kennedy) — 307
Anonymous, *Wild Swan* (tr. by Charles W. Kennedy) — 308
Anonymous, *Deor's Lament* (tr. by Charles W. Kennedy) — 309
Anonymous, *I Have a Gentle Cock* — 310
Geoffrey Chaucer, *Chaucer's Wordes unto Adam, His Owne Scriveyn* — 310
Geoffrey Chaucer, *The Complaint of Chaucer to his Purse* — 310

RENAISSANCE — 311

Authorized (King James) Version, *Psalm 91*	311
Thomas Campion, *There Is a Garden in Her Face*	312
Thomas Carew, *A Song*	312
Richard Crashaw, *On our Lord crucified, naked and bloody*	313
John Donne, *The Dream*	313
John Donne, *Farewell To Love*	314
John Donne, *Song: Go and Catch a Falling Star*	315
Michael Drayton, *How Many Paltry, Foolish, Painted Things*	316
George Herbert, *The Altar*	316
George Herbert, *Vanity (I)*	317
Robert Herrick, *Delight in Disorder*	317
Robert Herrick, *Upon Prue, His Maid*	318
Robert Herrick, *The Vine*	318
Henry Howard, *Earl of Surrey, Complaint of a Lover Rebuked*	319
Ben Jonson, *Song: Come, My Celia*	319
Ben Jonson, *Still to Be Neat*	319
Richard Lovelace, *La Bella Bona Roba*	320
Richard Lovelace, *To Lucasta, Going to the Wars*	320
Christopher Marlowe, *The Passionate Shepherd to His Love*	321
Andrew Marvell, *The Definition Of Love*	321
Andrew Marvell, *The Picture of Little T. C. in a Prospect of Flowers*	322
John Milton, *How Soon Hath Time*	323
John Milton, *When I Consider How My Light Is Spent*	324
Sir Walter Raleigh, *The Nymph's Reply To The Shepherd*	324
William Shakespeare, *Sonnet 18: Shall I Compare Thee To A Summer's Day?*	325
William Shakespeare, *Sonnet 29: When In Disgrace With Fortune And Men's Eyes*	325
William Shakespeare, *Sonnet 33: Full Many A Glorious Morning Have I Seen*	326
William Shakespeare, *Sonnet 129: Th' Expense Of Spirit In A Waste Of Shame*	326
William Shakespeare, *Sonnet 146: Poor Soul, The Center of My Sinful Earth*	327
Sir Philip Sidney, *Leave Me, O Love*	327
Sir Philip Sidney, *Loving In Truth*	327
Robert Southwell, *The Burning Babe*	328
Edmund Spenser, *Like as a Huntsman*	328
Edmund Spenser, *One Day I Wrote Her Name Upon the Strand*	329
Sir John Suckling, *Out upon It!*	329
Edmund Waller, *Song: Go, Lovely Rose*	330
Sir Thomas Wyatt, *Whoso List To Hunt*	330

RESTORATION AND EIGHTEENTH CENTURY — 331

    Joseph Addison, *Ode: The Spacious Firmament* — 331
    William Collins, *Ode to Evening* — 331
    John Dryden, *To the Memory of Mr. Oldham* — 333
    Oliver Goldsmith, *An Elegy On the Death Of A Mad Dog* — 333
    Oliver Goldsmith, *When Lovely Woman Stoops to Folly* — 334
    Thomas Gray, *Ode On The Death Of A Favorite Cat, Drowned In A Tub of Gold Fishes* — 335
    Alexander Pope, *Ode on Solitude* — 336
    Jonathan Swift, *A Description of a City Shower* — 336
    Jonathan Swift, *A Description of the Morning* — 338
    Jonathan Swift, *The Day Of Judgement* — 338

ROMANTIC AND VICTORIAN PERIOD — 339

    William Blake, *The Garden Of Love* — 339
    William Blake, *The Little Black Boy* — 339
    William Blake, *Song: How Sweet I Roam'd* — 340
    George Gordon, Lord Byron, *Prometheus* — 341
    George Gordon, Lord Byron, *She Walks in Beauty* — 342
    Samuel Taylor Coleridge, *Kubla Khan* — 343
    Emily Dickinson, *The Bustle in a House* — 344
    Emily Dickinson, *I Died For Beauty* — 344
    Emily Dickinson, *The Last Night That She Lived* — 345
    John Keats, *Bright Star, Would I Were Steadfast as Thou Art* — 345
    John Keats, *Ode To A Nightingale* — 346
    Percy Bysshe Shelley, *England in 1819* — 348
    Walt Whitman, *Cavalry Crossing A Ford* — 348
    Walt Whitman, *A Noiseless Patient Spider* — 349
    William Wordsworth, *It is a Beauteous Evening, Calm and Free* — 349
    William Wordsworth, *The World Is Too Much with Us* — 350

    Matthew Arnold, *Requiescat* — 350
    Robert Browning, *Soliloquy Of The Spanish Cloister* — 350
    Thomas Hardy, *The Darkling Thrush* — 352
    Thomas Hardy, *Hap* — 353
    Gerard Manley Hopkins, *Carrion Comfort* — 354
    Gerard Manley Hopkins, *The Windhover* — 354
    A. E. Housman, *Into My Heart An Air That Kills* — 354
    A. E. Housman, *On Moonlit Heath And Lonesome Bank* — 355
    A. E. Housman, *Terence, This Is Stupid Stuff* — 356
    Christina Rossetti, *In an Artist's Studio* — 357
    Dante Gabriel Rossetti, *Barren Spring* — 358
    Alfred, Lord Tennyson, *Break, Break, Break* — 358
    Alfred, Lord Tennyson, *The Eagle* — 359

MODERN AND CONTEMPORARY — 359

A. R. Ammons, *The City Limits*	359
A. R. Ammons, *So I Said I am Ezra*	360
A. R. Ammons, *Winter Scene*	360
John Ashbery, *My Erotic Double*	361
W. H. Auden, *Lullaby*	362
W. H. Auden, *Epitaph on a Tyrant*	362
W. H. Auden, *The Love Feast*	362
Imamu Amiri Baraka, *Preface To A Twenty Volume Suicide Note*	363
John Berryman, *A Professor's Song*	364
Elizabeth Bishop, *The Armadillo*	364
Robert Bly, *Driving To Town Late To Mail A Letter*	365
Gwendolyn Brooks ("*Thousands—killed in action*")	366
John Ciardi, *Men Marry What They Need. I Marry You*	366
Stephen Crane, *I Saw A Man Pursuing The Horizon*	366
Stephen Crane, *The Wayfarer*	367
Robert Creeley, *The Window*	367
E. E. Cummings, "*next to of course god america i*"	368
E. E. Cummings, *she being Brand*	368
E. E. Cummings, *when serpents bargain for the right to squirm*	369
James Dickey, *Adultery*	370
James Dickey, *Cherrylog Road*	371
Paul Laurence Dunbar, *We Wear The Mask*	373
Robert Duncan, *Poetry, A Natural Thing*	374
Richard Eberhart, *The Groundhog*	375
Richard Eberhart, *The Horse Chestnut Tree*	375
T. S. Eliot, *The Love Song of J. Alfred Prufrock*	376
Robert Frost, *Neither Out Far Nor In Deep*	380
Robert Frost, *The Road Not Taken*	380
Allen Ginsberg, *A Supermarket In California*	381
Nikki Giovanni, *On Hearing "The Girl with the Flaxen Hair"*	381
Anthony Hecht, *More Light! More Light!*	382
Ted Hughes, *Wodwo*	383
Richard Hugo, *Missoula Softball Tournament*	384
Randall Jarrell, *A Camp in the Prussian Forest*	384
X. J. Kennedy, *Nude Descending A Staircase*	385
Kenneth Koch, *Permanently*	386
Stanley Kunitz, *Careless Love*	386
Denise Levertov, *The Ache of Marriage*	387
Denise Levertov, *Losing Track*	387
Philip Levine, *Animals Are Passing from Our Lives*	388
Robert Lowell, *Memories of West Street and Lepke*	389
Robert Lowell, *Skunk Hour*	390
Archibald Macleish, *You, Andrew Marvell*	391

CONTENTS

William Meredith, *Winter Verse for His Sister*	392
Gary Miranda, *Listeners at the Breathing Place*	393
Howard Nemerov, *The Goose Fish*	393
Linda Pastan, *You Are Odysseus*	394
Sylvia Plath, *The Applicant*	395
Sylvia Plath, *Mirror*	396
Sylvia Plath, *Morning Song*	396
Ezra Pound, *The Bath Tub*	397
Ezra Pound, *In A Station Of The Metro*	397
Adrienne Rich, *The Roofwalker*	397
Edward Arlington Robinson, *Mr. Flood's Party*	398
Theodore Roethke, *Dolor*	400
Theodore Roethke, *I Knew A Woman*	400
Anne Sexton, *Song For A Lady*	401
Anne Sexton, *Us*	401
Louis Simpson, *The Man Who Married Magdalene*	402
W. D. Snodgrass, *Dr. Joseph Goebbels*	403
W. D. Snodgrass, *Old Apple Trees*	403
William Stafford, *Bess*	405
William Stafford, *Traveling Through the Dark*	406
Wallace Stevens, *Anecdote Of The Jar*	406
Wallace Stevens, *The Emperor Of Ice-Cream*	406
Dylan Thomas, *And Death Shall Have No Dominion*	407
Dylan Thomas, *The Force That Through The Green Fuse Drives The Flower*	408
Diane Wakoski, *Uneasy Rider*	408
Reed Whittemore, *The Line of an American Poet*	409
Richard Wilbur, *Cottage Street, 1953*	410
Richard Wilbur, *Love Calls Us To The Things Of This World*	411
Richard Wilbur, *Piazza Di Spagna, Early Morning*	411
William Carlos Williams, *Nantucket*	412
William Carlos Williams, *The Yachts*	412
James Wright, *A Blessing*	413
Richard Wright, *Between The World And Me*	414
William Butler Yeats, *Sailing to Byzantium*	415
William Butler Yeats, *The Second Coming*	416
William Butler Yeats, *The Wild Swans At Coole*	417

PART ONE

1

THE POEM, THE POET, THE READER

EATING POETRY

Ink runs from the corners of my mouth.
There is no happiness like mine.
I have been eating poetry.

The librarian does not believe what she sees.
Her eyes are sad
and she walks with her hands in her dress.

The poems are gone.
The light is dim.
The dogs are on the basement stairs and coming up.

Their eyeballs roll,
their blond legs burn like brush.
The poor librarian begins to stamp her feet and weep.

She does not understand.
When I get on my knees and lick her hand,
she screams.

I am a new man.
I snarl at her and bark.
I romp with joy in the bookish dark.

Mark Strand (b. 1934)

 This poem by Mark Strand describes an act that strikes us as absurd—eating poetry. "You must be joking," is our first response—and an appropriate one, for purposeful kidding is Strand's method here. Yet we are reluctant to trust our intuition. This can't be, we say. Still, Strand's poem seems more like a joke than a poem because, for many people, reading poetry has been a serious, heavy, sometimes painful, and rather joyless activity. If we look at it more closely, however, "Eating Poetry" seems to want to destroy many of our preconceived notions about poetry, how we read it, and why we read it. Let's look at the particulars of the poem again.
 We have all been in libraries and seen librarians, but it is unlikely that

any of us have ever witnessed anything quite as strange as the scene that unfolds in the library of this poem.

Someone has been "eating poetry." At least, that's what seems to be happening. Ink is running from his mouth. The poems are gone. The librarian is upset. She is pacing up and down with her hands in her pockets, stamping her feet and weeping. To complicate matters further, dogs suddenly appear from the basement stairs, eyeballs rolling and legs burning. Then the speaker himself begins acting like a dog. He kneels and licks the librarian's hand. When she screams, he snarls at her and romps, barking, into the darkness.

This much we know from the poet's vivid description of the scene. However, the poem raises many questions that are left unexplained by this summary of the literal situation—questions that we may have been formulating subconsciously and attempting to answer as we first read "Eating Poetry." For example, how can we explain the speaker's strange behavior? What does it mean to be "eating poetry"? How do all the details of the poem fit together, and what do they mean? Let's see if we can resolve some of these questions as we read through the poem again.

Since the word "poetry" appears in the title and is mentioned several other times in the poem, and since all the speaker's actions result from his "eating poetry," we suspect that one of the main concerns of the work is poetry itself, or rather the ways in which it can affect people who actively and enthusiastically *experience* poems. For such readers, poetry becomes something vital, nourishing, and powerful—something that can bring pleasure, arouse the most elemental impulses, even transform people in fundamental ways. Perhaps that is why the speaker pictures himself as an eater of poetry, why he feels as contented as a well-fed dog, and why he abandons all restraint.

It is not surprising that the librarian is disturbed, for this joyously irreverent act of "eating poetry" challenges the conventional assumptions that a library is a place for quiet, scholarly study and reserved behavior, and that a librarian's role is to watch over books and enforce rules. If we have any doubts about where Strand's own sympathies lie, the language of the poem should dispel them. For the speaker tells of his transformation from man to beast to "new man" in a dynamic vocabulary (eating, burning, barking, snarling, romping) that not only conveys his excitement but invites the reader to experience similar pleasures.

In your own reading of "Eating Poetry" you may have asked slightly different questions and arrived at different conclusions. That is to be expected, even welcomed. Poems live, and their strength and power invite us to interpret and understand them.

If you have caught some of the enthusiasm of Mark Strand's poem and identified with the speaker, you have already begun to "taste" poetry and to experience one of the surprises of art: its power to transport the reader to an imagined world that has a reality all its own. But even if you are not yet ready to "romp with joy in the bookish dark," you needn't be discouraged. You may yet be ready to experience the pleasures of poetry.

But why bother? Most people assume that poetry is difficult and often come to consider it unnecessary as well—impractical, irrelevant, sentimental, and a waste of time. It won't cement the deal that will make a million. It runs counter to the dispassionate scientific analysis much of our training has instilled in us. It won't automatically make us better lawyers, nurses, teachers, architects, lovers, or parents. The vast majority live without it and do fine. English majors may enjoy poetry, but—so the argument goes—no one else should have to deal with it.

That's quite a list, and some of the charges may be true—but not all of them. And the ones that are true are also true of many other activities we enjoy. Dancing, swimming, moviegoing, TV-watching, any recreation, any of the arts, in fact, anything we do that is not required by our roles could be considered unnecessary, if by "living" we mean "surviving" on the most minimal level.

But human beings have always wanted to do more than is required of them merely as animals. Not content simply with what we needed, we have striven for what we wanted. The history of civilization is the uneven calendar of our successes. We live in comfortable houses rather than caves, wear clothes to increase our appeal rather than just keep warm, and spend increasing amounts of money on vacations, entertainment, and sports. All of these, which are hardly necessities, fall under the category of "play," and play can have its unexpected practical benefits.

Poetry, from one perspective, is sheer play. Almost any information conveyed by poetry could be conveyed more clearly and directly in prose. (Firemen, for example, are unlikely to quote poems as directions to people they're rescuing from a burning building.) In fact, poetry doesn't exist primarily to convey information or contribute factual knowledge. No nutritionist would suggest "Eating Poetry" as background reading. No worker at a suicide-prevention hotline would give the following advice:

RÉSUMÉ

Razors pain you;
Rivers are damp;
Acids stain you;
And drugs cause cramp.
Guns aren't lawful;
Nooses give;
Gas smells awful;
You might as well live.

Dorothy Parker
(1893–1967)

In contrast with a literal statement or an expository essay, a poem is not intended to relate directly to the real world; instead, it tends to build a fictional world around itself and invites us as readers to piece together that closed environment and then live for a moment in it, before sending us back to the real world. The mental and imaginative energy required to participate in this process is one of the reasons poetry is sometimes difficult for many of us.

Yet, despite the difficulty of reading poetry (perhaps even because of it), the effort is worthwhile. Poems usually move from an experience to an insight into it, and so they can restructure our way of looking at our language, ourselves, our world, and our relationships with each other. A poem can open new dimensions of "reality" as no other means of communication can, calling into question our assumptions and forcing a crisis that requires a new, creative view of things. A poem can sharpen our sensitivity to detail, exercise our imagination in problem solving, and discipline our ability to infer from facts. Perhaps even more important, it can provide an intrinsic aesthetic pleasure. To paraphrase Wallace Stevens, the twentieth-century American poet who was also executive vice president of Hartford Accident and Indemnity Company, a poem can help us live our lives. It can help us know more fully what being human is about. If so, poetry is among the highest and most sophisticated forms of play—and one of the most beneficial.

It is also one of the most primitive. The earliest surviving literature of most of the world's cultures is poetry. Intensity of emotion, whether elation or depression, finds its natural expression in poetry. Poetry's rhythms echo the human heartbeat; its images, our sense impressions; its sounds, our human voice; its expressions, our emotions; and its stories, our myths. Poetry helps us gain insight into the things we see around us. Sound becomes sense; sight becomes insight.

Because the poetic impulse is so fundamental, it has found outlets not only in the polished written verse of the literary artist but also in the songs of primitive warriors and hunters, in the chants of religious devotees, in folk songs and ballads that deal with everything from unrequited love to the pleasures of drinking rye whiskey, and in the popular lyrics written, played, and sung by the modern minstrels of the "top forty." Although verse meant to be sung or spoken is usually less complex, less tightly constructed, and more repetitious than most written poems, it often speaks with an artistry of its own. To exclude examples from oral tradition arbitrarily would be to ignore the existence of a rich vein of poetry, including the Homeric epics and *Beowulf,* all of which existed as oral formulaic poetry before becoming fixed in a single written version.

Poems come in all sizes, shapes, and styles. Their subjects are everything that human senses experience, reason comprehends, feelings embrace, and imagination creates. Certain forms predominate in one era, but their popularity may fade in the next. Poets employ the form they find most appropriate for the experience they write about, within the context of the society in which they live.

Poets, too, are all manner of people. They are seldom the moony, delicate creatures popularly imagined, sitting in corners penning poems. They are often more active and more aware of the significance of their actions than most of us; they are in touch with themselves and their feelings and can help us know our own better. Among the poets represented here are scientists, soldiers, ghetto residents, farmers, college teachers, housewives, publishers, priests, medical doctors, unwed mothers, advertising executives, and deck hands on tramp steamers. They are male and female; moral, immoral, and amoral; unpleasant and pleasant; heterosexual, homosexual, and asexual. They are Chicano, Wasp, Black, Oriental, American Indian, Canadian, European, British, American.

Whatever else they might be, poets are people who can organize their experiences and their reactions into word patterns. Words are their media just as colors, musical tones, metals, and clay are the media of other artists. Since poetry is language at its most precise and condensed, skilled poets have a special attitude toward words and are expertly aware of subtle differences in meaning, sound, and tone; they understand the possibilities of the words most of us fail even to examine. They employ the same words we all do, but the intensity as well as the virtuosity with which they use them seems to create a different language.

Poets manipulate ordinary words to fit unusual situations; they make words double back on themselves with irony and ambiguity. Their words always mean more than they seem to on first reading and politely shatter many of our accepted definitions. In sum, poets generate a special vehicle called **poetic language,** *ordinary language used in an extraordinary and expert way that powerfully engages the reader and effects the desired response.*

The relationship between the poet, the poem, and the reader is complex. The impetus to write a poem may be an experience or a reaction to an experience that is meaningful to the poet. Sometimes poems are a means by which poets come to an understanding of themselves, their feelings, or their reactions to experiences; in other words, poets may not so much describe an experience as undergo an experience. They may or may not know how they are going to conclude when they start the poem. A poem may lead to one conclusion in first draft but to another in revision. Whatever the poet's experience and intent, the process of writing a poem involves restructuring an original experience into an artistic one by means of the many techniques and devices with which this book is concerned. Sometimes poets do not realize the ramifications of their work when they have finished a poem, and for this and other reasons poets may not be the best authority on their poems. They may know what they intended, but a finished poem has its own independent existence, and it is the poem rather than the poet to which the reader responds.

The communication between writer and reader is not direct in the poem. Unlike the scientific writer or preacher, both of whom tell their audience directly what to think or feel, the poet does not intend primarily to inform the reader. Like a choreographer, a poet creates a poem as a patterned process with an indirect and cumulative effect on the reader. To put it another way, a poem is less like a pane of glass than a prism; it is not seen through but looked at for itself, with its light refracted in various colors at various angles. Likewise, the "I" and "you" of a poem are not automatically the poet and reader. Rather, the poem is often presented "in the form of someone not the poet addressing someone not ourselves. . . ."[1] In a sense, we readers are listening in on an imaginary conversation.

Good poems require good readers—readers who participate actively, who open themselves to experiencing the poems and to appreciating the means by which the poems achieve their effects. Some poems can communicate without difficulty to readers uninitiated in the craft of poetry. More complex poems reveal themselves more slowly and require greater effort from their readers. If readers are active participants in a poem, they become creators of a reading of that work, rather than consumers of a finished product.

Although the difficulty of a poem is by no means in direct proportion to its worth, generally speaking a poem that reveals itself easily and completely on first reading has less to offer than one that becomes richer each time it is read. Tennis would be easier without the interference of a net, but the sport would hardly be as interesting or develop as much skill.

Appreciation of the value, craft, and meaning of poetry is the objective of this book. Instruction in the set of conventions used to read poetry is necessary to this end, but readers who know all the literary terms and answer all the questions raised but do not genuinely and creatively respond to the individual poems have failed to understand the purpose of the book.

On the other hand, it is unreasonable to suppose that a person who knows nothing about poetry can respond as fully or as maturely as one who appreciates the techniques and traditions with which a poet works. Because poetry is a structure dependent on special conventions, a book on poetry is a guide to the special kind of reading required to make sense of the conventions. If the term "convention" bothers you, remember, for example, that you accept without confusion an instant replay and that you routinely drive in the righthand lane. Both are conventions, agreements between participants, rules of the game. Like any other activity, poetry has a set of conventions. Although skill in analyzing a poem is not a guarantee of real involvement, it is a most promising setting for it.

Consequently, each of the first nine chapters in this book concentrates on

---

[1] Robert Scholes, *Structuralism in Literature: An Introduction* (New Haven and London: Yale University Press, 1974), p. 28.

poems that exemplify a certain poetic technique. Each first presents a poem, reminds you of what you probably already understand about it, presents questions and discussion to help you identify the technique most apparent in the poem, and then defines the term under consideration. Each chapter moves in an informally inductive manner from the known to the unknown, from the specifics of one poem to a generalization about that poem and others as well. Questions are provided so that you can formulate your own responses before you read someone else's opinions. For your own benefit, do not skip the questions. Answer them informally but carefully before reading the discussions.

This format does not imply that any response different from the editors' is automatically in error. Since there is no final authority in commenting on literature (for reasons to be discussed later), any response supported by the poem and not contradicted by it is valid. One response can, however, be more precise and accurate than another.

Although terminology should not become the most important feature of this book, the development of a critical vocabulary is a prerequisite to a mature discussion of a poem. It need not be a greater obstacle than the vocabulary of a sport or a recipe.

A poem is not material on which you can practice speed-reading. The more tightly constructed and controlled the poem, the more readings it will demand and reward. Until the ear of your imagination is keen enough to hear the play of sounds (and after that as well), it is wise to *read aloud* each poem to hear its music.

Most poems are best read in a natural voice, with normal stress and rhythm but with respect for the poem. There is no need to break excessively the flow of a sentence at the end of a line of poetry unless the sense of the sentence or a strong mark of punctuation (period, colon, semicolon, exclamation mark, dash) requires it. On the other hand, do not rush on from line to line. If you read a poem naturally, the time required for the eye to get from one line to the next will produce the slight pause that is appropriate.

> The librarian does not believe what she sees. (pause)
> Her eyes are sad (slight pause)
> And she walks with her hands in her dress. (pause)

The meaning of the sentences is of utmost importance; the natural speech rhythms are reinforced by and played off against the poetic rhythms and line lengths, not to make the poem difficult but to make it different from ordinary communication. The poetic rhythm should be observed, but not emphasized in a singsong pattern. Reading poems aloud becomes easier and more enjoyable with practice.

The procedure for analyzing a poem also becomes easier with practice. The study of one poem makes the next easier, although each poem requires its own kind of attention and treatment and each reader brings to the poem his or her own experiences and insight. By and large, the discussions of individual poems in this book should provide a model for the process by which a poem is analyzed for a particular technique. An analysis from any point of view focuses on the specific details of the poem and how they set up an appropriate response in an informed reader. The poem should be allowed to speak for itself and should be approached on its own terms.

The poet provides in the poem the **context** or *frame of reference for the poem, to which all the details contribute and by which all the details are colored.* Although no one reads a poem in a vacuum (poets don't write in a vacuum), it is best to allow the poem to provide as much of its own context as possible, rather than making it an extension of your own mood. It is also important to guard against drawing conclusions that the poem does not support. One detail taken out of context can be made too important and distort the reading of the poem. Because the poem speaks as a whole structure, respond to all its details, not just to one or two. Someone who cited one or two examples of the speaker's bizarre behavior as evidence that "Eating Poetry" is a case history of literal insanity, for example, or construed the amusing confrontation between the poetry-eater and the librarian as a plea for stronger police security (or dog control) in libraries would obviously have missed the point of the poem.

The following poem illustrates some of the elements that any analysis should consider.

ACQUAINTED WITH THE NIGHT

I have been one acquainted with the night.
I have walked out in rain—and back in rain.
I have outwalked the furthest city light.

I have looked down the saddest city lane.
I have passed by the watchman on his beat   5
And dropped my eyes, unwilling to explain.

I have stood still and stopped the sound of feet
When far away an interrupted cry
Came over houses from another street,

But not to call me back or say good-by;   10
And further still at an unearthly height,
One luminary clock against the sky

Proclaimed the time was neither wrong nor right.
I have been one acquainted with the night.

Robert Frost (1874–1963)

The first element we notice is the ***title***. Some poems untitled by the poet are known by their first lines, but if the poet supplies a title it often denotes the basic contents of the poem, just as the title of a book does. Some titles are literal statements of subject or attitude; others repeat a major image of the poem; but all are important. The title "Acquainted with the Night" is a phrase from the first line that is repeated in the last line of the poem. The repetition suggests importance; its choice as title indicates its centrality to the meaning of the poem. Why is it important to the poem? What meanings does it convey?

When we begin reading the poem we should not skip over any word or phrase we can't make sense of. Unfamiliar words, or even familiar words that seem to be used in special ways, should be looked up in a *dictionary*. We should also take the time to test all possible meanings, explicit and implicit, for their appropriateness. Although all the words and phrasings of "Acquainted with the Night" are similar to those of ordinary speech, several deserve further thought. Of the many associations of the word "night," for example, which seem appropriate here? Which don't? Which associations are appropriate for "luminary," "right," and "unearthly"?

We should never be afraid to try out variant meanings of the words in a poem. The poet often intends more than one meaning. In fact, the richness of meaning in poetic language is one of the reasons for its effectiveness. Although scientific language—even expository prose—attempts to eradicate multiple meanings in order to zero in on one precise intent, poetic language has the opposite aim: it plays with all possible meanings and relishes ***ambiguity:*** *the capacity of a word to generate thought in several directions at once and to suggest multiple meanings, several of which may be appropriate in the given context.* Rather than the result of imprecise thinking or fuzzy wording, ambiguity in artistic language is the result of the poet's sensitivity to the vehicle and the liveliness of his or her word choice. The importance of using a dictionary to be certain of all possible meanings cannot be stressed too much. *Expect* the poet to intend multiple meanings of individual words, phrases, and whole poems.

"Acquainted with the Night," although seemingly straightforward, contains ambiguities on several levels. The word "night" certainly refers to the period of a twenty-four-hour span when the sun is not visible. It suggests as well a time of mental or emotional darkness for the speaker. It may even reach beyond the human sphere of right and wrong to a sense of existential isolation within which the speaker feels *ultimately* alone. Thus, the one word "night," the phrase "acquainted with the night," and the whole poem prompt by their ambiguity several levels of awareness, much the way a pebble dropped in a pool creates concentric rings. The possibilities of a word are never exhausted by just one definition.

One of the surest means of clarifying difficult passages is to paraphrase. To ***paraphrase*** is to *restate the passage as accurately as possible in our own prose,* keeping the images, tense, and person of the original intact but supplying our own wording and word order. An elaborate paraphrase of a whole poem is almost never necessary or even desirable. In fact, since the essence of a poem includes its diction and phraseology, it is ultimately unparaphrasable and is never captured in other words. On the other hand, whatever we read we sift through and reorganize mentally until we grasp its meaning; in this sense paraphrase is a natural act. If used as an aid in understanding rather than an end in itself, it is a legitimate activity. Consider, for example, the usefulness of this approach in interpreting these puzzling lines from "Acquainted with the Night":

> And further still at an unearthly height
> One luminary clock against the sky
> Proclaimed the time was neither wrong nor right.

Since both the poem and the sentence are ambiguous, the sentence is open to a variety of interpretations, which will affect a paraphrase. The following two are possibilities:

> And still farther away, so high in the sky that it was eerie, one lighted (broken?) clock showed an hour that was neither the wrong time nor the right time.

> And still farther away, so high in the sky that it couldn't be on earth, one shining celestial body by which we measure time (the moon?) announced that this moment in the speaker's life (or the historical era in which he lived?) was of no concern to the rest of the universe.

As you seek to grasp the surface-level meaning of the lines, you may become aware that meaning resides not only in the definitions of the words but also in such elements as the situation behind the poem, the way the thoughts are organized, the tone, the imagery, and the sound and metrical patterns. In other words, content is inseparable from form. Nevertheless, even from a first reading we gradually see a pattern in the details and form an idea of both (1) the **subject** or *topic* and (2) the **theme,** *the central idea, description, or mood the poem develops concerning the subject.* Theme includes what the poet has to say about the subject; it is keyed to the poet's purpose in writing the poem. Although the subject may be captured in a single word, a statement of theme normally requires a full phrase or sentence.

Some poems contain an overt statement of the theme; others require us to infer a theme from the elements of the poem by turning the specific literal details into a more generalized statement about the subject, a redescription of the poem. Still others (for example, descriptions or humorous stories) may not require a statement beyond themselves. Frost's poem quoted above may be said to have as its *subject* personal isolation or desolation. Although the sentence "I have been one acquainted with the night" comes closest to an overt statement of *theme*, it seems inadequate. Perhaps a more complete statement of theme may be inferred: The experience of isolation on a personal level may be an indication of human isolation on a cosmic level. Mark

Strand's poem at the beginning of the book is about "eating" or experiencing poetry. But the theme is much more specific. Strand implies that *experiencing* poetry can radically change a person.

No pat statement, of course, embraces a whole poem. Even the quickest comparison of the above statements illustrates the injustice abstract statement does to a poem. Since literature usually contains ambiguities, not everyone will agree with any one statement. A range of meanings is both expected and desirable. The same person reading the same poem at different times—or even at one sitting—will find different meanings. No poem has only one meaning now and forever. There are, however, limits to the range of possibilities; the poem does not mean some things. "Eating Poetry" is not about picking grapefruit; it is not even about dogs or librarians. Nor is "Acquainted with the Night" about romance. A valid statement of theme is neither too specific nor too general for the working of the poem. Although isolating the theme is an invaluable exercise, its importance should neither be exaggerated nor allowed to become pat. Nor is the theme a moral. Sermons preach, but most good poems do not.

No one will like every poem in this book; the editors don't. Taste is an arbitrary and unpredictable phenomenon that differs from person to person and era to era. Some poems strike us because of our past experience, the traditions of our rearing, or our present dilemmas. Some works that don't seem important to us at one time will suddenly become resonant years later. Other poems, which leave us cold, will be someone else's favorites. In any case, we do not have to love a poem to admire its artistry. There should be enough poems here to satisfy most people's taste. Some poems have been chosen for their overall impact; others because they illustrate a certain poetic device; still others because they are beautifully crafted. It is important to remember that although we happen not to like a subject or attitude or style, the poet has the right to make his or her own choices. Even when we hate a poem's point of view, we can admire its effectiveness. With such an attitude, we will be more sophisticated readers than those who simply say "I like it" or "I hate it."

The following are poems many people consider effective. They are presented without questions or comment so that you can meet them on their own terms from the perspectives discussed in this chapter. You may find this summary of these perspectives helpful in understanding the poems. As you read the following chapters, you will add new concepts to those you have already learned.

1. Read the poem aloud first, listening to the way it sounds.
2. As you read it again silently, keep your mind alert in order to observe all the following (though not necessarily in this order):

a. Notice conspicuous details and signals of meaning
   b. Concentrate on the meaning of each sentence
   c. Decide how each sentence relates to the preceding ones
   d. Observe the pattern of ideas and details that is developing
   e. Speculate on the subject and the theme of the poem
3. Look up any unfamiliar words in the dictionary, allowing for multiple meanings made possible by the context of the sentence and the whole poem.
4. Decide on the meaning(s) of the title and its relationship to the poem.
5. Paraphrase any word groups that are troublesome, without straying from the context.
6. Reread the whole poem in the context of your speculation about subject and theme. If your hypothetical statement has left any details unaccounted for, go back to step #1. If you are satisfied, go on to #7.
7. State the subject of the poem and, in a precisely worded phrase or sentence, the theme of the poem.

THE DOUBLE PLAY

In his sea-lit
distance, the pitcher winding
like a clock about to chime comes down with

the ball, hit
sharply, under the artificial   5
banks of arc lights, bounds like a vanishing string

over the green
to the shortstop magically
scoops to his right whirling above his invisible

shadows   10
in the dust redirects
its flight to the running poised second baseman

pirouettes
leaping, above the slide, to throw
from mid-air, across the colored tightened interval,   15

to the leaning-
out first baseman ends the dance
drawing it disappearing into his long brown glove

stretches. What
is too swift for deception   20
is final, lost, among the loosened figures

jogging off the field
 (the pitcher walks), casual
in the space where the poem has happened.

>   *Robert Wallace* (b. 1932)

WHEN I WAS ONE-AND-TWENTY

When I was one-and-twenty
    I heard a wise man say,
'Give crowns and pounds and guineas°   °*British currency,*
    But not your heart away;   *in order of value*
Give pearls away and rubies   5
    But keep your fancy free.'
But I was one-and-twenty,
    No use to talk to me.

When I was one-and-twenty
    I heard him say again,   10
'The heart out of the bosom
    Was never given in vain;
'Tis paid with sighs a plenty
    And sold for endless rue.'
And I am two-and-twenty,   15
    And oh, 'tis true, 'tis true.

>   *A. E. Housman* (1859–1936)

INCIDENT

(*For Eric Walrond*)

Once riding in old Baltimore,
    Heart-filled, head-filled with glee,
I saw a Baltimorean
    Keep looking straight at me.

Now I was eight and very small,   5
    And he was no whit bigger,
And so I smiled, but he poked out
    His tongue, and called me, "Nigger."

I saw the whole of Baltimore
    From May until December;   10
Of all the things that happened there
    That's all that I remember.

>   *Countee Cullen* (1903–1946)

AFTER GREAT PAIN, A FORMAL FEELING COMES

After great pain, a formal feeling comes—
The Nerves sit ceremonious, like Tombs—
The stiff Heart questions was it He, that bore,
And Yesterday, or Centuries before?

The Feet, mechanical, go round—　　　　　　　　　5
A Wooden way
Of Ground, or Air, or Ought°—　　　　　　　　°nothingness
Regardless grown,
A Quartz contentment, like a stone—

This is the Hour of Lead—　　　　　　　　　　10
Remembered, if outlived,
As Freezing persons, recollect the Snow—
First—Chill—then Stupor—then the letting go—

　　　　　　　Emily Dickinson　(1830–1886)

2

THE SPEAKER, THE AUDIENCE, THE SITUATION

AT SEVENTEEN

I learned the truth at seventeen
That love was meant for beauty queens
and high school girls with clear-skinned smiles
who married young, and then retired
The valentines I never knew   5
The Friday night charades of youth
were spent on one more beautiful
At seventeen, I learned the truth

And those of us with ravaged faces
lacking in the social graces   10
desperately remained at home
inventing lovers on the phone
who called to say 'Come dance with me'
and murmured vague obscenities
It isn't all it seems at seventeen   15

A brown-eyed girl in hand-me-downs
whose name I never could pronounce
said 'Pity please the ones who serve
'Cause they only get what they deserve'
The rich-relationed hometown queen   20
marries into what she needs
The guarantee of company
and haven for the elderly

Remember those who win the game
They lose the love they sought to gain   25
in debentures of quality
and dubious integrity
Their small-town eyes will gape at you
in dull surprise when payment due
exceed accounts received at seventeen   30

To those of us who knew the pain
of valentines that never came

>   and those whose names were never called
>   when choosing sides for basketball
>   It was long ago, and far away   35
>   The world was younger than today
>   and dreams were all they gave for free
>   to ugly duckling girls like me
>
>   We play the game, and when we dare
>   to cheat ourselves at solitaire   40
>   Inventing lovers on the phone
>   Repenting other lives unknown
>   that call and say 'Come dance with me'
>   and murmur vague obscenities
>   at ugly girls like me, at seventeen   45

Janis Ian (b. 1950)

Janis Ian's "At Seventeen" has won a number of awards and become a popular classic. But many people who have heard it—even those who have resisted the mind-relaxation induced by the music and actually listened to the words—are probably unaware that these song lyrics stand on their own as a poem.

Since it was composed to be transmitted orally and to be accompanied by music, the song exhibits traditional characteristics of oral literature: it is more loosely constructed, more repetitious, and less complex than many poems intended to be read and reread from the page. Nevertheless, it reveals several techniques poets use to great advantage.

The first word is the pronoun "I," and the word "me" appears several times. Since we all use these first-person pronouns to refer to ourselves, we can assume that someone is speaking and that whoever it may be is referring to him- or herself. The more poems we read, the more conscious we will become that every poem has a **persona:** *the "I" of the poem, the speaker, the literary creation whose voice is heard in the poem.*

"At Seventeen" raises a number of questions. Who is this "I" intruding into our world, demanding our attention? Is the speaker Janis Ian herself, telling of her own teenage years? Someone distinguishable from the poet? Or someone who resembles the singer yet has a separate and recognizable identity? It is important that we answer these questions, for in any poem the speaker is a means by which the poet orders the poem, expresses its theme, and shapes the reader's responses to words, actions, and attitudes.

To define the nature of the first-person voice of "At Seventeen," we need to answer some additional questions, such as these: What does the poem reveal about the speaker's age and sex? What do we learn about this individual's teenage years—particularly physical appearance, economic status, attitudes toward social rituals, dating, sexual encounters, and marriage? Can we determine whether the persona still has the same self-image and attitude toward life? Finally, how does the author use these details to influence our perceptions of the "truth" of life at seventeen?

The song itself provides unambiguous answers to most of these questions, encouraging us to envision a certain kind of speaker. Line 35, for instance, indicates that the speaker is older than seventeen. The experience related is "long ago, and far away" when "The world was younger than today." Exactly how much older, we don't know and don't need to know. The speaker is obviously a woman (she refers to "ugly duckling girls like me"). Further, a paraphrase of the two specific references to her physical appearance ("ravaged faces" in line 9 and "ugly duckling" in line 38) indicates that she still remembers herself as plain, inferior to beautiful girls, and unattractive to males. Although the speaker does not mention economic status, her many references to money betray financial insecurity and, perhaps, envy of the "rich-relationed hometown queen." She also seems to be socially insecure: "lacking in the social graces," she "desperately remained at home" playing solitaire, longing for valentines, and inventing imaginary lovers. Even when sides were chosen for basketball she indicates that she felt inferior.

Her attitude toward the social activities of others is cynical—again perhaps revealing her own insecurity or enduring bitterness. Ordinary Friday night dates she calls the "charades of youth," and she says that beauty queens marry only for "a guarantee of company" and for financial security. She also relives the loneliness of sitting at home cheating herself at solitaire, having to fantasize the activities she believes others participate in.

Although we know the teenage self of the persona very well by the end, we do not have comparable details about her present life. We don't know, for example, whether she still feels alienated, whether age and maturity have caused her to change her outlook, or whether she has learned to cope with things she cannot change. However, the clarity with which she recollects the past, the emotional undercurrent of her words, and the shift from past to present tense in the last section all suggest that she still feels deeply the pain and disillusion that she experienced as a teen-ager.

Anyone familiar with Janis Ian's music and aware of her background may be tempted to identify her with the persona. We know, for example, that Ian was older than seventeen when she composed the song (she was born in 1950, and "At Seventeen" was recorded in 1973) and, according to some of her biographers, Ian was herself a sensitive and insecure child who disliked school and had little opportunity to develop friendships because her family constantly moved from one city to another. Moreover, it is Janis Ian's voice that we hear singing "I learned the truth at seventeen," her face that appears on the album cover, her protests about the alienated individual that echo in the haunting melodies of most of her other songs.

Yet there are also significant differences between the persona and Janis Ian. The former seems completely isolated, but Ian became a celebrity at sixteen, when she wrote and recorded "Society's Child." The speaker was obviously single at seventeen, but when Ian was that age, she briefly abandoned her show business career and got married. And some of the speaker's attitudes—especially the assertion that "love was meant for beauty queens"—are contradicted by the lyrics of other songs on the same album.

Thus, even when we sense that the "I" of a poem is a very personal voice that echoes the emotions and attitudes of the poet, we should be willing to recognize that the persona of any poem is not the poet directly but the *artistic creation* of the poet, who must be granted the imaginative freedom to alter, omit, and arrange details, and even biographical facts. The term we have used to describe this voice derives from classical theater, where *persona* referred to a mask worn by the actor. It still carries with it the sense that whenever a person writes a work of literature, he or she is creating a voice, striking a pose, or donning a mask for a particular utterance on a particular occasion.

In Ian's song, our sense of theme is shaped by a persona who is a representative figure, a spokesperson for the many people—men and women—who have felt these same emotions, felt them so deeply that even in adulthood they have not escaped the painful memory of not belonging.

The next poem is radically different from "At Seventeen." Its language is tight rather than loose; its brevity creates an impact that can take our breath away; its subject is much more somber. The relationship between poet and persona is also quite different.

THE DEATH OF THE BALL TURRET GUNNER[1]

From my mother's sleep I fell into the State,
And I hunched in its belly till my wet fur froze.
Six miles from earth, loosed from its dream of life,
I woke to black flak° and the nightmare fighters.   °*exploding shells*
When I died they washed me out of the turret with a hose.   5

Randall Jarrell (1914–1965)

In "The Death of the Ball Turret Gunner," what distinctions do the circumstances force us to make between the author and the speaker? What

---

[1] According to Jarrell's own note to the poem, "A ball turret was a plexiglass sphere set into the belly of a B-17 or B-24, and inhabited by two .50 caliber machine-guns and one man, a short small man. When this gunner tracked with his machine-guns a fighter attacking his bomber from below, he revolved with the turret; hunched upside down in his little sphere, he looked like the fetus in the womb. The fighters which attacked him were armed with cannon firing explosive shells. The hose was a steam hose."

does Jarrell accomplish by using such a persona and by withholding the most crucial evidence until the end of the poem?

Obviously the speaker here is dead (the phrase "when I died" is in the past tense) and thus cannot be the poet. Jarrell published his poem in 1945; he lived until 1965. The temptation to say "Jarrell says in line . . ." is therefore inappropriate, even though this nightmare vision emerges from his own military experience in World War II. In fact, most of the impact of this poem is a result of our becoming aware in the last line that we are being addressed by an "I" who is a dead person. That is at least one reason we do not learn of the death until the last line. And the brutal act of washing the body out of the turret with a hose is described in such emotionless terms that it has an incredibly chilling effect.

The poem offers still more information about the gunner (presumably a man, since the setting is World War II combat) and his attitudes. What does he mean in line 1 when he says that he "fell into the State"? How do the words "hunched in its belly" and "wet fur" describe him? What relationship does he have with the State? Why does he speak of sleeping, dreaming, and waking?

Certainly the poem represents a brutal awakening on the part of the airman—an awakening to the realization of his own unimportance to the State, among other things. In sharp contrast to the humanized persona of the first line (notice the image of birth), the persona of the final lines is treated like a thing (even a messy obstacle) or at best an animal. Awakened from his human dreams of life, in midair he confronts the blackness of wartime death.

Because the airman himself tells the story, it has an immediacy that Jarrell could not have attained if he had assumed the role of a detached reporter and simply told us about the gunner's death. Also, by drawing us into the poem and allowing us to experience the meaning of war in this immediate and shocking way, he communicates more about its impersonality and horror than would be possible through any abstract thematic statement. What is even more remarkable is that Jarrell is able to distance himself from the speaker without sacrificing his own imaginative and emotional identification with the gunner.

From these two poems, then, we learn that a persona may be very close to the poet or distant from the poet and still speak in the first person ("I") as an apparent spokesperson for the author. In some works, however, a very different kind of relationship exists between the poet and the persona. As you read the next poem, look not only for details that reveal the character of the speaker but also for evidence that indicates whether or not he is the kind of man that the poet—or anyone else—would identify or sympathize with. The insights you gain from this inquiry should in turn clarify other, more obscure aspects of the poem.

MY LAST DUCHESS[1]
Ferrara

That's my last Duchess painted on the wall,
Looking as if she were alive. I call
That piece a wonder, now: Frà Pandolf's[2] hands
Worked busily a day, and there she stands.
Will't please you sit and look at her? I said   5
"Frà Pandolf" by design, for never read
Strangers like you that pictured countenance,
The depth and passion of its earnest glance,
But to myself they turned (since none puts by
The curtain I have drawn for you, but I)   10
And seemed as they would ask me, if they durst,
How such a glance came there; so not the first
Are you to turn and ask thus. Sir, 'twas not
Her husband's presence only, called that spot
Of joy into the Duchess' cheek: perhaps   15
Frà Pandolf chanced to say "Her mantle laps
Over my lady's wrist too much," or "Paint
Must never hope to reproduce the faint
Half-flush that dies along her throat": such stuff
Was courtesy, she thought, and cause enough   20
For calling up that spot of joy. She had
A heart—how shall I say?—too soon made glad,
Too easily impressed; she liked whate'er
She looked on, and her looks went everywhere.
Sir, 'twas all one! My favor at her breast,   25
The dropping of the daylight in the West,
The bough of cherries some officious° fool   °*fawning*
Broke in the orchard for her, the white mule
She rode with round the terrace—all and each
Would draw from her alike the approving speech,   30
Or blush, at least. She thanked men,—good! but thanked
Somehow—I know not how—as if she ranked
My gift of a nine-hundred-years-old name
With anybody's gift. Who'd stoop to blame
This sort of trifling? Even had you skill   35
In speech— which I have not —to make your will
Quite clear to such an one, and say, "Just this
Or that in you disgusts me; here you miss,

---

[1] Scholars have conjectured that the duke is modelled on a sixteenth-century Italian nobleman whose wife died under mysterious circumstances. Ferrara is a city near Venice.

[2] A fictitious name. Here, the painter is represented as a member of a monastic order ("Frà" means "Brother").

Or there exceed the mark"—and if she let
Herself be lessoned so, nor plainly set   40
Her wits to yours, forsooth, and made excuse
—E'en then would be some stooping; and I choose
Never to stoop. Oh sir, she smiled, no doubt,
Whene'er I passed her; but who passed without
Much the same smile? This grew; I gave commands; 45
Then all smiles stopped together. There she stands
As if alive. Will't please you rise? We'll meet
The company below, then. I repeat,
The Count your master's known munificence° °generosity
Is ample warrant that no just pretence   50
Of mine for dowry will be disallowed;
Though his fair daughter's self, as I avowed
At starting, is my object. Nay, we'll go
Together down, sir. Notice Neptune,° though, °Roman god
Taming a sea-horse, thought a rarity,   of the sea 55
Which Claus of Innsbruck[3] cast in bronze for me!

Robert Browning (1812–1889)

[3] A city in Austria noted for its bronzework. Claus, like Frà Pandolf, is fictitious.

We don't have to read very far to discover that the poet is not speaking in a personal voice here. Robert Browning was an English poet of the nineteenth century; the persona is an Italian duke of the sixteenth century. Even so, Browning could be using the duke as a spokesman, just as Jarrell uses the airman in "The Death of the Ball Turret Gunner." Let's see if the evidence of the poem supports such a reading.

In the duke's own estimation, he is worthy of the highest respect and admiration. He possesses great wealth, he has the prestige and power of high rank and a nine-hundred-year-old name, he is a collector of fine paintings and sculpture, and—if the eloquence and sophistication of his speech are any indication—he is also a man of considerable intelligence. Are we to suppose, then, that the poet shares the duke's high opinion of himself? Before making this assumption, let's look into the duke's words further to see if they reveal any unflattering characteristics. Consider, for example, his excessive pride and egotism, his treatment of other people, and his reasons for putting so much emphasis on his art collection.

Modesty is not one of the duke's virtues. Notice the frequency with which he uses the words "I" and "my":

> "That's my last Duchess . . ."
> "I call that piece a wonder . . ."
> "I said Frà Pandolf by design . . ."
> "None puts by the curtain I have drawn for you but I . . ."
> "I repeat . . ."
> "My object . . ."

This list is hardly complete, but it suggests the magnitude of the duke's egotism. His self-love is also evident in his comments about his aristocratic genealogy; in his contempt for anyone below his rank, such as the "officious fool" who broke a bough of cherries for the duchess; and in his disgust with the duchess for accepting such favors and failing to pay him the absolute devotion he believes he deserves. So great is his pride that he will not even "stoop" to inform her of his dissatisfaction. Moreover, as lines 45–46 imply, he is directly responsible for her death: "I gave commands/ Then all smiles stopped together."

Although the duke is the only speaker in this poem, he is not the only character in it. Present also is a specific **audience,** *the "you" of the poem to whom the persona speaks.* We become aware of this listener as early as line 5, but his identity becomes clear only in the last ten lines. Who is the "you" of the poem, and why has he come to the duke's palace? What motivates the duke to tell this individual the story of his previous duchess? Is there any evidence to suggest how the listener reacts to the duke's monologue or what he will report to his master?

Once we have recognized that the duke's audience is the emissary of a count who wishes to arrange a marriage between his daughter and the duke, the whole context of the latter's speech becomes clear. When the poem opens, the negotiations between the duke and the emissary are nearing an end. The "company"—presumably other members of the count's party—are waiting below, but before the two leave to rejoin the others, the duke asks the emissary to sit and look at the portrait of the duchess. Although the duke takes this opportunity to expound upon his wealth and breeding, his primary purpose is to emphasize that his next duchess must live in absolute and utter devotion to him if she wishes to avoid the fate of her predecessor.

Because the emissary's reactions are not recorded in the poem, we cannot be certain what he will report to the count, nor do we have any way of guessing how the count will respond. The envoy may have been taken in by the duke's persuasive speech and impressed with his family name and wealth. Even if the envoy brings back an unfavorable report, the count may be as indifferent to the well-being of his daughter as the duke was to the happiness of his last wife. Another possibility, however, is that the duke's chauvinistic self-portrait reveals more than he intended and that when the envoy narrates it, the count will break off the marriage negotiations that the duke is obviously hoping to complete.

Browning's method in "My Last Duchess" is much like that of a playwright who sets the scene, creates characters, and orders events without intruding into the imagined world of his creation. In fact, the term that best describes the poem is **dramatic monologue,** *a speech occasioned by a dramatic situation and delivered by an individualized character to an implied or identifiable listener within the poem.* It is a demanding technique, but Browning handles it with great skill to objectify the workings of a complex mind and to explore the effects of an excessive preoccupation with self.

The artistry of the poem is reason enough to study it carefully, but this work is also valuable for what it says about the limitations and excesses of human beings in any place or time. In our own society, there are people like the duke who are jealous and possessive, who judge others by their wealth and class rather than by their human worth, and who attempt to destroy that which they cannot understand. It makes no difference that some of them wear three-piece suits rather than the robes of aristocracy and live in penthouses instead of palaces.

Although Browning's poem leaves us with several unresolved questions, it is representative of poems that make explicit the identity of the persona and audience as well as the context. Many other poems are ambiguous on these points, however. In the work that follows there is very little we can be sure of.

HOW ANNANDALE WENT OUT

"They called it Annandale—and I was there
To flourish, to find words, and to attend:
Liar, physician, hypocrite, and friend,
I watched him; and the sight was not so fair
As one or two that I have seen elsewhere;   5
An apparatus not for me to mend—
A wreck, with hell between him and the end,
Remained of Annandale; and I was there.

"I knew the ruin as I knew the man;
So put the two together, if you can,   10
Remembering the worst you know of me.
Now view yourself as I was, on the spot—
With a slight kind of engine. Do you see?
Like this . . . You wouldn't hang me? I thought not."

Edwin Arlington Robinson (1869–1935)

In order to understand this poem, we need to answer several interrelated questions: Who or what is Annandale? Who is speaking in the poem? Whom does this person address? Where is the persona when he or she speaks these words? What circumstances motivate the monologue?

The words "him" (lines 4 and 7) and "man" (line 9) seemingly identify Annandale as a man, but he is also described in dehumanized, mechanical terms: "it," "apparatus," "wreck," "ruin." One way of interpreting these ambiguous references is to see Annandale either as the victim of an accident that has destroyed his human features and left only the suffering remnants of a man, or perhaps as someone suffering from an incurable disease. If such is Robinson's intent, the speaker's description of himself as "Liar, physician, hypocrite, and friend" would be literal. As a physician, he (if it is a he) realizes he cannot "mend" or cure Annandale; as a friend, he can merely delude Annandale with words of comfort, thus becoming a liar and hypocrite. His sense of helplessness is especially clear at the end of the first section (lines 1–8), where he describes the "hell" or suffering that lies between Annandale and "the end" (death).

It is not until the final section of the poem (lines 9–14) that we discover whom the persona is addressing or how Annandale "went out" (a euphemism for death), and even here the poem works through indirection and implication rather than explicit statement. What is the "slight kind of engine" that the persona refers to in line 13, and what connection does it have with the circumstances described in lines 1–8? Who would know "the worst" about the speaker, sit in judgment on his actions, and hang him?

If we paraphrase the words "slight kind of engine" as "small instrument" (perhaps a scalpel), we can make several assumptions about the context of the speaker's monologue. Apparently, he has relieved Annandale of his suffering by performing a mercy killing and is now attempting to explain the circumstances to someone who knows at least part of the story.

Who, we might ask, would be the likely audience for such a speech: a jury in a courtroom setting? A priest in the confessional? Another physician in a hospital? The reader perhaps? Since the setting is not described and there are not enough details to make the kind of inferences we did in "My Last Duchess," we have to assume that those facts are less important than the arguments advanced by the speaker. He defends himself—as anyone might—by asking those who judge him to think about Annandale's condition, put themselves in the speaker's place, and acquit him: " 'You wouldn't hang me? I thought not.' "

In both "My Last Duchess" and "How Annandale Went Out," the details that contribute to our knowledge of persona and audience also help to establish the underlying **situation** of the poem: *the physical setting, time of the action, social and historical context, and circumstances (including events that have occurred before the opening of the poem) that influence thought and action*. Although the two previous works require us to infer much of this information, some poems, such as the next, treat situation very explicitly.

THE END OF THE WEEKEND

A dying firelight slides along the quirt°   °*riding whip*
Of the cast-iron cowboy where he leans
Against my father's books. The lariat
Whirls into darkness. My girl, in skin-tight jeans,

THE SPEAKER, THE AUDIENCE, THE SITUATION

Fingers a page of Captain Marryat,°   °*writer of*   5
Inviting insolent shadows to her shirt.   *adventure*
                                                                                                                                                                              stories

We rise together to the second floor.
Outside, across the lake, an endless wind
Whips at the headstones of the dead and wails
In the trees for all who have and have not sinned.   10
She rubs against me and I feel her nails.
Although we are alone, I lock the door.

The eventual shapes of all our formless prayers,
This dark, this cabin of loose imaginings,
Wind, lake, lip, everything awaits   15
The slow unloosening of her underthings.
And then the noise. Something is dropped. It grates
Against the attic beams.
                     I climb the stairs,

Armed with a belt.   20
                A long magnesium strip
Of moonlight from the dormer cuts a path
Among the shattered skeletons of mice.
A great black presence beats its wings in wrath.
Above the boneyard burn its golden eyes.   25
Some small grey fur is pulsing in its grip.

                   Anthony Hecht (b. 1923)

    We can determine the basic facts of this poem by answering such questions as these: Where and when do the events of the poem take place? What individuals are present, how long have they been there, and what is their relationship to each other? Does the persona show any uneasiness before hearing the noise? What significance does the attic scene have for the speaker? What events are likely to occur after the final scene? Does the poem have a theme?

    The details of the poem clearly indicate that the speaker and his girlfriend are spending the weekend (note the title) at a two-story cabin that belongs to the persona's father and is situated in the woods, by a lake, close to a cemetery. At the beginning of the poem, the couple is in the library near a fireplace.

    Although the poem begins with a description of the old-fashioned cowboy bookends that support a row of the father's books, the speaker soon shifts his attention to his girlfriend, who is thumbing through an adventure story. They have obviously been at the cabin for some time because the fire is dying; nevertheless, it casts shadows that flippantly play on the girl's shirt and excite the boyfriend.

In stanzas 2 and 3, the scene shifts to the second floor. The seductive mood builds, but not without an undercurrent of apprehensiveness about the foreboding environment outside. Then, suddenly, comes the noise from the attic, the sound of "something . . . dropped," followed by a grating on the attic beams. Already nervous about the remote location of the cabin, the closeness of the cemetery, and the ominous wailing of the wind, the man climbs the stairs to the attic. Like a camera operator filming a scene from a suspense story, Hecht follows the speaker as he ascends the stairs, then cuts to the attic and fixes on the climactic scene, which we observe from the man's point of view.

The title lets us know that the noises from the attic and the fears they arouse will bring a premature end to the couple's weekend. But the thematic significance of the attic scene is less certain. Possibly the man identifies himself with the "great black presence" and his girlfriend with its victim, but support for this reading is weakened by the fact that the woman is as anxious to make love as her boyfriend. Presumably, she has willingly accompanied him to the cabin; they "rise together" to the bedroom, and there she "rubs against" him, inviting more intimate contact. That their lovemaking is interrupted might suggest a moralistic theme, but only one reference to sin occurs (line 10), and it lumps together "all who have and have not sinned." A more plausible interpretation is that the predator presiding over the "boneyard" of "shattered skeletons" is the embodiment of the persona's own fears, or that this vision of death in nature makes him aware of his own mortality and of the brevity of even the most pleasurable moments of life.

In Hecht's poem, as in the other works discussed in this chapter, ambiguity is not a defect but a conscious effect of an artistic method that allows us to see and hear what the speaker perceives—but forces us to interpret everything for ourselves. Ambiguity is particularly important in "The End of the Weekend" because giving a name to our "loose imaginings," as the speaker calls them, would mean removing the mystery—and fascination—from them.

Up to this point, it may seem that every poem has a distinctive persona and that most have identifiable audiences and fully defined contexts or situations. But as the next work illustrates, a poem can communicate effectively even though it has none of these elements.

SPRING IS LIKE A PERHAPS HAND

Spring is like a perhaps hand
(which comes carefully
out of Nowhere)arranging
a window,into which people look(while
people stare   5

arranging and changing placing
carefully there a strange
thing and a known thing here)and

changing everything carefully

Spring is like a perhaps   10
Hand in a window
(carefully to
and fro moving New and
Old things,while
people stare carefully   15
moving a perhaps
fraction of flower here placing
an inch of air there)and

without breaking anything.

E. E. Cummings (1894–1962)

How much can we determine about the persona of this poem? Is a specific audience, either inside or outside the framework of the poem, designated? Does the poem have a recognizable setting? Is there any indication of what motivates the speaker's words?

"Spring is like a perhaps hand" does not clearly reveal a specific persona, audience, or setting, except in minimal ways. Thus we may assume that its context is unimportant and that the author wishes to direct us to other issues, such as those suggested by the following questions: What human traits is spring endowed with? What are people doing while spring is "arranging and changing" things? What inferences can we make concerning the persona's attitude toward nature?

The central concern of Cummings' poem is the relationship between nature and human beings; the words "Spring Is Like a Perhaps Hand" imply a close relationship between the two, but the word "perhaps" qualifies the comparison. In fact, this extended analogy between unseen essence and tangible object illuminates the differences between natural and human powers. Spring—like a human hand—can arrange and change things, but its sphere is not restricted to department store windows, nor is it as careless and destructive as people often are. Coming out of "Nowhere," spring works gracefully, almost mystically, "arranging and . . . placing," changing "everything." Spring even has the power to create unity out of separateness, to join the "strange thing" and the "known thing," the "New and/Old things," carefully shaping all aspects of nature with a precision unavailable to the human hand. While people merely "look" and "stare," spring moves a "fraction of flower" and an "inch of air," always "carefully," without ever "breaking anything."

In this poem, then, meaning is imbedded in language, rather than in dramatic context. And because the poem lacks any signal of insincerity or irony, we may assume that the persona expresses attitudes that are in keeping with the philosophy of the author.

Building on our analysis of these specific works, we should now be able to draw some conclusions about how and why poets create speakers, audiences, and situations. Here are some suggestions to help you in your study of other poems:

1. To identify the speaker of a poem, notice the title and any other details that aid in identification. Note particularly the pronoun references.
    a. First-person pronouns (I, me, mine; we, us, our) not included within direct quotations usually identify the speaker: Characterize the speaker using the poem's details. Also, make inferences based on less explicit evidence. Be especially aware of details that create a separation between poet and persona, and determine what the poet accomplishes by constructing the poem from this point of view.
    b. The absence of first-person pronouns requires even further inference on your part. Notice details that indicate whether the voice of the persona is close to the poet's or not. Even if persona and poet are close, characterize the speaker only by the details in the poem. If the speaker is not fully described, the poet may be focusing directly on the subject, on an interpretation of it, or on the audience.
    c. Sometimes you will discover that a poem has more than one speaker. Look for quotation marks and other indicators that distinguish one speaker's words from another's.
2. To identify audience, note pronoun references and other details.
    a. Second-person pronouns (you, thou, thee, thine) normally indicate the audience. Characterize the audience by noting all explicit and implicit details. Determine whether the audience is a functional character inside the poem or simply you, the reader, outside the poem.
    b. The absence of second-person pronouns makes the precise audience indeterminable. Practically speaking, however, you can assume the audience to be the reader.
3. To identify the situation and context, be attentive to signals of time, place, past and anticipated events. Make as precise inferences as the poem allows. The absence of these signals leaves the situation ambiguous or indeterminable. If there is a specific situation, determine what it adds to the impact of the poem.

4. As you accumulate information, you will naturally form your own value judgments about speaker, audience, and situation. Verbalize your reactions and support them with details included in the poem (and also those excluded from it). Do the values asserted by the persona conflict with the poet's? Do they clash with your own?

Now, without more specific directions, study the following two poems using the concepts discussed in chapters 1 and 2. Be especially aware of the way each author's handling of speaker, audience, and situation shapes your responses to the poem.

HAWK ROOSTING

I sit in the top of the wood, my eyes closed.
Inaction, no falsifying dream
Between my hooked head and hooked feet:
Or in sleep rehearse perfect kills and eat.

The convenience of the high trees!   5
The air's buoyancy and the sun's ray
Are of advantage to me;
And the earth's face upward for my inspection.

My feet are locked upon the rough bark.
It took the whole of Creation   10
To produce my foot, my each feather:
Now I hold Creation in my foot

Or fly up, and revolve it all slowly—
I kill where I please because it is all mine.
There is no sophistry in my body: 15
My manners are tearing off heads—

The allotment of death.
For the one path of my flight is direct
Through the bones of the living.
No arguments assert my right: 20

The sun is behind me.
Nothing has changed since I began.
My eye has permitted no change.
I am going to keep things like this.

Ted Hughes (b. 1930)

HURT HAWKS

I

The broken pillar of the wing jags from the clotted shoulder,
The wing trails like a banner in defeat,
No more to use the sky forever but live with famine
And pain a few days: cat nor coyote
Will shorten the week of waiting for death, there is game without talons.   5
He stands under the oak-bush and waits
The lame feet of salvation; at night he remembers freedom
And flies in a dream, the dawns ruin it.
He is strong and pain is worse to the strong, incapacity is worse.
The curs of the day come and torment him   10
At distance, no one but death the redeemer will humble that head,
The intrepid readiness, the terrible eyes.
The wild God of the world is sometimes merciful to those
That ask mercy, not often to the arrogant.
You do not know him, you communal people, or you have forgotten him;   15
Intemperate and savage, the hawk remembers him;
Beautiful and wild, the hawks, and men that are dying, remember him.

II

I'd sooner, except the penalties, kill a man than a hawk; but the great redtail°   °redtailed hawk
Had nothing left but unable misery
From the bone too shattered for mending, the wing that trailed under his talons when he moved.   20
We had fed him six weeks, I gave him freedom,
He wandered over the foreland hill and returned in the evening, asking for death,
Not like a beggar, still eyed with the old
Implacable arrogance. I gave him the lead gift in the twilight. What fell was relaxed,
Owl-downy, soft feminine feathers; but what   25
Soared: the fierce rush: the night-herons by the flooded river cried fear at its rising
Before it was quite unsheathed from reality.

Robinson Jeffers (1887–1962)

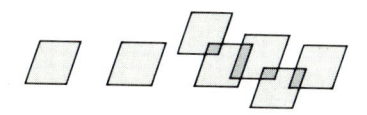

POEMS FOR FURTHER STUDY 1

THE UNKNOWN CITIZEN

*(To JS/07/M/378
This Marble Monument Is Erected by the State)*

He was found by the Bureau of Statistics to be
One against whom there was no official complaint,
And all the reports on his conduct agree
That, in the modern sense of an old-fashioned word, he was a saint,
For in everything he did he served the Greater Community. 5
Except for the War till the day he retired
He worked in a factory and never got fired,
But satisfied his employers, Fudge Motors Inc.
Yet he wasn't a scab or odd in his views,
For his Union reports that he paid his dues, 10
(Our report on his Union shows it was sound)
And our Social Psychology workers found
That he was popular with his mates and liked a drink.
The Press are convinced that he bought a paper every day
And that his reactions to advertisements were normal in every way. 15
Policies taken out in his name prove that he was fully insured,
And his Health-card shows he was once in hospital but left it cured.
Both Producers Research and High-Grade Living declare
He was fully sensible to the advantages of the Instalment Plan
And had everything necessary to the Modern Man, 20
A phonograph, a radio, a car and a frigidaire.
Our researchers into Public Opinion are content
That he held the proper opinions for the time of year;
When there was peace, he was for peace; when there was war, he went.
He was married and added five children to the population, 25
Which our Eugenist says was the right number for a parent of his
 generation,
And our teachers report that he never interfered with their education.
Was he free? Was he happy? The question is absurd:
Had anything been wrong, we should certainly have heard.

W. H. Auden (1907–1973)

QUESTIONS

1. Who or what is the speaker in this poem? Consider especially the implications of the epigraph and the frequent references to "our" and "we."
2. Is the persona addressing a specific or a general audience? Explain.
3. What is the context of the persona's remarks? Which occasion or situation, for example, might inspire them?
4. What is the "old-fashioned" meaning of the word "saint"? According to the persona, what is the "modern" meaning of this word? How does the unknown citizen conform to this modern definition of sainthood?
5. What does the speaker tell us about the unknown citizen's professional and personal life? How much do we learn about his thoughts and feelings?
6. Describe the persona's attitude toward the unknown citizen? Do you think the author shares the speaker's opinion, or does the poem suggest that a discrepancy exists between poet and persona? Explain.
7. Based on the evidence of the poem as a whole, do you agree with the persona's assertion that the citizen "had everything necessary to the Modern Man"? Why or why not?
8. What is the significance of the title?

NAMING OF PARTS

To-day we have naming of parts. Yesterday,
We had daily cleaning. And to-morrow morning,
We shall have what to do after firing. But to-day,
To-day we have naming of parts. Japonica°   °Japanese quince
Glistens like coral in all of the neighbouring gardens,   5
    And to-day we have naming of parts.

This is the lower sling swivel. And this
Is the upper sling swivel, whose use you will see,
When you are given your slings. And this is the piling swivel,
Which in your case you have not got. The branches   10
Hold in the gardens their silent, eloquent gestures,
    Which in our case we have not got.

This is the safety-catch, which is always released
With an easy flick of the thumb. And please do not let me
See anyone using his finger. You can do it quite easy   15
If you have any strength in your thumb. The blossoms
Are fragile and motionless, never letting anyone see
    Any of them using their finger.

And this you can see is the bolt. The purpose of this
Is to open the breech, as you see. We can slide it   20

Rapidly backwards and forwards: we call this
Easing the spring. And rapidly backwards and forwards
The early bees are assaulting and fumbling the flowers:
    They call it easing the Spring.

They call it easing the Spring: it is perfectly easy   25
If you have any strength in your thumb: like the bolt,
And the breech, and the cocking-piece, and the point of balance,
Which in our case we have not got; and the almond-blossom
Silent in all of the gardens and the bees going backwards and forwards,
    For to-day we have naming of parts.   30

Henry Reed (b. 1914)

QUESTIONS

1. As you read the poem, note in each stanza an abrupt shift in subject matter, attitude, and sounds. Point to the breaks. Describe the lines before and after each break.
2. Given this analysis of each stanza, characterize the speaker(s) in each. What makes you think that (a) one person is speaking or (b) two people are speaking?
3. Does the audience shift with the break in each stanza? To whom does each part seem to be addressed?
4. In what physical setting(s) might such a speech take place? What is happening during the poem?
5. Certain lines in the first part of each stanza are repeated in the second part. What is the purpose of the repetition? The effect? Does the tone of the repeated phrase change? Does the meaning?
6. Several of the military instructions gather sexual implications in the poem. Isolate them. What is the point of such implications?
7. The poem implies an attitude toward its subject more general than the immediate context. What is it?

THE SUN RISING

      Busy old fool, unruly sun,
      Why dost thou thus
Through windows and through curtains call on us?
Must to thy motions lovers' seasons run?
      Saucy pedantic wretch, go chide   5
      Late schoolboys and sour prentices,°   °*apprentices*
Go tell court huntsmen that the King will ride
Call country ants to harvest offices;°   °*tasks*
Love, all alike, no season knows nor clime,
Nor hours, days, months, which are the rags of time.   10

>   Thy beams, so reverend and strong
>   Why shouldst thou think?
>   I could eclipse and cloud them with a wink,
>   But that I would not lose her sight so long;
>   If her eyes have not blinded thine,   15
>   Look, and tomorrow late tell me
>   Whether both the Indias of spice and mine[1]
>   Be where thou left'st them, or lie here with me.
>   Ask for those kings whom thou saw'st yesterday,
>   And thou shalt hear, All here in one bed lay.   20
>
>   She is all states, and all princes I;
>   Nothing else is.
>   Princes do but play us; compared to this,
>   All honor's mimic, all wealth alchemy.[2]
>   Thou, sun, art half as happy as we,   25
>   In that the world's contracted thus;
>   Thine age asks ease, and since thy duties be
>   To warm the world, that's done in warming us.
>   Shine here to us, and thou art everywhere;
>   This bed thy center is, these walls thy sphere.   30
>
>   *John Donne* (1572–1631)

[1] The East Indies were famous for their spices, the West Indies for precious metals.
[2] In this context, "alchemy" (a medieval form of chemistry, the chief aim of which was to find methods of turning base metals into gold) connotes fraud or false value.

QUESTIONS

1. The audience of this poem is much more fully characterized than that of most poems. List all the appositives, adjectives, and characteristics associated with it. How unusual is this compiled description?
2. Why are there so many references to time and space in this poem?
3. Who is talking to the audience? Although the persona speaks for more than one person in line 3, point to a line that tells the sex of the persona. Whom does "us" in line 3 include?
4. The first four and last two lines state the physical setting precisely. What is it? What time of day? What has happened before the time of the poem? Immediately preceding the poem?
5. Describe the persona's attitude to the audience in stanzas 1 and 2. Note the abrupt commands in these stanzas. Why does the persona feel as he does?
6. In what ways do the attitudes of both the persona and the audience change in stanza 3? What, then, is the relationship among the three stanzas? What, finally, is the theme of the poem?

SONNET 48: HOW CAREFUL WAS I, WHEN I TOOK MY WAY

How careful was I, when I took my way,
Each trifle under truest bars to thrust,
That to my use it might unusèd stay
From hands of falsehood, in sure wards of trust.
But thou, to whom my jewels trifles are, 5
Most worthy comfort, now my greatest grief,
Thou best of dearest, and mine only care,
Art left the prey of every vulgar thief.
Thee have I not locked up in any chest,
Save where thou art not, though I feel thou art, 10
Within the gentle closure of my breast,
From whence at pleasure thou mayst come and part.
    And even thence thou wilt be stol'n, I fear,
    For truth proves thievish for a prize so dear.

William Shakespeare (1564–1616)

SONNET 65: SINCE BRASS, NOR STONE, NOR EARTH, NOR BOUNDLESS SEA

Since brass, nor stone, nor earth, nor boundless sea
But sad mortality o'ersways their power,
How with this rage shall beauty hold a plea,
Whose action is no stronger than a flower?
O how shall summer's honey breath hold out 5
Against the wrackful siege of batt'ring days
When rocks impregnable are not so stout
Nor gates of steel so strong but Time decays?
O fearful meditation! where, alack,
Shall Time's best jewel from Time's chest lie hid? 10
Or what strong hand can hold his swift foot back?
Or who his spoil of beauty can forbid?
    O, none! unless this miracle have might,
    That in black ink my love may still shine bright.

William Shakespeare (1564–1616)

QUESTIONS

1. These two sonnets by Shakespeare provide an interesting contrast in point of view. Although both have the same author, probably concern the same beloved, and express fear for the ultimate loss of that person, they approach their subject quite differently. How many times and in

which lines are personal pronouns (I, my, me, thou, thee) used in each poem? Which poem has the effect of a personal statement addressed to an intimate? Which makes a broad generalization on the nature of all things beautiful?

2. Supply the details given and your own inferences about the persona in each poem. In what ways are they similar in both poems? How do they differ? Is one persona necessarily any closer to the poet than the other?

3. What is revealed about their audiences? Do they differ? Discuss the relationship between the speaker, the person talked about, and the audience of each.

4. Comment on the similarity of Sonnet 48, line 5, and Sonnet 65, line 10. Comment on the difference.

5. How much of the situation behind each poem is revealed?

6. Notice that the last line of both poems reverses the basic pattern isolated in question #1. The intimate sonnet closes with a proverbial generalization; the abstract one ends on a personal note. What is the purpose of these reversals?

DOVER BEACH

The sea is calm tonight.
The tide is full, the moon lies fair
Upon the straits; on the French coast the light
Gleams and is gone; the cliffs of England stand,
Glimmering and vast, out in the tranquil bay.   5
Come to the window, sweet is the night-air!
Only, from the long line of spray
Where the sea meets the moon-blanched land,
Listen! you hear the grating roar
Of pebbles which the waves draw back, and fling,   10
At their return, up the high strand,
Begin, and cease, and then again begin,
With tremulous cadence slow, and bring
The eternal note of sadness in.

Sophocles long ago   15
Heard it on the Ægæan,° and it brought   °*The sea on the*
Into his mind the turbid ebb and flow   *eastern side*
Of human misery; we   *of Greece*
Find also in the sound a thought,
Hearing it by this distant northern sea.   20
The Sea of Faith
Was once, too, at the full, and round earth's shore
Lay like the folds of a bright girdle furled.

> But now I only hear
> Its melancholy, long, withdrawing roar, 25
> Retreating, to the breath
> Of the night-wind, down the vast edges drear
> And naked shingles of the world.
>
> Ah, love, let us be true
> To one another! for the world, which seems 30
> To lie before us like a land of dreams,
> So various, so beautiful, so new,
> Hath really neither joy, nor love, nor light,
> Nor certitude, nor peace, nor help for pain;
> And we are here as on a darkling plain 35
> Swept with confused alarms of struggle and flight,
> Where ignorant armies clash by night.
>
> *Matthew Arnold* (1822–1888)

QUESTIONS

1. Dover, England, famous for its chalky cliffs, is only twenty-two miles from Calais, France, across the English Channel. Assembling the references to time and place in the poem, describe in detail the physical setting.

2. How many people are present? What is their relationship? Can you definitely tell which party is the persona and which the audience?

3. The self-contained scene is made more dramatic if we know something of the historical setting out of which the poem grew. It appeared in print in 1867, eight years after the publication of Charles Darwin's contribution to the theory of evolution, *On the Origin of Species,* a work whose impact on traditional religious belief was great. How does a knowledge of this contribute to your understanding of the situation in the poem?

4. In the second stanza, the persona refers to the Greek playwright Sophocles (c. 495–406 B.C.), who wrote great tragedies such as *Oedipus Rex.* What is the purpose of this allusion?

5. One of the techniques that give Arnold's poem its sense of chilling desperation is his use of terms connoting surface calm to describe a condition of inner turmoil. What are some of the words that create this tension?

6. Are the persona's attitudes justified by the circumstances to which he is reacting, or do his words reveal an excessive emotionalism? Explain.

THE DOVER BITCH   A Criticism of Life
for Andrews Wanning

So there stood Matthew Arnold and this girl
With the cliffs of England crumbling away behind them,
And he said to her, "Try to be true to me,
And I'll do the same for you, for things are bad
All over, etc., etc."   5
Well now, I knew this girl. It's true she had read
Sophocles in a fairly good translation
And caught that bitter allusion to the sea,
But all the time he was talking she had in mind
The notion of what his whiskers would feel like   10
On the back of her neck. She told me later on
That after a while she got to looking out
At the lights across the channel, and really felt sad,
Thinking of all the wine and enormous beds
And blandishments in French and the perfumes.   15
And then she got really angry. To have been brought
All the way down from London, and then be addressed
As a sort of mournful cosmic last resort
Is really tough on a girl, and she was pretty.
Anyway, she watched him pace the room   20
And finger his watch-chain and seem to sweat a bit,
And then she said one or two unprintable things.
But you mustn't judge her by that. What I mean to say is,
She's really all right. I still see her once in a while
And she always treats me right. We have a drink   25
And I give her a good time, and perhaps it's a year
Before I see her again, but there she is,
Running to fat, but dependable as they come.
And sometimes I bring her a bottle of *Nuit d'Amour*.°   °*perfume*

Anthony Hecht (b. 1923)

QUESTIONS

1. The title, the subtitle, the content, and the tone indicate that Hecht is writing an imitation of Matthew Arnold's "Dover Beach." What is Hecht spoofing: the philosophy expressed in Arnold's poem? Its style? Its tone?

2. Arnold called poetry "a criticism of life." Notice here the change in character of the two principals of the preceding poem. What characteristics does Hecht exaggerate or distort? What does he add?

3. Identify persona and audience in "The Dover Bitch." What is the persona's attitude toward Arnold's poem and its persona?

4. In Hecht's poem, how does the speaker feel about the girl? In what ways does this attitude differ from that of the speaker in Arnold's poem? Does Arnold's persona really treat the girl as "a mournful cosmic last resort"?

5. How does the fact that Hecht is a twentieth-century poet affect his response to the situation depicted in Arnold's poem?

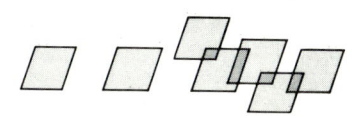

POEMS FOR FURTHER STUDY 2

BEDTIME STORY

Long long ago when the world was a wild place
Planted with bushes and peopled by apes, our
Mission Brigade was at work in the jungle.
    Hard by the Congo.

Once, when a foraging detail was active   5
Scouting for green-fly, it came on a grey man, the
Last living man, in the branch of a baobab°   °*tropical tree*
    Stalking a monkey.

Earlier men had disposed of, for pleasure,
Creatures whose names we scarcely remember—   10
Zebra, rhinoceros, elephants, wart-hog,
    Lion, rats, deer. But

After the wars had extinguished the cities
Only the wild ones were left, half-naked
Near the Equator: and here was the last one,   15
    Starved for a monkey.

By then the Mission Brigade had encountered
Hundreds of such men: and their procedure,
History tells us, was only to feed them:
    Find them and feed them;   20

Those were the orders. And this was the last one.
Nobody knew that he was, but he was. Mud
Caked on his flat grey flanks. He was crouched, half-
    armed with a shaved spear

Glinting beneath broad leaves. When their jaws cut 25
Swathes through the bark and he saw fine teeth shine,
Round eyes roll round and forked arms waver
    Huge as the rough trunks

Over his head, he was frightened. Our workers
Marched through the Congo before he was born, but 30
This was the first time perhaps that he'd seen one.
    Staring in hot still

Silence, he crouched there: then jumped. With a long swing
Down from his branch, he had angled his spear too
Quickly, before they could hold him, and hurled it 35
    Hard at the soldier

Leading the detail. How could he know Queen's
Orders were only to help him? The soldier
Winced when the tipped spear pricked him. Unsheathing his
    Sting was a reflex. 40

Later the Queen was informed. There were no more
Men. An impetuous soldier had killed off,
Purely by chance, the penultimate primate.
    When she was certain,

Squadrons of workers were fanned through the Congo 45
Detailed to bring back the man's picked bones to be
Sealed in the archives in amber. I'm quite sure
    Nobody found them

After the most industrious search, though.
Where had the bones gone? Over the earth, dear, 50
Ground by the teeth of the termites, blown by the
    Wind, like the dodo's.

                    George MacBeth (b. 1932)

NOTES FROM THE DELIVERY ROOM

Strapped down,
victim in an old comic book,
I have been here before,
this place where pain winces
off the walls 5
like too bright light.
Bear down a doctor says,
foreman to sweating laborer,
but this work, this forcing
of one life from another 10

is something that I signed for
at a moment when I would have signed anything.
Babies should grow in fields;
common as beets or turnips
they should be picked and held   15
root end up, soil spilling
from between their toes—
and how much easier it would be later,
returning them to earth.
Bear up . . . bear down . . . the audience   20
grows restive, and I'm a new magician
who can't produce the rabbit
from my swollen hat.
She's crowning, someone says,
but there is no one royal here,[1]   25
just me, quite barefoot,
greeting my barefoot child.

Linda Pastan (b. 1932)

[1] In lines 24–25, the speaker plays on the word "crowning," which refers to both childbirth (the stage at which the baby's head emerges) and the act of endowing someone with regal powers.

CRIMES OF PASSION: THE SLASHER

What I like most is when
the hemline rises
& they place the high heel,
usually the right,
onto the first step of the bus,   5
then, they grasp the small
rod, & pull themselves up. The nylons
flare like hot butter, & as that
thigh bulges slightly, & then
taut, I gently nudge her   10
& with the razor blade, one side
taped, as if a finger
were lovingly running from the back
of the knee toward the buttocks.
She will sometimes turn & smile,   15
feeling some part of herself freed,
only hours later does she learn
how deep my passion runs, the thick
blood of birth drips silently
to some cold floor,   20

    & in that pool, my face returns
    the wonderful smile, & then, I think,
    she probably screams. She will dream of me,
    & that is all
    anyone can ever ask.   25

Terry Stokes (b. 1942)

RAPE

There is a cop who is both prowler and father:
he comes from your block, grew up with your brothers,
had certain ideals.
You hardly know him in his boots and silver badge,
on horseback, one hand touching his gun.   5

You hardly know him but you have to get to know him:
he has access to machinery that could kill you.
He and his stallion clop like warlords among the trash,
his ideals stand in the air, a frozen cloud
from between his unsmiling lips.   10

And so, when the time comes, you have to turn to him,
the maniac's sperm still greasing your thighs,
your mind whirling like crazy. You have to confess
to him, you are guilty of the crime
of having been forced.   15

And you see his blue eyes, the blue eyes of all the family
whom you used to know, grow narrow and glisten,
his hand types out the details
and he wants them all
but the hysteria in your voice pleases him best.   20

You hardly know him but now he thinks he knows you:
he has taken down your worst moment
on a machine and filed it in a file.
He knows, or thinks he knows, how much you imagined;
he knows, or thinks he knows, what you secretly wanted.   25

He has access to machinery that could get you put away;
and if, in the sickening light of the precinct,
and if, in the sickening light of the precinct,
your details sound like a portrait of your confessor,
will you swallow, will you deny them, will you lie your way home?   30

Adrienne Rich (b. 1929)

ON READING POEMS TO A SENIOR CLASS AT SOUTH HIGH

Before
I opened my mouth
I noticed them sitting there
as orderly as frozen fish
in a package.   5

Slowly water began to fill the room
though I did not notice it
till it reached
my ears

and then I heard the sounds   10
of fish in an aquarium

and I knew that though I had
tried to drown them
with my words
that they had only opened up   15
like gills for them
and let me in.

Together we swam around the room
like thirty tails whacking words
till the bell rang   20
puncturing
a hole in the door

where we all leaked out.

They went to another class
I suppose and I home   25

where Queen Elizabeth
my cat met me
and licked my fins
till they were hands again.

D. C. Berry (b. 1947)

BATTER MY HEART, THREE-PERSONED GOD

Batter my heart, three-personed God, for you
As yet but knock, breathe, shine, and seek to mend;
That I may rise and stand, o'erthrow me; and bend
Your force to break, blow, burn, and make me new.

I, like an usurped town, to another due,　　　　　　5
Labor to admit you, but Oh, to no end;
Reason, your viceroy° in me, me should defend　　°representative
But is captived, and proves weak or untrue.
Yet dearly I love you and would be loved fain,°　　°willingly
But am betrothed unto your enemy;　　　　　　10
Divorce me, untie or break that knot again,
Take me to you, imprison me, for I,
Except° you enthrall° me, never shall be free,　　°unless
Nor ever chaste, except you ravish me.　　　　　°hold captive

     John Donne (1572–1631)

3
THEMATIC STRUCTURES

**THIS IS
JUST TO SAY**

I have eaten
the plums
that were in
the icebox

and which   5
you were probably
saving
for breakfast

Forgive me
they were delicious   10
so sweet
and so cold

William Carlos Williams (1883–1963)

    The "I" in this poem has taken the advice of nutritionists and selected fruit rather than junk food, probably for a midnight snack. Although we don't know the sex of this person, we know he or she feels the need to apologize for eating something that another person was apparently saving for the next morning's breakfast. The result of this situation is a note—the kind we might attach to the refrigerator door after everyone else has gone to bed, and we feel guilty over our indulgence. In fact, without changing a single word of the poem but simply writing it out linearly, we can make it look like a note:

> This is just to say I have eaten the plums that were in the icebox and which you were probably saving for breakfast. Forgive me—they were delicious, so sweet and so cold.

Yet none of us would read this note as a poem or the poem as simply a note. Even if we were to find the poem on our refrigerator door one morning, our response would be "Oh, a poem."

    Why is this so? Are there features of this group of words that set it off distinctly as "poem"? Is there anything about the content that makes it different? The kind of words used? The subject matter? Anything else? Should it even be called a poem?

Tradition has taught us to have certain expectations of a poem. We have a special attitude when we read one. Some of the characteristics we expect were mentioned in Chapter 1: poetic language, ambiguity, and theme. Others will be discussed later: tone, figurative language, sound patterns, rhythm, and rhyme. But for many people the characteristic most usually expected is significance of subject matter (though perhaps after reading Chapter 1 we can now allow the possibility of play).

If we look for heavy philosophical discussion in this poem, however, we are bound to be disappointed: all we find is a casual note apologizing for eating plums. When we check for other characteristics we find them reduced to a minimum: the language is not extraordinary; little about it is ambiguous; neither figurative language nor a definite rhyme scheme is apparent; and though the poem has tone, sound patterning, and rhythm, it has them to no greater degree than a prose passage might.

Williams's poem does have persona (the note writer), audience, and situation. And it does have theme—something like the inner conflict between immediately satisfying the senses and following the rules of social behavior. The senses initially win out (the plums are gone), but the sense of propriety ultimately demands an apology (therefore the poem is written). But even these characteristics are not unique to poetry, as is evident in the fact that they are still present when the poem is reduced to a note. If, then, "This Is Just to Say" is a poem, it would seem to be so on the most minimal level. Some people might quarrel with Williams about even calling it a poem and say that he has given the content a form it doesn't deserve.

William Carlos Williams (a doctor, by the way) was not, however, content to pour new wine into old bottles; he was continually seeking out new forms for his poems. Concerned with the nature of poetry, he wrote many poems that question—and make the reader question—what exactly makes a poem a poem.

"This Is Just to Say" is a case in point. Although it does little we expect of a poem, anyone looking at it would react as if it were a poem. Probably the main reason for this reaction is the way the work looks on the page: short lines grouped in stanzas surrounded by the silence of a great amount of white space. It looks so different from ordinary writing that, even before we read it, it shouts "I am a poem."

To summarize what sets this poem apart from prose, we might say (1) its line lengths conform to its own rules rather than, as prose does, to the margins of the page; (2) its lines are broken into stanzas, which are different from prose paragraphs; (3) it lacks the punctuation that we expect in prose and that we added when we turned the poem into a note; (4) its title slides down into the poem to become a part of it in a way a title couldn't do in a prose passage; (5) its word order, though the same as it might be in prose, is made particularly obvious because it is the basis on which the poem is broken into stanzas. The first stanza presents what has been done (the persona has eaten the plums); the second, the reason it

THEMATIC STRUCTURES 49

probably shouldn't have been done (the plums were being saved for breakfast); the third, the result of the act (the qualified apology the audience is asked to accept on the basis of the appeal to the senses).

The principle that we have been discussing in the preceding paragraph and that will be stressed throughout this chapter is **structure**, *the many kinds of patterns the poet uses to control and organize the matter of a poem and, consequently, the reaction of the reader.* Since the reader reacts to the total poem, not just the meaning of the words, the ways in which the poem is structured play a large part in creating its effect. The structures of a poem always do more than merely bear a message. It is therefore necessary that in reading a poem we become aware of how its features are organized.[1]

The subject of structure is so large and important that we need to break it down into two major categories. One is **formal patterns,** *the kinds of organization dependent on the physical properties (the form) of the words.* These patterns, which we may be tempted to call external to the thought of the poem, appeal to the senses for recognition. The lengths of lines and the division into stanzas, for example, are detected by the eye. Sound patterns, rhythm, and rhyme appeal to the ear. The other major category is **thematic structures,** *the kinds of organization dependent on meaning and the symbolic nature of words.* These patterns, often relating to content or idea and therefore considered internal, appeal to the intellect. That we can follow the poem's word order and can label each stanza by what it adds to the development of thought means that Williams has organized his work so that we can follow it intellectually.

Both the formal and the thematic structures help order the poem. They are integral parts of each other and are ultimately inseparable. But since this book is organized in response to the way a reader normally gets a grasp on a poem—first on the content and later on the more sophisticated principles of versification—it seems logical to postpone discussion of the formal patterns until Chapter 9 and to concentrate on the thematic structures here.

The content of any effective poem is organized by some means, as is any essay, novel, or dialogue. When we look for the thematic structure, we are looking, in effect, for an outline of the poem. Often one kind of structure will seem dominant; usually, however, the dominant structure will be supported by other kinds of structure. Sometimes several structures are so intermixed that we would have difficulty labeling one as dominant.

The following poem offers one example of the way that various thematic structures provide a design for the poet's utterance.

---

[1] We are indebted throughout this discussion to Terence Hawkes, *Structuralism and Semiotics* (Berkeley: University of California Press, 1977), pp. 139–140; Jonathan Culler *Structuralist Poetics* (Ithaca: Cornell University Press, 1975), pp.175–178; and Barbara Herrnstein Smith, *Poetic Closure* (Chicago: University of Chicago Press, 1968), pp. 255–260.

SIR PATRICK SPENCE

The king sits in Dumferling toune,°   °*town*
    Drinking the blude-reid° wine: °*blood-red*
"O whar° will I get guid° sailor,   °*where* °*good*
    To sail this schip of mine?"

Up and spak an eldern knicht,   5
    Sat at the kings richt° kne: °*right*
"Sir Patrick Spence is the best sailor,
    That sails upon the se."

The king has written a braid° letter,   °*broad*
    And signd it wi' his hand,   10
And sent it to Sir Patrick Spence,
    Was walking on the sand.

The first line that Sir Patrick red,
    A loud lauch° lauched he: °*laugh*
The next line that Sir Patrick red,   15
    The teir blinded his ee.°   °*eye*

"O wha is this has don this deid,
    This ill deid don to me;
To send me out this time o' the yeir,
    To sail upon the se?   20

"Mak hast, mak haste, my mirry men all,
    Our guid schip sails the morne."
"O say na sae, my master deir,
    For I feir a deadlie storme.

"Late late yestreen I saw the new moone   25
    Wi' the auld° moone in hir arme;   °*old*
And I feir, I feir, my deir master,
    That we will com to harme."

O our Scots nobles wer richt laith°   °*loath (reluctant)*
    To weet their cork-heild schoone;°   °*shoes* 30
Bot lang owre a'° the play wer playd,   °*But long ere all*
    Thair hats they swam aboone.

O lang, lang, may their ladies sit
    Wi' thair fans into their hand,
Or eir they se Sir Patrick Spence   35
    Cum sailing to the land.

O lang, lang, may the ladies stand
    Wi' thair gold kems° in their hair,   °*combs*
Waiting for thair ain° deir lords,   °*own*
    For they'll se thame na mair.   40

> Half owre°, half owre to Aberdour,   °*over*
>   It's fiftie fadom deip:
> And thair lies guid Sir Patrick Spence,
>   Wi' the Scots lords at his feit.
>
>   *Anonymous* (date unknown)

Regardless of whether this is a literarily polished version of a folk ballad, as some scholars argue, or an authentic oral-performance text, as others believe, it is of high artistic quality. One measure of its excellence is the anonymous poet's handling of structure, which we can better understand by trying to answer the following questions: What is the poet's basic means of organizing the thought of the poem? How does it begin? End? Get from beginning to end? Why do you think the material is structured in this way?

Once you have become accustomed to the Scottish dialect, notice how the sequence of events unfolds. The ballad begins with the king in his comfortable town seeking a skipper and sending a letter of command to Sir Patrick Spence (stanzas 1–3); it moves to Sir Patrick's grudging but decisive command to sail, despite his own misgivings and a sailor's warning of omens of disaster (stanzas 4–7); it ends with the nobles' ladies waiting in vain for the ship's noble crewmen, who lie dead at Sir Patrick's feet at the bottom of the ocean (stanzas 8–11). Like any story, this account of the shipwreck somewhere off the coast of Aberdeenshire, Scotland, has an overall **narrative** structure; it tells of a *series of events in a basically chronological order*. More specifically, within the first two major divisions (lines 1–28) the details follow the strict narrative sequence, but the way the scenes are spliced together and the details ordered after line 28 constitutes a different dimension.

How much transition is there between the first and second scenes? What kind of scene would you expect in a narrative tale that is missing between scenes 2 and 3 here? In what manner is the matter of this missing scene presented? What is the effect of this handling of stanzas 8–11?

The transitional elements that one might expect between scenes have been omitted. The abrupt shift between scenes 1 and 2 in lines 11–12 is closer to the technique of film than to narrative tale, but such shifts are characteristic of folk ballads. The transition between lines 28 and 29 is even more abrupt; in fact, the whole shipwreck likely occurs between these lines but is left unmentioned. Line 29 picks up the scene after the shipwreck and throws the catastrophe into a rather ironic perspective by alluding to three subscenes: the Scottish nobles who didn't want wet feet are survived by their dry hats; their ladies of luxury at home have lost their most precious possession; and the nobles themselves, who liked stooping to no one in life, lie in death at the feet of Sir Patrick Spence, who was aware of the dangers he faced but bravely obeyed the king's command. By shifting from a strict narrative to this series of reversals, the poet can comment on the narrative indirectly and then return to the final scene for the conclusion. Like many other poems, this one leads up to **closure:** *a statement which snaps the poem shut at the end, which gives finality to the issue, and which in retrospect the listener or reader realizes the poem has been building up to from the start.*

In "Sir Patrick Spence" the narrative structure clearly predominates; in other poems—for example, "Eating Poetry" and "My Last Duchess"—chronological order is subordinate to another pattern. Consequently, the two would not be called narrative poems.

Any pattern may act as a dominant structure or substructure in a poem. Although the narrative structure is dominant in "Sir Patrick Spence," it is not the only structure. It is supported, for example, by the ironic splicing (or *juxtaposition*) of subscenes after line 28 and by stretches of **dialogue.** Still another means the poet uses to structure the content is a very deliberate word order (or *syntax*). Notice that each line of the ballad is a self-contained phrase ending in punctuation rather than running on directly to the next line. Notice also that each stanza is a separate and complete sentence (stanza 6 contains two sentences) and that the close of each stanza is also the close of each sentence and the close of each subscene. In this way, each stanza is a separate unit with little transition to the next.

The final stanza presents a superb example of how word order is used for effect. The stanza presents the poem's most dramatic event—the death scene. Consequently, the poet builds the sentence so that the most dramatic detail is held till last. Suppose the final stanza were structured this way:

> For thair lies guid Sir Patrick Spence
>   Wi' the Scots lords at his feit,
> Haf owre, hal owre to Aberdour
>   Where it's fiftie fadom deip.

Although this rearrangement builds a perfectly good sentence, it puts the details in anticlimactic order and dilutes the final effect. In structuring the sentence as he did, the poet reveals an understanding of the importance of syntactic structure. The last overpowering detail effectively provides the poem's closing click.

In "Sir Patrick Spence" we see how the main structural pattern (the narrative pattern) is generated by the overriding purpose of telling a story but also how the substructures of juxtaposition of scenes, dialogue, and syntax support this pattern. Because the folk ballad was transmitted orally, it required a relatively uncomplicated set of simple structures, most of which we have investigated. With other purposes, other patterns come into play. Because written poems can sustain more structures played off against each other in more complex ways, we might find it beneficial to examine a literary work that contains a large number of patterns.

THE ENAMEL GIRL

Fearful of beauty, I always went
Timidly indifferent:

Dainty, hesitant, taking in
Just what was tiniest and thin;

Careful not to care
For burning beauty in blue air;

Wanting what my hand could touch—
That not too much;

Looking not to left nor right
On a honey-silent night;

Fond of arts and trinkets, if
Imperishable and stiff

They never played me false, nor fell
Into fine dust. They lasted well.

They lasted till you came, and then
When you went, sufficed again.

But for you, they had been quite
All I needed for my sight.

You faded, I never knew
How to unfold as flowers do,

Or how to nourish anything
To make it grow. I wound a wing

With one caress, with one kiss
Break most fragile ecstasies. . . .

Now terror touches me when I
Seem to be touching a butterfly.

Genevieve Taggard (1894–1948)

The "I" and "you" of the poem are apparent. The persona, called the enamel girl in the title, addresses an audience that has come and gone—probably a lover. Although the girl speaks as if she were addressing an audience physically near her, she is probably talking only to herself, sorting out her feelings in the aftermath of a failed relationship.

Consider, now, the different kinds of thematic patterns operating in this poem. What are the major units of the patterns? What are the characteristics of each unit? How do they relate to each other and to other patterns in the overall structure? Can you designate one pattern as dominant?

"The Enamel Girl" is an example of a poem in which several patterns work simultaneously, and it is therefore difficult to designate one as dominant. One of its structures is a time structure. Although it does not consist of a complex string of events like "Sir Patrick Spence" (which is clearly a narrative poem), "The Enamel Girl" does indicate progression of time: it begins and spends most of its time in the past tense ("I always went," line 1) but ends in the present ("I dream," line 26). Lines 1, 14, 15, 16, 17, and 25 advance the narrative substantially. But in a narrative poem we would expect more of the poem to be involved with the narrative; here, the other lines serve other purposes. The first twelve lines describe the speaker's mood. Lines 13–14 comment on the lasting quality of the "trinkets" in which she puts her trust. Lines 19–24 (except for the few time words) contain more of her self-accusations: she fears that she destroys anything she is involved with. Thus, most of the poem deals with something other than pure story. The ***chronological*** substructure seems to provide the framework on which more dominant structures depend.

From the tenses of the verbs and the arrangement of details, we can infer the time scheme and certain events:

> Past: Always a shy and apprehensive person, the speaker placed her confidence in "things" that she knew couldn't betray her. (lines 1–14)
> More recent past: She became involved with a person who displaced her interest in her former "things." (lines 15–18)
> Still more recent past: He went away, because of her awkwardness in a personal relationship, and she was left to depend once more on her stable "things"—things that no longer sustain her emotional life as they once did. (lines 19–24)
> Present: Now her former fears of involvement have grown to terror. (lines 25–26)

Implicit in this outline of the time scheme is another and probably more important structure, her ***analysis*** of her feelings:

> lines 1–14: the persona's past fear of involvement
> lines 15–18: her involvement with another person
> lines 19–24: the reasons for the loss of her involvement
> lines 25–26: her present terror of involvement

All the details of the poem are concerned with this subject, which seems to dominate the time structure and to include other substructures within it.

The ***syntax*** of this poem is very different from the short, punctuated lines of "Sir Patrick Spence." Here the first line of each stanza is incomplete by itself and must run on without pause to the next line for completion. In the first part of the poem each stanza is one orderly sentence;

THEMATIC STRUCTURES 55

but as the persona's terror builds, the order cannot hold. After the lover leaves (line 19), the syntax breaks out of the stanza pattern, until in line 24 it breaks off completely. In this way, the syntax reflects the persona's emotional instability. The design of the poem is also affected by the method of beginning stanzas 1–6 with parallel descriptive words and the almost musical counterpointing of "they," "you," and "I" in stanzas 7–13:

```
Fearful              I
Dainty
Careful
Wanting
Looking
Fond of
They
                     They
They                 You
          You
          You
I
You                  I
                     I
                     I

I
```

Another substructure is the **contrast** between the things the persona feels comfortable with and the things she doesn't; these are expressed in images (rather than literal statements) in the poem.

<u>What she can cope with</u> (dominant in the first part of the poem)
    what was tiniest and thin (small amounts)
    what her hand could touch (tangible things)
    arts and trinkets (inanimate objects)
<u>What she can't cope with</u> (dominant in the latter part)
    beauty
    burning beauty in blue air (the sun?)
    honey-silent night (romantic summer evenings?)
    "you" (therefore you faded like a flower)
    unfolding like a flower
    nourishing (a living thing)
    caressing a wing (of a bird)
    kissing fragile ecstasies
    touching a butterfly

From this list it becomes obvious that the persona feels safe only when dispassionately involved with inanimate things; in intense relationships with living things she fears that her awkwardness destroys the intimacy. No wonder she is unable to sustain a love relationship. Like the image in the title, she sees herself as an enamel-coated object—hard and brittle on the surface, causing what comes in contact with her to break. But from the reader's perspective, she is an enamel figurine—fragile and breakable herself. It is she who is destroyed by her attitude toward relationships.

Closure is effected in this poem after the ellipsis marks in line 24. It provides a sense of an ending to the poem on at least four levels: (1) in the chronological structure by finally reaching "now" (line 25) after dealing in the past; (2) in the analytical structure by explaining the speaker's resulting "terror" at the present; (3) in the syntactic structure by employing once again a self-contained stanza form; (4) in the image structure by ending on the most fragile image of all—a butterfly.

With this quick analysis we have found more than a half dozen structural devices interacting in the poem. There are still others, some of which you may have noticed on your own. Since the real experience the poet has translated into literary experience took place over time, the poet chooses a chronological framework; but, since the narrative is minor in significance compared with the emotional state of the speaker, the poet makes the analysis of feelings predominate over the chronological structure. In order to effect in the reader a sense of the speaker's state, the poet employs not only the various techniques of analysis but also the syntactic and image structures —thus bombarding the reader's intellect, sense of rhythm and sentence pattern, and visual sense. The persona's experience becomes a shared experience, in a way that no prose description of it could. The poem's structures play no small part in this achievement.

Sometimes it is sufficient simply to explain a situation in order to affect the audience or reader; in other instances the persona may have to go to greater lengths to convince a more resistant audience, as in the following poem.

TO HIS COY MISTRESS

Had we but world enough, and time,
This coyness, Lady, were no crime.
We would sit down, and think which way
To walk, and pass our long love's day.
Thou by the Indian Ganges'° side   °sacred river 5
Shouldst rubies find; I by the tide   in India
Of Humber° would complain. I would   °river in northeastern
Love you ten years before the Flood,   England
And you should, if you please, refuse
Till the conversion of the Jews.   10
My vegetable love should grow
Vaster than empires and more slow;
An hundred years should go to praise

Thine eyes, and on thy forehead gaze;
Two hundred to adore each breast,   15
But thirty thousand to the rest;
An age at least to every part,
And the last age should show your heart.
For, Lady, you deserve this state,
Nor would I love at lower rate.   20
     But at my back I always hear
Time's wingèd chariot hurrying near;
And yonder all before us lie
Deserts of vast eternity.
Thy beauty shall no more be found,   25
Nor, in thy marble vault, shall sound
My echoing song; then worms shall try
That long-preserved virginity,
And your quaint honor turn to dust,
And into ashes all my lust: 30
The grave's a fine and private place,
But none, I think, do there embrace.
     Now therefore, while the youthful hue
Sits on thy skin like morning dew,
And while thy willing soul transpires°   °*breathes* 35
At every pore with instant fires,
Now let us sport us while we may,
And now, like amorous birds of prey,
Rather at once our time devour
Than languish in his slow-chapped° power.   °*slowly* 40
Let us roll all our strength and all   *devouring*
Our sweetness up into one ball,
And tear our pleasures with rough strife
Through the iron gates of life:
Thus, though we cannot make our sun   45
Stand still, yet we will make him run.

Andrew Marvell (1621–1678)

Marvell's poem is deservedly one of the most famous in the English language. Its dramatic juxtaposition of humanity's three abiding preoccupations—love, time, and death—, the deliberateness of its words and sounds, and the audacity of its images have made an indelible impression on readers during the three hundred years since its composition. Yet the poem is treated gingerly in the schools because of its subject matter; only a few years ago one college instructor was suspended for treating (or perhaps mistreating) the poem in class. Its ambiguities are also remarkable. Many readers think they know what the poem does and what it means; meanwhile, centuries of literary critics cannot agree on its most obvious features. Is it a love poem? On the surface it certainly is, but a large number of people doubt that it is *ultimately* that. It is often labeled as an "invitation to love" or a "seduction piece," since the intent of the persona seems to be to convince his reluctant and reserved lady friend to join him in sex. It is often used as an example of the *carpe diem* tradition in literature (Latin for "seize the day"), which advocates the enjoyment of immediate pleasures (often love and/or sex) because of the brevity of time and the inevitability of death. But is that the poem's only or even primary purpose?

We don't need to answer all these questions in order to enjoy the poem, appreciate its artistry, and observe its basic structure (although, admittedly, its structural ambiguities contribute to the lack of consensus on it). Certain principles, at least, are apparent. We will concentrate on these. For example, what does the title tell us about the speaker and audience? Are any details of the physical setting included? What, on the surface at least, seems to be the persona's main intention in speaking? What design does he use to put across the point and achieve his desired effect?

No more definite physical setting than the whole world of time and space is indicated for this monologue from an amorous fellow to his "coy mistress"; nor do we know much about either person involved. In the seventeenth century the word "coy" did not necessarily mean "cunning" (though it could) nor the word "mistress" imply "loose morals" (though it might). Most probably the term "coy" meant only reluctant, modest, or shy; and the term "mistress," something as innocent as sweetheart or lady friend—it is the source of our titles Mrs., Miss, and Ms. Apparently the couple had not had sex (her virginity has been "long preserved"), and the poem is the man's attempt to convince the lady that they should.

He opts for the most rational means of persuasion available. What is that? Notice that the poem is divided into three stanzas and that each stanza has a very specific, logical theme and function. How would you describe the purpose of each? How do the details of each stanza relate to its purpose? How does each stanza relate to the other stanzas? They fit together in a very intricate pattern.

The first stanza opens with a conditional statement, a stipulation, a premise on which will depend the agreement the speaker hopes to set up with his mistress: "<u>IF</u> you and I could be sure of having sufficient time and space in our lifetimes to live at the pace and in the manner you propose, I would not call this reluctance on your part an injurious act or sin." The rest of the stanza (lines 3–20) supplies details that illustrate how, if these conditions were possible, he would spend centuries praising each of her attributes until finally, just before the end of time, she would give in to him. Such is the state she deserves, and he desires.

<u>BUT</u> such an ideal existence is not the human lot. Stanza 2 brings time

and the real world crushing in, in such a manner as to dissolve the agreement the persona in stanza 1 talked of setting up. Lines 20–24 give the reason the agreement won't work. Rather than ticking slowly, time flies swiftly, and future time and space will go on without him and her, for they will be dead. If the mistress intends to refuse until the end of time, she has a shock in store. All her attributes worthy of praise, past and present, will be non-existent in the future; her beauty, her virginity, her honor, as well as his song and his lust, will be turned to dust and ashes in the grave. Their time will be over, and the "fine and private place" that lovers seek for privacy will be reduced to the cramped and ghostly quiet space of a grave—not the ideal place for making love.

THEREFORE, NOW—he moves in with the logical conclusion—while they still have a little time and space left, now is the time to enjoy themselves and so defeat time. Though they cannot, like the god Zeus or the prophet Joshua, make time stand still (as the mistress had hoped in stanza 1), by doing what he proposes they can for the moment avoid being destroyed by it (as stanza 2 says they will be) by making time run faster (in enjoying themselves, as proposed in stanza 3), and thus (in the closure in lines 45–46) come as close as is humanly possible to the ideal existence of stanza 1.

It should be obvious from this rather lengthy paraphrase that the speaker carefully chooses each statement to fit into the pattern he uses to convince his mistress of his point, because he is building an **argument,** *a carefully reasoned sequence of premises leading logically to a conclusion.* In the first stanza he proposes that if certain conditions were met, he would accept an agreement with her; in the second, that these conditions could not possibly be met; and in the third, that since they can't agree on her point, they should agree on his.

The argumentative structure the persona builds is rigorously supported by the syntactic structure he uses. Notice the carefully placed logical connectives that introduce and relate the major ideas: *had we but* (meaning "if"), *but* (line 21), *now therefore* (line 33), and *thus* (line 45). If the mistress accepts the first premise, which she is glad to do, and if the speaker convinces her in stanza 2 that the conditions cannot be met, then she should see the logic of his conclusion in stanza 3. By so constructing his argument, the speaker hopes to trap her into accepting his proposition and his course of action. Even his choice of verbs is designed to have this effect: those in her proposal (stanza 1) are in the subjunctive or conditional mood (that is, they imply a state that can't or doesn't exist): *had we but, should,* and *would.* The stark realities of the future as he sees it (stanza 2) are emphatically presented in the future indicative mood: *shall.* Finally, his proposal (stanza 3) is in the present imperative mood: *let us.* Stanza 1 also shows the pair in separate activities. She does one thing while he does another. Stanza 2 depersonalizes their relationship altogether—not they, but their qualities are discussed. In contrast, stanza 3 proposes that they act together to defeat time. Thus, even the grammar of the poem (part of the syntactic structure) tries to force her to concede that he has the better plan.

The *image* structure adds a third layer of persuasion. Her ideal situation is described in pleasurable but separate and far-fetched activities that consume an inordinate amount of time and space. His vision of the future has no people—only dreadful things they are passively at the mercy of: deserts, vaults, worms, dust, ashes, and graves. But his proposition for the present is energetic, alive, and aggressive; he speaks of fire, sport, birds of prey, devouring, ball, and "tearing pleasures with rough strife."

Much more could be said about how the various structural features of the poem lend weight to the persona's argument and (he hopes) help to seduce the mistress. But something must also be said about the speaker's honesty. The logic he uses in his seduction speech is not as above-board and persuasive as he wants the mistress to think, and since he himself sets up the logical pattern, he should be logical about it. He chooses a form of syllogistic reasoning called *modus tollens,* which, by the principles of formal logic, ought to follow this pattern:

| If p, then q | (If we had time, this coyness would be no crime.) |
Not q	(But this coyness is a crime.)
Therefore, not p	(Therefore, we must have no time.)

But the speaker denies the antecedent (p:time), and the consequent (q:coyness is a crime) does not logically follow. In addition, not having time may be insufficient reason for calling the lady's coyness a crime. The speaker leaves no room for moral or other considerations. His logic then, as stated, is invalid. Moreover, he includes too many steps in the logical pattern of the poem. Even if he could dissuade the woman from her point of view, it does not follow that she must agree with his. There are other possible alternatives he doesn't mention, like involvement with someone else or interests completely unrelated to sex.

A poem that is tightly organized in a pattern obviously intended to appear logical that is not, however, logical raises several questions: Did the author mistakenly consider the argument logical? Was Marvell aware of the illogic and the speaker confused? Were both Marvell and the speaker aware and the mistress taken in by them? Or were all aware and playing a game of wit all along? Any of these could be true. It seems most likely, however, that in writing the poem Marvell was satirizing the genre of the seduction poem, which frequently used this kind of illogic. There are other features of the poem that seem inappropriate in an authentic seduction poem (if there is such a thing): the frightening imagery is more likely to scare off a woman than to bring her close; the subjects of time and death actually take over the poem and make the immediate conquest of this particular coy mistress at this particular time seem trivial. Perhaps through it all Marvell is making light of the seduction poem by implying that in seeming to make sex more important than mutability and mortality such a genre is rather short-sighted and ridiculous; maybe there are more important human concerns than seducing this one particular lady. Whatever the case, "To His Coy Mistress" serves well as an illustration of a poem with a dominant argumentative structure supported by several subordinate structures.

Our discussion of the various patterns the poet may employ to organize the content of the poem could go on indefinitely. Although we have focused on what are probably the most often used thematic structures (narrative, analysis, and argument, along with syntax and imagery), no pattern is disallowed and any number of subordinate patterns can support or be played off against a dominant pattern. What is subordinate in one poem may be dominant in another. The use of space (which plays a minor role in "To His Coy Mistress"), might become a dominant structure in a poem that is largely *description*. Some complex poems, rather than having one dominant structure, have multiple structures. In sum, poets control the development of poems in whatever way or ways are appropriate to their intention and the nature of the material.

Control is desirable—even necessary—to communication. On the most elementary level, if the words of a poem were not controlled by the poet's sense of word order, the poem would make no sense. But most of us are not so completely in control of our lives and actions as we'd like to think. Similarly, many contemporary poets realize that their poems fall short of being prophetic statements that they control and that the world waits impatiently to receive. Thus they may appear to underplay the importance of the attitude they project, sometimes by giving the impression that their poems are unstructured or that the structure has been reduced to a minimum. The following is an example.

MARIN-AN[1]

sun breaks over the eucalyptus
grove below the wet pasture,
water's about hot,
I sit in the open window
& roll a smoke.   5

distant dogs bark, a pair of
cawing crows; the twang

---

[1] Marin County is located just north of and across the Golden Gate Bridge from San Francisco. During the 1970s it became extremely chic, but when Snyder lived there in the 1950s it was mainly rural. Residents of the county are usually called Marinites. The suffix *-an* in Snyder's title may imply that the poem describes a situation characteristic of the Marin he knew.

of a pygmy nuthatch high in a pine—
from behind the cypress windrow
the mare moves up, grazing.

a soft continuous roar
comes out of the far valley
of the six-lane highway—thousands
and thousands of cars
driving men to work.

Gary Snyder (b. 1930)

    The speaker here, like the poet, seems to exercise little control. Even his activity (lines 4–5) illustrates his passiveness. The specifics of the poem seem to be randomly selected. No audience is apparent. No theme is stated. No real progression in time or idea occurs. No strong organizational pattern dominates the poem. The speaker is part of the background, and the poet almost erases himself. The poem stands on its details alone as they are perceived by the reader, without the poet's intervention.

    To create this effect, the poet has arranged the details so that structure is not obvious, and you feel you are taking part in the poem and making up your own mind. Details of the scene seem to hit your senses just as they do the speaker's—the sights, sounds, smells, tastes, and sensations of touch. What is your reaction to them? Which do you enjoy? Do you find any disturbing? If you were actually in the setting described by Snyder, what impression would it make on you? What conclusion about it would you draw?

    Notice that *you* are the active participant; the speaker and the poet make no value judgments for you. There is no argument to convince you, no statement of theme to tell you what to think. The poet's control seems minimal; he presents the details but makes no comment. But he does present the details. To do so, he chooses certain words and arranges the details in a certain order. His control is not as minimal as it appears.

    And the poem does have structure. How would you label it? To describe the scene, the poet subtly employs the technique of **contrast.** The first two stanzas introduce you to details from nature (among which the speaker subtly includes himself), while the third stanza offends you with the less pleasant aspects of modern industrialized civilization, its constant noises, traffic, and (worst of all) work. The speaker sits peaceful, alone, doing what he enjoys; the workers by the thousands are driven (with all the unpleasant associations of that word), perhaps against their wills, to work. In yet another way the description is organized; the poet presents first minerals, then vegetation, then animals, and finally humans. Why does he plant the speaker between the vegetables and the animals? As the details are arranged here, where would you prefer to be? Most probably you'd choose as does the persona. It may seem that you've made the choice yourself. But perhaps you have been led to make it by the poet's choice of structure.

Does the poem have closure? It would be in keeping with the poet's attitude toward this poem (and with modern poetry in general) that it not end with the finality of assertion of more traditionally structured poems— the "thus" of "To His Coy Mistress" or the "now" of "The Enamel Girl." Contemporary poets often shy away from resolution or conclusion. Indeed, "Marin-An" makes no such effort to tell you what to think. It presents its details and stops with the last of them. Yet the poem is so arranged that it needs no final comment to achieve its effect. After you, like the persona, have enjoyed the naturalness of the first two stanzas, the unnaturalness of the six-lane highway and the ugliness of work lead you to your own conclusion. Perhaps, in this instance your conclusion is predictable. In other poems, it may not be. But no matter how strongly some poets may protest, they are always in control of their poems to some degree.

There are no hard-and-fast rules for discovering the thematic structure(s) of a poem. But the following guidelines may help you remember the principles covered in this chapter.

1. As you read, be aware of words that signal one organizational pattern or another.
    a. A chronological or time structure is often indicated by
        1) such connective words as "meanwhile," "later," "soon," "at last," "then," etc.
        2) successive references to seasons, days, hours, etc.
        3) events in sequential order; changes in the persona's description or behavior
        4) change in verb tense from past to present, etc.
    If the main purpose of the poem seems to be to tell a story, the poem probably has a narrative structure.
    b. An analytical or expository structure may be indicated by
        1) the development of an idea or the explanation of a feeling
        2) the presence of expository devices that are also used in writing an expository essay (comparison and contrast, lists, juxtaposition of details, cause and effect, analogy, general to specific, specific to general)
    c. An argumentative structure may be indicated by
        1) tightly organized, logical development of ideas, giving reasons for accepting the main point
        2) a deductive pattern, inductive pattern, or thesis-antithesis-synthesis pattern

3) such connective words as "if, then," "since," "therefore," "thus," etc.
   d. A descriptive structure may be indicated by
      1) an accumulation of details of physical appearance
      2) successive specific references to space
   e. A syntactic structure may be indicated by
      1) conspicuous use of word order as a basis for development
      2) parallel construction of phrases
   f. An image structure may be indicated by
      1) appearance of a striking object, animal, or person at conspicuous points in the poem
      2) a network of related objects, etc., in the poem
2. Determine if one kind of structure is dominant and if others are used as supporting structures.
3. Divide the poem into the segments or units on which it is built (groups of lines or stanzas that cohere) and label them according to their function in the poem's development.
4. Describe the kind of closure in the poem.

In the next poem, try to investigate structure on your own. Since it is not divided into stanzas, you'll have to isolate the segments or units of thought and determine the relationship between them. Follow the guidelines listed above and then distance yourself from the details and see the patterns into which they fall. From your study of structure, what would you say is the theme of the poem? (By the way, a modernized version of the title might be "Living Together.")

LIVING IN SIN

She had thought the studio would keep itself;
no dust upon the furniture of love.
Half heresy, to wish the taps less vocal,
the panes relieved of grime. A plate of pears,
a piano with a Persian shawl, a cat   5
stalking the picturesque amusing mouse
had risen at his urging.
Not that at five each separate stair would writhe
under the milkman's tramp; that morning light
so coldly would delineate the scraps   10
of last night's cheese and three sepulchral bottles;
that on the kitchen shelf among the saucers
a pair of beetle-eyes would fix her own—
envoy from some village in the moldings . . .

Meanwhile, he, with a yawn, 15
sounded a dozen notes upon the keyboard,
declared it out of tune, shrugged at the mirror,
rubbed at his beard, went out for cigarettes;
while she, jeered by the minor demons,
pulled back the sheets and made the bed and found 20
a towel to dust the table-top,
and let the coffee-pot boil over on the stove.
By evening she was back in love again,
though not so wholly but throughout the night
she woke sometimes to feel the daylight coming 25
like a relentless milkman up the stairs.

Adrienne Rich (b. 1929)

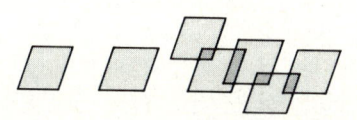

POEMS FOR FURTHER STUDY 1

THAT NIGHT WHEN JOY BEGAN

That night when joy began
Our narrowest veins to flush,
We waited for the flash
Of morning's levelled gun.

But morning let us pass, 5
And day by day relief
Outgrows his nervous laugh,
Grown credulous of peace,

As mile by mile is seen
No trespasser's reproach, 10
And love's best glasses reach
No fields but are his own.

W. H. Auden (1907–1973)

QUESTIONS

1. The people who call themselves "we" (line 3) seem to be related by the "love" of line 11. If the speakers are at present lovers, how did they ex-

pect their first night together (when joy began to flush their narrowest veins) to end? How did it end? What followed it?

2. Three words in the first line make direct or indirect reference to time, one of the structural elements in the poem. At what time did the event of the poem begin? When will it end? What has transpired in the meantime? Is the poem a narrative poem?

3. The words "narrowest" and "levelled" refer to physical space, another structural element. Isolate all other references to physical space. How do the space references at the end of the poem differ from those at the beginning? How did the differences come about? Does the poem contain a descriptive structural pattern?

4. In lines 3–4, the lovers expect to be greeted by a shot from a gun held by "morning." In line 10, they speak as if they've feared being trespassers (line 12) upon someone else's fields. If the lovers think of themselves as trespassers, who do they think owns the fields? Who in fact owns the fields? How far in time and space do his fields extend as seen through the field glasses in line 11? Complete the analogy. Is the poem based on an image structure?

5. On the basis of the trespassing analogy, what would you say is the theme of the poem?

A LECTURE UPON THE SHADOW

Stand still, and I will read to thee
A lecture, love, in love's philosophy.
    These three hours that we have spent
    Walking here, two shadows went
Along with us, which we ourselves produc'd;   5
But, now the Sun is just above our head,
    We do those shadows tread;
    And to brave clearness all things are reduc'd.
So, whilst our infant love did grow,
Disguises did, and shadows, flow   10
    From us, and our cares; but now 'tis not so.

That love hath not attain'd the high'st degree,
Which is still diligent lest others see.

Except our love at this noon stay,
We shall new shadows make the other way.   15
    As the first were made to blind
    Others, these which come behind
Will work upon ourselves, and blind our eyes.
If our love faint, and westwardly decline,

> To me thou, falsely, thine, 20
> And I to thee mine actions shall disguise.
> The morning shadows wear away,
> But these grow longer all the day,
> But oh, love's day is short, if love decay.
>
> Love is a growing, or full constant light; 25
> And his first minute, after noon, is night.

John Donne (1572–1631)

QUESTIONS

1. In what way is the poem a lecture? Who is the speaker? The audience? What is the lecture about? Outline its major points.
2. Explain how the shadows are both organizing principles of the poem and emblems of meaning. What meaning(s) do they have? See especially lines 9–19. Be as specific as you can.
3. What situation generates the poem? What have the people involved been doing? What do they do during the poem? Can you tell what they will do afterward?
4. What time is it (the "dramatic present") when the speaker speaks? How is this point in time significant thematically and structurally? Explain how Donne uses noon as a pivotal time.
5. Note the elaborate time pattern set up in the poem:
   a) During what period of the day and for how long has the couple been walking? In which direction? Where are their shadows?
   b) What time is it now? Where are their shadows?
   c) If the couple continues walking, how will their shadows be different?
   d) If they walk until night, how extensive will the shadows (or darkness) be?
6. Establish the analogy Donne sets up for each of these time spans. Fit all the lines of the poem into one time span or the other.
7. Paraphrase the last two lines of the poem. Now go back to line 1. In what way may it be said that the whole intent of the speaker lies in the first two words of the poem?

GAMBLING IN STATELINE, NEVADA

The great cracked shadow of the Sierra Nevada
Hoods over the last road.

I came down here from the side of
A cold cairn where a girl named Rachel

Just made it inside California   5
And died of bad luck.

Here, across from the keno° board,   °*card game*
An old woman
Has been beating a strange machine
In its face all day.   10

Dusk limps past in the street.
I step outside.
It's gone.
I finger a worthless agate
In my pocket.   15

James Wright (b. 1927)

QUESTIONS

1. Accidental? Loose? Random? Is any of these terms appropriate in describing the structure of this poem? Or is the casual arrangement of the poem more apparent than real? Explain the structure of the poem as you see it. Which poem discussed in the last section of the chapter does it resemble most?
2. The speaker of this poem is passive and self-effacing. How is this part of his organizational plan?
3. There are three human figures in the poem, and a couple of half-human ones. What have they in common? Would the elimination of the figure of dusk (line 11) seriously mar the poem?
4. What role does the mountain play in the organization of the poem? The time of day? The location in Nevada?
5. What traditional elements of structure has Wright dispensed with in writing the poem? Which has he employed?
6. Do you discern any progression, any steady building toward a climax or anticlimax? Explain.

SONNET 73: THAT TIME OF YEAR THOU MAYST IN ME BEHOLD

That time of year thou mayst in me behold
When yellow leaves, or none, or few, do hang
Upon those boughs which shake against the cold,
Bare ruined choirs° where late the sweet birds sang.   °*choir lofts*
In me thou seest the twilight of such day   5

As after sunset fadeth in the west,
Which by and by black night doth take away,
Death's second self, that seals up all in rest.
In me thou seest the glowing of such fire
That on the ashes of his youth doth lie,   10
As the deathbed whereon it must expire,
Consumed with that which it was nourished by.
    This thou perceiv'st, which makes thy love more strong,
    To love that well which thou must leave ere long.

William Shakespeare (1564–1616)

QUESTIONS

1. Paraphrase as much of the poem as you feel necessary in order to understand it. Then divide the lines into units or segments of thought and cite the line numbers of the units.

2. On what basis do the units relate to each other? What structural device is employed in ordering the units in lines 1–12?

3. How does the syntax of lines 1–12 support this structural device? Notice particularly the sentence structure at the beginnings of the units.

4. Which of the lines are grammatically complete in themselves and which run on to the next? Does this pattern reinforce the structural device we've been considering or is it played off against it?

5. Lines 1–4 speak of the end of a year; lines 5–8 of the end of a day; lines 9–12 of the end of a fire. According to the persona, each of these is to be found "in me." Since these references can hardly be taken literally (as the Enamel Girl is not really enamel), to what literal subject do these images seem to refer? Does the poem have an image structure?

FIRE AND ICE

Some say the world will end in fire,
Some say in ice.
From what I've tasted of desire
I hold with those who favor fire.
But if it had to perish twice,   5
I think I know enough of hate
To say that for destruction ice
Is also great
And would suffice.

Robert Frost (1874–1963)

QUESTIONS

1. Which of the main kinds of structure is/are at work here?
2. What are the specific theories alluded to in lines 1 and 2? Does Frost logically explore their implications? What is his purpose in including them?
3. It could be said that this poem has the "structure of surprise." What might this mean? Does the poem *seem* to work toward a preordained conclusion? If not, why?
4. Describe the effect of the run-on lines on the progress of the speaker's thinking.

EASTER WINGS

<pre>
       Lord, who createdst man in wealth and store,
            Though foolishly he lost the same,
                 Decaying more and more,
                      Till he became
                           Most poor: 5
                      With thee
                 O let me rise
            As larks, harmoniously,
       And sing this day thy victories:
Then shall the fall further the flight in me.   10

       My tender age in sorrow did begin;
            And still with sicknesses and shame
                 Thou didst so punish sin,
                      That I became
                           Most thin: 15
                      With thee
                 Let me combine,
            And feel this day thy victory;
       For if I imp my wing on thine,
Affliction shall advance the flight in me.   20
</pre>

George Herbert (1593–1633)

QUESTIONS

1. Look at the poem as it is printed; then turn it on its side. Comment on the formal structure of the poem.
2. What is the effect of the lines "Most poor" and "Most thin" upon the reader? What, if anything, does the visual pattern reinforce?
3. Explain how the line length (expansion and contraction) is used to support the meaning of the poem.

4. What does the word "imp" mean? How is it appropriate to the poem's context?
5. Is this poem merely a clever visual trick? Would it be more or less effective without the formal hieroglyphic pattern? Explain your response.

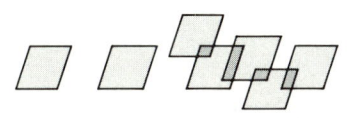

POEMS FOR FURTHER STUDY 2

UPON JULIA'S CLOTHES

Whenas in silks my Julia goes,
Then, then, methinks, how sweetly flows
That liquefaction of her clothes.

Next, when I cast mine eyes and see
That brave vibration, each way free,   5
O how that glittering taketh me!

Robert Herrick (1591–1674)

PRAYER (I)

Prayer: the church's banquet, angels' age,
    God's breath in man returning to his birth,
    The soul in paraphrase, heart in pilgrimage,
The Christian plummet sounding heaven and earth;
Engine° against th' Almighty, sinner's tower,   °weapon 5
    Reversèd thunder, Christ-side-piercing spear,
    The six-days' world transposing in an hour,
A kind of tune which all things hear and fear,
Softness, and peace, and joy, and love, and bliss,
    Exalted manna, gladness of the best,   10
    Heaven in ordinary,° man well dressed,   °daily life
The Milky Way, the bird of Paradise,
    Church bells beyond the stars heard, the soul's blood,
    The land of spices; something understood.

George Herbert (1593–1633)

40—	LOVE
middle	aged
couple	playing
ten	nis
when	the
game	ends
and	they
go	home
the	net
will	still
be	be
tween	them

Roger McGough (b. 1937)

ON DRIVING BEHIND A SCHOOL BUS FOR MENTALLY RETARDED CHILDREN

Full deep green
bloom-fallen spring
here outside,
for us.

They, 5
like winter-covered crocuses:
strange bright beauty
peeping through snow
that never melts—

(How quietly, 10
how quietly,
the bus.)

These flowers have no fragrance.
They move to an eerie wind
I cannot feel. 15
They rise, with petals fully opened,
from a twisted seed,
and neither grow
nor wither.

They will be taught 20
the colors of their names.

Grace Butcher (b. 1934)

LOVE SONG: I AND THOU

Nothing is plumb, level or square:
    the studs are bowed, the joists
are shaky by nature, no piece fits
    any other piece without a gap
or pinch, and bent nails
    dance all over the surfacing
like maggots. By Christ
    I am no carpenter. I built
the roof for myself, the walls
    for myself, the floors
for myself, and got
    hung up in it myself. I
danced with a purple thumb
    at this house-warming, drunk
with my prime whiskey: rage.
    Oh I spat rage's nails
into the frame-up of my work:
    it held. It settled plumb,
level, solid, square and true
    for that great moment. Then
it screamed and went on through,
    skewing as wrong the other way.
God damned it. This is hell,
    but I planned it, I sawed it,
I nailed it, and I
    will live in it until it kills me.
I can nail my left palm
    to the left-hand cross-piece but
I can't do everything myself.
    I need a hand to nail the right,
a help, a love, a you, a wife.

Alan Dugan (b. 1923)

STOPPING BY WOODS ON A SNOWY EVENING

Whose woods these are I think I know.
His house is in the village, though;
He will not see me stopping here
To watch his woods fill up with snow.

My little horse must think it queer
To stop without a farmhouse near

Between the woods and frozen lake
The darkest evening of the year.

He gives his harness bells a shake
To ask if there is some mistake. 10
The only other sound's the sweep
Of easy wind and downy flake.

The woods are lovely, dark, and deep,
But I have promises to keep,
And miles to go before I sleep, 15
And miles to go before I sleep.

Robert Frost (1874–1963)

4

TONE

MY ROOSEVELT COUPÉ

Coax it, clutch it, kick it
    in the gas was every dawn's
    scenario.
           Then off it bucked,
backfiring down the block to show 5
it minded.
          Each fender gleamed
a different hue of blue.
Each hubcap chose
    its hill to spin freewheeling 10
    into traffic.
           I fretted like a spouse
through chills and overboiling,
jacked my weekly flats
and stuffed the spavined seats 15
with rags.
        Leaking, the radiator
healed with swigs of Rinso,
brake fluid and rainwater.
            Simonized, 20
the hood stuck out like a tramp
in a tux.
        All trips were dares.
Journeys were sagas.
          From Norfolk 25
to New York and back,
I burned eleven quarts
of oil, seven fuses
and the horn.
          One headlight 30
dimmed with cataracts.
           The other
funneled me one-eyed
through darker darks than darkness . . .

>   O my Roosevelt coupé, my first,
>   my Chevrolet of many scars
>   and heart attacks, where are you
>   now?
>   Manhandled, you'd refuse
>   to budge.
>   Stickshifted
>   into low, you'd enigmatically
>   reverse.
>   Sold finally
>   for scrap, you waited on your treads
>   while I pocketed thirty
>   pieces of unsilver and slunk
>   away—Wild Buck Hazo
>   abandoning his first and favorite
>   mount, unwilling to malinger
>   long enough to hear
>   the bullet he could never fire.

Samuel Hazo (b. 1928)

Suppose you are sitting in class one morning and your English teacher announces that a poet has come to give a reading. The speaker enters the room, walks to the podium, clutches the lectern as if he were afraid it might run away and leave him standing naked in front of the audience and proceeds to read in a monotone without looking up from his manuscript—except to glance repeatedly at his watch. Immediately after finishing, he mutters something about being late for a flight and hastily leaves.

Unintentionally, the speaker has conveyed a definite attitude toward both his audience and his subject. He is saying, in effect, that he is bored, nervous, or both; that he is unable or unwilling to enliven his presentation and establish a rapport with his listeners; that he would rather be someplace else.

Now imagine a different scenario. This time the poet steps forward, walks briskly past the podium, and stands directly in front of the class. His posture is relaxed and his voice confident and good humored as he begins to recite from memory, "Coax it, clutch it, kick it/in the gas. . . ." During the recitation, he punctuates the poem with pauses and stresses, gestures emphatically to emphasize key words and ideas and never loses eye contact with you and the other members of the audience.

This is, in fact, the way Sam Hazo conducts a poetry reading—with an enthusiasm an audience can see, hear, and feel. At a reading, he is more than an anonymous voice droning on in poetic rhythms. But he can't be present each time the poem is read, and so he must employ techniques to compensate for his personal absence. We all compensate in a similar way. If we talk to someone in person, we supplement our words with pauses, pitch, volume, pace, tone of voice, gestures, and body language of various kinds. When we talk over the phone, though, we can't communicate gestures or body language, so we have to exaggerate the oral signals and often explain our meaning in other words. When we write, we can't communicate any of the oral signals; thus we compensate even more, using various written signals of meaning and attitude.

With what kinds of signals does Hazo communicate his attitude toward his subject in "My Roosevelt Coupé"? It is important to isolate and identify the techniques he uses. What generalizations about his attitude can you make on this basis?

Such signals are many and interwoven. Separating them may seem like unweaving a blanket, especially since more than one attitude may be conveyed at a time. But the more specific we are, the more we can appreciate the artistry of the communication. Let's look at just an example or two of each kind of signal (there are twelve of them).

The *word choice* (1) in the title is a good starting point. In order to grasp the full meaning of a word, we need to be attentive to both its **denotation,** or *explicit meaning,* and its **connotations,** *its associations or implications.* The denotation of the word coupé is car. But the real significance of the word lies in its connotations. The use of the French coupé rather than the American coupe creates the expectation of elegance. The *connotation* (2) of the name Roosevelt furthers that expectation: the Roosevelt family has long been synonymous with wealth, social prominence, and sophistication. Then, when the car is likened to other things, the *comparisons* (3) are not to lifeless things but to living creatures—mostly to a horse (it bucks, its seats are swollen joints, it has poor eyesight, it was its owner's "first and only mount," one he couldn't stand to shoot) and even to a wife ("I fretted like a spouse"). Other *details* (4) illustrate the care with which the car was treated. These signals and others reveal Wild Buck Hazo's untempered affection for his first automobile, an attitude many of us had toward the first major possession of our youth. No wonder, then, that when he had to abandon it to the junkyard he felt like a traitor, a fact that becomes clear in lines 45–49, where Hazo uses words with unflattering connotations such as "slunk" and "abandoning" as well as another device called **allusion:** *a reference to a person, place, literary work, historical event, or anything else that lies outside the immediate context, yet somehow adds meaning to it.* In this instance, the *allusion* (5) is to Judas' selling Christ for thirty pieces of silver.

But Wild Buck Hazo is not the speaker in the poem; the speaker is a more mature man looking back on his youthful experience. When we realize this, some of the details take on a different color. The term "Roosevelt" is not so much about elegance as about old age: the car was a Chevrolet built during the presidency of Franklin Delano Roosevelt (1933–1945). Its elegance existed only in the eyes of its youthful owner. Other details support this idea: the car's backfiring, the multicolored fenders, the loose hubcaps, the single headlight, and the oil consumption. The *exaggerations* (6) with which the poem is riddled (including the sentimental address to the car itself in lines 36–48) and the *amount of space* (7) devoted to the very real discomforts of the car make us aware that—speaking dispassionately—the car really wasn't worth keeping. Even the *physical appearance of the poem on the page* (8), with its broken lines and false starts, creates the sensation of how fitfully the car ran. And the whole *thematic organization* (9) moves from Hazo's intimacy with the car to a more objective observation at the end. The effect is to distance us from the experience, much as the speaker (the older Sam Hazo) is distanced from his first car and his younger self, so that now he can see them in perspective.

It is this perspective that the persona assumes he shares with the readers. The comic *incidents* (10), the colloquial *syntax* (11), and the whole *context* (12) of the poem create a rapport between the author and his readers, especially those who have owned a car like the one described: a high-mileage, low-performance, multihued clunker, fully warranted to consume enormous quantities of oil, break down inconveniently, hurl hubcaps into oncoming traffic, and shift its own gears inexplicably.

Thus, the poem reveals not only Wild Buck's attitude to his car but also Sam Hazo's attitude toward both Wild Buck and the car, and toward the audience of the poem as well. There is little question that the author intends the poem to be taken informally, humorously, yet affectionately, because he has carefully manipulated all the signals above (and others) to create this **tone**: *the author's attitude toward the subject matter, the speaker, and/or the audience.* A skillful poet can make a poem suggest more than (or even the opposite of) what it says on the page. The words of the poem may say one thing and the poet another, because tone is concerned with *how* the poem says what it says. It is not at all unusual to find the poet taking a different attitude from the speaker of the poem.

Failure to detect the exact shading of the tone can cause a complete misreading; therefore, when reading any poem, we need to pay attention to the author's tone of voice and describe it as precisely as possible in our own words, usually in more than just one word. Is the poet being sincere, sarcastic, or sentimental in relation to the subject matter? Is he or she amused, embarrassed, or angered by the persona? Does the poet take a condescending, critical, or sympathetic attitude toward you, the reader? A full description of tone takes all these topics into consideration.

Two poems on the same subject may have radically different tones and consequently very different meanings. Describe the tone of the next poem and point out features that support your description.

LIGHT SHINING OUT OF DARKNESS

God moves in a mysterious way,
    His wonders to perform;
He plants His footsteps in the sea
    And rides upon the storm.

Deep in unfathomable mines
    Of never-failing skill,
He treasures up His bright designs
    And works His sovereign will.

Ye fearful saints, fresh courage take;
    The clouds ye so much dread
Are big with mercy, and shall break
    In blessings on your head.

Judge not the Lord by feeble sense,
    But trust Him for His grace:
Behind a frowning providence
    He hides a smiling face.

His purposes will ripen fast,
    Unfolding every hour;
The bud may have a bitter taste,
    But sweet will be the flower.

Blind unbelief is sure to err,
    And scan His work in vain;
God is His own interpreter,
    And He will make it plain.

William Cowper (1731–1800)

Although the subject matter of Cowper's poem is abstract and vast, the points it makes are clear and the speaker's attitude is unambiguous. In contrast to "My Roosevelt Coupé," the poem is written in very formal diction, in which colloquialisms would be out of place. Line lengths are carefully planned and regular, with each stanza containing only one formal sentence. Comparisons are to things in nature: sea, storm, mines, clouds, and flowers. The speaker stands as a kind of interpreter between God and humanity. Everything he says seems intended to be taken at face value. Even the thematic organization builds formal support for the position taken: it is constructed as generalization (stanzas 1–2), application (stanzas 3–5), and refutation of opposing points of view (stanza 6). These features contribute to a serious, formal tone, a positive attitude, and a sincerely religious theme: although God's ways are incomprehensible and may seem unjust to His people, His acts are part of His grand design, which is ultimately just and benevolent; therefore, His people need to trust Him. If the poem seems fit for a worship service, no wonder; it is one of Cowper's eighteenth-century Olney Hymns and still appears in the hymnal of many Christian denominations.

The following poem has the same subject: God's ways of dealing with humans and their attitude toward Him. How likely is this poem to be incorporated into a Sunday service? Isolate what makes this poem different from Cowper's. Describe the tone.

PSALM

The Lord feeds some of His prisoners better than others.
It could be said of Him that He is not a just god but an indifferent god.
That He is not to be trusted to reward the righteous and punish the unscrupulous.
That He maketh the poor poorer but is otherwise undependable.

It could be said of Him that it is His school of the germane that
    produced the *Congressional Record*.   5
That it is His vision of justice that gave us cost accounting.

It could be said of Him that though we walk with Him all the days of our
    lives we will never fathom Him
Because He is empty.

These are the dark images of our Lord
That make it seem needful for us to pray not unto Him   10
But ourselves.
But when we do that we find that indeed we are truly lost
And we rush back into the safer fold, impressed by His care for us.

                                                 Reed Whittemore (b. 1919)

The poem is called a psalm, which like a hymn is a sacred song intended for worship. The title, the subject matter, the psalmlike line lengths, and the Biblical syntax (for example, "He maketh," "all the days of our lives") induce the reader to expect a formal religious poem like Cowper's. By the seventh word of the first line, however, this expectation is destroyed: a poem of worship would hardly call human beings God's prisoners or refer to God as indifferent (i.e., uninterested as well as impartial), untrustworthy, undependable, and empty. We may assume, then, that although the poet is employing the trappings of a formal religious poem, his attitude does not accord with one. Supporting this assumption are references to such unreligious topics as the *Congressional Record* and cost accounting (the careful estimation of costs before a project is contracted for). What to Cowper is God's smiling face is here a dark image: saints are prisoners; mysteriousness is indifference. The poets' attitudes toward the same religious experience are very different.

Nevertheless, Whittemore's poem ends with the same situation as Cowper's: with human beings putting their trust in God. The change occurs in the last stanza. Notice the thematic organization. Line 1 states what the speaker considers to be the fact: God's dealings with human beings are unjust. The rest of the poem concerns how human beings square that fact with belief in the benevolence of God. Lines 2–8 supply reasons that could be alleged for God's injustice. Lines 9–11 draw a seemingly logical conclusion, but lines 12–13 supply the real conclusions people often do draw. The reversal in lines 12–13 is explained by line 12: When we discontinue belief in God, we are left with only ourselves and are thus truly (existentially) alone, and so we rush back to the safety of the fold.

But how are we to take this last line—as a valid or invalid reason for clinging to a belief in God? Its tone is central to the tone of the whole poem, and it is itself based on ambiguities: for example, safety is not necessarily the greatest good; *impressed* can mean "stamped" or "forced into service" (i.e., drafted) as well as "deeply affected"; and "His care for us" is not very great as it is expressed in the rest of the poem. What signals help us know how to interpret the line? Probably the surest guide is the whole context of the poem. It is hardly a conventional, positive psalm. Although elsewhere certain words are intentionally ambiguous ("it could be said," "indifferent"), the poem emphasizes lack of care and the reasons not to depend on God. If so, the last line shows human beings' fear of being on their own, their rationalization of God's injustice, and their weakness in seeking the safety of the fold.

Certainly the tone can't be called religious; the poem expresses skepticism about the very basis of religion and about humanity's reasons for being religious. The poet, the speaker, and the human race are categorized together, and the poem is as much a comment on human nature as divine nature. To Whittemore, God's mysterious ways are a cover-up for indifference or, worse yet, nonexistence; to Cowper, of course, Whittemore's skepticism would be blind unbelief, which is sure to err. Nothing has been resolved in the imagined debate between the two poems.

Sometimes nothing gets resolved within a single poem. William Blake's "The Clod and the Pebble" illustrates the difficulty in determining the *author's* attitude in a poem related by one or more dramatized speakers that are obviously distinct from the poet.

THE CLOD AND THE PEBBLE

"Love seeketh not Itself to please.
Nor for itself hath any care,
But for another gives its ease,
And builds a Heaven in Hell's despair."

So sung a little Clod of Clay   5
Trodden with the cattle's feet,
But a Pebble of the brook
Warbled out these metres meet:

"Love seeketh only Self to please,
To bind another to Its delight,   10
Joys in another's loss of ease,
And builds a Hell in Heaven's despite."

William Blake (1757–1827)

Within the imaginative boundaries of a work of literature, even inanimate objects can be endowed with speech and reason, and so the Clod and the Pebble argue about love. What philosophy is expressed by each, and why is it appropriate to the speaker? Are there suggestions that Blake identifies with one viewpoint more than the other? What would you call the tone? How does the thematic organization reinforce the tone?

The Clod and the Pebble both convey in simple, melodic language attitudes that are appropriate to each. The Clod of Clay—an elemental substance trodden underfoot by the lowliest animals, yet infinitely flexible and enduring—sings of a humble, selfless love; the Pebble of the brook answers by advocating a self-absorbed, possessive love that—like itself—is hard, inflexible, and cold.

The mythic significance of clay (which in the sacred stories of many cultures is the substance from which human life was created) and the idealistic philosophy attributed to it might influence some readers to accept this speaker as a spokesman for Blake. Other readers, however, might construe the word "meet" (i.e., appropriate) in line 8 as an authorial endorsement of the Pebble's viewpoint and also find significant Blake's placement of the Pebble's speech at the end, the position usually reserved for the strongest and most important argument. Neither of these interpretations is really convincing, for the poem is symmetrical in virtually every respect. Blake devotes four lines to the Clod of Clay and four to the Pebble's response. Moreover, both the language and structure of the two stanzas are parallel. Each line of the Pebble's discourse refers to a corresponding line in the Clod's speech, for the most part in identical language reordered or redefined to refute the argument of the initial speaker. We can see just how tightly controlled and closely related these lines are by examining them side by side:

> Love seeketh not Itself to please
> Love seeketh only Self to please
>
> Nor for itself hath any care
> To bind another to Its delight
>
> But for another gives its ease
> Joys in another's loss of ease
>
> And builds a Heaven in Hell's despair
> And builds a Hell in Heaven's despite

This pattern is echoed in the second stanza, where two lines are devoted to the Clod and two to the Pebble. Verbally, the word "sung" in line 5 is balanced by "warbled" in line 7, and the language of the entire stanza is uniformly descriptive and expository rather than judgmental. In fact, none of the signals isolated in the poems we discussed earlier in the chapter gives a clue to Blake's view in this poem—only their *absence* does. Consequently, the attitude conveyed is one of impartiality, of weighing the two sides without opting for either one and without reconciling them. The dialogue is related by an observer close to the scene yet not intimately involved in it. We readers are set up to see the situation from the onlooker's point of view.

In the poem Blake acknowledges the reality of both the Clay's song of innocence and the Pebble's song of experience. The two attitudes toward love—and life—are opposite and irreconcilable. Blake's attitude is not ambiguous but ambivalent; he seems to be neutral toward both the speakers and their speeches, allowing us to ponder both sides by giving them equal weight. Perhaps we conclude that neither philosophy is adequate but both are necessary and that the real truth lies in the opposition between the two.

The next poem also concerns nature, but notice the difference in tone.

DESIGN

> I found a dimpled spider fat and white,
> On a white heal-all,° holding up a moth   °*a wildflower*
> Like a white piece of rigid satin cloth—
> Assorted characters of death and blight
> Mixed ready to begin the morning right,   5
> Like the ingredients of a witches' broth—
> A snow-drop spider, a flower like a froth,
> And dead wings carried like a paper kite.

> What had that flower to do with being white,
> The wayside blue and innocent heal-all?
> What brought the kindred spider to that height,
> Then steered the white moth thither in the night?
> What but design of darkness to appall?—
> If design govern in a thing so small.
>
> Robert Frost (1874–1963)

10

In a sense, nature speaks here, too, not in human language ascribed to personified objects but through the pattern or "design" of small, seemingly insignificant things: a spider, a moth, and a flower. What does the persona find so intriguing about this scene? Is the language in which he describes it subjective or objective? Straightforward or ironic? What words or combinations of words create this effect?

Because moths and other insects are the usual prey of spiders, the death of a single moth hardly seems significant—yet in this poem such a seemingly unimportant event assumes cosmic importance.

The poem begins almost casually, with the persona's discovery of the spider and the dead moth framed against the petals of the "heal-all," a small summer wildflower. From the very first line, the perplexing and disturbing makeup of this scene is apparent. The spider—the agent of death—is "dimpled" and "fat," words often used to describe babies. The flower is "innocent," and its name suggests that it has creative or life-giving powers, yet it attracts the moth to its fatal encounter with the spider. All are white—a color that has strong traditional associations of innocence—but the spider's whiteness and the heal-all's camouflage aid the spider in capturing its prey, whose own whiteness does not seem a protection. The color takes on still more ominous overtones as a result of the contrasts within word clusters: "snowdrop spider," "flower like a froth," and "dead wings carried like a paper kite." Snowdrops and flowers are beautiful; paper kites are the playthings of children. But "spider," "froth" (suggesting, among other things, mad dogs foaming at the mouth), and "dead wings" have the opposite connotations. Perhaps even more startling is the unexpected statement that this scene of "death and blight" is "right." Even without a discussion of the uses of irony, which will be described in Chapter 5, we can recognize a discrepancy between the usual meanings of many of these words and their associations in this particular poem.

Throughout the first stanza, the tone is one of fascination and muted horror, held in balance by pervasive irony that jars the persona—and therefore the reader—into a new perception of nature and the design or plan behind it. Does this tone change in the second stanza? What is the significance of the questions at the beginning of the stanza? How does the persona answer them in the next-to-last line? What is the significance of the final line?

At the beginning of stanza 2, the persona begins testing the hypothesis implicit in the first stanza: that the flower, the moth, the spider, and—by implication—the other elements of nature, including human beings, do not control their own destiny. They are but the "ingredients of a witches' broth," stirred by the unseen hand of an impersonal power that "brought" the spider and "steered" the moth in the darkness of night toward the darkness of death.

The conclusion "What but design of darkness to appall?" momentarily changes the uncertainty of lines 1–12 into a terrifying certainty, but the tone shifts again in line 14 with the revelation that something exists even more appalling than a "design of darkness"—the possibility that no principle of order governs the universe at all. Because the last line is itself conjectural, the persona does not reach a single, conclusive answer to his questions about the design of the universe. But for the reader sensitive to the poem's resonant, intricately patterned language and attentive to its ironic, shifting tone, "Design" communicates a vision of nature that is frighteningly different from the widely accepted concept of a benevolent and ordered universe.

If the interpretation of tone in poetry is often difficult, it is nonetheless necessary because tone and theme are so closely related that to misread one is to distort the other.

Here are some suggestions to help you deal accurately with tone:

1. Referring back if necessary to the guidelines at the end of Chapter 2, identify the voice (or voices) of the poem, the subject, the audience, and the situation.
2. Look closely at the persona's language as well, its connotations and its denotations.
3. Notice first what the words and syntax reveal about the speaker's attitude toward the reader. Do they create an effect similar to the colloquial, informal language of "My Roosevelt Coupé," or do they produce a more formal tone, like that of Cowper's hymn?
4. Next, think of a word or phrase that describes the speaker's attitude toward the subject, the audience within the poem (if one exists), and himself or herself. We have already used many such words, either in noun or in adjective form, throughout this chapter: <u>humorous</u>, <u>serious</u>, <u>affectionate</u>, <u>embarrassed</u>, <u>angry</u>, <u>condescending</u>, <u>critical</u>, <u>sympathetic</u>, <u>skeptical</u>, <u>questioning</u>, <u>impartial</u>, <u>ambiguous</u>, <u>ambivalent</u>, <u>fascinated</u>, <u>appalled</u>, <u>ironic</u>. And we could easily expand the list by adding such

words as <u>fearful</u>, <u>horrified</u>, <u>melancholy</u>, <u>energetic</u>, <u>excited</u>, <u>bored</u>, and so on.

5. In poems that have two or more speakers, notice whether their words convey similar or different attitudes. If you find descrepancies, observe whether the structure emphasizes one viewpoint more than another or whether the number of lines, the syntax, and other structural details create a balance such as we observed in "The Clod and the Pebble."

6. If there is a single persona, read carefully to determine whether he or she expresses a consistent viewpoint or whether there are shifts and contradictions. Changing or contrasting attitudes can sometimes be accounted for by the structure of the poem. A change from religious doubt to faith, for example, might evolve logically from a chronological pattern, a causal relationship, a formal argument, or another structure. But in some poems, the author leaves conflicts unresolved in order to suggest that the persona is shallow, confused, indecisive, unstable, or—conversely—that such ambiguities reflect a penetrating insight into the complexities and dislocations of life.

7. Decide whether the speaker's attitudes coincide with those of the poet. If no discrepancy exists in the language, incidents, structure, or context of the poem, then the persona's attitudes are also the poet's. If the poet intends to create a tone different from that of the speaker, this should also be apparent.

Taking into account all these suggestions, analyze the tone of Michael Dennis Browne's "Paranoia."

PARANOIA

When you drive on the freeway, cars follow you.

Someone opens your mail, two hands
that come out of your shirt-sleeves.

Your dog looks at you, he does not like you.

At the driving test the cop is tired. He has sat up   5
all night, screening your dreams.

If you go to the zoo, be sure to take your passport.

Everywhere you go, the dog goes with you. Beautiful women
come up to you and ask for the dog's telephone number.

You take a girl to a concert of Russian music; on the way   10
up the steps, she falls in love with one of the pickets.

You go to teach; everyone who passes you in the corridor
knows you never finished *Tristram Shandy*.
You are the assistant professor no one associates with.

At the yoga class you finally get   15
into the lotus position.
You are carried home.
When you close your eyes in meditation, all you see is breasts.

When you turn the refrigerator to de-frost, the TV drips.

Across the street, the pigeons call softly to each other   20
like the FBI on a stakeout.

When you walk to the post office and see the flag at half-mast,
you know you have died.

Michael Dennis Browne (b. 1940)

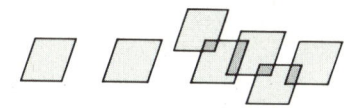

POEMS FOR FURTHER STUDY 1

THE THREE RAVENS

There were three ravens sat on a tree,
    Downe, a downe, hay downe, hay downe,
There were three ravens sat on a tree,
    With a downe,
There were three ravens sat on a tree,   5
They were as blacke as they might be,
    With a downe, derrie, derrie, derrie, downe, downe.

The one of them said to his mate,
"Where shall we our breakfast take?"—

"Downe in yonder greene field,   10
There lies a knight slain under his shield.
"His hounds they lie downe at his feete,
So well they their master keepe.

"His haukes they flie so eagerly,
There's no fowle dare him com nie."°   °*nigh* 15

Downe there comes a fallow doe,°   °*small, light brown*
As great with yong° as she might goe.   *European deer*
    °*young*

She lift up his bloudy hed,
And kist his wounds that were so red.

She got him up upon her backe,   20
And carried him to earthen lake.°   °*dike*

She buried him before the prime,
She was dead herselfe ere even°-song time.   °*evening*

God send every gentleman,
Such haukes, such houndes, and such a leman.°   °*sweetheart* 25

Anonymous (date unknown)

THE TWA CORBIES

As I was walking all alane,°   °*alone*
I heard twa° corbies making a mane;°   °*two* °*moan*
The tane° unto the t'other say,   °*one*
"Where sall° we gang° and dine to-day?"—   °*shall* °*go*

"In behint yon auld° fail° dyke,   °*old* °*earthen* 5
I wot there lies a new-slain knight;
And naebody kens° that he lies there,   °*knows*
But his hawk, his hound, and lady fair.

"His hound is to the hunting gane,
His hawk, to fetch the wild-fowl hame,   10
His lady's ta'en another mate,
So we may mak° our dinner sweet.   °*make*

"Ye'll sit on his white hause-bane,°   °*breast bone*
And I'll pick out his bonny blue een:°   °*eyes*
Wi' ae lock o' his gowden hair,   15
We'll theek° our nest when it grows bare.   °*thatch*

"Mony a one for him makes mane,
But nane sall ken where he is gane:
O'er his white banes, when they are bare,
The wind sall blaw for evermair."—   20

Anonymous (date unknown)

QUESTIONS

1. "The Three Ravens" and "The Twa Corbies" are traditional folk ballads, which are at least two centuries old. Like other forms of oral ex-

pression, these ballads have undergone changes over time. Do they tell different stories, or do they seem to be variants of the same narrative?

2. How do the anonymous authors (or performers) of the two works set the scene at the beginning? Does the narrative method of each ballad establish a close or distant relationship between the audience and the situation?

3. In "The Three Ravens," who seems to be speaking in the last two lines? What is the tone of these lines? Are any comparable sentiments expressed in "The Twa Corbies"?

4. Compare the plots of the two ballads, paying particular attention to the circumstances of the knight's death and the significance of the non-human participants.

5. In "The Three Ravens," the actions of the doe are the focus of over half the poem, but in "The Twa Corbies," there is no doe. Who is there instead? What is the significance of this variation?

6. The last two lines of "The Three Ravens" seem to be an explicit statement of the theme and tone of this ballad. Does the ending of "The Twa Corbies" have similar or different implications? Would you agree or disagree with the observation of one ballad scholar that the latter is a cynical version of the former?

AN ELEGY ON THAT GLORY OF HER SEX, MRS. MARY BLAIZE

Good people all, with one accord,
    Lament for Madam Blaize,
Who never wanted a good word—
    From those who spoke her praise.

The needy seldom passed her door,   5
    And always found her kind;
She freely lent to all the poor—
    Who left a pledge behind.

She strove the neighbourhood to please,
    With manners wondrous winning,   10
She never follow'd wicked ways—
    Unless when she was sinning.

At church, in silks and satins new,
    With hoop of monstrous size,
She never slumbered in her pew—   15
    But when she shut her eyes.

>   Her love was sought, I do aver,
>   By twenty beaux and more;
>   The king himself has followed her—
>   When she has walked before.   20
>
>   But now her wealth and fin'ry fled,
>   Her hangers-on cut short all;
>   Her doctors found, when she was dead,—
>   Her last disorder mortal.
>
>   Let us lament, in sorrow sore,   25
>   For Kent Street well may say,
>   That had she lived a twelvemonth more,—
>   She had not died to-day.
>
>   *Oliver Goldsmith* (1730–1774)

QUESTIONS

1. An elegy generally means a formal, dignified poem that laments a death and ends with a philosophical acceptance of it. What, then, does this title imply is the situation described in this poem? How much information is given about the persona? Who is the audience?

2. Although it is short, the poem still has overall structural divisions. Label them. In addition, each stanza has an internal organization pattern. Comment on it.

3. Lines 2 and 4 of each stanza have fewer syllables than lines 1 and 3. What effect is created by this pattern? Would longer lines and a less singsong pattern seem more appropriate for an elegy? Explain.

4. Which words and phrases are ambiguous? Which seem inappropriate for an elegy?

5. Your answers to questions 2, 3, and 4 may make you dubious about this poem as a formal lament on the death of someone important. Is Mrs. Blaize worth an elegy? What seems to be the poet's attitude toward her? How do you suppose he wants you to feel about the poem? What might be his intention?

6. The term *burlesque* refers to a work that ridicules a subject, style, or convention by treating it in an inappropriate manner. During the eighteenth century, when Goldsmith lived, the somber elegy was an extremely popular and overused form. Do you suppose Goldsmith is burlesquing the elegy form here? How would you describe his tone?

ELEGY FOR JANE
My Student, Thrown by a Horse

I remember the neckcurls, limp and damp as tendrils;
And her quick look, a sidelong pickerel smile;
And how, once startled into talk, the light syllables leaped for her,
And she balanced in the delight of her thought,
A wren, happy, tail into the wind,   5
Her song trembling the twigs and small branches.
The shade sang with her;
The leaves, their whispers turned to kissing;
And the mold sang in the bleached valleys under the rose.

Oh, when she was sad, she cast herself down into such a pure depth,   10
Even a father could not find her:
Scraping her cheek against straw;
Stirring the clearest water.

My sparrow, you are not here,
Waiting like a fern, making a spiny shadow.   15
The sides of wet stones cannot console me,
Nor the moss, wound with the last light.

If only I could nudge you from this sleep,
My maimed darling, my skittery pigeon.
Over this damp grave I speak the words of my love: 20
I, with no rights in this matter,
Neither father nor lover.

Theodore Roethke (1908–1963)

QUESTIONS

1. How important is the dedication? Does it set our expectations? Disappoint them? Would removal of the dedication change our understanding of the poem?
2. Where does a shift of tone occur in the poem? How does it modulate our feelings toward the subject?
3. Describe the emotional value of "limp and damp."
4. Roethke, or the speaker, sees Jane as a "sparrow," "wren," and "pigeon." What is the tonal effect of such comparison?
5. Elegies traditionally provide some form of consolation for the radical and painful loss involved with death. In Whitman's great elegy "When Lilacs Last in the Dooryard Bloomed," for example, Lincoln lives in memory, eternally returning with the seasonal perfume of lilac he is associated with in the poem. Is there any consolation in Roethke's poem?

AN ELEMENTARY SCHOOL CLASSROOM IN A SLUM

Far far from gusty waves these children's faces.
Like rootless weeds, the hair torn round their pallor.
The tall girl with her weighed-down head. The paper-
seeming boy, with rat's eyes. The stunted, unlucky heir
Of twisted bones, reciting a father's gnarled disease,   5
His lesson from his desk. At back of the dim class
One unnoted, sweet and young. His eyes live in a dream
Of squirrel's game, in tree room, other than this.

On sour cream walls, donations. Shakespeare's head,
Cloudless at dawn, civilized dome riding all cities.   10
Belled, flowery, Tyrolese valley.° Open-handed map   °*in the Alps*
Awarding the world its world. And yet, for these
Children, these windows, not this world, are world,
Where all their future's painted with a fog,
A narrow street sealed in with a lead sky,   15
Far far from rivers, capes, and stars of words.

Surely, Shakespeare is wicked, the map a bad example
With ships and sun and love tempting them to steal—
For lives that slyly turn in their cramped holes
From fog to endless night? On their slag heap, these children   20
Wear skins peeped through by bones and spectacles of steel
With mended glass, like bottle bits on stones.
All of their time and space are foggy slum.
So blot their maps with slums as big as doom.

Unless, governor, teacher, inspector, visitor,   25
This map becomes their window and these windows
That shut upon their lives like catacombs,
Break O break open till they break the town
And show the children to green fields, and make their world
Run azure on gold sands, and let their tongues   30
Run naked into books, the white and green leaves open
History theirs whose language is the sun.

Stephen Spender (b. 1909)

QUESTIONS

1. What do the children described in lines 1–6 have in common? What tone is established by the words "rootless weeds," "pallor," "weighed-down head," "paper-seeming," "twisted bones," and "gnarled disease"? What two meanings of "reciting" are appropriate in line 5?

2. How does the child sitting in the back of the room differ from the other children? Contrast the environment of the classroom and the child's dream world.
3. What are the "donations" mentioned in line 9? Are they meaningful in this environment? Why or why not?
4. Are stanzas 1 and 2 similar or different in tone?
5. When the speaker says that the children's faces are "far from gusty waves" (line 1) and that they are "sealed in with a lead sky,/Far far from rivers, capes, and stars of words" (line 16), what kinds of distance might he be referring to? Explain.
6. What shift in tone occurs in stanza 3? Which words mark this change? What emotions does the language of this stanza arouse in the reader?
7. What specific audience is addressed in the final stanza? What further changes in tone are evident?

A STUDY OF READING HABITS

When getting my nose in a book
Cured most things short of school,
It was worth ruining my eyes
To know I could still keep cool,
And deal out the old right hook   5
To dirty dogs twice my size.

Later, with inch-thick specs,
Evil was just my lark:
Me and my cloak and fangs
Had ripping times in the dark.   10
The women I clubbed with sex!
I broke them up like meringues.

Don't read much now: the dude
Who lets the girl down before
The hero arrives, the chap   15
Who's yellow and keeps the store,
Seem far too familiar. Get stewed:
Books are a load of crap.

Philip Larkin (b. 1922)

QUESTIONS

1. Describe the tension or contrast established between the title and body of the poem. Does the poem alter any expectations aroused by the title?

2. Locate the clichés in this poem. What is their function? Is the poet aware of them?

3. What meanings does the word "ripping" have?

4. Describe the sort of person the speaker is. Does any discrepancy exist between what the speaker says and what the author means? Explain.

5. How does the speaker's attitude toward himself change from one stanza to the next?

6. What word or phrase best describes the tone of the poem as a whole?

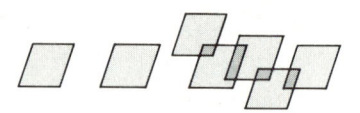

POEMS FOR FURTHER STUDY 2

FERN HILL

Now as I was young and easy under the apple boughs
About the lilting house and happy as the grass was green,
    The night above the dingle° starry,   °*small, wooded*
        Time let me hail and climb   *valley*
        Golden in the heydays of his eyes,   5
And honoured among wagons I was prince of the apple towns
And once below a time I lordly had the trees and leaves
        Trail with daisies and barley
    Down the rivers of the windfall light.

And as I was green and carefree, famous among the barns   10
About the happy yard and singing as the farm was home,
    In the sun that is young once only,
        Time let me play and be
        Golden in the mercy of his means,
And green and golden I was huntsman and herdsman, the calves   15
Sang to my horn, the foxes on the hills barked clear and cold,
        And the sabbath rang slowly
    In the pebbles of the holy streams.

All the sun long it was running, it was lovely, the hay
Fields high as the house, the tunes from the chimneys, it was air   20
    And playing, lovely and watery
        And fire green as grass.
    And nightly under the simple stars

As I rode to sleep the owls were bearing the farm away,
All the moon long I heard, blessed among stables, the night-jars 25
    Flying with the ricks, and the horses
        Flashing into the dark.

And then to awake, and the farm, like a wanderer white
With the dew, come back, the cock on his shoulder: it was all
    Shining, it was Adam and maiden, 30
        The sky gathered again
    And the sun grew round that very day.
So it must have been after the birth of the simple light
In the first, spinning place, the spellbound horses walking warm
    Out of the whinnying green stable 35
        On to the fields of praise.

And honoured among foxes and pheasants by the gay house
Under the new made clouds and happy as the heart was long,
    In the sun born over and over,
        I ran my heedless ways, 40
    My wishes raced through the house high hay
And nothing I cared, at my sky blue trades, that time allows
In all his tuneful turning so few and such morning songs
    Before the children green and golden
        Follow him out of grace, 45

Nothing I cared, in the lamb white days, that time would take me
Up to the swallow thronged loft by the shadow of my hand,
    In the moon that is always rising,
        Nor that riding to sleep
    I should hear him fly with the high fields 50
And wake to the farm forever fled from the childless land.
Oh as I was young and easy in the mercy of his means,
        Time held me green and dying
    Though I sang in my chains like the sea.

Dylan Thomas (1914–1953)

SPRING

To what purpose, April, do you return again?
Beauty is not enough.
You can no longer quiet me with the redness
Of little leaves opening stickily.
I know what I know. 5
The sun is hot on my neck as I observe
The spikes of the crocus.
The smell of the earth is good.

It is apparent that there is no death.
But what does that signify?
Not only under ground are the brains of men
Eaten by maggots.
Life in itself
Is nothing,
An empty cup, a flight of uncarpeted stairs.
Is is not enough that yearly, down this hill,
April
Comes like an idiot, babbling and strewing flowers.

Edna St. Vincent Millay (1892–1950)

OF DE WITT WILLIAMS ON HIS WAY TO LINCOLN CEMETERY°

°*a cemetery in Chicago*

He was born in Alabama.
He was bred in Illinois.
He was nothing but a
Plain black boy.

Swing low swing low sweet sweet chariot.
Nothing but a plain black boy.

Drive him past the Pool Hall.
Drive him past the Show.
Blind within his casket,
But maybe he will know.

Down through Forty-seventh Street:
Underneath the L,°
And—Northwest Corner, Prairie,
That he loved so well.

°*Chicago's elevated railway*

Don't forget the Dance Halls—
Warwick and Savoy,
Where he picked his women, where
He drank his liquid joy.

Born in Alabama.
Bred in Illinois.
He was nothing but a
Plain black boy.

Swing low swing low sweet sweet chariot.
Nothing but a plain black boy.

Gwendolyn Brooks (b. 1917)

VANDERGAST AND THE GIRL

Vandergast to his neighbors—
the grinding of a garage door
and hiss of gravel in the driveway.

He worked for the insurance company
whose talisman is a phoenix
rising in flames . . . *non omnis moriar*.
From his desk he had a view of the street—

translucent raincoats, and umbrellas,
fluorescent plate-glass windows.
A girl knelt down, arranging
underwear on a female dummy—

sea waves and, on the gale,
Venus, these busy days,
poised in her garter-belt and stockings.

*

The next day he saw her eating
in the restaurant where he usually ate.

Soon they were having lunch together
elsewhere.

   She came from Dallas.
This was only a start, she was ambitious,
twenty-five and still unmarried.
Green eyes with silver spiricles . . .
red hair. . . .

   When he held the car door open
her legs were smooth and slender.

'I was wondering',
she said, 'when you'd get round to it',
and laughed.

*

Vandergast says he never intended
having an affair.

    And was that what this was?
The names that people give to things. . . .
What do definitions and divorce-court proceedings
have to do with the breathless reality?

O little lamp at the bedside
with views of Venice and the Bay of Naples,
you understood! *Lactona* toothbrush
and suitcase bought in a hurry,
you were the witnesses of the love
we made in bed together.

Schrafft's Chocolate Cherries, surely you remember
when she said she'd be true forever,

and, watching 'Dark Storm', we decided
there is something to be said, after all,
for soap opera, 'if it makes people happy.'

*

The Vandergasts are having some trouble
finding a buyer for their house.

When I go for a walk with Tippy
I pass the unweeded tennis court,
the empty garage, windows heavily shuttered.

Mrs. Vandergast took the children
and went back to her family.

And Vandergast moved to New Jersey,
where he works for an insurance company
whose emblem is the Rock of Gibraltar—
the rest of his life laid out
with the child-support and alimony payments.

As for the girl, she vanished.

Was it worth it? Ask Vandergast.
You'd have to be Vandergast, looking through his eyes
at the house across the street, in Orange, New Jersey.
Maybe on wet days umbrellas and raincoats
set his heart thudding.

    Maybe
he talks to his pillow, and it whispers,
moving red hair.

In any case, he will soon be forty.

      Louis Simpson (b. 1923)

THE TYGER

Tyger! Tyger! burning bright
In the forests of the night,
What immortal hand or eye
Could frame thy fearful symmetry?

In what distant deeps or skies   5
Burnt the fire of thine eyes?
On what wings dare he aspire?
What the hand dare seize the fire?

And what shoulder, and what art,
Could twist the sinews of thy heart?   10
And when thy heart began to beat,
What dread hand? and what dread feet?

What the hammer? what the chain?
In what furnace was thy brain?
What the anvil? what dread grasp   15
Dare its deadly terrors clasp?

When the stars threw down their spears
And watered heaven with their tears,
Did he smile his work to see?
Did he who made the Lamb make thee?   20

Tyger! Tyger! burning bright
In the forests of the night,
What immortal hand or eye
Dare frame thy fearful symmetry?

      William Blake (1757–1827)

SONG: WHY SO PALE AND WAN?

Why so pale and wan, fond lover?
    Prithee, why so pale?
Will, when looking well can't move her,
    Looking ill prevail?
    Prithee, why so pale?   5

Why so dull and mute, young sinner?
    Prithee, why so mute?
Will, when speaking well can't win her,
    Saying nothing do't?
    Prithee, why so mute?   10

> Quit, quit for shame! This will not move—
>   This cannot take her.
> If of herself she will not love,
>   Nothing can make her:
> The devil take her!

        Sir John Suckling (1609–1642)

POEM IN WHICH MY LEGS ARE ACCEPTED

Legs!
How we have suffered each other,
never meeting the standards of magazines
                or official measurements.

I have hung you from trapezes,
    sat you on wooden rollers,
        pulled and pushed you
                with the anxiety of taffy,
and still, you are yourselves!

Most obvious imperfection, blight on my fantasy life,
strong,
plump,
never to be skinny
or even hinting of the svelte beauties in history books
                or Sears catalogues.

Here you are—solid, fleshy and
white as when I first noticed you, sitting on the toilet,
            spread softly over the
                  wooden seat,

having been with me only twelve years,
                yet
as obvious as the legs of my thirty-year-old gym teacher.

Legs!
O that was the year we did acrobatics in the annual gym
    show.
How you split for me!
            One-handed cartwheels
            from this end of the gymnasium to
              the other,
            ending in double splits,
legs you flashed in blue rayon slacks my mother bought
    for the occasion

and tho you were confidently swinging along,
the rest of me blushed at the sound of clapping.

Legs!
How I have worried about you, not able to hide you,
embarrassed at beaches, in highschool
                when the cheerleaders' slim brown legs
                              spread all over
                              the sand
                              with the perfection
                              of bamboo.
I hated you, and still you have never given out on me.

With you
I have risen to the top of blue waves,
with you
I have carried food home as a loving gift
                        when my arms began un-
                        jelling like madrilenne.

Legs, you are a pillow,
white and plentiful with feathers for his wild head.
You are the endless scenery
behind the tense sinewy elegance of his two dark legs.
You welcome him joyfully
and dance.
And you will be the locks in a new canal between
    continents.
                The ship of life will push out of you
                and rejoice
                    in the whiteness,
                    in the first floating and rising of water.

                            Kathleen Fraser (b. 1937)

5

INCONGRUITY

ON THE VANITY OF EARTHLY GREATNESS

The tusks that clashed in mighty brawls
Of mastodons, are billiard balls.

The sword of Charlemagne the Just
Is ferric oxide, known as rust.

The grizzly bear whose potent hug 5
Was feared by all, is now a rug.

Great Caesar's dead and on the shelf,
And I don't feel so well myself!

Arthur Guiterman (1871–1943)

Mutability, or the transience of earthly things, is a theme that has long fascinated writers. It is reflected in Hamlet's "Alas, poor Yorick" speech; in Macbeth's vision of life as a "walking shadow, a poor player/ That struts and frets his hour upon the stage/ And then is heard no more"; in the ruin and desolation that mock the tyrant-king of Shelley's "Ozymandias," whose shattered monument proclaims, "Look on my works ye mighty and despair." It is also the theme of Arthur Guiterman's "On the Vanity of Earthly Greatness," a very different kind of work.

How would you describe the tone of Guiterman's poem? In what way is this tone influenced by the poet's choice and arrangement of words? By the structure of the poem?

The tone of the poem is unmistakably humorous, not because there is anything inherently funny about mastodons, grizzly bears, or warrior-heroes like Charlemagne and Caesar but because the first line in each stanza clashes with the second. The effect that Guiterman achieves by this means is called *incongruity—a disparity or discrepancy that results from the juxtaposition of conflicting or incompatible objects, incidents, words and associations, tones, points of view, or other elements in a work of literature.* Without at this point attempting to name and define the specific forms that literary incongruity can take, let's see how Guiterman achieves this effect in "On The Vanity of Earthly Greatness" and what he seeks to accomplish with it.

The first stanza begins with the clash of enormous, Ice-Age beasts, then shifts abruptly and anticlimactically to billiard balls that sit passively on a table or clink unmajestically together when someone jabs them with a pool cue. The incongruity is made even more emphatic by the correspondence in sound between the final words in each line: "mighty brawls" and "billiard balls." Similarly, in stanza 2, the grandeur of the first line is deflated by the matter-of-fact, nonheroic language of the second, which reminds us that even the sword of a conqueror ultimately turns to ordinary "ferric oxide" and asks us to pair "Charlemagne the Just" with that indisputable sign of deterioration, "rust." Equally striking is the discrepancy in stanza 3 between a live grizzly bear, an animal noted for its strength and ferocity, and the inert rug made from its fur, a discrepancy that Guiterman underscores by rhyming "potent hug" with "rug." In the final stanza, the author modifies the basic structural pattern by drawing a parallel between another obvious example of earthly greatness, Julius Caesar, and the speaker. Caesar is already "on the shelf," presumably as a piece of statuary, and—as the speaker puts it—"I don't feel so well myself." The implication, of course, is that ordinary human beings are as subject to the processes of change and decay as the great and mighty.

Despite its light tone and its limited treatment of the mutability theme, "On the Vanity of Earthly Greatness" is worth reading, not only because it is amusing but also because its humorous incongruities serve a larger purpose, enabling us to laugh at conditions we cannot change and to put our own pretensions or ambitions in perspective.

Although the term itself may be unfamiliar, almost everyone has either heard at one time or another something incongruous or used language to evoke incongruity, for it is one of the chief ingredients in the oral humor of both children and adults. Incongruity is the basis of riddle-jokes, such as the one in which the performer asks, "How do you stop a charging elephant?" and then replies, "Take away his American Express card." It is apparent too in spoofs of "Mother Goose" in which Mary takes her lamb to school between two hunks of bread and Little Miss Muffet turns aggressor and eats the spider when it sits down beside her. Humorous adaptations of proverbs also rely on incongruity: "Familiarity breeds attempt." "Absence makes the heart go wander." "Do not enumerate your fowl until the process of incubation has been finalized."

The "charging elephant" riddle illustrates a form of incongruity called a *pun—a play on words requiring the reader or listener to perceive a discrepancy between two or more meanings in the same word.* "Charging," of course, means both "rushing" and "using a credit card," and the humor of the pun results from the double meaning and the absurdity of the situation it brings to mind. The other examples of oral humor cited earlier are all a form of *parody, the conscious imitation of the style, language, or ideas of another author or work with the intent of ridiculing or gently mocking the original.* The incongruity stems from the listener's awareness of both versions and ability to recognize differences in their tone, purpose, or theme. Let's turn to literary puns and parodies and see if they work in similar ways.

Although puns have sometimes been regarded as an inferior form of wit and art, many poets have used them. The technique was especially popular during the English Renaissance, when it was employed for both comic and serious purposes by poets of such stature as Shakespeare, who endowed many of the tragic heroes and romantic couples of his poetic dramas with skill in punning, and John Donne, who made the pun a vehicle for both secular and religious themes.

Since the seventeenth century, however, the pun has become primarily a comic device, as in this epitaph by the twentieth-century British poet Hilaire Belloc:

> When I am dead, I hope it may be said:
> His sins were scarlet, but his books were read.

Belloc makes his point about fame with the same economy of words as an oral punster, but with more subtlety of technique. What purpose do the first two rhymes serve? What associations of the word "scarlet" are relevant to understanding Belloc's poem? In which word does the pun occur? What is its significance?

In line 1, the words "dead" and "said" create an expectation of the sound that will occur in the final word of the second line, and the word "scarlet" in line 2 predisposes us to think of the color red when we get to the end of the line, even though logic tells us that "red" and "read" have totally different meanings. By forcing both meanings into the same sense unit, and by placing the pun at the very end of the last line, Belloc achieves two purposes. He releases the humor at the most emphatic point in the poem, and in the process he calls attention to the word that is most important to his theme: the hope that his works will outlive him.

Puns can usually be understood from their context, but a *parody* has meaning only if the reader or listener recognizes the work being imitated and remembers it well enough to match it, imaginatively, with the parody. Thus the task of literary parodists is more difficult than that of oral parodists, for an audience is more likely to recognize a variation of a familiar nursery rhyme or proverb than an imitation of a literary work, no matter how important the work or its author. See if you can identify the specific poem that inspired Kenneth Koch's "Variations on a Theme by William Carlos Williams."

VARIATIONS ON A THEME BY WILLIAM CARLOS WILLIAMS

I

I chopped down the house that you had been saving to live in next summer.
I am sorry, but it was morning, and I had nothing to do
and its wooden beams were so inviting.

                            II
We laughed at the hollyhocks together
and then I sprayed them with lye.   5
Forgive me. I simply do not know what I am doing.

                            III
I gave away the money that you had been saving to live on for the next ten
    years.
The man who asked for it was shabby
and the firm March wind on the porch was so juicy and cold.

                            IV
Last evening we went dancing and I broke your leg.   10
Forgive me. I was clumsy, and
I wanted you here in the wards, where I am the doctor!

                                        Kenneth Koch (b. 1925)

    To confirm that Koch's poem is a parody, rather than a serious extension of a Williams's theme, turn to the first page of Chapter 3 and reread "This Is Just to Say." What similarities in language do you find? What does each of Koch's variations have in common with the act described in Williams' poem? Even more important, what are the discrepancies between the two works in tone and theme?

    Even though Williams's poem is divided into a different number of lines and consists of one section rather than four, the parallels are unmistakable. Both are related in the first person by a speaker who has acted selfishly and is both explaining and justifying his action to the person who has been affected by it. Other resemblances become evident if we compare the diction and sentence structure of the two works. Koch's references to "the house that you had been saving" and "the money you had been saving" parallel Williams's description of "the plums . . . which you were probably saving for breakfast"; Koch's phrase "so juicy and cold" echoes Williams's "so sweet and so cold"; and the words "Forgive me" occur in both. Koch even brings Williams, a physician as well as a poet, into the poem as the clumsy and self-interested doctor of the fourth stanza.

    A reader, aware of these resemblances, will also be struck by the disparity between the commonplace, relatively harmless act of eating plums and the comically exaggerated variations on this theme: chopping down houses, spraying hollyhocks with lye, giving away another person's money, and finally breaking someone's leg. This discrepancy in tone also underscores the thematic differences between the two poems. In Koch's view, Williams is sympathetic to the plum-eater's philosophy; the parodist, however, attacks the assumption on which it rests by playfully pointing up the serious infringements of others' rights that could be justified if the principle of self-gratification were carried to its logical extreme.

Other forms of incongruity also present a challenge to both the reader and the poet, but for different reasons. Observe, for example, how Richard Lovelace exploits apparent contradictions in "To Althea From Prison."

TO ALTHEA FROM PRISON

When Love with unconfinèd wings
    Hovers within my gates
And my divine Althea brings
    To whisper at the grates;
When I lie tangled in her hair   5
    And fettered to her eye,
The gods that wanton° in the air   °*frolic*
    Know no such liberty.

When flowing cups run swiftly round,
    With no allaying° Thames,°   °*alleviating* °*chief* 10
Our careless heads with roses bound,   *river of England*
    Our hearts with loyal flames;
When thirsty grief in wine we steep,
    When healths and draughts go free,
Fishes that tipple in the deep   15
    Know no such liberty.

When, like committed linnets,° I   °*caged finches*
With shriller throat shall sing
The sweetness, mercy, majesty,
    And glories of my King;   20
When I shall voice aloud how good
    He is, how great should be,
Enlargèd winds that curl the flood
    Know no such liberty.

Stone walls do not a prison make,   25
    Nor iron bars a cage;
Minds innocent and quiet take
    That for an hermitage.
If I have freedom in my love
    And in my soul am free,   30
Angels alone, that soar above,
    Enjoy such liberty.

        Richard Lovelace (1618–1658)

An aristocrat and a loyal supporter of Charles I of England during the long struggle between the King and the Puritans, Lovelace was twice imprisoned for his political allegiances, first in 1641 and again in 1646. Is this poem a realistic account of his prison experiences, or does the setting function in some other way? How prominent a role does Althea play? Does the speaker describe her physically, or does he represent her as a spiritual ideal? What relationship does she have to the values that the speaker affirms in each stanza?

Scattered throughout the poem are words that suggest a prison locale: "gates," "grates," "stone walls," "prison," "iron bars," "cage." But the setting never becomes tangible, and neither the persona nor his beloved is ever individualized or described in physical terms. Rather, the poet develops a carefully constructed intellectual argument that affirms a number of closely related values—love, friendship, physical pleasures, and patriotism—through a series of **paradoxes**: *statements or situations that appear to be contradictory but on closer analysis prove to be true.*

The situation of the poem is itself paradoxical, for despite the fact that the speaker is literally a prisoner, he repeatedly asserts that he is freer than "the gods that wanton [frolic] in the air," "fishes that tipple in the deep," and "enlargèd winds that curl the flood." The closure is even more emphatic: "Angels alone, that soar above,/Enjoy such liberty."

How can a person be imprisoned and free at the same time? The situational paradox turns on the word "liberty," which in the context of the poem means not the absence of physical restraints but the freedom to love (stanza 1), to enjoy human fellowship and physical pleasures (stanza 2), and to proclaim "The sweetness, mercy, majesty,/And glories of my King" (stanza 3).

Within this framework, Lovelace further defines the nature and value of these ideals. The first to be defined (stanza 1) is love, which is expressed, paradoxically, in language suggestive of captivity. The context makes it clear that the words "tangled" and "fettered" describe not the bondage of actual imprisonment, but the bonds of love, which are emblematic of spiritual freedom.

The second stanza is more difficult to interpret because the pronoun references and situation are ambiguous. "Our careless heads" and "our hearts" may refer to Althea and the speaker, thus reemphasizing the lovers' bond described in stanza 1. But the references to "flowing cups" (i.e., cups filled to the top) and "healths and draughts" that "run swiftly round" (i.e., passed from one person to another) suggest a larger gathering of people, sitting at leisure, drinking from goblets filled with undiluted wine ("no allaying Thames"), and offering toasts. Regardless of how we interpret the situation, the speaker leaves no doubt that these pleasures, too, are essential to his "liberty."

The word takes on patriotic associations in the third stanza. In keeping with the paradoxical situation of the poem as a whole, the speaker identifies with "committed linnets," which sing more sweetly in captivity than when they are free.

In the final stanza, Lovelace draws together the three strands of the argument with the verbal paradoxes "Stone walls do not a prison make/Nor iron bars a cage." Literally, of course, prisons *are* built of stone and cages constructed of iron bars. But in the logic of the poem, walls and bars can enclose only the body. If one has freedom in love and soul, he can make a hermitage of a prison and attain a joyousness comparable to that of the angels.

Although some readers find Lovelace's style rather stiff and artificial, the paradoxes, abstract diction, and elaborate comparisons that he employs are well suited to a formal, intellectual argument. Yet despite this intellectual control—or perhaps because of it—Lovelace's poem conveys less emotional intensity than the poem that follows: William Wordsworth's "She Dwelt Among the Untrodden Ways." In reading it, think about some of these questions: Is Lucy comparable in any way to Althea? Is the nature of the relationship between Lucy and the speaker ever explicitly defined? What incongruities do you find in the poem? Are they cast in the form of paradoxes, or does Wordsworth employ some other technique?

SHE DWELT AMONG THE UNTRODDEN WAYS

She dwelt among the untrodden ways
    Beside the springs of Dove,°   °*the name of*
A Maid whom there were none to praise   *several rivers*
    And very few to love: *in England*

A violet by a mossy stone   5
    Half hidden from the eye!
—Fair as a star, when only one
    Is shining in the sky.

She lived unknown, and few could know
    When Lucy ceased to be;   10
But she is in her grave, and, oh,
    The difference to me!

William Wordsworth (1770–1850)

Unlike the divine Althea, Lucy is a simple country girl, "a violet by a mossy stone" rather than an angel of love. Furthermore, the poem reveals surprisingly little about the qualities that make her worthy of commemoration and even less about the relationship between her and the speaker. He does not describe Lucy's physical, intellectual, or spiritual attributes, nor do we know whether he speaks as a father, brother, suitor, or interested bystander.

The poem reveals a great deal through implication, however—especially through the implied contrast between the persona's attitude toward Lucy and that of her neighbors. To proceed further, we need to ask some additional questions. What relevance do the words "untrodden," "none to praise," and "unknown" have to this contrast? What is the purpose of the comparison in stanza 2? Do you think the diction of the last few lines of the poem is strong enough to convey all the speaker feels for Lucy?

In lines 1, 3, and 9, Wordsworth uses a specific form of incongruity known as **overstatement** (or **hyperbole**), *an exaggeration of emotion or content.* We find words that are more emotionally intense than the literal situation seems to call for. To say that the "ways" (paths) were literally "untrodden" would be to argue that no one—not even Lucy—had ever walked them. Similarly, she could not be absolutely unknown if even a "few could know" when she died, and an apparent discrepancy also exists between the assertion that "there were none to praise" Lucy and the implication (in line 4) that there were at least some who loved her.

In three instances, overstatement serves an important artistic function. It intensifies our awareness of Lucy's isolation from others and at the same time heightens our perception of the contrast between their inability to recognize her value and the speaker's high estimation of her worth.

His personal feelings, on the other hand, take the form of **understatement,** *language that says less than the situation seems to call for.* Understatement does not necessarily involve an emotional response, but in this poem notice the discrepancy between the emotions that the speaker feels and the seemingly unemotional language in which he discloses that Lucy is dead. He can only say that she has "ceased to be." This understatement is succeeded by another of greater magnitude: "and, oh,/The difference to me." In isolation, "difference" would be an unexpressive or, at best, neutral word, but in relation to what has gone before, it reveals the inadequacy of language to convey the most powerful of human emotions. In this way, Wordsworth communicates much by saying little.

Both overstatement and understatement are forms of **verbal irony,** *a mode of speech or writing in which the usual or expected meanings of words are in some way modified or reversed.* In judging whether a statement is ironic, we seldom rely on the language alone, however. It would not be ironic to say that the surface of Venus is untrodden or that the authorship of the folk ballad "Sir Patrick Spence" is unknown; we perceive these as overstatements in "She Dwelt Among the Untrodden Ways" because the context makes them so.

Sometimes this context extends beyond the situation of the poem itself, as in Donald Baker's "Formal Application":

FORMAL APPLICATION
The poets apparently want to rejoin the human race
                    TIME

I shall begin by learning to throw
the knife, first at trees, until it sticks
in the trunk and quivers every time;

next from a chair, using only wrist
and fingers, at a thing on the ground,   5
a fresh ant hill or a fallen leaf;

then at a moving object, perhaps
a pieplate swinging on twine, until
I pot it at least twice in three tries.

Meanwhile, I shall be teaching the birds   10
that the skinny fellow in sneakers
is a source of suet and bread crumbs,

first putting them on a shingle nailed
to a pine tree, next scattering them
on the needles, closer and closer   15

to my seat, until the proper bird,
a towhee, I think, in black and rust
and gray, takes tossed crumbs six feet away.

Finally, I shall coordinate
conditioned reflex and functional   20
form and qualify as Modern Man.

You see the splash of blood and feathers
and the blade pinning it to the tree?
It's called an "Audubon Crucifix."

The phrase has pleasing (even pious)   25
connotations, like *Arbeit Macht Frei,*
"*Molotov Cocktail,*" and *Enola Gay.*

                    Donald Baker (b. 1923)

This deeply ironic poem alters the meanings of familiar words, undercuts or reverses the reader's expectations, and calls into question many conventional assumptions about the human race. The title is a good place to begin our analysis of it. What "application" is Baker referring to? What is the connection between the title and the epigraph? How do they relate to the dramatic situation of the poem?

One kind of application is the type that people submit when they are seeking a job or attempting to gain admittance to an organization: a formal statement of qualifications. In this sense, "application" is consistent with the words "rejoin" (epigraph) and "qualify" (line 21). Assuming that the persona identifies with the poets mentioned in the quote from *Time* magazine, we can infer that the actions described in lines 1–21 constitute his "formal application" for readmission to the human race.

When reading the poem for the first time, when did you become aware of what the speaker intended to do to "qualify as Modern Man"? Were you shocked by his actions? Would you agree that such deceitfulness and violence are typical of the human race, or do you feel that this assertion is merely a rationale for an individual act of cruelty?

The poem begins quite innocently. The epigraph implies a reconciliation between the alienated artist and the human community, and little in the speaker's words or actions in the introductory scene (stanzas 1–3) indicates his intentions. His manner is friendly and familiar; his language consists of simple, colloquial words ("pieplate," "twine," "pot it"); and even his knife-throwing practice seems harmless because the targets are trees, ant hills, leaves, and the like.

With the introduction of the parallel action—the luring of birds to a distance of about six feet (easy throwing distance)—Baker begins to undercut our initial responses to the persona. Yet even these intimations of the dark design that informs the persona's actions do not prepare us for the killing of the towhee, partly because the picture of a harmless, innocent creature dying in a "splash of blood and feathers" is particularly repellent but more so because such a discrepancy exists between the act and the mechanical, coldly rational language used to describe it. Throwing the knife simply involves coordinating "conditioned reflex" with "functional form." All it takes is a little practice, which he demonstrates by tracing the stages of his progress from novice to expert, from outcast to acceptable member of the human race. With the culminating action of stanzas 7 and 8 comes a dramatic *reversal of earlier expectations,* **situational irony,** which in turn releases the many verbal ironies of the poem—that is, if the reader is aware of the contextual meanings of the language and is able to identify the historical and biographical allusions in the last two stanzas.

In addition to the primary meaning discussed earlier, "application" means diligence or effort; ironically, the narrator applies himself to the task of learning how to kill. To "qualify" is to demonstrate excellence or accomplishment; he qualifies as a member of the human race by demonstrating his ability to deceive and destroy. The phrase "Audubon crucifix" does have "pleasing (even pious)" overtones because it joins the name Audubon with a sacred object depicting Christ on the cross. The situation imparts a disturbing, ironic meaning to these words, however, for despite the findings of recent biographers, who have pointed out that Audubon took pleasure in killing animals and in watching such sports as bear-baiting, the popular response to the man remains very favorable. Furthermore, the religious implications of the words "crucifix" and "pious" are perverted by the grotesque image of a bloody cross formed by the intersection of the knife blade and the body of the bird. (There is a parallel as well between Christ suffering on the cross and the small bird pinned to the tree.)

We are now left with the problem of interpreting the meaning of the phrases in the last two lines of the poem. Without reference to the historical context of these words, would you agree with the persona that "Arbeit Macht Frei" (freedom through work), "cocktail," and the name "Enola Gay" have pleasant connotations? The political slogan expresses an ideology that most people would approve, at least in principle; "cocktail" brings to mind tall, icy glasses and the relaxed, convivial atmosphere of a party; and the name Enola Gay is melodic and suggestive of happiness. Now let's examine these phrases in another light. The idealistic slogan was part of the political jargon of the German Nazi party, which was responsible for the deaths of millions before and during World War II. A Molotov cocktail is a firebomb. Named for Stalin's foreign minister, this weapon has long been used both in large-scale combat and in guerilla warfare. And *Enola Gay* was the American plane that dropped the atomic bomb on the civilian population of Hiroshima.

By the end of the poem, we have traveled a great distance—from the localized environment where a "skinny fellow in tennis shoes" hones his skills with a knife to Calvary, the Nazi concentration camps, and the battlefields and bombed cities where human beings have systematically destroyed one another.

Baker's ironic method is well suited to the exploration of the perverse and violent impulses he associates with modern man. Irony is, in fact, the chief instrument of **satire**, a term applicable to *any work that seems to expose human frailties and that attempts to bring about reform by holding up to ridicule the customs, values, or institutions of society*. Whether the persona is aware of the ironic implications of his words and actions is difficult to determine. If we perceive a close identification between Baker and his persona, we would assume that the latter is speaking with *an emphatic, unmistakable irony* called **sarcasm** and that his "formal application" to rejoin the human race is exactly the opposite: a formal explanation of why some people have become alienated from their fellow human beings. But it is also possible that Baker is using an ironic mask, a character who so completely assumes the identity of modern man that he is unaware of the irony of his own words. Read in this way, the poem has a chilling effect much like that of Jonathan Swift's eighteenth-century satire "A Modest Proposal," which is narrated by a character who in calm, rational, and matter-of-fact language advocates cannibalism as the solution to the economic and social problems of Ireland. Readers familiar with Sophocles' *Oedipus* or Browning's dramatic poems (e.g., "My Last Duchess" in Chapter 2 or "Soliloquy of the Spanish Cloister" in Part III) might also perceive a form of **dramatic irony**, which results from *the discrepancy between* *a character's perceptions or assumptions and those of the audience or reader.* Despite the ambiguous nature of the poet/speaker relationship, one thing is clear: in the context of this poem, "Modern Man" and "human race" are synonymous with "deceiver" and "killer."

Perhaps we can now draw some general conclusions about incongruity, its functions in poetry, and what a reader should look for to see if a particular word or circumstance is incongruous. Whether used sparingly in an otherwise straightforward poem or as a sustained, reiterative pattern, incongruity is a flexible instrument, that serves equally well the needs of the humorist and the serious writer, the entertainer and the philosopher.

In some poems, incongruity is so obvious that we recognize and react to it instinctively, as if we were watching people slipping on banana peels, walking into doors, or throwing custard pies in one another's faces. In other works, however, incongruity is less obvious, and the poet makes greater demands on the reader.

Even the most skilled readers sometimes mistake incongruity for straightforward discourse, particularly in poems in which the writer requires the audience to bring to the poem a knowledge of some other field. Nonetheless, there are ways to improve your ability to recognize irony, paradox, and the other specific forms of incongruity discussed in this chapter.

1. Your first task, as always, is to understand the basic facts of the poem: speaker/audience relationships, thematic structure, and the meaning and associations of words.
2. With these details in mind, look for the signals of tone discussed in the preceding chapter.
3. Notice whether words, actions, structure, tone, and the other aspects of the poem are consistent in themselves and in relation to one another.
4. If you sense a discrepancy of any kind, see if you can apply one of the terms that we have defined and illustrated in this chapter.
5. To facilitate such an analysis, make a mental note whenever
    a. the traditional or expected meaning of a word seems inappropriate to its context
    b. the expected outcome of an action differs from the actual outcome
    c. the speaker's words and actions are contradictory
    d. the same speaker uses different types of language (e.g., a formal, learned vocabulary alternating with vulgar, obscene language)
    e. a single word conveys two or more contradictory or logically unrelated meanings
    f. a serious subject is treated humorously or a humorous subject seriously

g. a trivial subject is projected in elevated or heroic language (a technique called *mock heroic*)
h. words, actions, or circumstances seem contradictory but prove to be compatible
i. the title and/or internal evidence of a particular work recalls the manner and the substance of another author or poem
j. words convey either less or more than the circumstances seem to require
k. your own knowledge of past, present, or future conditions is superior to that of the persona and/or other important figures in the poem.

Before going on to the readings sections, see how many clues to incongruity you can find in the poem below, which specific types of it Shelley uses, and—most important—what functions they serve.

OZYMANDIAS

I met a traveller from an antique land
Who said: Two vast and trunkless legs of stone
Stand in the desert. Near them, on the sand,
Half sunk, a shattered visage lies, whose frown,
And wrinkled lip, and sneer of cold command   5
Tell that its sculptor well those passions read
Which yet survive, stamped on these lifeless things,
The hand that mocked them and the heart that fed;
And on the pedestal these words appear:
"My name is Ozymandias,[1] king of kings: 10
Look on my works, ye Mighty, and despair!"
Nothing beside remains. Round the decay
Of that colossal wreck, boundless and bare,
The lone and level sands stretch far away.

Percy Bysshe Shelley (1792–1822)

[1] The allusion here is to Rameses II, Egyptian ruler of the thirteenth century B.C.

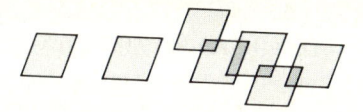

POEMS FOR FURTHER STUDY 1

BUICK

As a sloop with a sweep of immaculate wing on her delicate spine
And a keel as steel as a root that holds in the sea as she leans,
Leaning and laughing, my warm-hearted beauty, you ride, you ride,
You tack on the curves with parabola speed and a kiss of goodbye,
Like a thoroughbred sloop, my new high-spirited spirit, my kiss.   5

As my foot suggests that you leap in the air with your hips of a girl,
My finger that praises your wheel and announces your voices of song,
Flouncing your skirts, you blueness of joy, you flirt of politeness,
You leap, you intelligence, essence of wheelness with silvery nose,
And your platinum clocks of excitement stir like the hairs of a fern.   10

But how alien you are from the booming belts of your birth and the smoke
Where you turned on the stinging lathes of Detroit and Lansing at night
And shrieked at the torch in your secret parts and the amorous tests,
But now with your eyes that enter the future of roads you forget;
You are all instinct with your phosphorous glow and your streaking hair.   15

And now when we stop it is not as the bird from the shell that I leave
Or the leathery pilot who steps from his bird with a sneer of delight,
And not as the ignorant beast do you squat and watch me depart,
But with exquisite breathing you smile, with satisfaction of love,
And I touch you again as you tick in the silence and settle in sleep.   20

Karl Shapiro (b. 1913)

ALAS, POOR BUICK[1]
(A companion to "Buick," by Karl Shapiro)

You were no mere slip of a grille,
You buck-toothed beauty. No sloop either,
More hull than keel, you wallowed
Oversprung around corners. Like a fat whore
You gave a soft ride, drunk on gas—   5

---

[1] The title alludes to Hamlet's address to the skull of a court jester unearthed by a gravedigger in *Hamlet* V.i.

Yet you turned my head, lathe-like,
To love your wheelness; it never waned
Under my waxing. I felt manly with you, sweetie,
Like in the ads. I was me, in command,
The flying phallus of your hood ornament.   10
But as your mileage grew those charms foundered.
You floundered on spongy shocks,
Clattered in low gear, teeth missing,
Rattled rusted, rheumatic fenders,
Chattered with your palsied clutch. And now,   15
As their acetylene teeth gnaw your cast-off body,
Junkmen finger your secret parts.

Ron Ellis (b. 1941)

QUESTIONS

1. Comparison is both an organizing and a tone-establishing principle. Explain how this principle is applicable to these two poems.

2. Shapiro writes in the present tense throughout his poem; Ellis uses the past tense except in the last two lines, where he shifts to the present. What is the significance of each writer's handling of verb tenses? Consider whether the conclusion of "Alas, Poor Buick" alters our experience of shared pleasure in our early identification with the speaker and whether the ending establishes the speaker's *real* attitude or makes it more ambiguous.

3. Describe the theme and tone of each work.

4. In his parenthetical note to the title "Alas, Poor Buick," Ellis says that his poem is a "companion" to Shapiro's "Buick." In light of your comparison of the two poems, do you feel that Ellis is parodying Shapiro's poem? If so, what features of "Buick" might Ellis be parodying, and why?

5. Which of the types of incongruity discussed in this chapter are used in these two poems? What does each author accomplish through these techniques?

6. What are the chief similarities and differences between these two poems about cars and the one by Sam Hazo—"My Roosevelt Coupé"—which introduces Chapter 4 ("Tone")?

SUCCESS IS COUNTED SWEETEST

Success is counted sweetest
By those who ne'er succeed.
To comprehend a nectar
Requires sorest need.

> Not one of all the purple Host 5
> Who took the Flag today
> Can tell the definition
> So clear of Victory
>
> As he defeated—dying—
> On whose forbidden ear 10
> The distant strains of triumph
> Burst agonized and clear!
>
> *Emily Dickinson* (1830–1886)

QUESTIONS

1. Emily Dickinson's poem reveals its meaning through paradox. Provide a prose paraphrase of that paradoxical truth.
2. How is this basic paradox amplified through stanzas 2 and 3?
3. In what way are the military metaphors appropriate? Are they forced—too incongruous? Explain.
4. Is Dickinson's use of paradox similar to that of Richard Lovelace in "To Althea From Prison," discussed in the first section of this chapter? Why or why not?

SONNET 94: THEY THAT HAVE POWER TO HURT AND WILL DO NONE

> They that have power to hurt and will do none,
> That do not do the thing they most do show,
> Who, moving others, are themselves as stone,
> Unmoved, cold, and to temptation slow;
> They rightly do inherit heaven's graces 5
> And husband° nature's riches from expense;° °save °waste
> They are the lords and owners of their faces,
> Others but stewards of their excellence.
> The summer's flower is to the summer sweet
> Though to itself it only live and die; 10
> But if that flower with base infection meet,
> The basest weed outbraves° his dignity:° °surpasses °worth
>   For sweetest things turn sourest by their deeds;
>   Lilies that fester smell far worse than weeds.
>
> *William Shakespeare* (1564–1616)

QUESTIONS

1. Is there a discrepancy between the appearance of the person who has "the power to hurt" and his emotional or behavioral state?

2. The second quatrain alludes to a New Testament parable. Does Shakespeare use the parable ironically? Does the parable urge us "to husband nature's riches from expense"?
3. Is the poem a condemnation of people who refuse to risk potential corruption by playing it safe? Or is this too much of a simplification?
4. Is Shakespeare's attitude toward the "lords and owners of their faces" one of pure admiration? Explain.
5. The self-sufficient man described by Shakespeare arouses paradoxical feelings and is perhaps himself in a paradoxical situation. Comment. Explain how the last six lines potentially undermine the tentative admiration extended by the speaker for the "unmoved" friend in lines 1–8.

THE COLLAR

I struck the board and cried, "No more!
    I will abroad!
What? shall I ever sigh and pine?
My lines and life are free, free as the road,
    Loose as the wind, as large as store.°   °*abundant supply* 5
      Shall I be still in suit?
    Have I no harvest but a thorn
    To let me blood and not restore
What I have lost with cordial° fruit?   °*invigorating*
      Sure, there was wine   10
    Before my sighs did dry it; there was corn
      Before my tears did drown it.
      Is the year only lost to me?
        Have I no bays° to crown it?   °*laurels*
No flowers, no garlands gay? All blasted?   15
        All wasted?
    Not so, my heart; but there is fruit,
      And thou hast hands.
    Recover all thy sigh-blown age
On double pleasures: leave thy cold dispute   20
Of what is fit and not. Forsake thy cage,
      Thy rope of sands,
Which petty thoughts have made, and made to thee
    Good cable, to enforce and draw,
      And be thy law,   25
While thou didst wink and wouldst not see.
      Away! take heed:
      I will abroad.
Call in thy death's-head° there; tie up thy fears.   °*reminder*
      He that forbears   *of death* 30

> To suit and serve his need,
> Deserves his load."
> But as I raved and grew more fierce and wild
> At every word,
> Methought I heard one calling, *Child!* 35
> And I replied, *My Lord.*

George Herbert (1593–1633)

QUESTIONS

1. Whom is the speaker addressing? What is incongruous about his mode of address? What is the nature of his complaint?
2. Line 33 is a critical boundary line in this poem, for it reminds us of a disparity. What is the disparity?
3. How do the present and past feelings of the speaker contrast?
4. Describe the irony of the poem's title. Is the title literal or figurative?
5. Is the freedom Herbert speaks of paradoxical? How so? Does it bear any resemblance to that described by Lovelace in "To Althea From Prison"? Do these descriptions seem similar to popular notions of freedom?
6. What does "suit" in line 6 mean?
7. How do references to "fruit," "flowers," "corn," "wine," and "garlands" serve the purposes of contrast?

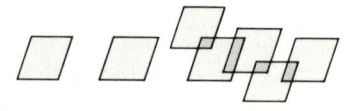

POEMS FOR FURTHER STUDY 2

PLAYBOY

> High on his stockroom ladder like a dunce
> The stock-boy sits, and studies like a sage
> The subject matter of one glossy page,
> As lost in curves as Archimedes once.
>
> Sometimes, without a glance, he feeds himself. 5
> The left hand, like a mother-bird in flight,
> Brings him a sandwich for a sidelong bite,
> And then returns it to a dusty shelf.

What so engrosses him? The wild décor
Of this pink-papered alcove into which
A naked girl has stumbled, with its rich
Welter of pelts and pillows on the floor,

Amidst which, kneeling in a supple pose,
She lifts a goblet in her farther hand,
As if about to toast a flower-stand
Above which hovers an exploding rose

Fired from a long-necked crystal vase that rests
Upon a tasseled and vermilion cloth
One taste of which would shrivel up a moth?
Or is he pondering her perfect breasts?

Nothing escapes him of her body's grace
Or of her floodlit skin, so sleek and warm
And yet so strangely like a uniform,
But what now grips his fancy is her face,

And how the cunning picture holds her still
At just that smiling instant when her soul,
Grown sweetly faint, and swept beyond control,
Consents to his inexorable will.

Richard Wilbur (b. 1921)

LOVE POEM

My clumsiest dear, whose hands shipwreck vases,
At whose quick touch all glasses chip and ring,
Whose palms are bulls in china, burs in linen,
And have no cunning with any soft thing

Except all ill-at-ease fidgeting people:
The refugee uncertain at the door
You make at home; deftly you steady
The drunk clambering on his undulant floor.

Unpredictable dear, the taxi drivers' terror,
Shrinking from far headlights pale as a dime
Yet leaping before red apoplectic streetcars—
Misfit in any space. And never on time.

A wrench in clocks and the solar system. Only
With words and people and love you move at ease.
In traffic of wit expertly manoeuvre
And keep us, all devotion, at your knees.

Forgetting your coffee spreading on our flannel,
Your lipstick grinning on our coat,
So gayly in love's unbreakable heaven
Our souls on glory of spilt bourbon float.   20

Be with me, darling, early and late. Smash glasses—
I will study wry music for your sake.
For should your hands drop white and empty
All the toys of the world would break.

John Frederick Nims (b. 1914)

BELLS FOR JOHN WHITESIDE'S DAUGHTER

There was such speed in her little body,
And such lightness in her footfall,
It is no wonder her brown study°   °*thoughtful pose*
Astonishes us all.

Her wars were bruited in our high window.   5
We looked among orchard trees and beyond
Where she took arms against her shadow,
Or harried unto the pond

The lazy geese, like a snow cloud
Dripping their snow on the green grass,   10
Tricking and stopping, sleepy and proud,
Who cried in goose, Alas,

For the tireless heart within the little
Lady with rod that made them rise
From their noon apple-dreams and scuttle   15
Goose-fashion under the skies!

But now go the bells, and we are ready,
In one house we are sternly stopped
To say we are vexed at her brown study,
Lying so primly propped.   20

John Crowe Ransom (1888–1974)

"OUT, OUT—"[1]

The buzz saw snarled and rattled in the yard
And made dust and dropped stove-length sticks of wood,

---

[1] The allusion is to Macbeth's famous "Out, out, brief candle" speech, which he makes near the end of the play after learning of his wife's death.

Sweet-scented stuff when the breeze drew across it.
And from there those that lifted eyes could count
Five mountain ranges one behind the other
Under the sunset far into Vermont.
And the saw snarled and rattled, snarled and rattled,
As it ran light, or had to bear a load.
And nothing happened: day was all but done.
Call it a day, I wish they might have said
To please the boy by giving him the half hour
That a boy counts so much when saved from work.
His sister stood beside them in her apron
To tell them "Supper." At the word, the saw,
As if to prove saws knew what supper meant,
Leaped out at the boy's hand, or seemed to leap—
He must have given the hand. However it was,
Neither refused the meeting. But the hand! –
The boy's first outcry was a rueful laugh,
As he swung toward them holding up the hand,
Half in appeal, but half as if to keep
The life from spilling. Then the boy saw all—
Since he was old enough to know, big boy
Doing a man's work, though a child at heart—
He saw all spoiled. "Don't let him cut my hand off—
The doctor, when he comes. Don't let him, sister!"
So. But the hand was gone already.
The doctor put him in the dark of ether.
He lay and puffed his lips out with his breath.
And then—the watcher at his pulse took fright.
No one believed. They listened at his heart.
Little—less—nothing!—and that ended it.
No more to build on there. And they, since they
Were not the one dead, turned to their affairs.

Robert Frost (1874–1963)

THE GARDEN OF LOVE

I went to the Garden of Love,
And saw what I never had seen:
A chapel was built in the midst,
Where I used to play on the green.

And the gates of this chapel were shut,
And "Thou shalt not" writ over the door;
So I turned to the Garden of Love
That so many sweet flowers bore.

And I saw it was filled with graves,
And tombstones where flowers should be;
And priests in black gowns were walking their rounds,
And binding with briars my joys and desires.

William Blake (1757–1827)

ARMS AND THE BOY[1]

Let the boy try along this bayonet-blade
How cold steel is, and keen with hunger of blood;
Blue with all malice, like a madman's flash;
And thinly drawn with famishing for flesh.

Lend him to stroke these blind, blunt bullet-leads
Which long to nuzzle in the hearts of lads,
Or give him cartridges of fine zinc teeth,
Sharp with the sharpness of grief and death.

For his teeth seem for laughing round an apple.
There lurk no claws behind his fingers supple;
And God will grow no talons at his heels,
Nor antlers through the thickness of his curls.

Wilfred Owen (1893–1918)

[1] The opening words of Virgil's *Aeneid*, a heroic epic praising prowess in battle, translate as "Arms and the man I sing. . . ."

WAR IS KIND

Do not weep, maiden, for war is kind.
Because your lover threw wild hands toward the sky
And the affrighted steed ran on alone,
Do not weep.
War is kind.

Hoarse, booming drums of the regiment,
    Little souls who thirst for fight,
    These men were born to drill and die.
    The unexplained glory flies above them,
    Great is the Battle-God, great, and his Kingdom—
    A field where a thousand corpses lie.

Do not weep, babe, for war is kind.
Because your father tumbled in the yellow trenches,
Raged at his breast, gulped, and died,
Do not weep.
War is kind.

  Swift blazing flag of the regiment,
  Eagle with crest of red and gold,
  These men were born to drill and die.
  Point for them the virtue of slaughter,   20
  Make plain to them the excellence of killing,
  And a field where a thousand corpses lie.

Mother whose heart hung humble as a button
On the bright splendid shroud of your son,
Do not weep.   25
War is kind.

       Stephen Crane (1871–1900)

6
IMAGE AND ABSTRACTION

ON A WITHERED BRANCH

On a withered branch
   a crow has settled—
      autumn nightfall.

Matsuo Bashō (1644–1694)
(trans. by Harold G. Henderson)

SACRIFICE

Though love repine, and reason chafe,
There came a voice without reply,—
" 'Tis man's perdition to be safe,
When for the truth he ought to die."

   Ralph Waldo Emerson (1803–1882)

Each of these poets sets for himself the difficult task of communicating an experience or insight within the space of only a few lines. Neither poet has the opportunity for extended argument or elaborate illustrations; both must rely on a few well chosen words to convey the desired effect. Notice, though, the differences in how they proceed and what they are able to accomplish through their respective methods.

The most significant difference between the two poems is their language. Which writer uses words that appeal primarily to the senses? Which employs language that requires an intellectual response?

Bashō's poem is a *haiku*, a centuries-old Japanese art form usually characterized by a structure of three lines and seventeen syllables and by precise, concrete language. One of the masters of this form, Bashō creates word pictures that remind us of delicate Japanese brush paintings. With a few deft strokes, he sketches the particulars of a natural scene—a withered branch, a crow, the coming of night—and the composite picture they form. These same words also suggest much that is not specifically described: the barrenness of an autumn landscape, the blackness of the crow, the merging of this small patch of blackness with the vast darkness of the night. Each of these tangible details is an **image**: *a word or group of words that stimulates one or more of the physical senses.* The word also has two plural forms, *images* and *imagery.* We can say, for example, that each line of Bashō's poem contains an *image,* that the poem is composed of a series of *images,* or that it is rich in *imagery.*

125

We need a different kind of terminology to describe the language of Emerson's poem. He relies almost exclusively on **abstract language:** *language that is intangible rather than image-producing, general rather than particular.* We cannot visualize "sacrifice," "love," "reason," or "truth" the way we can picture the scene Bashō describes; nor can we really hear in any tangible way the "voice" that speaks in the final two lines because the emphasis falls on what is said rather than on the sensations produced by the words.

These dissimilarities in language can be explained, at least in part, by the differing purposes of the two poets. What would seem to be Bashō's chief objective? What does Emerson seek to accomplish? Is their language appropriate to their purpose?

Bashō seeks to capture a moment of personal observation and discovery, so that his readers can re-create the scene in their own imaginations and interpret it through their own experience. To some, the imagery may suggest the interrelatedness of seemingly diverse elements of nature; to others, it may convey the beauty and grandeur of simple, familiar things; to still others it may reflect the cyclical processes of nature: the crow will awaken in the morning, darkness will give way to the light of day, and the withered branch will blossom again in the spring. Bashō himself does not step in to interpret the scene or to make an overt thematic statement. Yet these meanings are possible because they are consistent with the language of the poem.

In contrast, Emerson begins with an abstract, philosophical statement and hopes—or perhaps assumes—that we will either accept it without question (note that the voice through which he presents his theme speaks "without reply") or supply our own examples to explain what the poem does not specify. In one sense, the abstractness and indefiniteness of the diction are appropriate because he seeks to communicate on an intellectual level a paradox of universal validity: "'Tis man's perdition to be safe,/ When for the truth he ought to die."

This kind of language has its limitations, not because abstractness is necessarily a sign of artistic weakness, but because in this particular poem Emerson does not clarify his generalizations with images, illustrations, or definitions. As a result, his language keeps us at too great a distance, forces us to provide too much of the evidence necessary to define what kind of "truth" justifies the sacrifice of human life, and leaves us with a sense of vagueness and incompleteness we do not feel when we read Bashō's poem.

As we have noted, one measure of Bashō's skill is his ability to create images that have a strong visual impact. In this respect, the literary use of the word "image" coincides with popular usage. We refer to a reflection in a mirror as an *image,* watch the *image* on a television screen, and speak of people's children as the very *image* of their parents.

Sight, though, is only one of the senses to which poetic imagery may appeal. It can also serve as a stimulus to the sense of hearing, touch, taste, smell, and even internal sensations such as pain, thirst, or hunger. The technical terms for images that appeal to the five primary senses are as follows: visual images (sight), auditory images (hearing), tactile images (touch), gustatory images (taste), and olfactory images (smell). It is important to recognize what sensations the poet seeks to evoke and why. Notice, for example, the different types of imagery that Gary Snyder uses in the next poem.

DRINKING HOT SAKÉ

Drinking hot saké
                toasting fish on coals
    the motorcycle
out   parked in the rain.

Gary Snyder (b. 1930)

    Let's see how this poem compares with Bashō's. Are there any abstract words in Snyder's free adaptation of the haiku form? Does each word convey a single sense impression, or do some words appeal to several senses at once? If you were to use only one or two words to describe the total effect of the poem's imagery, which would you choose?

    Snyder, like Bashō, uses images that enable us to visualize a scene. We can see one or more people drinking wine from steaming cups and cooking fish over an open fire as the rain falls outside. It is also natural for us to supply other details, such as the number of people present and the kind of structure that would provide shelter from the rain. Some readers might imagine a simple lean-to or shed; others, a cabin with a fireplace.

    The words that create these visual impressions also engage our other senses. The phrases "drinking hot saké" and "toasting fish on coals" appeal to the sense of taste and smell as well as to sight. Also, the words "hot" and "coals" evoke feelings of warmth that contrast with our imagined sense of the chill and discomfort of the rain. And even though the poem is without explicit references to sound, we can imagine the sound of the falling rain and possibly the contrast between the silence of a motorcycle at rest and the roar of the machine with the throttle open. Here, as in Bashō's poem, everything is communicated through imagery. No one steps in to interpret or to tell us how to respond. However, even if we choose different words to describe our impressions (e.g., comfort, conviviality, satisfaction, well-being), we are all likely to feel the same pleasurable sensations of the words.

    Although *haiku* and other short poems often work exclusively through imagery, longer works usually necessitate the use of abstract words and general statements in association with concrete language. In reading the next poem, think about the kinds of words the poet uses. Which are abstract? Which appeal to the senses? Do any words convey several sense associations simultaneously?

NIGHT JOURNEY

Now as the train bears west,
Its rhythm rocks the earth,
And from my Pullman berth
I stare into the night
While others take their rest.　　　　　　　　　　5
Bridges of iron lace,
A suddenness of trees,
A lap of mountain mist
All cross my line of sight,
Then a bleak wasted place,　　　　　　　　　　10
And a lake below my knees.
Full on my neck I feel
The straining at a curve;
My muscles move with steel,
I wake in every nerve.　　　　　　　　　　15
I watch a beacon swing
From dark to blazing bright;
We thunder through ravines
And gullies washed with light.
Beyond the mountain pass　　　　　　　　　　20
Mist deepens on the pane;
We rush into a rain
That rattles double glass.
Wheels shake the roadbed stone,
The pistons jerk and shove,　　　　　　　　　　25
I stay up half the night
To see the land I love.

Theodore Roethke (1908–1963)

"Night Journey" begins and ends with the powerful, thrusting surge of a train that propels its passengers from some unnamed point of departure to an unspecified destination, somewhere in the West. The vagueness is intentional, for the poem is concerned not with beginnings and endings but with an on-going process of observation and discovery. From the vantage point of the speaker, we first see the other passengers "take their rest," and then we turn our gaze to the world of excitement and wonder that flashes by outside the window of the Pullman car.

Out of context, the words "I wake in every nerve" might be an empty exaggeration, but the imagery of the poem immediately defines and clarifies the persona's meaning. Speaking in the present tense, he brings us instantly into intimate contact with the tangible reality of the train and the landscape. The verbs—"rocks," "thunder," "rush," "rattles," "shake," "jerk," and "shove"—create **kinesthetic images,** *images of movement* that not only produce a mental picture of the train hurtling through ravines and over mountain passes but compel us to feel the rocking and jerking of the cars and the force of the train "straining at a curve" and to hear the grate of steel on steel, the sound of "roadbed stone" shifting under the weight of the locomotive, the rattle of rain on glass. As the observer gazes into the darkness, he responds to other stimuli: trees, mist, "bleak wasted places," ravines and mountains, the spurt of light from a beacon that swings "from dark to blazing bright," and "bridges of iron lace," an image that not only evokes a mental picture but arouses two different sensations—the hardness and coldness of iron and the soft, delicate texture of lace.

This dazzling array of images builds toward the generalized statement of meaning in the last two lines: "I stay up half the night / To see the land I love." What, precisely, does he love about the land? The content of his imagery, as well as its sensory overtones, should help us decide. Many of Roethke's images are drawn from nature: trees, mountains, gullies, ravines, rain. Others are associated with man-made objects: bridges, Pullman cars, pistons, wheels, beacons. They are not in conflict, however; all are part of the panorama that gives meaning to the concluding sentence and leads us to the realization that what he loves about the land is its beauty, its vastness, its mystery, its power to awaken his faculties and to illuminate the essential oneness of nature, people, and machines.

To this point, we have studied one poem that is totally abstract and three that are composed wholly or predominantly of images. As you read the next poem, notice the types of language that the author uses and their relationship to one another.

DULCE ET DECORUM EST

Bent double, like old beggars under sacks,
Knock-kneed, coughing like hags, we cursed through sludge,
Till on the haunting flares we turned our backs
And towards our distant rest began to trudge.
Men marched asleep. Many had lost their boots   5
But limped on, blood-shod. All went lame; all blind;
Drunk with fatigue; deaf even to the hoots
Of tired, outstripped Five-Nines° that dropped behind.   °*skells*

> Gas! GAS! Quick, boys!—An ecstasy of fumbling,
> Fitting the clumsy helmets just in time; 10
> But someone still was yelling out and stumbling
> And flound'ring like a man in fire or lime . . .
> Dim, through the misty panes and thick green light,
> As under a green sea, I saw him drowning.
>
> In all my dreams, before my helpless sight, 15
> He plunges at me, guttering, choking, drowning.
>
> If in some smothering dreams you too could pace
> Behind the wagon that we flung him in,
> And watch the white eyes writhing in his face,
> His hanging face, like a devil's sick of sin; 20
> If you could hear, at every jolt, the blood
> Come gargling from the froth-corrupted lungs,
> Obscene as cancer, bitter as the cud
> Of vile, incurable sores on innocent tongues,—
> My friend, you would not tell with such high zest 25
> To children ardent for some desperate glory,
> The old Lie: Dulce et decorum est
> Pro patria mori.

Wilfred Owen (1893–1918)

Centuries ago, the Roman poet Horace wrote the words *"Dulce et decorum est / Pro patria mori":* "Sweet and fitting it is to die for one's country." Are these words abstract or concrete? Can you find any passages in Owen's poem that support this patriotic sentiment? In each of the four stanzas, which words and incidents contradict the attitudes expressed by the Latin motto? What does Owen's imagery reveal about the reality of war and death?

These important questions lead us to the central conflict in the poem: the conflict between death in the abstract and death as reality; between noble-sounding but empty abstractions like "sweet," "fitting," and "glory" and images that mirror the suffering of individuals caught up in the horror of an actual war. The falsity of the Latin motto sounds in the coughing and cursing of the men; in their stooped posture and slow, painful movements; in the dehumanizing physical conditions that are as much the soldiers' enemy as the adversary they never see.

In stanza 1 (and in the stanzas that follow), each word is exactly suited to its purpose, both in its sensory impact and in its connotations. In the opening lines, for example, Owen "sees" with both the eye and the imagination. Literally the men are "bent-double" and "knock-kneed," but this observation simultaneously suggests images that are not part of the literal situation—"old beggars" and "coughing like hags." By joining these separate images through the word "like" (see the discussion of *simile* in the following chapter), Owen creates a picture of men prematurely aged and enfeebled by the long and purposeless march that has taken them only as far as the "haunting flares" and then—in retreat—toward their "distant rest." "Sludge" has the same exactness. A word with a similar denotation is "mud," but "sludge" has a wider range of connotations. It is a thick, slimy, foul-smelling ooze, and the sound of the word is as hard and discordant as its association. If we are aware of these connotations, we can understand why the men "cursed," rather than simply marched, through it. Other vivid images follow. "Blood-shod" graphically describes the physical condition of the men, whose feet are literally coated with blood. "Hoots" is a word that not only simulates the sound of gas-shells but creates the impression that the shells are mocking and taunting the soldiers, and there is a terrible irony in the muffled sound of shells falling "softly behind," unheard by men whom fatigue has made "deaf" and "blind."

Suddenly, the slow, dreamlike atmosphere dissolves. The imagery grows more agitated, more violent. The frenzied cry "Gas! Gas! Quick boys!" shocks the soldiers into action, and we see—as the narrator saw—the frantic movement, the "ecstasy of fumbling" that means safety for all but one man. Now we hear his voice "yelling out," see him "stumbling and flound'ring" through the sea-green gas, and imagine what the dying man must have felt: suffocation and an internal sensation analogous to being burned by "fire or lime."

Protected by his mask, the speaker has survived the gas attack, but nothing can protect him from the nightmare images that flash through his dreams before his always "helpless sight." Because the imagery of the poem brings us close to the action and admits us into the speaker's dreams, we too can see the doomed man plunging, "guttering, choking, drowning," and we can identify with the observer's helplessness.

At this point we realize the speaker has been addressing a specific audience, someone he refers to as "you" and "my friend." This realization raises additional questions: What attitude toward war does this listener have? Why has the narrator been telling him about the gas attack and its aftereffects? Does the context suggest that the listener is the speaker's friend?

The poem tells us only that the listener shares Horace's philosophy, that he repeats it with "high zest," and that his words are addressed to "children ardent for some desperate glory." Whether this person is a civilian, a soldier who has never witnessed a scene like the one described, or a representative of everyone who has accepted and perpetuated this "old lie," the speaker draws him into these "smothering dreams" and compels him to "pace / Behind the wagon that we flung him [the victim] in" to see what death really is. There is no sweetness or nobility in the "writhing" of the victim's eyes, in the sound of "gargling" blood, or in the "bitter" discharge of "froth corrupted lungs" which the observer describes in terms of something even more abhorrent: "vile, incurable sores on innocent tongues."

Only after he has re-created every appalling detail of this episode for the person he addresses with apparent irony as "my friend" does the speaker draw the conclusion that has been implicit in every sense-assailing image: *"Dulce et decorum est / Pro patria mori"* is an old and enduring lie.

Owen's method, then, is to contrast image and abstraction, rather than to harmonize them as Roethke does. But his imagery does have a comparable function in creating an unforgettable impression of reality.

Imagery can also serve the opposite purpose and make tangible the world of imagination—a world such as the one that Thomas Lux creates in "The Midnight Tennis Match."

THE MIDNIGHT TENNIS MATCH
Note: *In midnight tennis each player gets three serves rather than the usual two.*

You are tired
of this maudlin country club
and you are tired of his insults.
You'd like to pummel his forehead
with a Schweppes bottle   5
in the sauna, but instead
you agree, this time,
to meet him at midnight
on the tennis court.

When you get there   10
you can't see him
but you know he is waiting
on the other side of the net.
You consider briefly
his reputation.   15

You have first serve
so you run toward the net
and dive over it.
You land hard on your face.
It's not a good serve: looking up   20
you can barely see his white shorts
gleam in the darkness.

You get up, go back
to your side of the net
and dive over again.   25

IMAGE AND ABSTRACTION

This time you slide
to within a few feet of him.
Now you can make out his ankles,
the glint of the moon
on his white socks.   30

Your last serve is the best:
your chin stops one inch
from the tip of his sneakers.
Pinheads of blood
bloom across your chest.   35
You feel good crawling
back to your side again.

Now it is his turn
and as he runs toward the net
you know he's the fastest man   40
you've ever seen.

His dive is of course flawless.
He soars by you,
goes completely off the court
and onto the lawn,   45
demolishing a few lounge chairs.
To finish, he slides
brilliantly onto the veranda.

You go up and sit beside him
and somehow   50
you don't feel too humiliated:
he is still unconscious.
At least now you know why
he is undefeated. It's
his sensitive, yet brutal, contempt.   55
With a similar contempt
you pour a gallon of water on his face.
He still has two more serves—

Thomas Lux (b. 1946)

Although the title and the accompanying note suggest that midnight tennis is a strange sport, still, a match *could* be played at midnight (on lighted courts, that is), and it is conceivable that two players *might* decide to modify the official rules of tennis to allow "three serves rather than the usual two." Having whetted our curiosity without giving away the really crucial distinction between regulation tennis and the midnight version, Lux introduces the competitors and sets the scene for the big match.

At the outset of the poem, does Lux fill in any background details to explain the tension between the two competitors? Does he describe the setting and "players" in precise physical detail? How extensively does he use imagery in lines 1–9?

Lux scarcely mentions the setting. He does refer to a "country club," but he doesn't say whether it has fluted columns and marble statues or a modern facade of steel and glass, whether it sits on a hundred-acre site far beyond the city limits or on a small patch of ground next to the freeway, or if it has one tennis court or fifty. The words "sauna" and "Schweppes" are more specific, but even though their connotations are appropriate to the country club setting, their main function is to make us visualize a comically absurd scene in which the "you" of the poem imagines himself avenging some unspecified insults by pummeling his opponent with a bottle of tonic. It is this competitive instinct—characteristic of both men—that Lux wishes to stress, not their physical features, their past encounters, or their country club.

But why, we might ask, does he go to the trouble of imagining a sport that is not merely implausible but humanly impossible? Let's see if the description of the match provides any answers.

Beginning with line 10, we cross the boundary that separates the relatively familiar environs of country clubs and saunas from the strange world of midnight tennis, which is played without lights, balls, rackets, or the usual restraints of gravity.

In describing the match itself, Lux combines literal statements ("You have first serve," "Now it is his turn," etc.) and abstractions ("reputation," "flawless," "humiliated," "brutal," "contempt") with graphic visual images. Picture, if you will, someone standing on a tennis court, peering over the net at an opponent who is completely obscured by the darkness. Now imagine how he would look rushing toward the net, diving over it, landing on his face and sliding across the surface, returning to his side of the net and "serving" himself two more times. Even more ludicrous is the idea of the "winner" soaring beyond the end-line, "demolishing a few lounge chairs," and sliding "brilliantly onto the veranda."

Somehow, these images don't coincide with the high seriousness with which the opponents approach the match or with such assertions as these:

> "Your last serve is your best" (this is the one that carries him to the
> "tips of his opponent's sneakers" and scrapes his chest so badly that
> "pinheads of blood / bloom").
> "You feel good" (the "server" has to crawl back to his side of the
> net).
> "His dive is of course flawless" (could a headlong dive over a tennis
> net look graceful under any circumstances?).

In making the midnight tennis match imaginatively convincing, Lux achieves at least two other effects. By insistently addressing one of the players as "you," he places the reader on court rather than in the gallery, thus emphasizing that the competitive instinct is a basic human drive—not just a characteristic of trained athletes or country club combatants. The midnight tennis match also dramatizes his central theme: that when competition is merely an outlet for relieving boredom, venting hostilities and petty jealousies, or humiliating others, both victor and loser are ridiculous.

Certainly, that is the impression left by this absurdly comical game, which settles nothing. Though unconscious, the winner maintains an air of "brutal contempt," and his opponent, though defeated, expresses a "similar contempt" by pouring a bucket of water over his adversary's face. The final absurdity is that the match doesn't end with the already convincing triumph of the superior performer: "He still has two more serves."

Remembering both the concepts and examples introduced in this chapter, let's see if we can establish some general guidelines for reading other poems.

1. As you read a poem, allow yourself to respond to its language with your senses as well as your intelligence. You will probably do this subconsciously anyway because the senses are the body's conduits to the mind.
2. If there are any words that do not convey sensory associations (e.g., abstractions such as "hope," "fear," "courage," "love," "faith"), examine the context in which they are used. You may occasionally encounter a poem like Emerson's "Sacrifice," which is all abstraction, but more often you will discover that the poet has combined abstract language with image-bearing words. If so, notice whether the imagery clarifies or defines abstractions, projects conflict, or creates incongruity.
3. When you encounter words that do stimulate the senses, pause to consider the associations of the imagery. Often a single word or phrase conveys a whole range of sensations (e.g., the words "hot saké" in Snyder's poem appeal to sight, touch, taste, smell, and the internal sensation of warmth).
4. Notice also the field or domain from which the images are drawn and the frequency with which similar images occur: clusters or patterns of imagery may be central to the development of tone and theme.

A writer's skill in using imagery cannot be measured simply by counting images and tabulating the percentage of abstract and concrete words. A more reliable index is whether the language is appropriate to the poet's purpose. You will be in a better position to make such judgments after reading the next two chapters, which discuss literal, figurative, and symbolic uses of imagery.

As a test of your ability to distinguish abstract from concrete language and to recognize different imagistic effects, read the excerpts below. Then turn back to the chapter in which each appears and study how each passage functions in context:

1. . . . the almond-blossom
    Silent in all of the gardens and the bees going
      backwards and forwards . . . .

    (Henry Reed, "Naming of Parts," Chapter 2)

2. Listen! you hear the grating roar
    Of pebbles which the waves draw back, and fling,
    At their return, up the high strand . . . .

    (Matthew Arnold, "Dover Beach," Chapter 2)

3. My little horse must think it queer
    To stop without a farmhouse near
    Between the woods and frozen lake
    The darkest evening of the year.

    (Robert Frost, "Stopping by Woods on a Snowy Evening," Chapter 3)

4. To what purpose, April, do you return again?
    Beauty is not enough.
    You can no longer quiet me with the redness
    Of little leaves opening stickily.
    I know what I know.

    (Edna St. Vincent Millay, "Spring," Chapter 4)

5. Swift blazing flag of the regiment,
    Eagle with crest of red and gold,
    These men were born to drill and die.
    Point for them the virtue of slaughter,
    Make plain to them the excellence of killing,
    And a field where a thousand corpses lie.

    (Stephen Crane, "War Is Kind," Chapter 5)

Now go on to D. H. Lawrence's "Piano." Be especially attentive to the sensory appeal of its language and the ways in which this imagery influences your interpretation of tone and theme.

PIANO

Softly, in the dusk, a woman is singing to me;
Taking me back down the vista of years, till I see

IMAGE AND ABSTRACTION

A child sitting under the piano, in the boom of the tingling strings
And pressing the small, poised feet of a mother who smiles as she sings.

In spite of myself, the insidious mastery of song 5
Betrays me back, till the heart of me weeps to belong
To the old Sunday evenings at home, with winter outside
And hymns in the cosy parlour, the tinkling piano our guide.

So now it is vain for the singer to burst into clamour
With the great black piano appassionato. The glamour 10
Of childish days is upon me, my manhood is cast
Down in the flood of remembrance, I weep like a child for the past.

D. H. Lawrence (1885–1930)

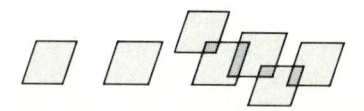

POEMS FOR FURTHER STUDY 1

FIGURE

He would slump to his knees, now that his agonies
were accomplished, would fall but for the chain that binds
    him to the tall columnar tree.

His head hangs heavily away to one side; we
cannot see his face. The dead weight of 5
    the quelled head has pulled

the haltering chain tight. A clothesline nooses
both wrists, forcing his arms in an arrowing angle
    out behind him. Stripes

of blood like tribal markings run from naked 10
shoulder to naked waist. We observe that his jeans are torn
    at the groin;

that the lower links of the chain cut deeply into
the small of his back and counter the sag, the downthrust.
    And the chain, we observe the chain— 15

the kind that a farmer might have had use for or a man with
a vicious dog. We have seen its like in hardware
    stores; it is cheap but strong

and it serves and except for the doubled length of it lashing
him to the blighted tree, he would slump to his knees, in total   20
   subsidence fall.

He is a scythe in daylight's clutch. Is gnomon.
Is metaphor of a place, a time. Is our
   time geometrized

Robert Hayden (b. 1913)

QUESTIONS

1. What is the meaning of "gnomon"?
2. Describe the situation and central image of the poem. Are there supporting images? If so, what are they?
3. The particulars of a poem often move toward universals. What theme or emotion does the imagery of this poem establish and support?
4. Is there any dramatic point to the poet's presentation of images? Or are they presented randomly?
5. Although the poem is primarily descriptive and objective, what is the poet's attitude toward what he describes?
6. Does the figure's physical position resemble that of any other well-known "figure"?
7. Comment on the meaning of the last stanza.

THE RED WHEELBARROW

so much depends
upon

a red wheel
barrow

glazed with rain   5
water

beside the white
chickens.

William Carlos Williams (1883–1963)

QUESTIONS

1. How many abstract words are there in this poem?
2. Does the poem appeal to one or to more senses? Which?

3. Although this poem is essentially objective and almost unmetaphorical, the poet still reveals his attitude toward the subject. How?
4. Is the wheelbarrow really the subject?
5. Why has Williams divided the word "wheelbarrow" in the body of the poem?
6. What is the theme of the poem?

THE TAXI

When I go away from you
The world beats dead
Like a slackened drum.
I call out for you against the jutted stars
And shout into the ridges of the wind.   5
Streets coming fast,
One after the other,
Wedge you away from me,
And the lamps of the city prick my eyes
So that I can no longer see your face.   10
Why should I leave you,
To wound myself upon the sharp edges
   of the night?

Amy Lowell (1874–1925)

QUESTIONS

1. Make a list of the images in this poem.
2. What do most of these images have in common?
3. Explain the appropriateness of the auditory image in "beats like a slackened drum."
4. What feelings do you get from the poem? How do the images contribute to that feeling?
5. Robert Penn Warren has said that a poem is "some kind of vital image, a vital and evaluating image. . . ." What kind of experience does the imagery of this poem evaluate? What abstract statement does it implicitly make?

THE KRAKEN

Below the thunders of the upper deep,
Far, far beneath in the abysmal sea,
His ancient, dreamless, uninvaded sleep
The Kraken° sleepeth: faintest sunlights flee   °*Scandinavian*
About his shadowy sides; above him swell   *sea monster* 5

       Huge sponges of millennial growth and height;
       And far away into the sickly light,
       From many a wondrous grot and secret cell
       Unnumbered and enormous polypi
       Winnow with giant arms the slumbering green.   10
       There hath he lain for ages, and will lie
       Battening upon huge sea-worms in his sleep,
       Until the latter fire shall heat the deep;
       Then once by man and angels to be seen,
       In roaring he shall rise and on the surface die.   15

            Alfred, Lord Tennyson (1809–1892)

QUESTIONS

1. What are the meanings of "kraken," "polypi," "winnow," and "battening"?
2. What kind of drama do the images in this poem create? Does what you see remind you of any films? Which, or what kind? What kind of music might accompany these images?
3. One poet, Stanley Plumly, described an image as "an idea with a body." What is the idea behind this poem?
4. "The Kraken" contrasts images of light and darkness. Why?
5. Water has often been associated with the unconscious in modern psychology and psychiatry. What does this poem reflect about the human mind?

TO AUTUMN

Season of mists and mellow fruitfulness,
    Close bosom-friend of the maturing sun;
Conspiring with him how to load and bless
    With fruit the vines that round the thatch-eaves run;
To bend with apples the mossed cottage-trees,   5
    And fill all fruit with ripeness to the core;
        To swell the gourd, and plump the hazel shells
    With a sweet kernel; to set budding more,
And still more, later flowers for the bees,
Until they think warm days will never cease,   10
        For Summer has o'er-brimmed their clammy cells.

Who hath not seen thee oft amid thy store?
    Sometimes whoever seeks abroad may find
Thee sitting careless on a granary floor,
    Thy hair soft-lifted by the winnowing wind;   15

Or on a half-reaped furrow sound asleep,
    Drowsed with the fume of poppies, while thy hook
        Spares the next swath and all its twinèd flowers:
And sometimes like a gleaner thou dost keep
    Steady thy laden head across a brook;   20
    Or by a cider-press, with patient look,
        Thou watchest the last oozings hours by hours.

Where are the songs of Spring? Aye, where are they?
    Think not of them, thou hast thy music too—
While barréd° clouds bloom the soft-dying day,   °banded with   25
    And touch the stubble-plains with rosy hue;   different colors
Then in a wailful choir the small gnats mourn
    Among the river sallows,° borne aloft   °willows
        Or sinking as the light wind lives or dies;
And full-grown lambs loud bleat from hilly bourn;   30
    Hedge crickets sing, and now with treble soft
    The redbreast whistles from a garden-croft;
        And gathering swallows twitter in the skies.

John Keats (1795–1821)

QUESTIONS

1. What categories of images exist in "To Autumn"? Make a list of the visual, auditory, and tactile images.

2. Do certain images dominate in each stanza? Explain.

3. Do you notice any progression in the imagery?

4. What human attributes does Keats associate with autumn? Which words establish this relationship?

5. What is the theme of this poem? How does the imagery reveal the speaker's attitude toward what he presents?

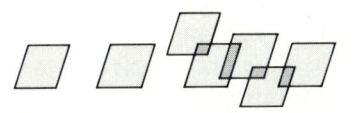

POEMS FOR FURTHER STUDY 2

A DEEP-SWORN VOW

Others because you did not keep
That deep-sworn vow have been friends of mine;

Yet always when I look death in the face,
When I clamber to the heights of sleep,
Or when I grow excited with wine,   5
Suddenly I meet your face.

William Butler Yeats (1865–1939)

AS YOU LEAVE ME

Shiny record albums scattered over
the livingroom floor, reflecting light
from the lamp, sharp reflections that hurt
my eyes as I watch you, squatting among the platters,
the beer foam making mustaches on your lips.   5

And, too,
the shadows on your cheeks from your long lashes
fascinate me—almost as much as the dimples:
in your cheeks, your arms and your legs:
dimples . . . dimples . . . dimples . . .   10

You
hum along with Mathis—how you love Mathis!
with his burnished hair and quicksilver voice that dances
among the stars and whirls through canyons
like windblown snow. sometimes I think that Mathis   15
could take you from me if you could be complete
without me. I glance at my watch. it is now time.

You rise,
silently, and to the bedroom and the paint:
on the lips red, on the eyes black,   20
and I lean in the doorway and smoke, and see you
grow old before my eyes, and smoke. why do you
chatter while you dress, and smile when you grab
your large leather purse? don't you know that when you
leave me I walk to the window and watch you? and light   25
a reefer as I watch you?   and I die as I watch you
disappear in the dark streets
to whistle and to smile at the johns.°   °*prospective customers*

Etheridge Knight (b. 1933)

THE DIVINE IMAGE

To Mercy, Pity, Peace, and Love
All pray in their distress;
And to these virtues of delight
Return their thankfulness.

For Mercy, Pity, Peace, and Love
Is God, our father dear,
And Mercy, Pity, Peace, and Love
Is man, his child and care.

For Mercy has a human heart,
Pity a human face,
And Love, the human form divine,
And Peace, the human dress.

Then every man, of every clime,
That prays in his distress,
Prays to the human form divine,
Love, Mercy, Pity, Peace.

And all must love the human form,
In heathen, Turk, or Jew;
Where Mercy, Love, and Pity dwell
There God is dwelling too.

William Blake (1757–1827)

THE HUMAN ABSTRACT

Pity would be no more
If we did not make somebody Poor;
And Mercy no more could be
If all were as happy as we.

And mutual fear brings peace
Till the selfish loves increase:
Then Cruelty knits a snare,
And spreads his baits with care.

He sits down with holy fears,
And waters the ground with tears;
Then Humility takes its root
Underneath his foot.

Soon spreads the dismal shade
Of Mystery over his head;
And the Catterpiller and Fly
Feed on the Mystery.

And it bears the fruit of Deceit,
Ruddy and sweet to eat;
And the Raven his nest has made
In its thickest shade.

> The Gods of the earth and sea
> Sought thro' Nature to find this Tree;
> But their search was all in vain:
> There grows one in the Human Brain.
>
> *William Blake* (1757–1827)

THE FISH

wade
through black jade.
    Of the crow-blue mussel-shells, one keeps
    adjusting the ash-heaps;
        opening and shutting itself like   5
an
injured fan.
    The barnacles which encrust the side
    of the wave, cannot hide
        there for the submerged shafts of the   10
sun,
split like spun
    glass, move themselves with spotlight swiftness
    into the crevices—
        in and out, illuminating   15
the
turquoise sea
    of bodies. The water drives a wedge
    of iron through the iron edge
        of the cliff; whereupon the stars,°   °*starfish* 20
pink
rice-grains, ink-
    bespattered jelly-fish, crabs like green
    lilies, and submarine
        toadstools, slide each on the other.   25
All
external
    marks of abuse are present on this
    defiant edifice—
        all the physical features of   30
ac-
cident—lack
    of cornice, dynamite grooves, burns, and
    hatchet strokes, these things stand
        out on it; the chasm-side is   35

dead.
Repeated
    evidence has proved that it can live
    on what can not revive
        its youth. The sea grows old in it.   40

        Marianne Moore (1887–1972)

PRELUDES

I

The winter evening settles down
With smell of steaks in passageways.
Six o'clock.
The burnt-out ends of smoky days.
And now a gusty shower wraps   5
The grimy scraps
Of withered leaves about your feet
And newspapers from vacant lots;
The showers beat
On broken blinds and chimney-pots,   10
And at the corner of the street
A lonely cab-horse steams and stamps.
And then the lighting of the lamps.

II

The morning comes to consciousness
Of faint stale smells of beer   15
From the sawdust-trampled street
With all its muddy feet that press
To early coffee-stands.
With the other masquerades
That time resumes,   20
One thinks of all the hands
That are raising dingy shades
In a thousand furnished rooms.

III

You tossed a blanket from the bed,
You lay upon your back, and waited;   25
You dozed, and watched the night revealing
The thousand sordid images
Of which your soul was constituted;
They flickered against the ceiling.
And when all the world came back   30

And the light crept up between the shutters
And you heard the sparrows in the gutters,
You had such a vision of the street
As the street hardly understands;
Sitting along the bed's edge, where
You curled the papers from your hair,
Or clasped the yellow soles of feet
In the palms of both soiled hands.

IV

His soul stretched tight across the skies
That fade behind a city block,
Or trampled by insistent feet
At four and five and six o'clock;
And short square fingers stuffing pipes,
And evening newspapers, and eyes
Assured of certain certainties,
The conscience of a blackened street
Impatient to assume the world.

    I am moved by fancies that are curled
Around these images, and cling:
The notion of some infinitely gentle
Infinitely suffering thing.

    Wipe your hand across your mouth, and laugh;
The worlds revolve like ancient women
Gathering fuel in vacant lots.

T. S. Eliot (1888–1965)

7

FIGURATIVE LANGUAGE

IT DROPPED SO LOW—IN MY REGARD

It dropped so low—in my Regard—
I heard it hit the Ground—
And go to pieces on the Stones
At bottom of my Mind—

Yet blamed the Fate that flung it—*less* 5
Than I denounced Myself,
For entertaining Plated Wares
Upon my Silver Shelf—

Emily Dickinson (1830–1886)

This one-sentence poem prints its facts quickly and sharply on our consciousness. Something—"it"—has fallen and shattered, and the persona blames herself (lines 1–6). The last two lines tell us why she does so and also identify "it": On the shelf used for displaying genuine silverware (a silver shelf, like a linen closet or trash can, is one made *for* silver, not of it), the speaker has placed not a piece of real silver but something far less precious, mere "plated wares."[1] This is the "it" that has fallen and shattered on the stone floor, and the persona blames herself more than fate for the accident because she "entertained" the piece among the silver pieces—she set it up where it never belonged. She reviles herself for being naive or deceived or unobservant enough to fail to detect its falseness.

But phrases in the poem are still left unaccounted for by this explanation. According to the persona, where exactly did the plate drop and shatter? (*Regard* can mean "esteem" or "respect" as well as "sight.") This piece of silver plate dropped not to a kitchen floor but to the bottom of the speaker's mind. We had best reexamine our assumption that the poem describes a literal plate falling off a literal shelf. Perhaps we are dealing with a poem that employs a *figurative* level of language, not just the expected literal level.

If the event described is not to be taken literally, what is the speaker *actually* talking about *in terms of* a piece of plated ware dropping off a shelf? What are the characteristics of silverware not shared by plated wares? What might each represent, especially in terms of relative worth? What are we to

---

[1] Although some critics have assumed that Dickinson erred in suggesting that a piece of silver plate would break, the plate that goes "to pieces" here is probably a china dish plated to resemble silver, a technique popular in the nineteenth century.

make of the silver shelf? The falling and shattering? The persona's attitude towards herself?

Clearly both "it" (the false silver incorrectly regarded as authentic) and its falling exist only in the mind. The poem recounts a mental process. If silverware, highly regarded for its beauty and worth, represents a mental construct, whose value is determined by the speaker's attitude, perhaps the silver shelf is something like her mental system of values or a place of high regard. If so, the piece of false silver would be an esteemed item that has fallen in value, a value the persona had lost faith in and now recognizes as false. Although we might be tempted to assign a single, specific meaning to each of these mental images, the poem does not invite us to go this far. The most we can say is that the subject of Dickinson's poem is an abstract mental process—loss of faith or confidence in some ideal, belief, or cause.

If we read the poem in this way, all the details make sense, whereas a literal interpretation of plates and shelves does not account for the words "in my Regard" and "at bottom of my Mind." Why, though, does Dickinson use this approach? Why doesn't she just state in literal terms what the speaker has become disillusioned with and what has caused this change of attitude?

Perhaps the most important reason is that the speaker cannot find a general or abstract way to describe her feelings and thoughts; thus she fashions them instead in terms of familiar, tangible things. There is nothing unique about this process; on the contrary, people use figures of speech in verbal communications of every kind. We speak of people being "naked as a jaybird" or "eating crow." People who take risks have gone "out on a limb" and those who are in trouble are "up the creek without a paddle," "in hot water," or "behind the eightball." In the language of the sportscaster, a fast back doesn't run, he "flies," and a basketball player who makes a long shot scores from "downtown."

The figures of speech in Dickinson's poem are also drawn from familiar, domestic sources, but they are not among the commonplace formulas of spoken, colloquial language, nor are they used randomly and instinctively as conversational figures are. The words are part of an artistic construct, a means by which the poet compels our attention, gives us insight into a perennial human problem, and illuminates previously unperceived relationships.

Dickinson's poem uses the figurative level throughout, except in the two phrases mentioned ("Mind" and "Regard"). More common than such an extended figure is a specific *figure of speech, an individual, isolatable utterance that, by comparing two subjects not literally comparable, means something other than precisely what it says.* When D. H. Lawrence, in his predominantly literal poem "Piano," says "the heart of me weeps to belong/to the old Sunday evenings at home," most of the words can be taken at face value. But since hearts cannot literally weep, the likeness is figurative. An analogy is set up, but it is not a literal one.

In contrast to the examples discussed in the section on irony (Chapter 5), in which the disparity between two subjects is played on, the examples in this chapter are the result of the poet's making a *comparison* of two literal incomparables. Often a poem will operate entirely on the literal level except for two or three figures of speech. In fact, it is a good idea to take a poem's words at face value unless its language suggests that the poet is using a figure of speech.

The next poem is also rich in figurative language. Rather than using one extended figure, however, the poet—Langston Hughes—employs a series of figures of speech, each of which helps answer the question he poses in the first line: "What happens to a dream deferred?"

DREAM DEFERRED

What happens to a dream deferred?

Does it dry up
like a raisin in the sun?
Or fester like a sore—
And then run? 5
Does it stink like rotten meat?
Or crust and sugar over—
like a syrupy sweet?

Maybe it just sags
like a heavy load. 10

Or does it explode?

Langston Hughes (1902–1967)

The question that begins the poem has several implications. What does "deferred" mean? Which of the several definitions of "dream" is important in this context? In sentences like "I deferred my mortgage payment" or "The judge deferred the trial," we immediately see that "deferred" means postponed or delayed. But how can a dream be deferred?

Hughes' meaning becomes clearer if we recognize that "dream" means hope or aspiration as well as sleep-induced visions, and that something that is deferred is incomplete or unfulfilled. We might paraphrase the first line as "what happens to unrealized hopes?" and, by implication, to the people who possess them.

The answer to the initial question (line 1) comes in the form of other questions (lines 2–11) using figures of speech to define abstract concepts through more familiar, concrete images. What sense impressions do these images convey? What other associations do they have? What are the essential similarities between the two terms of each comparison?

The imagery in lines 2–11 has an immediate impact on the senses. We can visualize foods in the process of decay, open sores, and—less specifically—a "heavy load." The poem also evokes the stench of rotting meat, the taste and feel of sticky, syrupy confections, and the sound of an explosion. These sense impressions generate other associations. Shriveled fruit, rotten meat, and crusted sweets, like any spoiled foods, are useless and unrestorable. A festering, running sore is ugly and painful, usually infectious or cankerous, and dangerous if left untreated. A load so heavy that it sags is one that seems in danger of splitting open, spilling its contents, and crushing whatever or whoever bears it. And an explosion is a powerful, destructive force.

In what ways, then, does the imagery illuminate the meaning of a "dream deferred"? Dreams, Hughes seems to say, are valuable as long as those who hold them believe in the possibility of their fulfillment. Repeated disappointments, however, eventually destroy such belief. A dream can nourish the spirit as food nourishes the body but, like food, a dream is perishable. People sometimes do lose hope, and the poem suggests that once this has happened, a dream cannot be restored any more than the deterioration of food can be reversed. Even worse, despair born of frustration and delay may corrupt the dream itself, making it not only valueless but tormenting. In this sense, it becomes like a disease, rankling within as a sore festers without. And psychological or emotional problems, especially if they are neglected, can be as dangerous as virulent physical disease. Or, as lines 9–10 imply, a "dream deferred" may become an increasingly heavy burden on the spirit, so much so that it becomes unbearable. When that happens, it may "explode" in the release of violent emotions or actions that threaten others as well as the dreamer.

For the moment, let us rephrase lines 2–10 as statements rather than as questions. Lines 2–3 are representative, for they draw a comparison between two essentially unlike things. In this example, a dream deferred is (A) the **literal subject** being discussed, sometimes called the **tenor,** and a raisin in the sun is (B) the **figurative subject,** sometimes called the **vehicle,** that the literal subject is being compared with. Line 2 supplies as well (C) the **grounds** for this comparison: both will dry up, though in different ways. This comparison may be expressed in a formula:

$$\frac{\text{(A) a dream deferred} \quad \text{IS LIKE} \quad \text{(B) a raisin in the sun}}{\text{(C) both will dry up}}$$

or, more generally,

$$\frac{\text{(A) literal subject} \quad \text{IS LIKE} \quad \text{(B) figurative subject}}{\text{because of (C)}}.$$

A *figure of speech that expresses the likeness between two logically unlike things by means of an explicit connective such as "like," "as," "as if," "than," or "seems" is called a* **simile.** *It is different from a literal comparison such as* "a nectarine is like a peach" or "syrup is messier than sugar" in that its two terms are not literally comparable. But because the poet can use the device to point up an unseen similarity and reflect that quality back upon the subject, the simile is one of the most often used figures of speech. The following examples taken from poems elsewhere in the book illustrate the variety and uses of simile. Set up the formula for each example.

1. . . . She woke sometimes to feel the daylight coming like a relentless milkman up the stairs.
2. Your mouth opens clean as a cat's.
3. . . . I gently nudge her/& with the razor blade, one side/taped, as if a finger/were lovingly running from the back/of the knee toward the buttocks.

Simile always makes its comparison explicit; it often leaves the grounds of comparison implicit. It may occur in its elemental form, as it does in these examples, or as an elaborate, extended figure. It may exist in isolation, or it may appear, as in "Dream Deferred," in a chain. What does Hughes accomplish by using figurative language to explain "What happens to a dream deferred?" Why do you think he phrases his figurative "answers" as questions rather than as declarative statements?

The forcefulness of the language suggests that the questions in the poem are rhetorical. These consequences may result when a dream is deferred because people respond to despair and frustration differently. Even though Hughes could have written specifically of the frustrations of black Americans or his own struggles as a black writer in a predominantly white society, he universalizes the situation and enables us to experience through our senses what happens when something of value is transformed into something useless. Thus the similes in this poem are far more than the literary equivalent of the decoration on a cake; they are the poem's substance.

In the next poem, Sylvia Plath makes use of a different figure of speech.

METAPHORS

I'm a riddle in nine syllables,
An elephant, a ponderous house,
A melon strolling on two tendrils.
O red fruit, ivory, fine timbers!
This loaf's big with its yeasty rising.   5
Money's new-minted in this fat purse.
I'm a means, a stage, a cow in calf.
I've eaten a bag of green apples,
Boarded the train there's no getting off.

Sylvia Plath (1932–1963)

This poem could easily have ended like a riddle with the question "What am I?" because, as the first line indicates, it *is* a riddle. To answer it, we must identify the real subject, just as we would for this more familiar traditional riddle:

> Little Nancy Edicott
> In a white petticoat
> With a red nose.
> The longer she stands the shorter she grows.
>
> (Answer: a candle)

The poem "Metaphors" gives all the information necessary for us to solve its riddle and provides certain clues along the way. The answer to it should not only tell us what "I" is but also identify the persona of the poem. Notice that lines 1–3 and line 7 offer a series of appositives of "I," while lines 8–9 describe activities that "I" has already accomplished. Line 4 is a direct address, and lines 5–6 refer in the third person to what seems to be another subject. These lines must somehow be related to the answer to the riddle.

What would the first line mean if taken literally? If taken figuratively? Note the words that are direct appositives of "I." Since the answer to the riddle could not possibly be all these things, we might assume that the appositives are meant figuratively. What characteristics do the appositives have in common? What is being addressed in line 4? How is each appositive in line 4 appropriate to that subject? How do the past actions mentioned in lines 8–9 add to your awareness of the answer? To what might "loaf" (line 5) and "purse" (line 6) refer? Why are these terms appropriate? What is the "money" being minted?

The first line, if taken literally, can refer to the line itself. The line is a riddle in nine syllables (that is, units of speech). Taken figuratively, the line could refer to the whole poem; it is a riddle in nine lines (that is, units of the poem). Otherwise, the line could refer to the answer of the riddle: some mystery or problem or puzzle that progresses over nine stages. Since human gestation is the most familiar phenomenon that occurs in nine stages or months, we might see if the other appositives support it. The appositives in lines 1–3 and 7 suggest something temporarily large and awkward that houses a tenant. The last appositive, "a cow in calf," indicates that what it is carrying is a fetus. Most probably, then, the appositives refer to a pregnant woman, and a pregnant woman is also both the answer to the riddle and the persona who tells it.

To test our hypothesis, we need to examine the other details of the poem. The direct address in line 4 does not contradict our hypothesis. Whether the ambiguous line 4 refers to the body of the persona herself or the fetus in her womb (it could do either), the three terms pick up the appositives from lines 2–3. Lines 5–6 could also have two subjects: the body of the persona in general or her belly in particular. In either case, by its bread-making/ coin-minting process, it is made larger by the action of forming a baby. In

FIGURATIVE LANGUAGE 153

lines 8–9, the persona proceeds from effect to cause. Everyone who has eaten green apples has also had the stomachache they cause. As children, some of us even heard the tale that pregnancy could be caused by eating green apples, a tale this poem humorously seems to verify. In line 9 the persona creates her own folktale: she has stepped aboard a special train whose only stations are the nine months and whose destination is inevitable.

 A pregnant woman, then, is not only (1) the answer to the riddle and (2) the persona of the poem but also (3) the literal subject of most of its figurative language. In contrast to the similes in Hughes' poem, in which the literal subject (A) is said to be *like* a figurative subject (B), Plath's literal subject (A) is said *to be* the figurative subject (B). Rather than merely being compared, the two terms share an identity. Such *a statement claiming two unlike things are identical* is a **metaphor.** Thus, the persona says

(A) <u>I</u> = (B) <u>riddle,</u>

the grounds of comparison (C) being perhaps the sharing of mysteriousness, the problems involved in both, the enigmas and paradoxes of both situations. In fact, all the appositives for "I" discussed earlier are used as different figurative subjects (or vehicles) for the one literal subject (or tenor). Each provides a further elaboration of how the speaker, a pregnant woman, sees herself. The literal subject of the metaphor remains the same while the figurative subject continually changes. Each of these, however, is a surface metaphor in which two stated nouns are joined by a form of the verb *to be:* I am a riddle, elephant, house, melon, means, stage, cow in calf.

 Line 5 presents a metaphor in another form (as do lines 4 and 6). Here the figurative subject is presented but the literal subject is implied. Stated as a formula, the metaphor would be something like this:

(A) <u>[I or body]</u> = (B) <u>loaf</u>
(C) big with yeasty rising.

Of course, what makes her "rise" is not yeast but the fetus. The implicit identification of yeast with fetus creates another metaphor; both are rapidly changing, growing things that cause what they are a part of to swell. In line 6, the persona or her body is a purse made large by the money (metaphor for fetus) it contains. Unlike the purse, however, the persona actually mints the money. The term "mint" is a metaphor for "create."

 The last two lines illustrate another point about metaphors: they often involve parts of speech other than nouns. In line 8, the verb phrase "eaten a bag of green apples" is the vehicle for the act of becoming pregnant, the same literal subject that is represented by "boarded the train there's no getting off" in line 9. Since "yeasty" (line 5) refers to the fetus, it is an example of an adjective used metaphorically. Any principal part of speech can be used as a metaphor, and either or both terms (literal or figurative subject:

A or B) may be implied rather than stated. Sometimes the figurative subject (B) of one metaphor will become the literal subject (A) of another. Consequently, the metaphor can be a highly varied and subtle instrument in the poet's hands.

Each of the following quotations, for example, contains at least one metaphor, but several different parts of speech are represented in the terms (A and B). Some have both literal and figurative subjects stated; others leave one or both implied. To determine how they are constructed, identify the terms of each metaphor and the grounds of comparison:

1. She is all States, and all princes, I. . . .
2. The Sea of Faith
   Was once, too, at the full. . . .
3. Who would have thought my shrivel'd heart
   Could have recover'd greennesse?
4. Now that the April of your Youth adorns
   The Garden of your Face. . . .
5. She lifts a goblet with her farther hand,
   As if about to toast a flower-stand
   Above which hovers an exploding rose
   Fired from a long-necked crystal vase.

Metaphor is an almost indispensable figure of speech, a basic example of the way language works, and it is close to the essence of poetry. More than a comparison or substitution or a statement that two logically unlike things are similar in some respect, a truly vital metaphor juxtaposes two entities in such a way that the two, without losing their separate identities, interact to form a new entity. To say as Jaques does in Shakespeare's *As You Like It* that "All the world's a stage,/And all the men and women merely players," makes us both see the world in a new light and redefine our sense of reality. By his use of metaphor, the poet organizes our view of his subject and makes us see it as he does. Philosopher Max Black compares the way a reader reads a poet's metaphor to the way a stargazer looks through a filter:

> Suppose I look at the night sky through a piece of heavily smoked glass on which certain lines have been left clear. Then I shall see only the stars that can be made to lie on the lines previously prepared upon the screen, and the stars I do see will be seen as organized by the screen's structure. We can think of a metaphor as such a screen and the system of "associated commonplaces" of the focal word as the network of lines upon the screen. We can say that the principal [or literal] subject is "seen through" the metaphorical expression—or, if we prefer, that the principal subject is "projected upon" the field of the subsidiary [or figurative] subject.[1]

---

[1] Max Black, *Models and Metaphors* (Ithaca: Cornell University Press, 1962), p. 41.

Sometimes, instead of using just an occasional metaphor or a series of different metaphors, the poet will build a whole section of a poem around one such figure of speech.

SWIMMER

I

Observe how he negotiates his way
With trust and the least violence, making
The stranger friend, the enemy ally.
The depth that could destroy gently supports him.
With water he defends himself from water. 5
Danger he leans on, rests in. The drowning sea
Is all he has between himself and drowning.

II

What lover ever lay more mutually
With his beloved, his always-reaching arms
Stroking in smooth and powerful caresses? 10
Some drown in love as in dark water, and some
By love are strongly held as the green sea
Now holds the swimmer. Indolently he turns
To float.—The swimmer floats, the lover sleeps.

Robert Francis (b. 1901)

Robert Francis's poem is, according to its title, about a swimmer. Although the title of any poem is important in indicating the poem's subject and its direction, we should also remember that the poet may be using words figuratively. If the title taken literally provides a consistent reading with nothing left unaccounted for, the literal level may be the intended one. If not, we should consider the figurative.

Trying the literal interpretation first, see if there are any terms referring to swimming. Actually, the poem includes quite a few: water, sea, drowning, depth, float, and swimmer. If the poet is talking about a real swimmer, however, he is employing a large number of terms that are not directly related to swimming, and these must be accounted for.

In stanza 1, for example, what words have no connection with swimming? Is there one field of human endeavor to which most or all of these words have reference? Why might the poet be using words from this subject matter to describe a swimmer? In what ways does this cluster of references enhance the reader's understanding of the persona's attitude to the swimmer? What relationship between the swimmer and the sea is thus established?

Notice the strong terms used in stanza 1: "violence," "stranger," "enemy," "ally," "destroy," "supports," "defends," "danger." Although some of these words could come from several fields of discourse, the accumulation of words forces the reader to think in terms of violence between enemies—the unfortunate human activity called warfare. But the first line portrays the swimmer not as a fighting soldier but as someone who "negotiates," turning the stranger into a friend, the enemy into an ally. Thus, he acts as a kind of diplomat in war, reconciling the enmity between opposing forces and creating friendship between them.

Of what relevance are these terms to the swimmer's action in the sea? Paraphrased, lines 4–7 indicate that a potentially destructive force has now become supportive, that the swimmer actually relies on what might have been his enemy to prevent his destruction, that by swimming calmly and expertly he uses the sea, which could drown him, to keep himself from drowning. The literal level works.

Thus, the persona, apparently an onlooker watching a swimmer in a sea, directs the audience, perhaps someone standing nearby, to observe the swimmer, whom the persona admiringly compares with a diplomat carefully creating peace and friendship in a potentially violent situation. To crystallize his own reaction to the artistry he sees, the poet through the persona reaches out for a comparison and isolates the figure of the mediator between nations. By doing so he not only understands his own reaction better but also creates for the audience a new and fresh appreciation for the swimmer's art.

The device employed to achieve this purpose is, of course, metaphor, but metaphor used differently from the way Plath used it. Plath's poem includes a separate figurative subject in almost every line. Francis's single figurative subject controls the whole stanza through an *extended metaphor*. In addition, whereas Plath's poem stated the figurative subjects but kept the literal subject undisclosed, "Swimmer" discloses its literal subject in the title but implies its figurative subject through a cluster of terms used to describe the swimmer (i.e., the grounds of comparison). Francis creates an *implied metaphor*. In terms of our formula it may be expressed thus:

(A) swimmer = (B) [diplomat]
(C) [the specific words indicating a negotiator in warfare]

The reader supplies the submerged figurative subject, a diplomat.

Stanza 2 employs a different method from stanza 1. Which word in the stanza establishes one of the terms in this figure? What are the literal and figurative subjects? Does the literal subject change from stanza 1 to 2? Since the first sentence is elliptical ("more mutually" than what?), supply the missing term in the comparison. Is this form a metaphor or simile? Isolate the supporting terms of the figurative subject in the rest of the stanza. How does this cluster enrich the reader's understanding of the literal subject?

Line 8 supplies one term of the stanza's basic analogy—a lover. But the elliptical sentence compares the lover with the swimmer: "What lover ever lay more mutually / With his beloved [than the swimmer does with the sea] . . . ." The second half of the sentence can be read either literally (as about a lover) or figuratively (as about the swimmer). As a lover's arms literally seem to stroke "in smooth and powerful caresses," so do the swimmer's "always-reaching arms" seem to lightly touch the water in his swimming strokes. The swimmer and the sea, like lovers, lie prone in a mutual embrace. As swimming can cause an incompetent swimmer to drown, so love can overwhelm ("drown") an incompetent at love. Conversely, as the water supports the expert swimmer, so love supports the authentic lover. The act of love accomplished, the lover lazily turns over to sleep. His swimming done, the swimmer turns on his back to float with ease.

The extended figure

(A) swimmer   [is like]   (B) lover
(C) [actions in common: lying down, stroking, being held, resting]

is stated completely, except for the linking word. Since this analogy functions like an extended metaphor but is technically a simile in elliptical form, either term is appropriate.

But the whole of the poem is greater than either of its stanzas alone. The structure or progression of thought carried by the images reveals the persona's increasing understanding of and admiration for the swimmer. In stanza 1, what might have been seen at first as an antagonistic relationship is seen by the persona as a relationship between friends or allies; in stanza 2, however, he recognizes that the relationship is even more mutual and more intimate than that: the swimmer and the sea exist in a bond of love. Any expert swimmer would agree.

In addition to being instructive about the uses of metaphor and simile, "Swimmer" contains other figures of speech. In the extended simile in stanza 2, not only is the swimmer compared to a lover, but the sea is talked about in human terms. The sea is a lover lying with her swimmer-lover, being caressed by his arms, and in turn holding him. Such a *comparison in which a thing, an abstraction, or an animal is endowed with human characteristics is a metaphor called* **personification.** Personification is a frequently used technique that gives quick impact to lifeless things and concepts (note that the sea in stanza 1 is also personified, as stranger, friend, enemy, and ally). Personification can be analyzed by our formula and, like a metaphor, may appear as any part of speech. The following examples of it are taken from poems discussed elsewhere in this book. Explain each by the formula:

1. . . . the Fate that flung it . . . .
2. . . . For entertaining Plated Wares . . . .
3. A melon strolling on two tendrils.

Closely related to metaphor is the construction in line 4 of "Swimmer." Referring to the sea, the persona says "The depth that could destroy gently supports him." Actually it is the sea that could destroy the swimmer, not the depth. But since the depth of a sea adds to its terror, the poet uses a term associated with the sea in place of the sea itself. This construction is called **metonymy,** *a figure of speech that substitutes something associated with the literal subject for that subject.* For example, an agent may be substituted for its act, an effect for its cause, space for time. When Cleopatra, in Shakespeare's *Antony and Cleopatra,* is about to meet her much desired death by placing asps to her bosom, she says of the man who brings them to her, "He brings me liberty." Literally, they are only asps, but to her they are what she associates with them—her liberty—so she substitutes the effect for the cause.

Sometimes metonymy takes a very specific form, as in the following poem.

THE HAND THAT SIGNED THE PAPER

The hand that signed the paper felled a city;
Five sovereign fingers taxed the breath,
Doubled the globe of dead and halved a country;
These five kings did a king to death.

The mighty hand leads to a sloping shoulder,   5
The finger joints are cramped with chalk;
A goose's quill has put an end to murder
That put an end to talk.

The hand that signed the treaty bred a fever,
And famine grew, and locusts came;   10
Great is the hand that holds dominion over
Man by a scribbled name.

The five kings count the dead but do not soften
The crusted wound nor stroke the brow;
A hand rules pity as a hand rules heaven;   15
Hands have no tears to flow.

Dylan Thomas (1914–1953)

What is the literal subject of Thomas's poem? Why do you think he calls attention to "the hand that signed the paper" rather than referring to the *person* who performs the act? What is the speaker's attitude toward this individual? What abstract words does Thomas use? How does he give them concreteness? In what ways is the poem ironic?

Thomas censures any tyrannical power as lacking human vision and compassion. Because "tyranny" is an abstraction and hence difficult to relate to, he personalizes it in the king; then, to imply that the use of such power could not involve the whole human being, he again depersonalizes it by focusing on only the king's hand, unconnected to a heart or to tear ducts. The resulting vision of the poem is that of a blind, callous, disembodied hand dispensing unconscionable injustice and death.

This effect is achieved by the poet's substituting a part of the tyrant's body (his hand) for the king as a whole, a particular kind of metonymy called **synecdoche**, *a figure of speech in which a part of something is used for the whole, the whole for a part, or a material for the object made from the material.* It is the device employed in expressions such as "I've lost my wheels" (for automobile), "I want a sheepskin" (for diploma), and "I bought some new threads" (for the clothes made of them). Sometimes metonymy and synecdoche are so close as to be indistinguishable. The following are examples from poems earlier in the book. Can you isolate the figure of speech and label each?

1. [He] had everything necessary to the Modern Man,
   A phonograph, a radio, a car and a frigidaire.
2. . . . high school girls with clear-skinned smiles . . . .
3. A great black presence beats its wings in wrath.
   Above the boneyard burn its golden eyes.
   Some small grey fur is pulsing in its grip.
4. . . . This grew; I gave commands:
   Then all smiles stopped together.

Now let's return to Thomas's poem, looking more specifically, this time, at the intricate ways in which Thomas uses synecdoche and metonymy. The strong hand of tyrannical power is ironically contrasted with the weakly sloping shoulder and the arthritic joints. And not only does the hand represent the body, but a whole chain of figures is developed in a hierarchy something like this:

A goose's quill is actually the instrument that makes the marks on the papers; but it is here a metonym for

five sovereign fingers, the human agent that moves it; the fingers are a synecdoche for

the hand, which in turn is a synecdoche for

the tyrant, whose brain actually directs the movement of the hand; but the tyrant himself is a physical container for

political power and tyranny in general, the abstraction behind the poem, which in line 15 is extended to include

God's tyrannical power over the creatures under His dominion.

In fact, so strong are the synecdoches and the cultural associations we hold with them that they take on symbolic significance.

By this point, it should be obvious that figurative language is not merely an embellishment to literal discourse but a varied and extremely flexible instrument by which the poet captures the essence of an experience and conveys it vividly and emphatically.

Cast in a variety of specific forms, figures of speech may be concise or extended, simple or complex, immediate or cumulative in impact. A single device can play a dominant role in a poem, as does simile in "Dreams Deferred," metaphor in "Metaphors," and synecdoche in "The Hand That Signed the Paper." Usually, however, several devices function together, as in Francis's "Swimmer."

Not all poems rely so heavily on figurative language, of course. But simile, metaphor, and the other devices we have examined are used in most poetry because they can express so much in such brief compass. In only eleven lines, Hughes evokes a dynamic and compelling image of waste and disillusionment, and Thomas says more about despotism and its effects in his short poem than many other writers have been able to express in entire books.

As you study other poems, you may find the following checklist an aid in dealing with their figurative language:

1. Be aware of the potential multiple meanings of words. Use a second meaning if it fits the context. Determine if the words make sense on the literal level. If some words can't be taken literally, determine if they are figures of speech. Decide which is the literal and which the figurative level.
2. Isolate statements comparing two subjects that can't literally be compared. Notice not only nouns but also verbs, adjectives, and adverbs. Be sure you detect both the stated and implied figures. Decide what is the literal subject, the figurative subject, and the grounds for comparing the two.
3. Label the figure by comparing it with models such as these:
    a. Simile: literal subject *is like* figurative subject (expressed comparison using *like, as, as if, than, seems*). For example, "Time is like a bird."
    b. Metaphor: literal subject *is* figurative subject (expressed or implied identity). For example, "Time is a bird." "Time flies." "The wings of time."
    c. Personification: a *nonhuman* literal subject talked about in terms of a *human* figurative subject. For example, "Death is the Grim Reaper." "The Villain Time." "Death's scythe."
    d. Metonymy: an *unexpressed* literal subject talked about in terms of something closely *associated* with it. For example, "The White House says . . ." "I like to read Shakespeare."
    e. Synecdoche: an *unexpressed* literal subject talked about in terms of one of its *parts,* a specific *example* of it, or the *material* from which

it is made. For example, "All hands on deck!" "Get a Kleenex." "Change your linens."
4. Determine whether the figure of speech is extended beyond the single reference (for example, if the mode of discussion or subject of the grounds of comparison remains unchanged) so that it could be called an extended or controlling figure.
5. Most importantly, as you deal with the figures, be aware of what they contribute to the effect of the poem.

With these suggestions in mind, read the next poem, May Swenson's "The Watch." Identify the types of figurative language used and consider what they reveal about the speaker, the situation, the speaker's attitude, and the theme of the poem as a whole.

THE WATCH

When I
took my
watch to the watchfixer I
felt privileged but also pained to watch the operation. He
had long fingernails and a voluntary squint. He   5
fixed a magnifying cup over his
squint eye. He
undressed my
watch. I
watched him   10
split her
in three layers and lay her
middle—a quivering viscera—in a circle on a little plinth. He
shoved shirtsleeves up and leaned like an ogre over my
naked watch. With critical pincers he   15
poked and stirred. He
lifted out little private things with a magnet too tiny for me
to watch almost. "Watch out!" I
almost said. His
eye watched, enlarged, the secrets of my   20
watch, and I
watched anxiously. Because what if he
touched her
ticker too rough, and she
gave up the ghost out of pure fright? Or put her   25
things back backwards so she'd
run backwards after this? Or he

                might lose a minuscule part, connected to her
                exquisite heart, and mix her
                up, instead of fix her.   30
                And all the time,
                all the time-
                pieces on the walls, on the shelves, told the time,
                told the time
                in swishes and ticks,   35
                swishes and ticks,
                and seemed to be gloating, as they watched and told. I
                felt faint, I
                was about to lose my
                breath—my   40
                ticker going lickety-split—when watchfixer clipped her
                three slices together with a gleam and two flicks of his
                tools like chopsticks. He
                spat out his
                eye, lifted her   45
                high, gave her
                a twist, set her
                hands right, and laid her
                little face, quite as usual, in its place on my
                wrist.   50

                                                May Swenson (b. 1919)

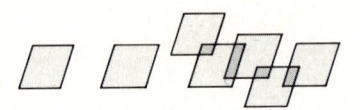

POEMS FOR FURTHER STUDY 1

THE CREATURE

This morning something
Perched like a bird
On my left shoulder,
And was silent.
If I brushed it away,   5
It reappeared
Like a premonition.
If I ran,
It clawed deep

Into my coat, 10
My wool coat,
And closed its eyes—
Or what I thought
Were its eyes.
So, here I was 15
Walking the town
Perplexed like a priest,
My neck stiff
As a new beard,
And no friend 20
Waving Hola!
That afternoon
I prayed and lit
A candle for the spirit
Of my wife 25
Dead two years,
And still this
Creature tightened
And yawned
Into my ear. 30
At supper in my room,
It ate my bread
And the handle
Of a sharp knife.
To that I said Enough! 35
And left hatless
For the cantina,
Where again the creature
Lay on my shoulder
Like the hand of someone 40
Bearing grief.

Gary Soto (b. 1952)

QUESTIONS

1. What is the literal situation of this poem? Which elements are figurative?
2. Is the "creature" an identifiable species of animal life, or does it seem more akin to such otherworldly beings as the demonic bird in Edgar Allan Poe's "The Raven"?
3. What technique does Soto employ in lines 1–4? By what means does he sustain this figure of speech throughout the poem? How does this figure of speech differ from those in lines 2–9 of "Dream Deferred"?

4. In most similes, the second term of the comparison is more concrete than the first. Identify a figure in this poem in which this pattern is reversed. For what purpose does Soto use this technique?
5. Locate a figure of speech in which both terms can be visualized. What purpose does it serve?
6. Does the poem give any indication of why the "creature" suddenly appears and stays with him everywhere?

EX-BASKETBALL PLAYER

Pearl Avenue runs past the high-school lot,
Bends with the trolley tracks, and stops, cut off
Before it has a chance to go two blocks,
At Colonel McComsky Plaza. Berth's Garage
Is on the corner facing west, and there,   5
Most days, you'll find Flick Webb, who helps Berth out.

Flick stands tall among the idiot pumps—
Five on a side, the old bubble-head style,
Their rubber elbows hanging loose and low.
One's nostrils are two S's, and his eyes   10
An E and O. And one is squat, without
A head at all—more of a football type.

Once Flick played for the high-school team, the Wizards.
He was good: in fact, the best. In '46
He bucketed three hundred ninety points,   15
A county record still. The ball loved Flick.
I saw him rack up thirty-eight or forty
In one home game. His hands were like wild birds.

He never learned a trade, he just sells gas,
Checks oil, and changes flats. Once in a while,   20
As a gag, he dribbles an inner tube,
But most of us remember anyway.
His hands are fine and nervous on the lug wrench.
It makes no difference to the lug wrench, though.

Off work, he hangs around Mae's luncheonette.   25
Grease-grey and kind of coiled, he plays pinball,
Sips lemon cokes, and smokes those thin cigars.
Flick seldom speaks to Mae, just sits and nods
Beyond her face toward bright applauding tiers
Of Necco Wafers, Nibs, and Juju Beads.   30

John Updike (b. 1932)

FIGURATIVE LANGUAGE

QUESTIONS

1. What does the poem tell us about Flick's present situation? Consider details such as his job and what he does after work.
2. How does Flick's present life contrast with his past?
3. What is significant about the names of places and people: Flick, Pearl Avenue, Colonel McComsky Plaza, Berth's Garage, Mae's luncheonette, the Wizards?
4. Stanza 2 is an extended figure of speech. What technique does Updike use here? What does it reveal about Flick? What contrast does it suggest?
5. This technique appears again in the last two lines of the poem, when the speaker says that Flick nodded "toward bright applauding tiers/Of Necco Wafers, Nibs, and Juju Beads." Does it have the same function as the figure of speech in stanza 2? Does it reveal Flick's thoughts, or only those of the speaker?
6. What type of figurative language does Updike employ in each of the following statements: "the ball loved Flick"; "His hands were like wild birds"; "Grease-gray and kind of coiled, he plays pinball"? What do they reveal about Flick?
7. Taking into account these details—plus the literal elements of the poem—what is the speaker's attitude toward Flick?

SONNET 130: MY MISTRESS' EYES ARE NOTHING LIKE THE SUN

My mistress' eyes are nothing like the sun;
Coral is far more red than her lips' red;
If snow be white, why then her breasts are dun;
If hairs be wires, black wires grow on her head.
I have seen roses damasked, red and white,   5
But no such roses see I in her cheeks;
And in some perfumes is there more delight
Than in the breath that from my mistress reeks.
I love to hear her speak, yet well I know
That music hath a far more pleasing sound.   10
I grant I never saw a goddess go;
My mistress, when she walks, treads on the ground.
    And yet, by heaven, I think my love as rare
    As any she belied with false compare.

William Shakespeare (1564–1616)

QUESTIONS

1. Each of the first three lines suggests and yet simultaneously denies a likeness between a physical feature of the speaker's mistress—eyes, lips, and breasts—and an element of nature: the sun, coral, and snow. If these comparisons were stated affirmatively, what visual impressions would they convey?
2. In line 4, does the speaker say that his love's hair is like black wire, or does he question the validity of this comparison?
3. What additional characteristics of his mistress does the speaker refer to in lines 5–12? What other comparisons does he reject? Why? How does the structural pattern of these lines differ from that of lines 1–4?
4. What words associated with the speaker's mistress have unfavorable connotations? How can the persona's use of such words and his refusal to compare his love's breath with perfume, her voice with music, etc., be reconciled with his praise for her in the closing couplet?
5. Is the language of the last two lines abstract or concrete? Literal or figurative? In this context, what does "belied" mean? What is the meaning of the phrase "false compare"? Does it suggest that figures of speech like the ones the persona refuses to use are too conventional to be meaningful, that there is too little similarity between the things being compared, or that they are inadequate for some other reason?

OVERWEIGHT POEM

biscuits with honey running down into the deep crevices
thick dark bread cut into fresh chunks and butter waving over the terrain,
red berries and yellow cream

am I thinking of these things
or you?   5

Love fills my body,
all the crevices
for the first time. And I feel
heavy
like the September limbs of an   10
apple tree.

Feel opulent

and don't like this opulence.

Coming from a man who knows less than I,
one who, like my father, talks big   15
and goes away;
one who, like my father, loves deep, a lot,

and goes away / has many others.
And I want it all.
A man who is everything. 20
Everything I can find in the refrigerator,
or the fruit bin, or the oven, or the larder, or the cup-
board, everything in the silverware chest, the freezing compartment;
I want him to be handsome and brilliant and
making a mark on the world, rich, responsible, 25
older. Someone to rescue me.

The British Museum, perhaps.

Something that will last well.
My favorite foods do not keep well;
must be gotten fresh each week 30

I never know how far
for the sake of wisdom
to carry a metaphor.

Diane Wakoski (b. 1937)

QUESTIONS

1. Which of the five senses does the imagery of lines 1–3 appeal to? Do the appetizing foods described in these lines seem literal or figurative (note the speaker's questions in lines 4 and 5)?

2. What similarities in language exist between lines 1–3 and lines 6–8? What is the implied metaphor in lines 6–8? In lines 8–11, Wakoski employs two other types of figurative language. What are they? Taken together, what do the figures of speech in lines 6–11 reveal about the persona and her attitude toward the person mentioned in line 5?

3. In the long central stanza, what are the figurative vehicles by which the speaker attempts to explain what she wants in a man? What other means does she use to accomplish this purpose?

4. The next-to-last stanza returns to the ostensible subject of lines 1–3: food. Are the "favorite foods" of the persona literal or figurative? Does she herself have difficulty answering this question?

5. In several lines, especially the conclusion, the speaker raises an issue similar to that explored in "Sonnet 130": "how far . . . to carry a metaphor" (or, by implication, any other figure of speech). Are the figures of speech in this poem carried too far? Do they have a definite purpose? Explain.

FOR MY LOVER, RETURNING TO HIS WIFE

She is all there.
She was melted carefully down for you

and cast up from your childhood,
cast up from your one hundred favorite aggies.°   °*marbles*

She has always been there, my darling.   5
She is, in fact, exquisite.
Fireworks in the dull middle of February
and as real as a cast-iron pot.

Let's face it, I have been momentary.
A bright red sloop° in the harbor.   °*masted ship* 10
My hair rising like smoke from the car window.
Littleneck clams out of season.

She is more than that. She is your have to have,
has grown you your practical your tropical growth.
This is not an experiment. She is all harmony.   15
She sees to oars and oarlocks for the dinghy,°   °*rowboat*

has placed wild flowers at the window at breakfast,
sat by the potter's wheel at midday,
set forth three children under the moon,
three cherubs drawn by Michelangelo,   20

done this with her legs spread out
in the terrible months in the chapel.
If you glance up, the children are there
like delicate balloons resting on the ceiling.

She has also carried each one down the hall   25
after supper, their heads privately bent,
two legs protesting, person to person,
her face flushed with a song and their little sleep.

I give you back your heart.
I give you permission—   30

for the fuse inside her, throbbing
angrily in the dirt, for the bitch in her
and the burying of her wound—
for the burying of her small red wound alive—

for the pale flickering flare under her ribs,   35
for the drunken sailor who waits in her left pulse,
for the mother's knee, for the stockings,
for the garter belt, for the call—

the curious call
when you will burrow in arms and breasts   40
and tug at the orange ribbon in her hair
and answer the call, the curious call.

> She is so naked and singular.
> She is the sum of yourself and your dream.
> Climb her like a monument, step after step.   45
> She is solid.
>
> As for me, I am a watercolor.
> I wash off.

Anne Sexton (1928–1974)

QUESTIONS

1. Does the persona seem to be thinking to herself throughout the poem, or do you envision a dramatic situation such as a farewell scene between the speaker and her lover?
2. How much does the speaker reveal about her lover and their past relationship? Does she give more emphasis to the man or to his wife? Is this emphasis consistent with the expectations raised by the title?
3. What does the speaker mean when she says that her lover's wife "was melted carefully down for you/ and cast up from your . . . one hundred favorite aggies"? What figure of speech is Sexton using here? What other figures does she use for similar purpose?
4. In stanzas 4–7, which details clarify the meaning of the statement "She is more than that"? More specifically, what does the speaker mean by the words "She . . . has grown you your practical your tropical growth" and "She sees to oars and oarlocks for the dinghy"?
5. What is the purpose of the allusion to Michelangelo, the great Renaissance sculptor and painter, and to the painted ceiling of the Sistine Chapel?
6. Beginning with line 31, what change in tone occurs? Explain.
7. In the figures of speech that the persona uses in lines 9–12 and 47–48, what are the different vehicles she uses to describe herself? How do these figures of speech contrast with those that the persona associates with her lover's wife?
8. Taking into account the language and structure of the poem as a whole, describe the persona's attitude toward her lover, his wife, and herself.

THE CANONIZATION

> For God's sake hold your tongue, and let me love,
>   Or chide my palsy, or my gout,
> My five gray hairs, or ruined fortune, flout,
>   With wealth your state, your mind with arts improve,
>   Take you a course,° get you a place,   °pursue   5
>   Observe His Honor, or His Grace,   a career

Or the King's real, or his stampéd face°   °*face stamped*
    Contemplate; what you will, approve,   *on a coin*
    So° you will let me love.   °*as long as*

Alas, alas, who's injured by my love?   10
    What merchant's ships have my sighs drowned?
Who says my tears have overflowed his ground?
    When did my colds a forward spring remove?
        When did the heats which my veins fill
        Add one more to the plaguy bill?°   °*list of* 15
Soldiers find wars, and lawyers find out still   *plague victims*
    Litigious men, which quarrels move,
    Though she and I do love.

Call us what you will, we're made such by love;
    Call her one, me another fly,   20
We're tapers too, and at our own cost die,°   °*expire/have*
    And we in us find th' eagle and the dove.   *orgasm*
        The phoenix° riddle hath more wit   °*legendary bird that*
        By us: we two being one, are it.   *rises from its own ashes*
So to one neutral thing both sexes fit.   25
    We die and rise the same, and prove
    Mysterious by this love.

We can die by it, if not live by love,
    And if unfit for tombs and hearse
Our legend be, it will be fit for verse;   30
    And if no piece of chronicle we prove,
        We'll build in sonnets pretty rooms;
        As well a well-wrought urn becomes
The greatest ashes, as half-acre tombs;
    And by these hymns, all shall approve   35
    Us canonized for love

And thus invoke us: You, whom reverend love
    Made one another's hermitage;
You, to whom love was peace, that now is rage;
    Who did the whole world's soul contract, and drove   40
        Into the glasses of your eyes
        (So made such mirrors, and such spies,
That they did all to you epitomize)
    Countries, towns, courts: Beg from above
    A pattern of your love!   45

              John Donne (1572–1631)

QUESTIONS

1. What kinds of figures of speech does the poet employ in stanza 1 to offer flippant alternatives to his attacker, and how does he use them?
2. Stanza 2, which refutes criticism by insisting that the speaker's love does the world no harm, belittles the exaggerated clichés (called **Petrarchan conceits**) that were current in Donne's time. Are lines 11–17 used figuratively or literally? Explain in detail.
3. Having dispensed with critic and criticism, the persona in stanza 3 seeks an adequate metaphor for the kind of love he and "she" have. After trying three clichéd metaphors (lines 20–22), he hits on an adequate one: He and she make sense of the riddle of the phoenix. Recall or research information that will enable you to make sense of the reference. The words "die" and "rise" have reference on several levels: in religion they refer to death and resurrection; in sex they are slang for orgasm and tumescence; in mythology they refer to the phoenix's death by fire and resurrection from its ashes. In religious matters the word "mysterious" means something that is beyond understanding but nevertheless true. The extended, exaggerated, and intellectual metaphor of the phoenix is a good example of what is called a *metaphysical conceit*. Trace the complex logic of the transformation in stanza 3.
4. If, like religious martyrs, the lovers die as a result of their love, they will nevertheless love beyond their death. What kinds of memorials will there be of them (stanza 4)? Why are these appropriate?
5. Who utters the prayer in stanza 5? To whom is it addressed? What is being requested of these "saints"? How much use of paradox do you find in this poem?
6. How does the title relate to the poem? Explain it as a metaphor or (more specifically) metaphysical conceit. Critics have said this poem *is* what it talks about. In what sense is the poem a canonization?

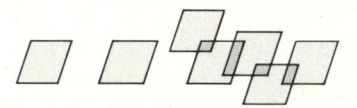

POEMS FOR FOR FURTHER STUDY 2

ULYSSES

To this much-tossed Ulysses,° never done
    With woman whether gowned as wife or whore,
Penelope° and Circe° seemed as one:
She like a whore made his lewd fancies run,
    And wifely she a hero to him bore.

°*Greek hero whose wanderings are recounted in Homer's epic* The Odyssey
°*Ulysses' wife* °*a legendary sorceress* 5

172   FIGURATIVE LANGUAGE

<pre>
Their counter-changings terrified his way:
    They were the clashing rocks, Symplegades,
Scylla and Charybdis° too were they;   °legendary monster
Now they were storms frosting the sea with spray   and whirlpool
    And now the lotus orchard's filthy ease.   10

They multiplied into the Sirens'° throng,   °the mythic tempt-
    Forewarned by fear of whom he stood bound fast, resses who lured sailors
Hand and foot helpless at the vessel's mast,   to destruction with
Yet would not stop his ears: daring their song   their singing
    He groaned and sweated till that shore was past.   15

One, two and many: flesh had made him blind,
    Flesh had one pleasure only in the act,
Flesh set one purpose only in the mind—
Triumph of flesh and afterwards to find
    Still those same terrors wherewith flesh was racked.   20

His wiles were witty and his fame far known,
Every king's daughter sought him for her own,
    Yet he was nothing to be won or lost.
    All lands to him were Ithaca:° love-tossed   °Ulysses' native land
He loathed the fraud, yet would not bed alone.   25
</pre>

Robert Graves (b. 1895)

ULYSSES

<pre>
It little profits that an idle king,
By this still hearth, among these barren crags,
Matched with an agèd wife, I mete and dole
Unequal laws unto a savage race
That hoard, and sleep, and feed, and know not me.   5
I cannot rest from travel; I will drink
Life to the lees. All times I have enjoyed
Greatly, have suffered greatly, both with those
That loved me, and alone; on shore, and when
Through scudding drifts the rainy Hyades°   °star cluster 10
Vexed the dim sea. I am become a name;   by which the
For always roaming with a hungry heart   ancients predicted
Much have I seen and known—cities of men   rainy weather
And manners, climates, councils, governments,
Myself not least, but honored of them all—   15
And drunk delight of battle with my peers,
Far on the ringing plains of windy Troy.
I am a part of all that I have met;
Yet all experience is an arch wherethrough
</pre>

Gleams that untraveled world whose margin fades 20
Forever and forever when I move.
How dull it is to pause, to make an end,
To rust unburnished, not to shine in use!
As though to breathe were life! Life piled on life
Were all too little, and of one to me 25
Little remains; but every hour is saved
From that eternal silence, something more,
A bringer of new things; and vile it were
For some three suns to store and hoard myself,
And this grey spirit yearning in desire 30
To follow knowledge like a sinking star,
Beyond the utmost bound of human thought.

    This is my son, mine own Telemachus,
To whom I leave the scepter and the isle—
Well-loved of me, discerning to fulfill 35
This labor, by slow prudence to make mild
A rugged people, and through soft degrees
Subdue them to the useful and the good.
Most blameless is he, centered in the sphere
Of common duties, decent not to fail 40
In offices of tenderness, and pay
Meet adoration to my household gods
When I am gone. He works his work, I mine.

    There lies the port; the vessel puffs her sail;
There gloom the dark, broad seas. My mariners, 45
Souls that have toiled, and wrought, and thought with me—
That ever with a frolic welcome took
The thunder and the sunshine, and opposed
Free hearts, free foreheads—you and I are old;
Old age hath yet his honor and his toil. 50
Death closes all; but something ere the end,
Some work of noble note, may yet be done,
Not unbecoming men that strove with Gods.
The lights begin to twinkle from the rocks;
The long day wanes; the slow moon climbs; the deep 55
Moans round with many voices. Come, my friends,
'Tis not too late to seek a newer world.
Push off, and sitting well in order smite
The sounding furrows; for my purpose holds
To sail beyond the sunset, and the baths 60
Of all the western stars, until I die.
It may be that the gulfs will wash us down;
It may be we shall touch the Happy Isles° °*the kingdom*
And see the great Achilles, whom we knew. *of the dead*

Though much is taken, much abides; and though 65
We are not now that strength which in old days
Moved earth and heaven, that which we are, we are—
One equal temper of heroic hearts,
Made weak by time and fate, but strong in will
To strive, to seek, to find, and not to yield. 70

Alfred, Lord Tennyson (1809–1892)

A SIMILE FOR HER SMILE

Your smiling, or the hope, the thought of it,
Makes in my mind such pause and abrupt ease
As when the highway bridgegates fall,
Balking the hasty traffic, which must sit
On each side massed and staring, while 5
Deliberately the drawbridge starts to rise:

Then horns are hushed, the oilsmoke rarefies,
Above the idling motors one can tell
The packet's smooth approach, the slip,
Slip of the silken river past the sides, 10
The ringing of clear bells, the dip
And slow cascading of the paddle wheel.

Richard Wilbur (b. 1921)

BESTIARY FOR THE FINGERS OF MY RIGHT HAND

I

Thumb, loose tooth of a horse.
Rooster to his hens.
Horn of a devil. Fat worm
They have attached to my flesh
At the time of my birth. 5
It takes four to hold him down,
Bend him in half, until the bone
Begins to whimper.

Cut him off. He can take care
Of himself. Take root in the earth. 10
Or go hunting with wolves.

II

The second points the way.
True way. The path crosses the earth,

The moon and some stars.
Watch, he points further.
He points to himself.

III

The middle one has backache.
Stiff, still unaccustomed to this life;
An old man at birth. It's about something
That he had and lost,
That he looks for within my hand,
The way a dog looks
For fleas
With a sharp tooth.

IV

The fourth is mystery.
Sometimes as my hand
Rests on the table
He jumps by himself
As though someone called his name.

After each bone, finger,
I come to him, troubled.

V

Something stirs in the fifth
Something perpetually at the point
Of birth. Weak and submissive,
His touch is gentle.
It weighs a tear.
It takes the mote out of the eye.

Charles Simic (b. 1938)

LOVE (III)

Love bade me welcome, yet my soul drew back,
    Guilty of dust and sin.
But quick-eyed Love, observing me grow slack
    From my first entrance in,
Drew nearer to me, sweetly questioning
    If I lacked anything.

"A guest," I answered, "worthy to be here";
    Love said, "You shall be he."
"I, the unkind, ungrateful? Ah, my dear,
    I cannot look on thee."

Love took my hand, and smiling did reply,
   "Who made the eyes but I?"

"Truth, Lord, but I have marred them; let my shame
   Go where it doth deserve."
"And know you not," says Love, "who bore the blame?"   15
   "My dear, then I will serve."
"You must sit down," says Love, "and taste my meat."
   So I did sit and eat.

                  George Herbert (1593–1633)

I TASTE A LIQUOR NEVER BREWED

I taste a liquor never brewed—
From Tankards scooped in Pearl—
Not all the Vats upon the Rhine
Yield such an Alcohol!

Inebriate of Air—am I—   5
And Debauchee of Dew—
Reeling—thro endless summer days—
From inns of Molten Blue—

When "Landlords" turn the drunken Bee
Out of the Foxglove's door—   10
When Butterflies—renounce their "drams"—
I shall but drink the more!

Till Seraphs swing their snowy Hats—
And Saints—to windows run—
To see the little Tippler   15
Leaning against the—Sun—

          Emily Dickinson (1830–1886)

DEPARTMENTAL

An ant on the tablecloth
Ran into a dormant moth
Of many times his size.
He showed not the least surprise.
His business wasn't with such.   5
He gave it scarcely a touch,
And was off on his duty run.
Yet if he encountered one
Of the hive's enquiry squad
Whose work is to find out God   10

And the nature of time and space,
He would put him onto the case.
Ants are a curious race:
One crossing with hurried tread
The body of one of their dead 15
Isn't given a moment's arrest—
Seems not even impressed.
But he no doubt reports to any
With whom he crosses antennae,
And they no doubt report 20
To the higher-up at court.
Then word goes forth in Formic:
"Death's come to Jerry McCormic,
Our selfless forager Jerry.
Will the special Janizary° °*Members of* 25
Whose office it is to bury *an elite fourteenth*
The dead of the commissary *century Turkish*
Go bring him home to his people. *military unit*
Lay him in state on a sepal.
Wrap him for shroud in a petal. 30
Embalm him with ichor° of nettle. °*fluid*
This is the word of your Queen."
And presently on the scene
Appears a solemn mortician;
And taking formal position, 35
With feelers calmly atwiddle,
Seizes the dead by the middle,
And heaving him high in air,
Carries him out of there.
No one stands round to stare. 40
It is nobody else's affair.

It couldn't be called ungentle.
But how thoroughly departmental.

Robert Frost (1874–1963)

8

SYMBOL

STRANGE FITS OF PASSION

Strange fits of passion have I known:
And I will dare to tell,
But in the lover's ear alone,
What once to me befell.

When she I love looked every day   5
Fresh as a rose in June,
I to her cottage bent my way,
Beneath an evening-moon.

Upon the moon I fixed my eye,
All over the wide lea;   10
With quickening pace my horse drew nigh
Those paths so dear to me.

And now we reached the orchard-plot;
And, as we climbed the hill,
The sinking moon to Lucy's cot   15
Came near, and nearer still.

In one of those sweet dreams I slept,
Kind Nature's gentlest boon!
And all the while my eyes I kept
On the descending moon.   20

My horse moved on; hoof after hoof
He raised, and never stopped:
When down behind the cottage roof,
At once, the bright moon dropped.

What fond and wayward thoughts will slide   25
Into a Lover's head!
"O mercy!" to myself I cried,
"If Lucy should be dead!"

William Wordsworth (1770–1850)

    This is one of Wordsworth's most accessible poems, if not his most memorable. Coming to it from the study of figurative language, though, we should find it informative. We as readers overhear someone recounting his experience—someone (presumably a man) who is in love with a girl named Lucy and who will tell his tale only to another lover. Why does he limit himself to "the lover's ear alone"? What kind of experience is he describing? What structural patterns help organize the telling?

Since the experience the speaker has had involves his momentary fears about the safety of the person he loves, he probably assumes that only one also in love will understand his confusion of joy and doubt. At a time like this the two emotions are held in a kind of suspension: as his journey takes him closer to Lucy his excitement rises and his "sweet dreams" increase, but at this moment of greatest expectation he fears that his hopes will be unfulfilled. Our life experiences have taught us that we can't expect too much happiness, that just when we seem to have happiness within our grasp we often have it snatched from us. The speaker's fear is the ultimate one: that the source of his happiness might even have died.

The poem does not indicate how the journey turned out—whether the speaker got to Lucy's house and whether she was alive or dead. In other words, the outcome of the experience and the literal truthfulness of the speaker's premonition are unimportant to the poem. Rather, it is the experience and the way it happened that the poet is concerned with.

The poem is structured so that the heart of the experience is withheld until the last stanza. The first stanza is a direct statement to the poem's fictional audience; by singling out this one "fit of passion" from the others that he has known, the speaker readies the hearer for his tale. Stanzas 2–6 recount in narrative form the episodes leading up to the experience, and the last stanza makes the emotion in question explicit.

If we look back at the first six stanzas, however, we find we are well prepared for the revelation of the final stanza. What devices are employed to set up the experience? Does anything in the rest of the poem foreshadow the abrupt conclusion in stanza 7?

The first stanza prepares us for an unusual experience concerning love, but it does not define the nature of that experience. In fact, the metaphor "fits of passion" (which if taken literally could mean an attack of suffering or even disease) might make a twentieth-century audience think first of sexual desire, since the word "passion" has for us become more narrowly defined. Although amorous feelings are certainly evident, they are not the fit of passion the speaker is referring to. Love motivates the journey and is its end, and references to this love in each stanza make its benign presence felt throughout. But the "strangest" fit of passion comes suddenly in stanza 7 as an outburst of a different emotion—a troublesome and powerful one. The references to love do not account for the climactic closure.

Neither do the geographical references nor the several figures of speech. Cottage, moon, meadow, paths, orchard, and hill are pleasant references, especially as they bring him ever nearer to his lover. Like his horse's pace, his pulse must beat faster as he nears his goal. The simile "fresh as a rose in June," the metaphors "bent my way" and "those sweet dreams I slept," and the personification "kind nature" create a sense of serenity and well-being as the poem moves on.

And yet we *are* prepared for the sudden rush of the last stanza. What prepares us? Which words or sequence of words seems to trigger the sudden outburst of emotion in stanza 7? You have probably noted that the main image left unaccounted for in our discussion is the image of the *moon,* which recurs throughout the poem. There is nothing remarkable about the presence of the moon in the situation described: the event takes place outdoors on a clear evening, where the image of the moon is appropriate. And yet the poet repeatedly refers to the moon with several different descriptive words, as if it had a purposefulness of its own. In line 8 we are told simply that the journey is taking place "beneath an evening moon." In line 9 the speaker fixes his eye upon the moon. As he climbs the hill near Lucy's cottage, the moon—either literally or in an optical illusion or both—begins to sink nearer and nearer to the cottage (lines 13–16). In line 20 it descends even further, until by line 24 it drops (as if no longer connected to the cosmic system) completely behind the cottage and is thus obliterated from view. It is this development that causes the irrational thought—which the speaker characterizes as foolish and perverse—to go through his mind:

> "O mercy!" to myself I cried,
> "If Lucy should be dead!"

Is there a logical connection between a moon or a descending moon and a death? Not even an ardent astrologer would say so. Certainly, no observable cause-and-effect relationship exists, nor are the physical features of the two similar. Yet the speaker makes a connection, and the connection doesn't seem absurd or even illogical, because both the moon and the act of descending have symbolic significance for us. The moon and its descent seem to acquire a special significance to the speaker as he watches it and the poet as he employs it. To the speaker the moon becomes more than a heavenly body; to the reader it is more than an image in the poem; to both, its descent is more than a simple action. By some special connection, these *things* are associated in the mind with *ideas,* in the way that dream images are associated with meanings. And as the speaker sees them and the poet uses them, we as readers react to the ideas behind them as well as to the things themselves. If the speaker saw the moon only as a literal moon, it would stir no particular feeling in him. But to him the moon seems to be associated with his love. Similarly, the moon's quick dropping out of sight would merely indicate the natural course of events, or else an optical illusion, were it not for the association he has of the death of something with the motion of descending. The moon together with its descending pattern suggests to the speaker that his Lucy may have died. He reacts to the descending moon as symbol. And the poet, as he constructs the poem, sets the reader up to react to the descending moon not merely as image or action but as **literary symbol:** *a reference to a concrete image, object, character, pattern, or action which, by virtue of the mental associations it evokes, suggests meanings in addition to and often more significant than its literal meaning.* The additional meanings that the image of the moon and the act of its falling have for the speaker are what make the moon a symbol for him; as the poet repeats the speaker's experience, the descending moon takes on symbolic value for the reader. The meadow is merely a meadow; it has no meaning other than the literal. It is only an image in the poem. The same is true of paths, orchard, and hill. But the descending moon is different. It appeals to the senses like an image, but unlike an image it requires interpreting. It is (A_1) the descending moon (the image, the literal material subject, the vehicle) but at the same time it is *also* the idea (the abstract concept, the feeling, the tenor) that it evokes by association, in this case (A_2) the death of the beloved. In the last lines we read the two meanings simultaneously because (here, at least) the speaker makes explicit the connection between the two. As the speaker discovers the symbolism during the course of his experience, we discern it in the way he presents it to us.

The image (A_1) and the idea (A_2) are mentioned together in this poem; Wordsworth makes the meaning of his symbol explicit. More often, the meaning is left implicit—only the image (A_1) is given and readers must search their memories for associations that lend it significance (A_2), so that the symbol can open up the poem. In other words, the symbol most often appears as only

$$(A_1) \text{ literal subject}$$

without a direct interpretation. But because of previous mental associations we have with the image and because the poet has constructed the poem so that the literal subject does not suffice in the context, we mentally search for a larger meaning for the image:

$$(A_2) \text{ the idea (s) suggested by the literal subject}$$
$$(A_1) \text{ literal subject}$$

If we compare formulas we should be able to differentiate between *image*, *metaphor*, and *symbol* in their appearance and the way they work:

Image: (A) literal subject

Metaphor: (A) literal subject = (B) figurative subject

Symbol: (A_2) the idea (s) suggested by the literal subject
(A_1) literal subject

As a literary symbol is different from images and figures of speech in appearance, it is also different in its origins. In contrast to them, a symbol is not entirely the product of the creative conscious mind. Its beginnings are more ancient, its origins less conscious, its mechanism and meaning more mysterious. Its source, according to psychologists like Freud and Jung, is the unconscious. Symbols are communicated to our consciousness through dreams. In fact, all of us are already acquainted with symbols from our dreams. In dreaming, symbols are produced involuntarily and spontaneously. We dream of snakes, of falling, of being chased, of opening doors—things that have little meaning to us literally, and so have to be interpreted symbolically. Since similar symbols recur in the dreams of people of different times, nationalities, and backgrounds, psychologists are able to see some meaning in the specific dream of an individual. Yet since each individual—and his or her experience—is unique, the exact meaning of any dream symbol is not dogmatically fixed; it is open-ended and extends over a range of possibilities. The same is true of a literary symbol. It reaches from a concrete image to an abstraction but can never be completely and accurately narrowed down to one equivalence. It is the whale in *Moby Dick,* the "A" in *The Scarlet Letter,* the albatross in "The Rime of the Ancient Mariner." It eludes exact definition. The symbol is unlike the figures of speech also in that, rather than becoming trite with repetition, it actually acquires its meaning through repetition.

Symbols dominate not only our dreams but also our waking lives. Societies, religions, institutions, and individuals make conscious use of symbols. Symbols are derived from all aspects of our environment—nature, animal life, human behavior, the human body, and human artifacts. A flag with fifty stars and thirteen stripes is symbolic of the United States; one with a rising sun symbolizes Japan. In the 1960s, the raised fist was associated with the black power movement and the dove with the peace movement. The cross, the fish, the apple, the rainbow, bread, and wine have symbolic meaning for Christians. A bishop carries a staff to symbolize his authority in the church; the president of a university carries a mace. People in love send each other single roses, exchange wedding bands, and become sentimental over drawings of red hearts. A groom carries his bride over the threshold. To most of us, darkness symbolizes ignorance, the unknown, or death; light is knowledge, civilization, or life; a road, the course of life; a river, time; spring, new life; winter, death; dawn, a beginning; dusk, an ending or death. People pass out cigars to symbolize the birth of a baby and hang wreaths on doors to indicate a death. We have even become adept at interpreting subtle body language as symbolic behavior. We live surrounded by symbols, because humans are symbol-conscious animals.

Nevertheless not all objects or actions are symbolic; it would be absurd to assume so. So we take objects literally if the literal level suffices. A wink may indicate merely the presence of something in someone's eye, a white handkerchief only the presence of a cold. Nor should we expect all images to be literary symbols, nor all poems to be symbolic. It is wise to take an image on a literal level unless, as in Wordsworth's poem, the literal level doesn't suffice and the poet prepares us for a symbol.

The sources of poets' symbols are substantially the same as those of society at large—their symbols come from their dreams, their culture, their own experience, their imagination. They use symbols to suggest a meaning beyond the literal, to make an abstract idea more intelligible, to intensify emotional impact. Some symbols appear to be so basic to our nature and our experience that they are universally recognized. Others are less broad in their appeal because they have significance for a cultural tradition, religion, or institution.

Poets may make use of any of these symbols, or they may create their own private symbols in their poems. Like any poem, a poem that contains symbols is an amalgam of inherited tradition and individual insight. The following is an example.

ELDORADO

> Gaily bedight,
> A gallant knight,
> In sunshine and in shadow,
> Had journeyed long,
> Singing a song, 5
> In search of Eldorado.
>
> But he grew old—
> This knight so bold—
> And o'er his heart a shadow
> Fell as he found 10
> No spot of ground
> That looked like Eldorado.
>
> And as his strength
> Failed him at length,
> He met a pilgrim shadow— 15
> "Shadow," said he,
> "Where can it be,
> This land of Eldorado?"
>
> "Over the Mountains
> Of the Moon, 20
> Down the Valley of the Shadow,
> Ride, boldly ride,"
> The shade replied—
> "If you seek for Eldorado!"

Edgar Allan Poe (1809–1849)

Which details in the poem can be taken on the literal level? Which should be approached as metaphors? Which as symbols? Are any of the symbols so general in their application and appeal that they can be said to have universal significance? In what way is the poem as a whole symbolic?

On a first reading we might assume that (except for the metaphor "shadow" in line 9) everything up to the appearance of the "pilgrim shadow" (shade? ghost?) in line 15 could be taken literally. But lines 15–24 cause us to examine our assumptions, and we begin to see that the obstacles to a literal interpretation of "Eldorado" are numerous. Even if we assume that the knight is a specific, real figure, that he has literally "journeyed long,/ Singing a song,/ In search of Eldorado," and that the object of his search is an actual city of gold, the subsequent repetitions of the word "Eldorado," the appearance of a supernatural agency, and the reference to a place where no man could ride, the "mountains of the moon," suggest that the poem has other than literal dimensions.

The changes in meaning in the repetition of the word "shadow" are enlightening. On a first reading we have no reason to take the reference in line 3 as anything but an image. But in line 9, the shadow is obviously a metaphor, and by line 21 it has become a symbol, "the Valley of the Shadow." In all probability there is no valley so named on the face of the earth. Rather, we remember the phrase from the twenty-third Psalm: "Yea, though I walk through the valley of the shadow of death, I will fear no evil: for thou art with me; thy rod and thy staff they comfort me." The identification of this phrase with death is ancient as well as modern, and in variant forms it has symbolic significance beyond the Judeo-Christian tradition. In fact, the phrase is so widely recognized that hardly anyone reading the poem could fail to take it symbolically. And as it is symbolic, the ending of the poem makes us reexamine the knight, his journey, and the poem as a whole.

Both the knight and his journey have far-reaching significance, for both are **archetypal symbols:** *symbols that have enduring and universal meanings, because they derive from a conscious or unconscious recognition of the commonalities of human experience.* In other words, while each of these symbols is specific and individual, behind each is a large, general pattern exemplified in a whole category of symbols.

If we look beyond the specifics of the poem, the universal pattern on which "Eldorado" is based is that of the hero and the quest, a pattern that occurs again and again in the oral and written traditions of different cultures. The relevant aspect of the hero's life story is the initiatory journey that leads from childhood to adulthood, from innocence to experience, from life to death and afterlife. The object of the quest varies. But whatever its ultimate purpose, the quest requires the hero to perform miraculous tasks or overcome obstacles that delay its fulfillment. Often, he is aided by a wise old man who serves as a tutor or guide. When the hero accomplishes his purpose, he either returns to redeem his people or completes the progression from life to death.

Poe's knight is such a quester, embarking on the journey of experience. At the beginning of the poem, he is "gaily bedight," "gallant," and hopeful. Within the space of a few lines, he grows old and disillusioned. Age and loss of faith become the obstacles he must overcome. Like the archetypal hero, the knight has a guide, the "pilgrim shadow," who tells him where to seek Eldorado, but the poem ends ambiguously, without the fulfillment of the quest and without the redemptive return to society.

Because the hero in his various manifestations passes through the same stages of life we do, he represents all of us; his immersion in experience is a reflection of our own. The value of archetypal symbols lies in their power to awaken this sense of shared experience. Consequently, the categories of symbols usually considered archetypal include bigger-than-life personages or broad general patterns such as the earth-mother, the fertility god, death and rebirth, the hero and his quest.

In literature archetypal symbols appear in various guises determined by their cultural contexts. The knight, for example, is a cultural as well as a universal symbol; or, more precisely, he is a cultural representation of the archetype of the hero. Poe gives no physical description of the knight. Yet, for most American or European readers, the word instantly recalls an armored warrior on horseback and—more important—the ideals associated with him: chivalry, idealism, loyalty, courage, strength.

The knight has traditionally been an admirable figure; but what of Eldorado? Is the object of his quest commensurate with his heroic role? Do any words help to define what Eldorado represents?

"Eldorado," the word that both gives the poem its title and concludes each stanza with a reminder of the knight's failure to discover what he has sought, is a multilayered symbol. To sixteenth-century explorers, Eldorado was a reality—a city of gold that supposedly existed somewhere in the jungles of South America. But to the audience of Poe's time, as well as to readers of later generations who have been nurtured by the oral and written traditions of Western civilization, Eldorado is synonymous with any desired goal of human life—wealth, opportunity, contentment, the ideal. For American readers of the late 1840s, the symbolism may have been even more specific; a short time before the publication of the poem, the California gold rush had begun, and Poe may have had it in mind when he composed the poem in 1849.

Although we can't be certain of the exact meaning that Eldorado holds for the knight, the poem does tell us that it is difficult, perhaps impossible, to attain. In dwelling on the knight's sense of futility (lines 9–12, 16–18), and the apparent irony of the pilgrim shadow's words, is Poe suggesting that the quest is meaningless, or does he imply that its fulfillment is less important than the search and the striving?

Read in one way, the words of the pilgrim shadow are mocking and pessimistic. If Eldorado lies "over the mountains/Of the moon," it is physically unattainable. If it is located "down the Valley of the Shadow," it cannot be reached except through death. The same symbols could also suggest a more optimistic reading: The poem may be both an acknowledgment of the impossibility of attaining the ideal on earth and an affirmation of the questing spirit and the ultimate attainment of immortality.

Archetypal symbols are by nature few in number. Less universal in appeal but more numerous are symbols recognizable by smaller groups of people as common to their experience, although not shared by the whole human race. These symbols are also available to poets. The following poem presents some examples.

TO AN ATHLETE DYING YOUNG

The time you won your town the race
We chaired you through the market-place;
Man and boy stood cheering by,
And home we brought you shoulder-high.

To-day, the road all runners come, 5
Shoulder-high we bring you home,
And set you at your threshold down,
Townsman of a stiller town.

Smart lad, to slip betimes away
From fields where glory does not stay 10
And early though the laurel grows
It withers quicker than the rose.

Eyes the shady night has shut
Cannot see the record cut,
And silence sounds no worse than cheers 15
After earth has stopped the ears:

Now you will not swell the rout
Of lads that wore their honours out,
Runners whom renown outran
And the name died before the man. 20

So set, before its echoes fade,
The fleet foot on the sill of shade,
And hold to the low lintel up
The still-defended challenge-cup.

>And round that early-laurelled head
>Will flock to gaze the strengthless dead,
>And find unwithered on its curls
>The garland briefer than a girl's.
>
>*A. E. Housman* (1859–1936)

25

The poem is a eulogy addressed to a champion runner and local hero who died young and famous. It is spoken by his fellow townsmen as they carry him in procession to his grave. The eulogy praises not only the athlete's physical victory in the games but also his moral victory in death. He is a "smart lad" in that, rather than living long enough to wear out his honor, he has died at the height of his fame. As a consequence, he has achieved victory not merely over a few human competitors in a foot race but over the great enemies of humanity and human accomplishment—time and the transitoriness of renown. His fame will outlast his lifetime, rather than vice versa.

The poem is structured on the parallel between the two "victory" processions. In stanzas 1 and 2 the analogy is set up: As we neighbors carried you back to your home on our shoulders after your victory in the foot race, so today we carry you to your final resting place after your victory in the larger race to death. Stanzas 3 to 5 praise the wisdom of the youth in winning the ultimate race against time, rather than staying in the merely human competition, where fame is short-lived. Finally, stanzas 6 and 7 urge the youth to enter his new home in the earth as a victor, as he did his old one above earth, for he has achieved a permanent, not just a temporary, victory.

Thus, the poem is a *eulogy* (praise for the deceased) but hardly an *elegy* (lament for the deceased). The tone of voice is sincere in respect to the dead youth, though cynical in respect to the permanence of life's accomplishments. Paradoxically, what is usually considered the occasion for distress and sorrow is an occasion for congratulations and joy here.

In what ways does the imagery support the paradoxical situation? Discuss the imagery in stanzas 1 and 2. Which are metaphors, which simply images? Explain the difference between them. Why are the same terms used in both stanzas? What is the extended metaphor behind the whole poem?

The first stanza is a masterpiece of literal description. Although vivid images make the event almost visible, the stanza contains no figures of speech. In contrast, stanza 2 has many metaphors. In support of the paradox, the images used literally in stanza 1 become the metaphors of stanza 2. Literally there is no one single "road all runners run." Nor is there a literal threshold or literal "stiller town" to which the corpse is carried. The terms "road," "runners," "home," "threshold," "townsmen," and "town" are all used metaphorically. Applying the vocabulary of running to the usually sad event of death makes the paradox obvious. This is no typical attitude for a funeral.

The analogy and the metaphors set up in the first two stanzas are continued in the next three. Since the same terms are used in both registers (winning a foot race and dying victoriously), many of the statements are intended to be read on two levels simultaneously. In general, though, the stanzas seem to be talking about larger issues of life than running a race. The "fields where glory does not stay," the "shady night," the earth which stops the ears, and the name dying before the man are references to the transience of fame and life (the tenor) in terms of running a race (the vehicle).

The last two stanzas, which continue the extended metaphor, indicate the basis for considering the central event a victory: whereas the fruits of winning a human competition are short-lived, the results of the lad's dying at the height of his fame will be a permanent monument to his victory. As he lies in his grave with his challenge-cup on his chest, he will forever be holding the cup up to the "low lintel" of the casket lid (or the dirt over his head), much as he did in that brief time when his townsmen brought him home after the race. Moreover, his honor, his renown, his name will never die; he will always be a hero to his townsmen. Thus, the poem "proves" its contention that the athlete's final act is his most outstanding success, and the metaphor begun in stanza 2 is sustained throughout the poem.

Within the controlling metaphor and in addition to the incidental metaphors are several symbols. Note, for example, stanza 3:

> Smart lad, to slip betimes away
> From fields where glory does not stay
> And early though the laurel grows
> It withers quicker than the rose.

Which of these images could be called a metaphor? A symbol? How must they be interpreted to make the statement consistent? Why does the poet mention the laurel and the rose? What relationship do they have to a race?

If we take "fields" literally, both "laurel" and "rose" seem appropriate but "glory" does not, since glory cannot grow in a field. If we take "fields" as a metaphor for a human lifetime, "glory" is appropriate but "laurel" and "rose" are not, since they do not "grow" there. Cultural associations of the two terms, however, help explain their usage. Both "laurel" and "rose" have a long history of symbolic significance, which stanza 7 indicates is to be remembered in the context of the poem.

From the time of the ancient Greeks and Romans, the laurel (specifically the bay laurel, or *Laurus nobilis*) has been a symbol of victory and honor. It was associated in myth with Apollo (the god of light, moral purity, order, prophecy, music, and poetry) after he spent seven years in a grove of bay trees to atone for taking the life of the Delphian python. In his honor the leaves of the bay tree were woven into wreaths for prizes in the Pythian games. Because of the broad scope of Apollo's influence, the wreath was also given for competitions in music, art, and poetry, and became the symbol of important offices. Although few people today are given a wreath of laurel as a prize, the symbolism of the laurel is part of our vocabulary. We speak of "resting on one's laurels" and of a "poet laureate." Most of us are familiar with paintings and sculptures of Nero, Napoleon, and Dante with laurel wreaths on their heads symbolizing superiority in their field, and we understand the symbolism of the term because it has come down to us as part of our heritage from the Greeks. Nations that are not within the Western traditions, such as Nepal or Sierra Leone, would probably not recognize the laurel as a symbol and consequently would have difficulty understanding lines 11–12 and 25–28 of this poem, for A. E. Housman has employed a **conventional symbol,** *a symbol that has a shared meaning for a particular culture, nation, or group of people and that has been traditionally used with this meaning.* Such symbols as the American eagle and the status-loaded Cadillac are basic to the American tradition but not necessarily to that of another country. At Jewish wedding celebrations, the smashing of a glass is symbolic of consummation and consequently of fertility, whereas at weddings that reflect Celtic ritual, the guests throw rice at the couple or tie shoes to the bumper of the car, actions with the same symbolic import. The Roman Catholic Church indicates by the color of smoke from a Vatican chimney whether or not a new Pope has been elected. These are conventional symbols of the cultures or groups that employ them.

The open-ended nature of the literary symbol precludes such automatic and precise assignment of a specific meaning. Rather, the symbol suggests a range of possibilities. Because Apollo is the god of various fields, the laurel could symbolize achievement in art, poetry, music, or politics as well as athletics. It might even symbolize chastity, since it was also associated with the nymph Daphne who, to escape romantic pursuit by Apollo, was changed into a bay tree. But the context of the extended metaphor is a foot race, and the laurel is consequently interpreted as a prize for victory in athletic competition: it is the prize the lad receives for beating time while still honored.

Another conventional symbol is the rose, which in Western culture has symbolized such qualities as beauty, love, passion, martyrdom, and even death. The Virgin Mary has been called the rose of heaven, and Robert Herrick has instructed young virgins to gather "rosebuds while ye may," implying that beauty and love are short-lived. Housman pretty clearly instructs us to think in terms of beauty, for he mentions the flower's transience and associates the rose with a girl. Thus, lines 11–12 might be paraphrased as "Although success in athletics comes early (in youth), it is briefer than even beauty." In lines 25–28, however, by the miracle of the athlete's dying strong and famous in his youth, those who died old and weak gather around him to see the symbol of his fame—which usually does not last as long as a girl's beauty—still unwithered in his grave.

Several other terms also could be interpreted as symbols because, as the poem demonstrates, the line between metaphor and symbol is not clear-cut, and the two devices often work hand-in-hand. In fact, a symbol is almost always supported by other images and figures of speech. The challenge-cup in line 24 is fairly clearly a symbol of victory because it is conventionally used as one and because it has no other meaning in this poem. The terms "threshold" (line 6) and "sill" (line 22) are often used as symbols of the passage from life to death. Here, however, they are an integral part of the extended analogy of the poem and, like the low lintel (line 23), might better be thought of as metaphors that take on symbolic shading. The "road all runners come" (line 5) and the "shady night" (line 13) would seem to be still closer to metaphor and less appropriately labelled symbols.

In the examples mentioned, Housman made use of conventional symbols appropriate to the subject of his poem. Since they were generally recognized public symbols, he had only to mention them for us to catch their meaning. If he had chosen to develop a private rather than a public symbol, however, his technique as well as his intention would have been different, as the following poem demonstrates.

FENCE WIRE

Too tight, it is running over
Too much of this ground to be still
Or to do anything but tremble
And disappear left and right
As far as the eye can see   5

Over hills, through woods,
Down roads, to arrive at last
Again where it connects,
Coming back from the other side
Of animals, defining their earthly estate   10

As the grass becomes snow
While they are standing and dreaming
Of grass and snow.
The winter hawk that sits upon its post,
Feeling the airy current of the wires,   15

Turns into a robin, sees that this is wrong,
Then into a boy, and into a man who holds
His palm on the top tense strand
With the whole farm feeding slowly
And nervously into his hand.   20

If the wire were cut anywhere
All his blood would fall to the ground
And leave him standing and staring
With a face as white as a Hereford's.
From years of surrounding grain,   25

Cows, horses, machinery trying to turn
To rust, the humming arrives each second,
A sound that arranges these acres
And holds them highstrung and enthralled.
Because of the light, chilled hand   30

On the top thread tuned to an E
Like the low string of a guitar,
The dead corn is more
Balanced in death than it was,
The animals more aware   35

Within the huge human embrace
Held up and borne out of sight
Upon short, unbreakable poles
Wherethrough the ruled land intones
Like a psalm: properly,   40

With its eyes closed,
Whether on the side of the animals
Or not, whether disappearing
Right, left, through trees or down roads,
Whether outside, around, or in.   45

James Dickey (b. 1923)

How far into this poem can we read on a literal level? What indications are there that the fence wire is being used symbolically? What characteristics of it are important? What human endeavor incorporates these characteristics? Is Dickey employing a conventional symbol or creating one of his own instead in this poem?

The first two stanzas of the poem present us with a fairly objective description of taut fence wire that runs out of sight to the left and right before us "Over hills, through woods, / Down roads . . ." to return "from the other side of animals, defining their earthly estate." Thus the first two stanzas are—with the exception of several strongly connotative words—literal, and they establish an atmosphere of rural beauty and stillness. Not until the third stanza do we perceive some magic quality inherent in the wire. In touch with the "current of the wires," a hawk sits on its post and is turned "into a robin . . . / Then into a boy, and into a man who holds / His palm on the top tense strand" and seems to be nourished by the farm, which flows into him through the wire. The poet has begun to explore the symbolic possibilities of fence wire. But so far, it has been associated only with the idea of transformation—magical or imaginative transformation.

The idea that the wire is life-sustaining is returned to in the fifth stanza, a pivotal point in the poem, for here the beauty and equilibrium already established are potentially threatened. If the title and references to fence wire did not already hint at a larger meaning, stanza 5 undoubtedly suggests such a special significance by describing the devastating effects that would befall the man at the fence if the tight singing wire were cut. We learn that he would become lifeless, but not literally dead; he would become as dumb and white-faced as the Hereford to which he is compared. Is Dickey implying that the fence wire separates human beings from brutehood? Certainly he is using the wire to suggest some faculty more godlike than just tool-making ability. Still, how does he wish us to understand this wire?

In stanza 6, we are told that the humming wire holds everything within its perimeter—grain, cows, horses, machinery—from rust and the eroding influence of time: everything is held "high strung and enthralled." What are the implications of this phrase? Does fence wire have any conventional symbolic associations? Dickey, it seems, is suggesting that the fence wire somehow electrifies, makes more intense, holds in a state of dynamic suspension the things that it encloses. But what human endeavor is capable of doing this? Up to this point, the poet has described only the powers of the wire and its effect on various things; and since the wire has no traditional symbolic associations, it is difficult for a reader to identify what this object is meant to represent. Dickey has created a **personal symbol:** *a symbol that is unique to the user, rather than commonly or traditionally recognized.*

Because the symbol is private, that is, not interpretable without help, we expect the poet to supply the necessary details. In the seventh stanza, the fence wire, humming, is likened to a guitar string "tuned to an E." Here Dickey's intentions become more explicit; he has used terminology from the world of music or, more generally, from the world of art. The poet seems to be implying that art is that human endeavor which "arranges these acres," brings intense awareness, and holds everything suspended in time. The fence wire is still fence wire, but we are now ready to understand its symbolic dimensions. In lines 30–35, Dickey lyrically explains the cause-and-effect relationship:

> Because of the light, chilled hand
> On the top thread tuned to an E
> Like the low string of a guitar,
> The dead corn is more
> Balanced in death than it was,
> The animals more aware . . . .

It is art that brings balance, that makes us "more aware" and distinguishes us from animals. If art offers the possibility of a higher consciousness and enables us to participate more intensely in our own existence, it does so by unsettling our habitual, rational, plodding way of looking at the world. Notice the unusual syntax of the last stanzas, the hypnotic repetitions, the cadenced elaborations, and the floating, uncertain relations between subjects and verbs.

In the last two stanzas, what does the poet mean by "huge human embrace" and "short, unbreakable poles"? Why is the land "ruled"? Why does it intone "like a Psalm"? Why is it a personified land "with its eyes closed"?

The "huge human embrace" is another element in the several contrasts Dickey has drawn between human beings and animals; it refers literally to the man-made enclosure of fence wire but figuratively suggests the great capacity of art and/or the imagination to encompass and enhance, to make durable ("unbreakable") and visible ("held up") the mutable things it is in relationship with. By using a religious simile in line 40, Dickey may imply the sacred potential of art—its capacity for revelations, its ability to order ("ruled land") and embrace. The personified land "with its eyes closed" is an example of Dickey's Romantic imagination. Born in the rural South, James Dickey believes in the spirit of the land and believes that art reveals that spirit and gives voice to it.

Why does Dickey conclude his poem with a series of directional words and prepositions? He seems once again to be emphasizing the power of art to affect and transform whatever comes within its range. (For an interesting and engaging poem that also deals with the relation between art and reality, see Wallace Stevens' "The Anecdote of the Jar.") Art has dominion everywhere but reveals—gives the world voice and visibility—as if for the first time. While suggesting an infinite world beyond what can be seen and enclosed, art also reminds us of the latent possibilities in what can be seen and heard. Art is a great reminder.

Now that you are aware of the poem's symbolic dimensions, reread it, noticing the heavily connotative words you understood only literally in the first reading, words that define the nature and purpose of art: Art connects, feeds, arranges, holds, enthralls, balances, holds up, embraces, rules. Although Dickey chose to create his own symbol rather than one ready-made to his purpose, he has prepared us to see it as a symbol and has given us data by which we can assign meaning to it. For us the poem becomes an example of what it's talking about. *It* is what *it* defines.

Because symbols require, perhaps more than any other aspect of poetry, the active participation of the reader, they can be intimidating to the uninitiated. They can be fascinating to the accomplished reader, however, partially because symbols allow the skilled interpreter not only to understand the poem but also to supply information that makes the merely implicit perfectly explicit. Unfortunately, readers may also fall prey to all sorts of "fond and wayward thoughts" which, unlike those in Wordsworth's poem, "Strange Fits of Passion Have I Known," are not prompted by (or are inadequately prompted by) the details of the poem. Because symbols are often open-ended, they can be carried to extremes. To carry a symbol too far is to detract from the meaning and significance of a poem rather than enhance it.

The false art of "symbol hunting" is a danger to new readers, who can be lured down many dead ends by a symbolic hare crossing their paths. Reader, be warned: not every poem is symbolic or contains a symbol. Most, in fact, do not. Even if a poem contains a symbol, it is likely that not every image in the poem is symbolic. Even the images that almost definitely are symbols should not be carried beyond the range of meaning that the details of the poem require or suggest. Not every road is the road of life, nor every journey a quest. Do not let the poem become an excuse for expounding on a topic you happen to be interested in. Allow the poem to say what it has to say and also to be silent when it has no intention to speak. The line between reading exhaustively and reading-in is a fine one, the proof of which is that not even the most astute literary critics agree completely about any one poem. The most sensible action for a new reader is to play it safe, to understate slightly rather than overstate, and to qualify statements with such words as "perhaps," "may be interpreted," and "suggests," rather than "is." Never base an entire interpretation on a conjecture or on one slight reference in a poem.

The following offers an opportunity to analyze a poem that may (or may not) contain symbols or be symbolic. Before you read the comment following it, see if you can arrive at your own interpretation.

ON FLUNKING A NICE BOY OUT OF SCHOOL

I wish I could teach you how ugly
decency and humility can be when they are not
the election of a contained mind but only
the defenses of an incompetent. Were you taught
meekness as a weapon? Or did you discover,
by chance maybe, that it worked on mother
and was generally a good thing—
at least when all else failed—to get you over
the worst of what was coming. Is that why you bring

these sheepfaces to Tuesday?   10
            They won't do.
It's three months work I want, and I'd sooner have it
from the brassiest lumpkin in pimpledom, but have it,
than all these martyred repentances from you.

John Ciardi (b. 1916)

Shortly after Ciardi published this poem in 1961, a student used it as a subject for a paper, which his professor forwarded to the poet for comment. The student's paper was well written, well organized, and insightful about the basic situation and mood of the poem. In fact, the paper indicated that the student had mastered many of the techniques of critical analysis and had a good grasp of the poem. Then he injected the phrase "on a deeper level" and began discussing the symbolism he saw in the poem.

According to the student's analysis, the poem is a teacher's response to a student's attitude toward classwork but also evolves into a tirade against both the matriarchal principle in American society in contrast with the patriarchal, and a meek Christian attitude toward life in contrast with the forcefulness expressed in Norse mythology. According to the student's reading of the poem, the word "Tuesday" becomes a symbol for Tyr, the Norse god of battle, and by extension it becomes a symbol for the patriarchal principle and even for the teacher. The reference to Tuesday (he says) is juxtaposed against a list of references symbolizing Christianity—"election," "meekness," "mother," "sheepfaces," and "martyred"—with the reference to mother (the Virgin Mary) indicating the matriarchal basis of institutionalized Christianity. He suggests the poem implies that the kind of Christianity which teaches that God's love must be earned is superior to the kind which teaches that God's love is for all. His conclusion is that the poem is a plea for individual responsibility. A teacher prefers an upstart who works to a "nice boy" who doesn't.

Ciardi commented on the paper in his role as poetry editor of the *Saturday Review*. His reaction to the student's analysis of the poem is pertinent to our discussion of symbolism.

> What astonishes me about all this is its combination of acumen and obtusity. The conclusions are right enough, yet all sorts of things are incidentally wrong. . . .
>
> Somewhere between precision and fumble, moreover, this student decided to turn a corner that wasn't there. Obviously the boy had been reading up on Norse mythology and he happened to be loaded up on Tyr and Fenris.
>
> For all that about Tuesday is an obvious derailment. Had I said Monday he would probably have come on with moon symbolism, and so on through the week. . . .
>
> But I really shouldn't josh this boy. On something like the same level

he is exactly right about the Christian overtones of *election, meekness,* etc. Those words were all chosen for a purpose.

But how is a student to know he is right in one set of identifications and wrong in another? It is the residual teacher in me that asks that question, not the writer of the poem. And I think the teacher has a reasonable answer.

How do you *know,* asks the student, that *Tuesday* wasn't meant as a symbol? Because, says the teacher, that possibility is never returned to in the poem.

Any poet who intends a common word to acquire the extraordinary symbolic weight this student gives to *Tuesday* will reinforce that possibility somewhere else in the poem. The Christian overtones of the poem are a theme because they are developed into a theme. *Tuesday* is simply a day of the week because had the poet wanted to evoke Tyr, or Tiw, or Thing, he would have brought the phrasing back to that possibility somewhere else in the poem.[1]

Ciardi's comments on his own intention and on the way he would have prepared the reader for a symbol if he had wanted to should be taken seriously; for, as all the poems in this chapter have demonstrated, poets prepare readers to see the symbols they intend. As a checklist for identifying symbols, you may find the following helpful:

1. Be aware, as you read, that certain objects, patterns, and actions have for certain groups of people a significance beyond their literal meaning and that poets often incorporate these symbols in their poems.
2. Read any image that makes sense on a literal level as a literal image. You are usually safe in calling a device a symbol, however, if it passes *more than one* of these tests:
   a. The poet directs your attention to the term by repetition or by peculiar emphasis, so that the poem seems to make *more* of the image than it's worth.
   b. You are either already familiar with the symbolic associations of the term or the poem makes you think you ought to be.
   c. The literal meaning of the image will not suffice—as if the one remaining piece of a jigsaw puzzle will not fit the space that's left.
   d. You have difficulty paraphrasing the passage that the term appears in because the term will not be integrated on the same level with the rest of the terms in the passage.
   e. Reading the image as an implied metaphor leaves details unaccounted for.

---

[1] John Ciardi, "Manner of Speaking," *Saturday Review,* XLVIII (January 16, 1965), 19.

  f. Both supporting images and figures of speech direct your memory to associations outside the poem.
3. If you decide on the basis of the list that the poem contains a symbol, you may want to identify the scope of its significance.
  a. A symbol that seems to be based on an experience shared by all or most of the human race is an archetypal symbol.
  b. A symbol that has a shared meaning for a particular culture, nation, religion, fraternity, etc., is a conventional symbol.
  c. A symbol that is not publicly recognized but that the poet creates for the individual poem is a personal symbol.
4. In determining the meaning associated with a symbol, do not push beyond the support offered by the poem. Although a symbol can never be pinned down to one and only one exact meaning, there are *many* meanings that are inappropriate for any symbol. Go with conventional or archetypal associations unless the poet indicates otherwise. Sex and religion are rich sources of symbols, but not *every* poem contains a phallic symbol or a Christ figure.
5. Above all, consider why the poet has used a symbol and the effect it has on the poem and the reader.

 Now see if you can apply what you have learned about symbolism to Robert Frost's "Desert Places."

DESERT PLACES

Snow falling and night falling fast, oh, fast
In a field I looked into going past,
And the ground almost covered smooth in snow,
But a few weeds and stubble showing last.

The woods around it have it—it is theirs.   5
All animals are smothered in their lairs.
I am too absent-spirited to count;
The loneliness includes me unawares.

And lonely as it is, that loneliness
Will be more lonely ere it will be less—   10
A blanker whiteness of benighted snow
With no expression, nothing to express.

They cannot scare me with their empty spaces
Between stars—on stars where no human race is.
I have it in me so much nearer home   15
To scare myself with my own desert places.

       Robert Frost (1875–1963)

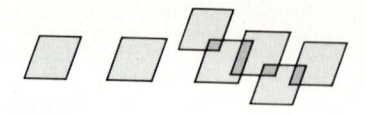

POEMS FOR FURTHER STUDY 1

THE MAGI

Now as at all times I can see in the mind's eye,
In their stiff, painted clothes, the pale unsatisfied ones
Appear and disappear in the blue depth of the sky
With all their ancient faces like rain-beaten stones,
And all their helms of silver hovering side by side,
And all their eyes still fixed, hoping to find once more,
Being by Calvary's turbulence unsatisfied,
The uncontrollable mystery on the bestial floor.

William Butler Yeats (1865–1939)

QUESTIONS

1. It is difficult to probe very deeply into Yeats's poetry without some knowledge of myth, a term that has been variously interpreted by folklorists, psychologists, and literary critics. Contrary to popular usage, in which the word means falsehood, the term **myth** usually designates a type of *oral-traditional narrative that has the following characteristics:*

   a. It is a sacred story accepted as truth by a large segment of the culture in which it is told.
   b. The events it recounts are set in a remote time and place.
   c. Its principal characters are gods or animals, though human beings sometimes play a significant role.
   d. The story is usually composed of archetypal motifs such as those explored earlier in this chapter.

Writers who have made literary use of myths have freely modified these elements, often interpreting ancient stories in the light of modern civilization or creating their own mythology using oral sources and their own imaginations. In what sense is the New Testament account of the wise men who journeyed to Bethlehem mythic? Does the poet seem to be drawing primarily from this source, or is he, in effect, creating his own myth? The questions that follow should lead to some tentative conclusions about Yeats's mythology and the artistry that shapes it.

2. Who is speaking in this poem? What does he "see in the mind's eye"?
3. Does Yeats picture the Magi on their way to Bethlehem or at some later time? What is the significance of this fact?
4. The persona envisions the Magi as "pale" men in "stiff, painted clothes" and "helms of silver," their faces "ancient . . . like rain-beaten stones." What is the tone of these words? Do these images serve only to describe the physical appearance of the wise men, or do they have other functions as well?
5. In lines 2 and 7, the Magi are described as "unsatisfied." Does the poem explain why?
6. What is the meaning of the phrase "Calvary's turbulence"? What are the symbolic associations of Calvary?
7. In his vision, the speaker imagines the wise men reunited after the crucifixion, seeking "once more" to find "the uncontrollable mystery on the bestial floor." In what sense would the Christ-child represent for them an "uncontrollable mystery"? What are the symbolic dimensions of their new journey? What is its object?

JOURNEY OF THE MAGI

'A cold coming we had of it,
Just the worst time of the year
For a journey, and such a long journey:
The ways deep and the weather sharp,
The very dead of winter.'   5
And the camels galled, sore-footed, refractory,
Lying down in the melting snow.
There were times we regretted
The summer palaces on slopes, the terraces,
And the silken girls bringing sherbet.   10
Then the camel men cursing and grumbling
And running away, and wanting their liquor and women,
And the night-fires going out, and the lack of shelters,
And the cities hostile and the towns unfriendly
And the villages dirty and charging high prices: 15
A hard time we had of it.
At the end we preferred to travel all night,
Sleeping in snatches,
With the voices singing in our ears, saying
That this was all folly.   20

Then at dawn we came down to a temperate valley,
Wet, below the snow line, smelling of vegetation;
With a running stream and a water-mill beating the darkness,

And three trees on the low sky,
And an old white horse galloped away in the meadow. 25
Then we came to a tavern with vine-leaves over the lintel,
Six hands at an open door dicing for pieces of silver,
And feet kicking the empty wine-skins.
But there was no information, and so we continued
And arrived at evening, not a moment too soon 30
Finding the place; it was (you may say) satisfactory.

All this was a long time ago, I remember,
And I would do it again, but set down
This set down
This: were we led all that way for 35
Birth or Death? There was a Birth, certainly,
We had evidence and no doubt. I had seen birth and death,
But had thought they were different; this Birth was
Hard and bitter agony for us, like Death, our death.
We returned to our places, these Kingdoms, 40
But no longer at ease here, in the old dispensation,
With an alien people clutching their gods.
I should be glad of another death.

T. S. Eliot (1888–1965)

QUESTIONS

1. The story recounted in "Journey of the Magi" is filtered through the consciousness of one of the Magi. How does this narrative method differ from that of Yeats? Is one approach more successful than the other, or is each appropriate to a different objective?

2. What parallels do you find between the journey and return of the wise men and the story told in Matthew 2:1–12? How does Eliot embellish the Biblical narrative?

3. To what extent does Eliot make use of archetypal symbols? Consider, for example, the literal and symbolic goals of the Magi's quest, the hardships they endured, whether they gained knowledge from their experience, and what happened to them when they returned to their kingdoms.

4. What seasonal images are there in "Journey of the Magi"? What are their traditional symbolic associations? What other images, figures of speech, or literal statements reinforce this universal pattern?

5. In the Christian context of this poem, what is the symbolic significance of the "three trees on a low sky"? The "white horse"? The men "dicing for pieces of silver"? Why do you think the speaker, who is looking back from the perspective of many years, associates these images with the journey *to* Bethlehem?

6. Lines 35–39 deal with the birth of Christ, but only in abstract, paradoxical language. What does the speaker mean when he says, "this Birth was / Hard and bitter agony for us, like Death, our death"? What is the other death he alludes to in the last line?

THE PILGRIMAGE

I traveled on, seeing the hill, where lay
    My expectation.
  A long it was and weary way:
  The gloomy Cave of Desperation
I left on the one, and on the other side   5
    The Rock of Pride.

And so I came to Fancy's Meadow, strowed
    With many a flower;
  Fain would I here have made abode,
  But I was quickened by my hour.   10
So to Care's Copse I came, and there got through
    With much ado.

That led me to the Wild of Passion, which
    Some call the Wold:
  A wasted place, but sometimes rich.   15
  Here I was robbed of all my gold,
Save one good angel, which a friend had tied
    Close to my side.

At length I got unto the Gladsome Hill,
    Where lay my hope,   20
  Where lay my heart; and climbing still,
  When I had gained the brow and top,
A lake of brackish waters on the ground
    Was all I found.

With that abashed, and struck with many a sting   25
    Of swarming fears,
  I fell and cried, "Alas, my King,
  Can both the way and end be tears?"
Yet taking heart I rose, and then perceived
    I was deceived.   30

My hill was further, so I flung away,
    Yet heard a cry,
  Just as I went: "None goes that way
  And lives." "If that be all," said I,
"After so foul a journey death is fair,   35
    And but a chair."

George Herbert (1593–1633)

QUESTIONS

1. The title implies that the poem will be a religious one. Which references support a religious reading? Is it specifically a Christian poem? Is it affirmative or negative? Does it have a happy ending? Explain.

2. The title also implies that the poem will have a narrative structure. Make a list of all the subject-verb combinations that advance the story line. Of how many events does the narrative consist?

3. If we take the poem on the literal level (i.e., a person on a pilgrimage to a holy shrine), it consists of numerous images of a physical landscape: hill, cave, rock, meadow, copse (i.e., thicket), and so forth. There are few figures of speech in between these images until the end of the poem. However, each of these sites in the landscape is labeled, for example, the "Cave of Desperation." What figure of speech does the added label create?

4. Are the labels from the expected physical domain of human experience, or are they from the emotional and spiritual domain? What difference do the labels make in your reading of the poem on the literal level? What is "the hill" the pilgrim seeks?

5. Whether you called the image-plus-label combinations metaphors or symbols, they clearly take on symbolic significance in the poem and make you read it on the spiritual *as well as* the physical level. Like a symbol, the poem itself makes reference to one level but its real meaning is on another. If *a whole poem is explicitly a consistent symbolic representation* (i.e., *with reading required on two levels or more*), it is called an **allegory.** Allegory is usually narrative and often religious or mythic in content. Nearly every image in it has a fixed and explicit abstract meaning. In fact, the concrete level is often merely the vehicle to make the abstract level vivid. Relatively few short poems employ this medium. The most famous examples are long narrative poems and prose pieces, such as *Faerie Queene* and *Pilgrim's Progress.* Christ's parables also have allegorical qualities. Is "The Pilgrimage" an allegory? Explain.

THE ALBATROSS
L'Albatros

Ofttimes, for diversion, the men of the crew
Capture albatross, vast birds of the seas
That accompany, at languid, leisurely pace,
Boats on their way through bitter straits.

Having scarce been taken aboard   5
These kings of the blue, awkward and shy,
Piteously their great white wings
Let droop like oars at their sides.

This wingèd voyager, how clumsy he is and weak!
He just now so lovely, how comic and ugly! 10
One with a stubby pipe teases his beak,
Another mimics, limping, the cripple who could fly!

The Poet resembles this prince of the clouds,
Who laughs at hunters and haunts the storms;
Exiled to the ground amid the jeering pack, 15
His giant wings will not let him walk.

Charles Baudelaire (1821–1867)
(trans. by Kate Flores)

QUESTIONS

1. When do we become aware that the poet wishes us to see the albatross more than literally?
2. Is the bird a personal symbol? Can you think of other poems or tales that use birds or flying in a similar way? What is unique about Baudelaire's handling of the bird?
3. The ideal is always defeated by the real—is this a fair summary of the symbolic content of the poem? Or can its meaning be narrowed further?
4. When Baudelaire says that the bird's giant wings hinder its walking, what sense does he intend beyond the literal one? Why does he compare the bird to a king and a prince?
5. Baudelaire anticipated the French Symbolist movement—which included Valéry Mallarmé, Verlaine, Rimbaud. Baudelaire wrote in "Correspondences" that the world is "a forest of symbols." *The Symbolist poem usually makes no direct statement* of the poet's emotions but finds instead an object or an outer landscape that will approximate or express the poet's inner mood or spiritual state. In what ways does "The Albatross" do or fail to do this?

AH SUN-FLOWER

Ah Sun-flower! weary of time,
Who countest the steps of the Sun,
Seeking after that sweet golden clime
Where the traveller's journey is done:

Where the Youth pined away with desire, 5
And the pale Virgin shrouded in snow,
Arise from their graves and aspire
Where my Sun-flower wishes to go.

William Blake (1757–1827)

QUESTIONS

1. Characterize the audience of the poem.
2. Is the sunflower a symbol? If so, of what? Support your answer.
3. Describe "that sweet golden clime." To what, in your opinion, does the phrase refer? Where does the sunflower wish to go? What effect does her desire have on her and her relationships?
4. Characterize the youth, the virgin, and their relationship. Comment on the term "snow."
5. Does the word "my" in line 8 help identify the speaker? Is his relationship to the sunflower reflected in any other relationship in the poem? In what tone of voice does he say "Ah!"
6. Which of the symbols would you consider archetypal, which conventional, which personal? Can any or all be pinned down to one meaning?
7. Does the effectiveness of this poem depend in part on its being a symbolic poem, or would it be more effective without the symbols?

GREEN WATER TOWER

W. S. Merwin (b. 1927)

A guest at Thanksgiving   said And you've got
a green water tower   with a blue 2 painted on it

it is there at the edge of the woods   on the hill to the east
at night it flattens   into the black profile of trees
clouds bloom from behind it   moonlight climbs through them   5
to the sound of pouring   far inside

in an east wind we wake hearing it   wondering where it is
above it the sky grows pale   white sun emerges
the green tower swells   in rings of shadow
day comes   we drink and stand listening   10

QUESTIONS

1. It has been said that art is simply an eloquent reminder. Can this statement in any way apply to "Green Water Tower"?
2. If the tower is symbolic, is it *personal* or *conventional* in its associations? Do the first two descriptive elements of the title have traditional symbolic value? Does the tower?
3. Is it accidental that the guest calls attention to the tower at Thanksgiving? What is the effect of the tower on the speaker? What is the relationship between the tower and what surrounds it?

4. The poem concludes with sunrise and at least two people drinking water while looking at the tower and listening to the sound of water "far inside." Does this have any particular significance?

5. Do all the details of a poem have to have symbolic value? The guest calls attention to the "blue 2 painted on it." Does this have any special significance?

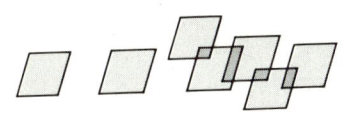

POEMS FOR FURTHER STUDY 2

THE HEAVY BEAR WHO GOES WITH ME
"the witness of the body"

The heavy bear who goes with me,
A manifold honey to smear his face,
Clumsy and lumbering here and there,
The central ton of every place,
The hungry beating brutish one   5
In love with candy, anger, and sleep,
Crazy factotum°, dishevelling all,   °someone
Climbs the building, kicks the football,   who performs
Boxes his brother in the hate-ridden city.   various duties

Breathing at my side, that heavy animal,   10
That heavy bear who sleeps with me,
Howls in his sleep for a world of sugar,
A sweetness intimate as the water's clasp,
Howls in his sleep because the tight-rope
Trembles and shows the darkness beneath.   15
—The strutting show-off is terrified,
Dressed in his dress-suit, bulging his pants,
Trembles to think that his quivering meat
Must finally wince to nothing at all.

That inescapable animal walks with me,   20
Has followed me since the black womb held,
Moves where I move, distorting my gesture,
A caricature, a swollen shadow,
A stupid clown of the spirit's motive,
Perplexes and affronts with his own darkness,   25
The secret life of belly and bone,

Opaque, too near, my private, yet unknown,
Stretches to embrace the very dear
With whom I would walk without him near,
Touches her grossly, although a word   30
Would bare my heart and make me clear,
Stumbles, flounders, and strives to be fed
Dragging me with him in his mouthing care,
Amid the hundred million of his kind,
The scrimmage of appetite everywhere.   35

Delmore Schwartz (1913–1966)

I SAW IN LOUISIANA A LIVE-OAK GROWING

I saw in Louisiana a live-oak growing,
All alone stood it and the moss hung down from the branches;
Without any companion it grew there uttering joyous leaves of dark green,
And its look, rude, unbending, lusty, made me think of myself,
But I wonder'd how it could utter joyous leaves standing alone there without its friend near, for I knew I could not,   5
And I broke off a twig with a certain number of leaves upon it, and twined around it a little moss,
And brought it away, and I have placed it in sight in my room;
It is not needed to remind me as of my own dear friends,
(For I believe lately I think of little else than of them,)
Yet it remains to me a curious token, it makes me think of manly love;   10
For all that, and though the live-oak glistens there in Louisiana solitary in a wide flat space,
Uttering joyous leaves all its life without a friend a lover near,
I know very well I could not.

Walt Whitman (1819–1892)

THE SNOW MAN

One must have a mind of winter
To regard the frost and the boughs
Of the pine-trees crusted with snow;

And have been cold a long time
To behold the junipers shagged with ice,   5
The spruces rough in the distant glitter

Of the January sun; and not to think
Of any misery in the sound of the wind,
In the sound of a few leaves,

Which is the sound of the land 10
Full of the same wind
That is blowing in the same bare place

For the listener, who listens in the snow,
And, nothing himself, beholds
Nothing that is not there and the nothing that is. 15

Wallace Stevens (1879–1955)

HYMN TO GOD MY GOD, IN MY SICKNESS

Since I am coming to that holy room
    Where, with Thy choir of saints for evermore,
I shall be made Thy music; as I come
    I tune the instrument here at the door,
    And what I must do then, think here before. 5

Whilst my physicians by their love are grown
    Cosmographers, and I their map, who lie
Flat on this bed, that by them may be shown
    That this is my southwest discovery
    Per fretum febris,° by these straits to die, °through the 10
                                                          strait of fever

I joy that in these straits I see my West;
    For though their currents yield return to none,
What shall my West hurt me? As West and East
    In all flat maps (and I am one) are one,
    So death doth touch the resurrection. 15

Is the Pacific Sea my home? Or are
    The Eastern riches? Is Jerusalem?
Anyan,° and Magellan, and Gibraltar, °*the Bering Strait*
    All straits, and none but straits, are ways to them,
    Whether where Japhet dwelt, or Cham, or Shem. 20

We think that Paradise and Calvary,
    Christ's cross, and Adam's tree, stood in one place;
Look, Lord, and find both Adams met in me;
    As the first Adam's sweat surrounds my face,
    May the last Adam's blood my soul embrace. 25

So, in his purple wrapped, receive me, Lord;
    By these his thorns give me his other crown;
And, as to others' souls I preached Thy word,
    Be this my text, my sermon to mine own:
    Therefore that he may raise the Lord throws down. 30

John Donne (1572–1631)

THE SICK ROSE

O Rose, thou art sick!
The invisible worm
That flies in the night,
In the howling storm,

Has found out thy bed   5
Of crimson joy
And his dark secret love
Does thy life destroy.

William Blake
(1757–1827)

9

FORMAL PATTERNS

SPRING AND FALL:
to a young child

Márgarét, are you gríeving
Over Goldengrove unleaving?
Leáves, líke the things of man, you
With your fresh thoughts care for, can you?
Áh! ás the heart grows older   5
It will come to such sights colder
By and by, nor spare a sigh
Though worlds of wanwood leafmeal lie;
And yet you wíll weep and know why.
Now no matter, child, the name: 10
Sórrow's spríngs áre the same.
Nor mouth had, no nor mind, expressed
What heart heard of, ghost guessed:
It ís the blight man was born for,
It is Margaret you mourn for.   15

Gerard Manley Hopkins (1844–1889)

Throughout this chapter, we will be studying a concept that was discussed briefly at the beginning of the third chapter: **formal patterns,** *the kinds of organization that are based on the physical properties of words— especially their appeal to sight and hearing—rather than on their meaning.* The main kinds of formal patterns are sound patterns, metrics, and verse forms. Of all the elements of poetry, these are the most difficult for most readers, largely because the critical vocabulary that describes them still employs terms reflecting its Greek and Latin origin. Nonetheless, it is worthwhile to look more closely at these patterns, for in many poems they are as essential to the poet's communication of ideas and emotions as the thematic structures discussed in Chapter 3 or the modes of poetic language investigated in other sections. As we become more aware of these formal structures and their relationships to other elements of a poem, we may find that they are not as mystifying as they first seem.

SOUND PATTERNS

Let's begin with sound effects, using as an example Gerard Manley Hopkins's "Spring and Fall: to a young child." This poem admirably illustrates

209

Hopkins's general observation that his "verse becomes all right" when "read . . . with the ears, as I always wish to be read."[1] Without thinking, as yet, about the meaning of the words, read the poem to yourself or, better still, read it aloud, pronouncing the words accurately. What recurrent consonent sounds do you hear? Which vowel sounds are repeated? Do these patterned repetitions extend from word to word? Line to line? In which words is an initial vowel or consonant sound repeated internally? What is the cumulative effect of these sounds? Do they slow the tempo or increase it? Do they instill a sense of calm or agitation? Is the tone they help create joyous or melancholy?

One of the sonic devices that Hopkins uses repeatedly in this poem is **consonance,** *which may be defined loosely as any kind of consonant repetition, regardless of whether the corresponding sounds occur in stressed or unstressed syllables, at the beginnings of words or within them.* A more restrictive definition would be *the exact or close repetition of consonant sounds before and/or after different vowel sounds.* The words "ghost guessed" in line 13, for example, satisfy both definitions. Note that the determinant of sound correspondence is pronunciation, not spelling. In this example, *gh* and *g* as well as the final *st* and *sed* are identical in pronunciation, though obviously different in spelling.

When the sound correspondence involves initial consonants in stressed syllables that are close to one another, the sonic pattern is called **alliteration.** In line 14, for example, the *b* in "blight" alliterates with the *b* in "born," but for most readers these sounds would not alliterate with "By and by" in line 7 because the latter are too far removed for the ear—or the imagination—to connect. Other examples of alliteration can be found in almost every line. Usually such repetition involves the initial consonants of different words ("Sorrow's springs . . . same," "mouth . . . Mind"), but the alliterative pattern also includes the consonant sounds that occur in the internal stressed syllables of such compound words as "Goldengrove" and "wanwood."

Hopkins also makes extensive use of **assonance,** *the correspondence in sound of vowels that occur in stressed syllables of nearby words.* In line 2, for example, the *o* of "over" is repeated and amplified in the long vowel sounds of "Goldengrove"; the prolonged *e* sounds of leafmeal are duplicated in the following line in the word "weep"; and—to cite but one more example—the long *i* of "sights" is echoed in the words "By and by" and "sigh" of the following line. The vowel repetition of line 7 is also a form of **rhyme,** *the correspondence of the final stressed vowel and any following sounds in two or more nearby words that have different consonant sounds preceding the vowel.* When the corresponding sounds are exact, as they are throughout Hopkins's poem, the author is using **true rhyme** (e.g., "by"/

---

[1] Robert Bridges, ed., *Poems of Gerard Manley Hopkins,* 2nd ed. (London: Oxford University Press, 1930), p. 97.

"si_gh_," "n_a_me"/"s_a_me," etc.). When the sounds are similar rather than identical, the result is **slant rhyme, or off-rhyme** (e.g., b_ar_/st_air_, t_orn_/b_urn_, etc. .

In line 7, Hopkins employs **internal rhyme,** *which is usually created by the placement of one rhyming word within a line and another at the end of the line.* More common is **end rhyme,** *in which the rhyming words occur at the end of their respective lines* (e.g., "gr_íeving_"/"unl_eaving_," "_older_"/ "c_older_," "n_a_me"/"s_a_me," and so forth). Assigning a different lowercase letter to each sound, we can describe the rhyme scheme of "Spring and Fall" in this way: aabbccdddeeffgg. Except for one triple rhyme, in lines 7–9, Hopkins writes in paired rhymes, which—together with alliteration and assonance—slow the tempo of the poem, causing us to enunciate each syllable, to linger on certain words, and to ponder the relationships formed by interlinked vowel and consonant sounds.

The vowel/consonant blends in the opening line—"Márgarét, are you gríeving"—focus attention on the young child mentioned in the subtitle and on her present situation: it is autumn, and she is weeping, without knowing why, for the falling leaves and the dying year. The end rhyme of lines 1–2 seals with sound the relationship between the child's emotion and the natural phenomenon that elicits it. A note of sadness can be heard in "Goldengrove" as well, but there is an aura, too, of enchantment, evoked by the clear, mellow vowel sounds and the liquid *l*'s that associate this word with "unl_ea_ving," "l_ea_ves," and "l_i_ke." These sounds are the perfect complement to the visual image of golden-leaved trees and the poignance of a child's grief.

In the next two lines, the complex sentence structure and inverted syntax break the spell for a moment, forcing an intellectual response to the speaker's rhetorical questions, which we might paraphrase in this way: Can you, in your youthful innocence, care as much for the falling leaves as for the things of humankind? Here, too, sound underscores meaning, especially at the beginning of line 3, where the alliteration of the first two words emphasizes an analogy between change in nature and change in the individual, an analogy that is further developed in the remaining lines. Before Margaret can perceive that truth, however, she must cross the boundary between childhood and adulthood: "Áh! ás the heart grows older / It will come to such sights colder." Linked by assonance, as well as by their adjacent position in the line, the words "gr_o_ws _o_lder" remind us of the inevitability of change, while the connection between the rhyming words "_older_" and "c_older_" simultaneously makes us think about the inevitable consequence of such change—the loss of compassion that makes the adult unresponsive even to the decay of countless forests—and the more chilling reminders of death.

In the next line, *w* and *l* alliteration, accompanied by prolonged vowel sounds, creates an auditory as well as a visual image of vast desolation in nature, which parallels—both in sound and meaning—the child's sorrow.

Before the sounds of "worlds of wanwood" and "leafmeal lie" have died out, we hear the emphatic "will weep" and the pivotal phrase "know why." This last repetition of the triple rhyme brings to mind the previous allusions to early innocence and points to the realization that Margaret will ultimately achieve: that whatever name one gives to sorrow, its "springs" (sources, cycles) are always the same; that birth is a blight because every living thing must die; that "It is Margaret you mourn for." The parallel structure of the final two lines, the repetition of words, the build-up of sonorous *or* and *ar* sounds all bring the poem to a close on the same note of sadness with which it began. Yet, in spite of this prevailing tone, the cumulative effect of Hopkins's language is **euphony**, *a smooth, melodic blend of harmonious sounds*. The opposite effect is known as **cacophony**, which is produced by *harsh, strident, discordant sounds*. To distinguish between the two, compare the language of "Spring and Fall" with such words as "guttering," "choking," and "gargling" in Wilfred Owen's "Dulce Et Decorum Est," in Chapter 6.

We can hear the mournful, dirgelike melody of "Spring and Fall" without analyzing Hopkins's patterned uses of sound, and we can feel its power without understanding exactly how he weaves this spell. But a knowledge of alliteration, assonance, and rhyme does help us to perceive the meaning behind the poet's words and to appreciate one of the many dimensions of his artistry.

For additional practice, read the short excerpts below and do the following:

1. Read the passages aloud so that you hear the sounds that the poet has sought to reproduce.
2. Determine which of the aural patterns discussed in this chapter is being used.
3. Decide whether the poet is using **euphony** or **cacophony**, and be able to justify why you think so.
4. Explain what tonal effect these sounds help to establish.
5. Read the poem from which each excerpt is drawn (all are included in earlier chapters), and explain the sonic and thematic connections between the part and the whole.

> I found a dimpled spider fat and white,
> On a white heal-all, holding up a moth
> Like a white piece of rigid satin cloth—
> Assorted characters of death and blight
> Mixed ready to begin the morning right. . . ."
> *from Robert Frost's "Design"*
> *(Chapter 4)*

The winter evening settles down
With smell of steaks in passageways.
Six o'clock.
The burnt-out ends of smoky days.
from T. S. Eliot's "Preludes"
(Chapter 6)

Nothing beside remains. Round the decay
Of that colossal wreck, boundless and bare
The lone and level sands stretch far away.
from Percy Bysshe Shelley's "Ozymandias"
(Chapter 5)

Born in Alabama.
Bred in Illinois.
He was nothing but a
Plain black boy.

Swing low swing low sweet sweet chariot.
Nothing but a plain black boy.
Gwendolyn Brooks' "Of De Witt Williams
on his way to Lincoln Cemetery"
(Chapter 4)

METRICS

Aided by a knowledge of sound patterns and by the other critical skills we have been developing in earlier chapters, we should now be able to tackle a more complicated aspect of formal structure, illustrated by William Butler Yeats's "The Song of Wandering Aengus":

THE SONG OF WANDERING AENGUS

I went out to the hazel wood,
Because a fire was in my head,
And cut and peeled a hazel wand,
And hooked a berry to a thread;
And when white moths were on the wing, 5
And moth-like stars were flickering out,
I dropped the berry in a stream
And caught a little silver trout.

When I had laid it on the floor
I went to blow the fire aflame, 10
But something rustled on the floor,
And some one called me by my name:
It had become a glimmering girl
With apple blossom in her hair

Who called me by my name and ran 15
And faded through the brightening air.

Though I am old with wandering
Through hollow lands and hilly lands,
I will find out where she has gone,
And kiss her lips and take her hands; 20
And walk among long dappled grass,
And pluck till time and times are done
The silver apples of the moon,
The golden apples of the sun.

William Butler Yeats (1865–1939)

The language of Yeats' poem is in one sense like that of ordinary speech and written prose, for in both we hear varying emphases, created by a pattern of stressed and unstressed syllables. To illustrate, let's begin with two simple examples: the name Abraham Lincoln and the familiar expression "rise and shine." If we use an accent mark (ˊ) to indicate the **stressed syllables** (*the speech units receiving emphasis*) and a slur (˘) to indicate the **unstressed syllables,** we can make a visual representation of the rhythmical pattern in the segments of speech:

Ábrăhăm Líncŏln

Ríse ănd shíne

We sometimes distinguish between the noun and verb forms of a word by a shift in stress: we accent the noun form on the first syllable (récŏrd, súspĕct), the verb form on the second (rĕcórd, sŭspéct). We also create different meanings in the same sentence by emphasizing different words. If we say, "I ám driving to school," we defy opposition; if we say, "I am drivíng to school," we emphasize the mode of transportation.

Although normal speech employs rhythm, it employs it very loosely, with only the normal pronunciation of words or the need to emphasize a particular word determining the placement of stress. The first sentence of the Gettysburg Address, for example, sounds something like this:

Fóurscóre ănd sévĕn yéars ăgŏ oŭr fáthĕrs bróught fórth ŏn thís cóntĭnĕnt ă néw nátiŏn, cŏncéived ĭn líbĕrty, ănd dédĭcătĕd tŏ the própŏsĭtiŏn thăt áll mén ăre créatĕd équăl.

Because stress is relative (sectional differences in pronunciation and differing intentions produce slightly different patterns), these markings are only generally meaningful; but they illustrate the free rhythm inherent in normal speech, prose, and even some poetry. Since poetry is a self-conscious use of language, however, it often employs rhythms in a more strictly patterned fashion than prose. Line 3 of "The Song of Wandering Aengus," for example, would fall in a pattern like this:

                    Aňd cút aňd péeled ă házĕl wánd . . .

Rather than merely following the loose rhythms of speech, the poet has obviously chosen and arranged his words to create a strict pattern of unstressed syllable followed by stressed syllable throughout the line, a much more orderly rhythm than that of normal speech. *The strict repetitive pattern of rhythm* found in some poetry is called **meter**. Meter is a kind of formal structure employed by some poets in all ages but most strictly adhered to in eras that emphasize order and decorum—for example, the eighteenth century in England. In our age poets are free to use or not to use strict meter, depending on their intention, their material, and their particular style. Strictly metered poetry creates an effect that is different from that of poetry with a looser rhythm. The closer the poem to song, the more likely it is to have meter. Since Yeats's poem is a song, it is likely to follow a regular pattern, which we can discern by marking the syllables. In line 3, marked above, the unstress/stress pattern (˘ ´) is repeated throughout the line. We have thus isolated *the basic metrical unit, or* **foot,** in the line, the smallest combination of a stressed syllable with one or more unstressed syllables. Next we need to determine the kind of foot we are dealing with.

English poetry, showing its classical heritage, uses four kinds of feet as the bases of meter:

Basic Feet	Stress Pattern	Example
1. **iambic foot** (n. *iamb*)	˘ ´	ă Fláme
2. **trochaic foot** (n. *trochee*)	´ ˘	sómethĭng
3. **anapestic foot** (n. *anapest*)	˘ ˘ ´	ŭndĕrnéath
4. **dactylic foot** (n. *dactyl*)	´ ˘ ˘	flíckĕrĭng

Any regularly metered poem in English will have one of these as its *basic foot* and is labeled by that foot.[1] Several substitute feet can also appear in poetry. The most frequently used are these:

---

[1] Regular meter in English poetry is based on both the placement of the accent and the number of syllables in a line. It is thus *accentual-syllabic*. Poems can be (and have been) written in which only the number of syllables per line is counted, without consideration of accent (*syllabic* meter), or in which only the number of accented syllables is counted, without consideration of the total number of syllables (*accentual* meter). A few poems have been written that, in imitation of Greek and Roman metrics, depend on the length of time required to pronounce the syllables rather than the number of either accents or syllables (*quantitative* meter). Since none of these is a major force in English metrics, they are not covered in this book. Likewise, discussion of the full number of possible substitute feet has been eliminated in favor of the three most often used. Except in rare instances, the beginning student of poetry need not be concerned with more than the feet discussed above. For a lucid and comprehensive study of meter, see Paul Fussell, Jr., *Poetic Meter and Poetic Form* (New York: Random House, 1979).

Substitute Feet	Stress Pattern	Example
5. **spondaic foot** (n. *spondee*)	́ ́	hóld tíght
6. **pyrrhic foot** (n. *pyrrhic*)	̆ ̆	ŏf ă

Substitute feet never occur as basic feet (i.e., no poem is written in spondaic meter) but are used to prevent a singsong monotony, to alter the tone of voice in the poem, to interrupt a thought, or to throw emphasis on the meaning of important words by breaking away from the expected rhythm. Sometimes poets will add an extra syllable to the beginning or end of a line, thus creating a *monosyllabic foot;* at other times they may cut off a syllable. In either case, we define the line by the prevailing pattern in the other lines.

It is obvious that the unstress/stress pattern repeated in line three of Yeats' poem is the iambic foot. Using a slant bar (/) to divide the line into feet (with no regard to word division), we find no substitute feet here at all. It is a thoroughly iambic line.

Ănd cút/ănd péeled/ă ház/ĕl wánd

In so marking, we also discover that the line consists of *four* iambic feet, and we need a label to describe the number of feet. The terms indicating the number of feet per line are these:

monometer	(one foot)	**pentameter**	(five feet)
dimeter	(two feet)	**hexameter**	(six feet)
trimeter	(three feet)	**heptameter**	(seven feet)
tetrameter	(four feet)	**octameter**	(eight feet)

Now we can label line 3 by the kind of foot that predominates and the total number of feet in the line: *iambic tetrameter.* We will discover this meter quite frequently in reading poetry. Even more frequently used is *iambic pentameter,* the most common meter in English. The iambic foot seems the most natural one for normal English speech rhythms, and pentameter seems to provide the most comfortable line length. Very few poems have lines that consistently run less than three feet or more than six.

Having described line 3, we can now determine if our description is typical of the poem as a whole. Mark the syllables in lines 9–12. What stress pattern is followed in each line? Are there any substitute feet? We should not expect every line to be so completely regular, for variation from the norm is pleasant. But since our poem is a song, we might expect it to be more regular than the usual poem. If we mark the first four lines of stanza 2, trying not to be arbitrary but remembering the basic iambic tetrameter pattern, we find a few possible substitute feet but the same basic meter:

> Whĕn Í/hăd láid/ĭt ŏn/the flóor
>
> Ĭ wént/tŏ blów/the fíre/ăfláme,
>
> Bŭt sóme/thĭng rús/tlĕd ŏn/the flóor,
>
> Ănd sóme/ŏne cálled/mĕ bў/mў náme.

The first foot in line 9, like the first feet in several other lines, could have been marked as a trochee (′ ˘). But line 10 is perfectly regular, and the pyrrhic feet in the other lines could have been marked as iambic. Marking the rest of the lines in stanza 2 would confirm our assumption about the meter. Without marking the rest of the poem, we can be confident that "The Song of Wandering Aengus" is written in eight-line stanzas of iambic tetrameter. We might add that lines 2 and 4 and lines 6 and 8 of each stanza rhyme.

What we have done is to scan the poem. **Scansion** is *the act of analyzing meter,* by marking the syllables, dividing the lines into feet, and noting the pattern of the lines (including rhyme, if any) within the stanzas. A few suggestions about scansion might be helpful. To determine the meter of a poem:

1. Choose a group of lines (or a stanza) from the middle of the poem. Lines at the beginning of a poem tend to be the least regular; for scansion you need lines representative of the whole poem.
2. Mark *stressed* syllables first. Normally they are the syllables given prominence in normal speech (e.g., sómethĭng) and monosyllabic words important to the meaning of the sentence (most often nouns and verbs; sometimes adjectives and adverbs).
3. Mark the other syllables as *unstressed,* usually including such non-content words as articles, prepositions, and pronouns (e.g., *a, the, of, to, and, my, to the, of the*).
4. See which of the four basic feet predominates and divide the lines using vertical bars so as to preserve as many of those basic feet as possible, without being overly mechanical. Some words may be capable of being pronounced more than one way (e.g., wónděrĭng or wónderĭng). The predominant rhythm pattern will determine the way such words should be pronounced. Divide the lines by *stress patterns,* not by words.
5. Notice the *substitute feet* and decide why they are used as they are. Do not be alarmed by shortened feet or an occasional added syllable or monosyllabic foot in a line. You are concerned with the *predominant* meter.

6. Count the total *number* of feet in each line.
7. Determine if each line in the stanza follows the basic meter. If line lengths differ, decide if a pattern emerges.
8. Check for a *rhyme* scheme, for example, ababcdcdefefgg.
9. Describe the *meter* of the poem.
10. Remember that even though the scansion of a poem may seem like a great task achieved, it is a preliminary act only. The real purpose of scanning is to help open up the poem so that its structural subtleties can be appreciated. To the modern sensibility, the mechanical meter is often less pleasurable than the meaningful variation from the meter.

The following lines will enable you to test your skills at scanning for meter. Describe the examples giving the kind of foot that predominates and the total number of feet in the line. Note any substitute feet that vary from the overall meter.

1. Give pearls away and rubies
   But keep your fancy free.

2. Half owre, half owre to Aberdour,
     It's fiftie fadom deip:
   And thair lies guid Sir Patrick Spence,
     Wi' the Scots lords at his feit.

3. Where the Youth pined away with desire,
   And the pale Virgin shrouded in snow,
   Arise from their graves and aspire
   Where my Sun-flower wishes to go.

4. . . . Till he became
        Most poor:
        With thee
     O let me rise . . . .

5. This is the forest primeval; but where are the hearts
       that beneath it
   Leaped like a roe, when he hears in the woodland the
       voice of the huntsman?

6. Piping down the valleys wild,
   Piping songs of pleasant glee,
   On a cloud I saw a child. . . .

Now that you have some experience in scanning lines that have a strict, identifiable meter, read the next poem and determine whether it conforms to any of the patterns already discussed.

THE FARING

Once over water, to you borne brightly,
Wind off the North Sea cold but
Heat-streaked with summer and honed by the dazzle
Of sun, and the Channel boat banging
The chop like a shire-horse on cobbles—thus I, 5
Riding the spume-flash, by gull cries ringed,
Came.

Came, and the harbor slid smooth like an oil-slick.
It was the gray city, but the gray roof-slates
Sang blue in the sun, and the sea-cliffs, 10
Eastward, swung in that blue wind. I came thus,
And I, unseen, saw. Saw
You,

And you, at the pier edge, face lifting seaward
And toward that abstract of distance that I 15
Yet was and felt myself to be, stood. Wind
Tugged your hair. It tangled that brightness. Over
Your breast wind tautened the blue cloth, your skirt
Whipped, your bare legs were brown. Steel
Rang on steel. Shouts 20
Rose in that language.
Later,

The quiet place. Roses. Yellow. We came there, wind
Down now, sea slopping the rocks, slow, sun low and
Sea graying, but roses were yellow, climbing 25
The wall, it was stone. The last light
Came gilding a track across the gray water from westward.
It came leveling in to finger the roses. One
Petal, yellow, fell, slow.

At the foot of the gray stone, like light, it lay. 30
High beyond roses, a gull, in the last light, hung.

The sea kept slopping the rocks, slow.

Robert Penn Warren (b. 1905)

Unlike Yeats's poem, which tells the story of a mysterious man in search of a woman whom he himself creates but cannot obtain until some illusory future world, "The Faring" captures the events of a rendezvous between a real man and a real woman and the attainment of their desires. But this reality—in which time seems to stop for the voyager and his love, even though "the sea keeps slopping the rocks"—is described with the same brilliance as the visionary quest of the Wandering Aengus.

Even at first glance we notice that the formal aspects of the two poems are as different as the tones. Yeats' "Song" looks orderly on the page: its line lengths and evenly divided stanzas create a sense of control and discipline. The line lengths and stanza divisions in Warren's poem, on the other hand, give the impression that the poem pays no heed to conventional form. To be certain this impression is valid, we need to try to scan the poem. Let us choose lines 8–13 from the middle of the poem. Can they be scanned? Is a predominant rhythm pattern established? How many feet are in each line? Do the lines rhyme? What conclusions can you draw from these lines? Check over the poem as a whole. Does this analysis bear out your conclusions? Describe the rhythm and versification of the poem.

Lines 8–13 might be marked thus:

> Cáme, aňd the hárbŏr slíd smóoth līke aň oíl-slick.
>
> It wăs the gráy cítў, bŭt the gráy roóf-slates
>
> Sáng blúe iň the sún, aňd the séa-cliffs,
>
> Eástwărd, swúng iň thăt blúe wind. Í cáme thús,
>
> Aňd Í, uňseén, sáw. Sáw
>
> Yóu. . . .

In marking the stress patterns of these lines we must allow ample room for individual differences. One person may not read the lines the same way twice. Certainly "came," the first syllable in "harbor," "smooth," and "oil" would be stressed, whereas "and," "the," the second syllable in "harbor," "like," and "an" wouldn't be. Whether "slid" and "slick" are stressed or not is an individual matter. The alliteration and assonance involved might encourage us to emphasize them. The opening words in line 9, "it was the," might be marked any of three ways: (˘ ˘ ˘), (ˊ ˘ ˘), (˘ ˊ ˘). If line 8 were marked in one particular way, we might see a pattern in it:

> Cáme, aňd the hárbŏr slíd smóoth līke aň oíl-slick.

We could call this a dactylic tetrameter line (with a substituted final trochee). But since none of the other lines in the stanza can be so scanned (only line 3 of the poem could possibly fit this pattern), we should be hesitant to label it. The fact that the number of stressed syllables and feet varies widely from line to line (from one stress in line 13 up to possibly seven in line 11) should indicate to us that the poem is not tetrameter as a whole. Lines 12–13, which contain no dactylic feet, indicate that the poem as a whole is not dactylic. We seem to be back where we started. But we can make some assumptions based on our analysis of stanza 2: that the poem cannot be scanned in the usual way because it is not in conventional meter; that line lengths vary greatly; that there is no end-rhyme; that no one basic foot predominates even though frequent use is made of a triple foot (two unstressed syllables with one stressed); that this foot seems sometimes to be anapestic and at others dactylic; and that the stanza is heavily stressed throughout.

If we marked every line, we could verify our assumptions because the poem—which seems on first glance more like the prose of the Gettysburg Address than like the strict meter of Yeats' poem—follows the rhythm of natural speech more than the meter of conventional poetry. Whereas Yeats achieved his effect by fitting his details into a ready-made case, Warren achieves his by seemingly springing open the case, or else by creating a unique enclosure for this particular poem. It is written in *a form that does not obey the rules of conventional meter concerning regular rhythm pattern and line length;* consequently, it must be called (for lack of a better term) **free verse.**

And yet it is far from free, in the sense of undisciplined or unprincipled. Like all good free verse poets, Warren sets up his own principles and abides by them faithfully. The problem for the artist is to decide what kind of principles to set up in place of conventional meters. We would not be exaggerating if we said that even though Warren's poem lacks strict meter and rhyme it is just as finely wrought as Yeats' poem and that the formal structures Warren uses more than compensate for those he lays aside.

For example, the triple foot (whether anapestic or dactylic) is used in juxtaposition with the spondaic measures. The doubled unstressed syllable with stress on either side (/ ⏑ ⏑ / ⏑ ⏑ /) creates a wavelike rhythm appropriate to the choppy tide of the English Channel, over which the boat is crossing. The rhythm of this triple foot is sometimes called "galloping measure," because it resembles the three-beat gait of horses in gallop. Perhaps not coincidentally, the rhythm of the boat "bánging / The chóp like ă shĭrehórse ŏn cóbblĕs" made the poet conscious of the simile of the galloping horse and the metaphor of the speaker "Rídiňg thĕ spúme-flásh" like some kind of ancient mythical god riding the waves, with a garland of gulls about his head. In counterpoint to the speed of the wave rhythm are the solid staccato stresses, which seem to concentrate around references to the lovers as they come in focus:

                                              thus I

   . . . bў gúll crĭes rĭnged, cáme.

  Cáme. . . .

  . . . .

                                      Í cáme thús,

  Aňd Í, uňseén, sáw. Sáw

  Yóu,

  Aňd yóu. . . .

If we can shift our analogy from music to painting, Robert Penn Warren seems to paint the background in the triple measure and the foreground figures in the bold strokes of stressed syllables—grouping up to five stresses together at points in the poem.

He seems also to have set off the human figures syntactically. When they are in focus, the phrases are shorter and the subjects and verbs of the sentences are closer together. Perhaps the distance of several lines between subject and verb (e.g., lines 5–7, 14–16) reflects the "abstract of distance" between them before they are together. In addition, Warren makes important use of *the breath-pause within a line, made necessary by punctuation, word meaning, or syntax,* a device called a **caesura.** Though at least one caesura can be found in practically every line, the device is used in clusters when the focus shifts from the waves to the slower activities of the lovers. We can mark these breaks in the lines by double lines (||):

And I, || unseen, || saw. || Saw
You
. . . .
The quiet place. || Roses. || Yellow. || We came there . . .
. . . .
          One
Petal, || yellow, || fell, || slow.

The poem's progression from rapid to slow is supported by both the imagery and the sound patterns. The first stanza—riding the waves—is full of bright actions, images, and banging sounds (*b, k, ch* sounds). In stanza 2, as the water smooths out near the harbor, the sounds become long and liquid:

and the harbor slid smooth like an oil-slick.
. . . .
swung in that blue wind

As excitement rises at the sight of his lover, the third stanza becomes crowded with startling verbs and nervous sounds: the wind tugs, tangles, tautens, and whips. Steel rings. Shouts rise. But, in the quiet place, both the images (roses, the last light, the gull) and the sounds (*h, l, o*) are quiet and slow.

Although the number of lines in the stanzas varies from one to nine and each stanza is a unit set off by itself, each section of the poem is linked to the stanza adjacent to it. The verb "came," which ends the first section, is repeated at the beginning of the second; "you," which occurs in line 14 and is repeated in line 15, serves as a bridge between stanza 2 and stanza 3; the adverb "later," which closes stanza 3, provides a transition to the next stanza and slows the pace, preparing for a radical change in tone; and the last three stanzas are held together by the quiet setting and by images of roses, gull, and stones, as "The sea kept slopping the rocks, Slow."

As "The Faring" demonstrates, laying aside meter does not necessarily mean letting down standards. In the best free verse, it means replacing a set of conventional principles with a set unique to that poem.

VERSE FORMS

Our study of poetic conventions would be incomplete without some consideration of a third aspect of formal structure: *verse forms.* A verse form is *any structural unit—a* **stanza,** *(most basically, a group of lines set off typographically as a unit) a part of a stanza or poem, or a complete poem—that has been used repeatedly by a number of writers or is so closely associated with a particular poem that the two are synonymous.* Lewis Turco, in *The Book of Forms,* identifies 175 different traditional forms in Anglo-American poetry alone—far more than we have space to discuss. We can, however, learn to recognize the distinguishing characteristics of some of the most widely used forms by paying close attention to three things: meter, rhyme scheme, and number of lines.

We have already encountered several different verse forms in the first two poems of this chapter. The type that predominates in "Spring and Fall" is the **couplet:** *a two-line unit, in any meter,*[1] *usually set off by rhyme.* The only variation occurs in lines 7–9, where we find a **triplet,** *a three-line unit created by adding to a couplet a line with the same end rhyme.* As Hopkins' use of these forms suggests, the triplet is usually subordinate to some other pattern (most often the couplet) rather than a primary element of structure. Compare also Swift's use of the couplet/triplet combination in "A Description of a City Shower" in Part III. A more frequently used three-line form, which is usually set off as a stanza, is the **tercet,** *which has a variable meter and often follows a rhyme scheme of aba.*

The most prevalent verse form in English and American poetry is the **quatrain,** *a four-line structure in any meter, with or without rhyme.* Among the most popular types are the **ballad stanza,** which consists of *alternating iambic tetrameter and trimeter lines rhymed abcb,* and the abba and abab patterns which are prevalent in many types of poems, especially the sonnet.

Quatrains are often set off as stanzas, but just as frequently they are used in multiples of two or three to create longer stanzaic units. Yeats' "The Song of Wandering Aengus," for example, is written in three eight-line stanzas, each composed of two quatrains that follow the rhyme pattern of the ballad stanza, but with four tetrameter lines that harmonize with the regularity of the rhythm, the balance of the two-part stanzas, and the symmetry of the poem as a whole.

---

[1] In "Spring and Fall," Hopkins employs an accentual meter, the complexities of which are beyond our scope here. A more often used combination of meter and verse form is the **heroic couplet,** which consists of *two iambic pentameter lines rhymed aa.* This form was made famous by the eighteenth-century poet Alexander Pope, who used heroic couplets in such works as the satiric epic *The Dunciad* and his verse translations of Homer's *Iliad* and *Odyssey.*

In some poems, different verse forms, or multiples of the same form, combine to create a distinctive **poetic form,** or **genre.** The poem below illustrates one of the best known genres, the sonnet. As you read it, note the number of lines in the poem as a whole. Then try to identify all aspects of its formal structure. There are no stanza divisions to guide you, so you will need to observe closely the rhyme scheme as well as other indicators of internal divisions such as end punctuation, transitions, or shifts in ideas or images. When you have finished, scan a few lines to determine whether there is a regular meter.

SONNET 60: LIKE AS THE WAVES MAKE TOWARDS THE PEBBLED SHORE

Like as the waves make towards the pebbled shore,
So do our minutes hasten to their end;
Each changing place with that which goes before,
In sequent toil all forwards do contend.
Nativity, once in the main of light, 5
Crawls to maturity, wherewith being crown'd,
Crooked eclipses 'gainst his glory fight,
And Time that gave doth now his gift confound.
Time doth transfix the flourish set on youth
And delves the parallels in beauty's brow, 10
Feeds on the rarities of nature's truth,
And nothing stands but for his scythe to mow.
    And yet to times in hope my verse shall stand,
    Praising thy worth, despite his cruel hand.

William Shakespeare (1564–1616)

We can tell at a glance that the poem has fourteen lines, twelve written in an alternating rhyme pattern and the final two in couplet form. In some editions of Shakespeare's sonnets, the last lines are not indented, but even without the typographical notation, we would know from the difference in verse form that the last two lines are distinct from the first twelve. Now let's see if this longer section has any clearly discernible subdivisions. The rhyme scheme indicates three equal segments—abab cdcd efef—and the periods at the ends of lines 4, 8, and 12 further emphasize the three-quatrain internal structure. On the basis of our findings, we can describe two aspects of the formal structure of the poem:

a
b   First Quatrain
a
b

```
c
d           Second Quatrain
c
d

e
f           Third Quatrain
e
f

g           Couplet
g
```

Turning our attention now to the meter of the poem, let's choose a few lines at random—4, 8, and 13, for example—and scan them:

In séquĕnt tóil aĺl fórwaȓds dó cŏnténd (line 4)

Aňd Tíme thăt gav́e dŏth nów hiš gíft cŏnfóund (line 8)

Aňd yét tŏ tiḿes iň hópe mẙ vérse shăll stánd (line 13)

In each of these lines, Shakespeare uses an extremely regular iambic pentameter meter. And if we scanned the other lines, we would find the same basic pattern, varied only by the trochaic substitutions that occur in the first foot of several lines ("Líke aš," "Cráwls tŏ," "Cróokĕd," etc).

What we have just described are the conventions of the **English, or Shakespearean, sonnet:** *a fourteen-line, iambic pentameter poem divided into three quatrains and one couplet, with a rhyme scheme of abab cdcd efef gg.* Adding two other terms to our critical vocabulary—the ***octave,*** *an eight-line form,* and the ***sestet,*** *a six-line unit*—we can also define a second major sonnet type, the **Petrarchan,** or **Italian, sonnet,** *which consists of fourteen iambic pentameter lines divided into an octave rhymed abba abba and a sestet rhymed cdcdcd or cdcdee.*

The Shakespearean and Petrarchan forms of the sonnet differ not only in rhyme but also in the degree of imbalance between the two sections. In the former, the imbalance is extreme (12 lines/ 2 lines); in the latter, the second part is only two lines shorter than the first. This structural principle also determines the position of the ***turn:*** *the shift in tone, theme, or imagery that marks the separation between burden and release, question and answer, problem and solution, etc.* In the Petrarchan sonnet, the turn comes at the beginning of the sestet. In the Shakespearean, it is usually delayed until the first line of the couplet.

As you encounter all these terms and definitions, you may question whether they are really important enough to justify the time and effort required to learn them. This is a valid concern, and it deserves further exploration.

Conventions can be limiting and deadening if they serve merely as an artificial framework on which to hang words and ideas. In the hands of a skilled poet, however, the apparent limitations of fixed forms become a means of artistic control and a source of emotional and intellectual power. Let's return to Shakespeare's sonnet and see how a genuine master of poetic forms makes these technical elements organic to the poem.

"Like as the Waves Make Towards the Pebbled Shore" illustrates admirably what Paul Fussell means when he says in *Poetic Meter and Poetic Form* that "the poet who understands the sonnet form is the one who has developed an instinct for exploiting the principle of imbalance."[1] In the first twelve lines, Shakespeare builds a seemingly irrefutable argument about the brevity of human life and the all-consuming power of time; in the final two lines, he surprises us with a new and apparently contradictory assertion. How does he exploit this structural imbalance? A close reading of the language and ideas of each section should give us some answers.

The quatrains that compose the first twelve lines are distinctive in imagery, but closely related in tone and theme. The first quatrain introduces the mutability theme through an extended simile likening the minutes in which existence is measured to "the waves that make towards the pebbled shore." The completion of the rhyme pattern in line 4, together with the period at the end of this line, brings the section to an emphatic close. At the same time, the final rhyming word, "contend," anticipates the conflict that is dramatized in the second quatrain through personified abstractions and images of light and darkness. "Nativity" struggles toward maturity, only to have this "crown" of youth removed by time; the "main of light" associated with youth is "eclipsed" by age and death. Again, the final rhyme-word ("confound") not only completes the thought of its own quatrain but also leaves us with a sense of unresolved tension that extends into the next section. Here, also, time is personified, but the impersonal power of the first quatrain and the perverse giver and taker of gifts portrayed in the second quatrain have been replaced by a menacing figure who pierces, cuts, feeds upon, and ultimately destroys beauty and life.

The momentum of these twelve lines carries over into the first word of the couplet—"And"—which suggests that the argument of the preceding quatrains will be continued in the final two lines. But the next word, "yet," signals the true turn, which in this poem marks a shift in tone from pessimism to a qualified optimism and a shift in theme from a concept of time as an unconquerable foe to a faith in the immortalizing power of poetry.

Despite its brevity, the couplet expresses its own truth, which is convincing for several reasons. The contrast between the first twelve lines and the last two is not as radical as it may first appear, because Shakespeare subtly foreshadows the turn and counterargument with such words as "contend" and "fight." Moreover, the triumph over time is presented as only a limited victory. For even though the verse of great poets may outlive them, it cannot

---

[1] Fussell, p. 115.

change the fact of human mortality. Finally, both the syntactic structure of the couplet and its rhyme force the two contrasting ideas into the same logical unit:

> . . . my verse shall stand
> . . . despite his cruel hand.

The metrical regularity of these parallel phrases links them even more closely with one another, as well as to the preceding twelve lines. The trochaic substitutions mentioned earlier also serve an important function because the surprise of the metrical variation gives added emphasis to significant words and relationships. The usually unemphatic connective "like" becomes important in line 1 because it introduces the simile on which the first quatrain is structured. In the second quatrain, the emphasis given to "crawls" in line 6 and "crooked" in line 7 stresses the importance of human struggle and the perversity of time (notice, too, the way in which alliteration links the two words and their connotations). And the strong stress of the first syllable of "Praising" in line 14 strikes the note of tribute and triumph on which the poem ends.

As this poem demonstrates, the real value of conventions is that they force the poet to discipline and condense thoughts, to choose words and create images that are precise and rich in connotation, and to harmonize rhyme, meter, and verse forms with meaning. These are challenges that have also intrigued many contemporary poets, among them Theodore Roethke. The form that he uses in the poem below is the *villanelle,* which is as complex and rigidly structured in its own way as the sonnet.

THE WAKING

I wake to sleep, and take my waking slow.
I feel my fate in what I cannot fear.
I learn by going where I have to go.

We think by feeling. What is there to know?
I hear my being dance from ear to ear.   5
I wake to sleep, and take my waking slow.

Of those so close beside me, which are you?
God bless the Ground! I shall walk softly there,
And learn by going where I have to go.

Light takes the Tree; but who can tell us how?   10
The lowly worm climbs up a winding stair;
I wake to sleep, and take my waking slow.

Great Nature has another thing to do
To you and me; so take the lively air,
And, lovely, learn by going where to go.   15

> This shaking keeps me steady. I should know.
> What falls away is always. And is near.
> I wake to sleep, and take my waking slow.
> I learn by going where I have to go.
>
> *Theodore Roethke* (1907–1963)

You can define the distinctive features of this poetic form by answering the following questions: How many stanzas are there? How many contain three lines and how many contain four? What is the rhyme scheme? Does each stanza have a different set of rhyming sounds, or do the rhymes overlap? Finally, what is the meter?

Originally popular in France in the sixteenth century, the villanelle has five tercets and a quatrain and only two rhymes throughout. The first line of the poem becomes the last line of the second and fourth tercet; the final line of the first tercet becomes the last line of the third and fifth tercet. These two lines function as a refrain and are repeated at the closure. With so much repetition and rhyme, the villanelle would appear villainously impossible for most poets, bringing them perilously close to a singsong, artificial sound.

Poets like Theodore Roethke and Dylan Thomas, however, have been unusually successful with this demanding medium. With its many repetitions, the form allowed Thomas to passionately implore his dying father, "Do Not Go Gentle Into That Good Night"—with rage, anger, love, and remorse achieving a kind of emotional crescendo in the last lines of the poem.

Now that we have identified the form of "The Waking," let's explore some of the ways in which the villanelle contributes to the development of Roethke's theme. What is the effect of the slow, regular rhythm? What purpose do the strong pauses at the ends of lines have? Describe the state of mind revealed by the paradox of line 1 and the mention of "fate" and "fear" in line 2. How does the first line of the second tercet reinforce and further describe the state of mind? How do you interpret this line?

Like Thomas, Roethke makes an ally of a potential enemy—frequent repetition. In a poem that, as the title suggests, celebrates a certain kind of awareness—awareness of human participation in the process of change, disintegration, and certain death—the repetitions and variations of the villanelle are excellently well suited to the content. The poem charts progress through life; its repetitions and rhythms imitate the labored cycles of the speaker's life and days. The regular meter and **end-stopped lines**—*lines that end with a strong pause or stress, usually marked by end punctuation, by the completion of the syntactic or logical pattern, or by other means*—create a sense of daily recurrence, of deliberate, step-by-step, forward movement. Each line represents a completed stage of the journey, this learning process of life.

Knowledge is not comprehensive, but piecemeal. As it emerges in the first paradoxical description, Roethke's ideal of awareness—an awareness that is further elaborated—is one of calm, joyful acceptance of our place in the scheme of "Great Nature." Roethke is not an ironist, and there is no bitterness in this line; he means the praise he speaks. The central dramatized opposition in the poem is between reason and intuition—an age-old conflict but an especially Romantic conflict, in which reason is seen as an enemy of understanding. In this respect and others, Roethke extends the themes of the Romantics Keats and Wordsworth into the twentieth century. Roethke places his faith in the power of intuition and emotion to discern purpose and permanence behind apparent purposelessness and transience. His skeptical view of reason, announced in the first line of the second tercet ("We think by feeling. What is there to know?"), is repeated with variation in the first line of the fourth tercet: "Light takes the Tree; but who can tell us how?"

One critic has said that "The Waking" is "a world in process about a world in process."[1] Can you explain what he means? What is Roethke suggesting in line 2 of the fourth tercet? How is this line related to lines 1 and 2 of the fifth tercet? Why does Roethke capitalize "Ground," "Tree," and "Great Nature"? Discuss lines 1 and 2 of the quatrain and their relation to the rest of the poem, especially the second line of the first tercet.

"The Waking" is informed with the idea of change and the process of change. In a world that continuously modifies its shape and external appearance before our eyes, Roethke seems to be saying, knowledge can only be tentative. The villanelle, then, with its changes, imitates the subject and theme of the poem. The worm is a token or emblem of change. Roethke identifies his speaker in the poem with one of the lowest forms of sensory awareness, the worm, which blindly "climbs up a winding stair." Here, as elsewhere throughout his poetry, Roethke uses the upward path to suggest an arduous, purifying journey of the spirit. The worm is also a reminder of death and the grave and the natural cycle in which we all participate, a reminder of the last part of the process described throughout the poem, especially in lines 1 and 2 of the fifth tercet: "Great Nature has another thing to do/To you and me. . . ." Since Roethke asserts the superiority of intuition over reason, it is appropriate that he compares himself to the blind worm, for both intuition and faith are often spoken of as "blind." Other lines also hint at the speaker's darkened journey: "Of those so close beside me, which are you?" Feeling, hearing, and smelling are the senses appealed to in this poem—surely one of Roethke's least visual poems and rightly so, for, here at least, appearances deceive.

"Ground," "Tree," and "Great Nature" are capitalized because they are important as abstractions: Roethke is interested in unchanging universals that are above or behind the flux of things and, as such, relate to his faith in the rightness of life's processes. The first two lines of the quatrain state

---

[1] Richard Blessing, *Theodore Roethke's Dynamic Vision* (Bloomington, Ind.: Indiana University Press, 1974), p. 223.

paradoxes that deal with the central theme of the poem: change. This is not the first time he uses paradox; in fact, the poem opens with a paradox—a device in keeping with Roethke's purposes. In a poem that emphasizes intuition over reason, the paradox is well suited to breaching the barriers of rational experience. Many of the parables of the New Testament present paradoxical experience and require an altogether different kind of understanding, namely faith.

But let's return to the first two lines of the quatrain: In a changing world of shifting shapes, motion *is* a kind of "steadiness," the only kind we know. The second line is also a paradox, celebrating the "always," the permanence of being behind the apparent changes of nature. The present is eternal, "always." Finally, then, we understand the basis of the speaker's strange faith, his sense of the rightness of this personal-impersonal cycle of growth, change, and disintegration, and why he "cannot fear," why he takes "his waking slow," why he takes so much pleasure in the "lively air."

Lawrence Ferlinghetti's "The Pennycandystore Beyond the El" illustrates a different kind of craftsmanship. After reading the poem carefully, compare its formal structures with those of the poems discussed earlier in the chapter. Which of them does "The Pennycandystore" most clearly resemble? Does Ferlinghetti display the kind of intellectual and artistic control that Shakespeare exercises in his sonnet or Roethke demonstrates in "The Waking"?

THE PENNYCANDYSTORE BEYOND THE EL

The pennycandystore beyond the El
is where I first
        fell in love
                with unreality
Jellybeans glowed in the semi-gloom   5
of that september afternoon
A cat upon the counter moved among
              the licorice sticks
     and tootsie rolls
  and Oh Boy Gum   10

Outside the leaves were falling as they died

A wind had blown away the sun

A girl ran in
Her hair was rainy
Her breasts were breathless in the little room   15

Outside the leaves were falling
        and they cried
             Too soon! too soon!

      Lawrence Ferlinghetti (b. 1919)

Unlike "The Song of Wandering Aengus" and "The Waking," "The Pennycandystore Beyond The El" is not cast in regular stanzaic form, but rather breaks unevenly into two parts separated by an isolated line. At first the lines give the appearance of being unmeasured, haphazard, like the free verse of Warren's poem. As we learned in studying that poem, such freedom is more apparent than real. T. S. Eliot, himself a practitioner of free verse, held that no verse was free for the poet who was interested in doing a good job and that rejection of rhyme did not necessarily mean ease and facility; in fact, it often put a greater strain on the language. This *seemingly unstructured but actually disciplined form is called* **open form**.

In order to determine some of the chief characteristics and uses of this kind of structure, see if you can answer these questions: In the absence of rhyme and meter, what alternatives are open to the poet? Why is the "pennycandystore" printed as one word? Is this type of printing functional or merely clever decoration? What is the effect of the steplike third and fourth lines, of lines 8, 9, and 10, and of the last two lines of the poem?

One technique available to the poet is **enjambment,** *the continuation of phrasing and meaning beyond the end of one line and into the next.* Unlike the end-stopped lines of "The Waking," the enjambed lines of Ferlinghetti's poem—together with the unorthodox typography, variant line lengths, and other devices—create stresses and pauses that either speed up or slow down the narrative flow and/or the way a reader proceeds through the poem (Warren uses all these methods in "The Faring"). "Pennycandystore" as one word has a childlike appeal; it has the carelessness and innocence of the poem's subject, a young boy teetering between the adult world and the world of childhood. By placing the word "El" (the name for an elevated railway) at the end of the first line, Ferlinghetti not only sets it in symbolic contrast to the childhood world of the "pennycandystore" but gives the latter more stress, more attention, and thus prepares for the speed of flight and escape in the next line with its two quick stresses: "is where I first . . . "

Throughout the poem, typography, such as the word "pennycandystore," and the steplike, falling lines that occur in three places have more than mere visual value (Warren uses this device in moderation). With beginning poets, such practice is often never more than artsy-craftsy decoration, typewriting rather than writing. But not with Ferlinghetti's poem, for beyond the visual value of these first falling lines—lines that prepare for a later visual and thematic echo—an enclosed atmosphere of slowness and silence is created and a sense of "unreality" as well. Ferlinghetti's manipulation of white space in lines 3 and 4 achieves several effects. First, the verse sentence is broken into elements and slowed, and the pauses are enforced both visually and aurally. Secondly, the elements "fell in love" and "with unreality" stand out and announce themselves as central themes and subjects. Lines 8, 9, and 10—backward-stepping lines—function in much the same way. They visually re-create the slow-motion hours of childhood and emphasize the longed-for and slowly savored candies, the magical and evocative names: "the licorice sticks/and tootsie rolls/and Oh Boy Gum." Finally, the segmented, descending line also makes it difficult for the reader to forget the cat slowly moving along the counter among these different candies. The line mimics the slow steps of the cat.

Consider the kinds of sound devices the poet uses in lines 5 through 10. Do the sounds reinforce the meaning of these lines? Why does Ferlinghetti isolate line 11? In terms of meter, how does the second half of the poem compare with the first half?

Lines 5, 6, and 7 offer the reader a succession of *o*-sounds, *l*-sounds, and *c*-sounds: "Jellybeans glowed," "semi-gloom," "afternoon," "moved among," "cat," "counter," "licorice sticks," "tootsie rolls," and "Oh Boy Gum." Thus the idea of "unreality" is made especially attractive by the poet's careful use of sound. Even "semi-gloom" has an appealing ring and seems to stand at odds with its usual connotation, for the boy is reluctant to leave his pleasant pennycandy Eden for the ambiguous and vaguely frightening world beyond the "little room."

Line 11 ("Outside the leaves were falling as they died") is isolated for several reasons. The slight narrative frame of a poem like "Pennycandystore" puts the burden of meaning on the images and their aura of suggestion. Isolated, the line insists on being noticed; the inevitable is made visual. This line parallels and is associated with something represented by the "El" —an intrusive and ambiguous reality. Line 11 also functions as a fulcrum on which the balance tips from the timelessness of childhood toward the speed of the adult world and the speaker's hesitant involvement with change, sex, and death.

In the second part of the poem, Ferlinghetti creates a sense of increased speed and urgency with four end-stopped lines. These lines are short, with no more than four stresses each. The effect is one of breathlessness. If the girl is out of breath from running, the boy is too in a sense; he is breathless with the new excitement of sex. Short lines reinforce the sense of urgency. Lines 13 and 14, for example, are little more than subject-verb statements; the words all monosyllabic but one. The girl with her "breathless breasts" and "rainy" hair has introduced a new element into the boy's life. He has not outgrown his taste for candy, but from now on he will be preoccupied with another kind of sweetness—the bittersweetness of sex, growth, change, and decay. The poem is a retrospective one, and Ferlinghetti laments that the loss of childhood happens "Too soon! too soon!"

In studying these technical aspects of poetry, we should always remember that a knowledge of versification is a means to an end, not an end in itself. The following suggestions may help you to learn not only to describe rhyme patterns and identify meters and verse forms but also to make the kinds of

FORMAL PATTERNS

judgments and distinctions that we have been discussing throughout this chapter:

1. As you read a poem for the first time, listen to the sounds of the words and the natural cadences of the lines. Then reread the poem, this time with an eye and ear for details.
2. If, during your reading, you were aware of vowel or consonant repetitions, underline or circle them to see if a pattern takes shape. You may find that sound correspondences serve to link key ideas, call attention to especially important words, or arouse pleasurable or repellent associations.
3. Referring back to the guidelines for scansion (p. 219) whenever necessary, determine whether the poem has meter or is written in free verse. If it is free verse, note the ways in which the poet compensates for the lack of fixed conventions: variations in line or stanza length, for example, or typographical devices like the avoidance of capital letters, omission of punctuation, and unusual patterning of lines, which in some poems run down the page or in zigzags rather than across. If the poem has meter, note the prevailing pattern and any significant variants.
4. Look for end-rhyme, taking care to mark each line so that when you have finished you can see at a glance whether any sounds are repeated and what patterns, if any, can be identified. If these patterns occur within a stanza or in a poem that has no stanza divisions, circle or bracket each segment, as we did with the Shakespearean sonnet.
5. If you discover that the poem has meter and/or rhyme, count the number of lines in the poem as a whole or in the segment of the poem you wish to identify. Then look in the appropriate columns of the forms chart that follows. If it isn't there, the poet may be using a form that isn't listed or creating a new form. If you are able to identify any one corresponding feature on the chart, examine the others as well. If line number, rhyme pattern, and meter match those of the passage or work you are investigating, you will find the name for the pattern in the far lefthand column.
6. Once you have identified the form, ask yourself these questions: Why might the poet have chosen this structure rather than another? What does formal structure contribute to the total effect of the poem? What evidence from the poem itself could be cited to support these conclusions?

The poems that are included in the two "Further Readings" sections at the end of this chapter will provide illustrations of many of the verse forms listed on the chart. But before going on to them, read the two short poems that follow the chart. Determine their forms and see how their meaning and tone would be affected if each were written in the form of the other.

Forms Chart[1]

Form	Number of Lines	Rhyme Scheme	Meter
Alexandrine	1	dependent on the form with which it is combined	iambic hexameter
couplet	2	aa	variable
heroic couplet	2	aa	iambic pentameter
triplet	3	aaa	variable
tercet	3	usually aba	variable
quatrain	4	variable	variable
ballad stanza	4	abcb	variable, but often iambic tetrameter in lines 1 and 3 and iambic trimeter in lines 2 and 4
other prevalent quatrain forms	4	abba or abab	iambic pentameter
quintet	5	variable	variable
limerick	5	aabba	lines 1, 2, and 5: anapestic trimeter; lines 4 and 5: anapestic dimeter
sestet	6	variable—but usually ababab or ababcc	variable
septet	7	variable	variable
rime royal	7	ababbcc	iambic pentameter
octave	8	variable	variable
ottava rima	8	abababcc	iambic pentameter
Spenserian stanza	9	ababbcbcc	lines 1–8: iambic pentameter; line 9: iambic hexameter (Alexandrine)

[6] Odes, elegies, and several other major forms have been omitted because they are defined principally by tone and content rather than by a set meter, rhyme scheme, or number of lines.

Form	Number of Lines	Rhyme Scheme	Meter
sonnet English, or Shakespearean, sonnet	14	variable	iambic pentameter
	14	ababcdcdefefgg	iambic pentameter
Petrarchan, or Italian, sonnet	14	abbaabbacdcdcd, abbaabbacdecde, and others	iambic pentameter
villanelle	19	5 tercets rhyming aba aba aba aba aba and a final quatrain rhyming abaa	variable, but often iambic pentameter
sestina	39	6 sestets and a final tercet, without rhyme but with repetition of the same words in a different order in each stanza	variable
terza rima	variable	interlocking tercets, usually ending in a couplet, e.g., aba bcb cdc dcd efe ff	usually iambic pentameter
blank verse	variable	unrhymed	iambic pentameter
free verse	variable	unrhymed	unmetered

THE SOUL SELECTS HER OWN SOCIETY

The Soul selects her own Society—
Then—shuts the Door—
To her divine Majority—
Present no more—

Unmoved—she notes the Chariots—pausing—
At her low Gate—
Unmoved—an Emperor be kneeling
Upon her Mat—

5

I've known her—from an ample nation—
Choose One—
Then—close the Valves of her attention— 10
Like Stone—

Emily Dickinson (1830–1886)

ME IMPERTURBE

Me imperturbe, standing at ease in Nature,
Master of all or mistress of all, aplomb in the midst of irrational things,
Imbued as they, passive, receptive, silent as they,
Finding my occupation, poverty, notoriety, foibles, crimes, less important than I thought,
Me toward the Mexican sea, or in the Mannahatta or the Tennessee, or far north or inland, 5
A river man, or a man of the woods, or of any farm-life of these States or of the coast, or the lakes or Kanada,
Me wherever my life is lived, O to be self-balanced for contingencies,
To confront night, storms, hunger, ridicule, accidents, rebuffs, as the trees and animals do.

Walt Whitman (1819–1892)

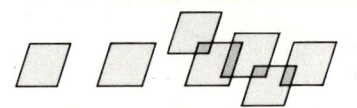

POEMS FOR FURTHER STUDY 1

A pretty young thing from St. Paul
Wore a newspaper gown to a ball.
The dress caught on fire
And burned her attire
Front page, sporting section, and all. 5

Anonymous

QUESTIONS

1. Scan the poem and describe the pattern of the meter.
2. What is the rhyme scheme?
3. Would you call the tone of the poem light or serious? Construct your own poem using exactly the meter and rhyme of this poem but supply-

ing serious content. What is the effect? Can you make a generalization about the effect of this verse form?

4. The verse form is called a **limerick**, *which consists of five lines rhyming aabba* (usually lines 1, 2, and 5 trimeter and lines 3 and 4 dimeter and usually with anapestic rhythm). As you discovered from the previous question, the limerick is suitable exclusively for humorous verse and, interestingly enough, is said to be one of few verse forms native to English (specifically, to Limerick, Ireland). It is a form capable of extraordinary indecency and hilarious sexual ingenuity, though it can also be as inoffensive as the nursery rhyme "Hickory Dickory Dock," which is a limerick.

ON FIRST LOOKING INTO CHAPMAN'S HOMER

Much have I traveled in the realms of gold,
And many goodly states and kingdoms seen;
Round many western islands have I been
Which bards in fealty° to Apollo[1] hold.   °fidelity
Oft of one wide expanse had I been told   5
That deep-browed Homer ruled as his demesne°;   °domain
Yet did I never breathe its pure serene
Till I heard Chapman speak out loud and bold;
Then felt I like some watcher of the skies
When a new planet swims into his ken;   10
Or like stout Cortez[2] when with eagle eyes
He stared at the Pacific—and all his men
Looked at each other with a wild surmise—
Silent, upon a peak in Darien.°   °Panama

John Keats (1795–1821)

[1] Apollo was the Greek god of sunlight, music, and poetry.
[2] The actual European discoverer of the Pacific was Balboa, not Cortez.

QUESTIONS

1. George Chapman published the first readable English translation of Homer's great Greek epic *Iliad* at the beginning of the seventeenth century. Keats' reaction to reading Chapman's Homer provides the situation of the poem. What does his imagery reveal about his attitude to the work? Does his mistake in line 11 detract from the poem? How is the imagery appropriate? Does it change during the poem? How? In what line?

2. Comment on the sound patterns in the poem and how they reinforce tone and meaning. In which section of the poem do sound patterns seem to cluster? Which line? Why?

3. What is the rhyme scheme?
4. Scan the poem. What is its basic meter? Identify and explain the substituted feet.
5. The nature of the imagery, the rhyme scheme, the thematic structure, and the tone shift into a different key at the beginning of one line. Identify the line—and the word that begins this turn.
6. What is the name of the form Keats uses, and why is this structure appropriate?

ODE TO THE WEST WIND

1

O wild West Wind, thou breath of Autumn's being,
Thou, from whose unseen presence the leaves dead
Are driven, like ghosts from an enchanter fleeing,

Yellow, and black, and pale, and hectic red,   5
Pestilence-stricken multitudes: O, thou,
Who chariotest to their dark wintry bed

The wingéd seeds, where they lie cold and low,
Each like a corpse within its grave, until
Thine azure sister of the spring shall blow

Her clarion o'er the dreaming earth, and fill   10
 (Driving sweet buds like flocks to feed in air)
With living hues and odors plain and hill:

Wild Spirit, which art moving everywhere;
Destroyer and preserver; hear, oh, hear!

2

Thou on whose stream, mid the steep sky's commotion,   15
Loose clouds like earth's decaying leaves are shed,
Shook from the tangled boughs of Heaven and Ocean,

Angels of rain and lightning: there are spread
On the blue surface of thine aëry surge,
Like the bright hair uplifted from the head   20

Of some fierce Maenad,[1] even from the dim verge
Of the horizon to the zenith's height,
The locks of the approaching storm. Thou dirge

---

[1] Maddened participant in rituals celebrating Dionysus, the Greek god of wine and fertility.

Of the dying year, to which this closing night
Will be the dome of a vast sepulcher, 25
Vaulted with all thy congregated might

Of vapors, from whose solid atmosphere
Black rain, and fire, and hail will burst: oh, hear!

3

Thou who didst waken from his summer dreams
The blue Mediterranean, where he lay, 30
Lulled by the coil of his crystálline streams,

Beside a pumice isle in Baiae's bay,
And saw in sleep old palaces and towers
Quivering within the wave's intenser day,

All overgrown with azure moss and flowers 35
So sweet, the sense faints picturing them! Thou
For whose path the Atlantic's level powers

Cleave themselves into chasms, while far below
The sea-blooms and the oozy woods which wear
The sapless foliage of the ocean, know 40

Thy voice, and suddenly grow gray with fear,
And tremble and despoil themselves: oh, hear!

4

If I were a dead leaf thou mightest bear;
If I were a swift cloud to fly with thee;
A wave to pant beneath thy power, and share 45

The impulse of thy strength, only less free
Than thou, O uncontrollable! If even
I were as in my boyhood, and could be

The comrade of thy wanderings over Heaven,
As then, when to outstrip thy skyey speed 50
Scarce seem a vision; I would ne'er have striven

As thus with thee in prayer in my sore need.
Oh, lift me as a wave, a leaf, a cloud!
I fall upon the thorns of life! I bleed!

A heavy weight of hours has chained and bowed 55
One too like thee: tameless, and swift, and proud.

5

Make me thy lyre, even as the forest is:
What if my leaves are falling like its own!
The tumult of thy mighty harmonies

Will take from both a deep, autumnal tone,   60
Sweet though in sadness. Be thou, Spirit fierce,
My spirit! Be thou me, impetuous one!

Drive my dead thoughts over the universe
Like withered leaves to quicken a new birth!
And, by the incantation of this verse,   65

Scatter, as from an unextinguished hearth
Ashes and sparks, my words among mankind!
Be through my lips to unawakened earth

The trumpet of a prophecy! O Wind,
If Winter comes, can Spring be far behind?   70

Percy Bysshe Shelley (1792–1822)

QUESTIONS

1. "Ode to the West Wind" is a Romantic poet's adaptation of the more complexly structured ode that originated with the Greek poet Pindar and was widely imitated by English poets of the seventeenth and eighteenth centuries. Like the traditional **ode**, Shelley's poem *is a long, serious, meditative work written in an elevated, formal style.* It is distinctive, however, in its stanzaic pattern and rhyme scheme. Study the form of the poem to determine whether each section has the same number of stanzas, whether the stanzas all have the same number of lines, and whether there is a consistent pattern of rhyme.

2. If you have analyzed the rhyme scheme accurately, you will have discovered a verse form called the **terza rima.** See if you can arrive at your own definition of this term inductively. If not, refer back to the forms chart.

3. How does the rhyme scheme help to link important words and ideas? What necessitates the changes in the last stanza of each section?

4. Is the meter of the poem as regular as its stanzaic pattern and rhyme scheme? Explain.

5. Throughout the first three stanzas, Shelley attempts to capture in words and their sounds the driving force and awesome power of the west wind. What are the technical means he uses to accomplish this objective? How successful is he?

6. In sections 4 and 5, the poem turns inward to the soul of the speaker. What visual and auditory connections exist between these two stanzas and the first three? What symbolic significance do "Winter" and "Spring" have in the last line of the poem?

MENDING WALL

Something there is that doesn't love a wall,
That sends the frozen-ground-swell under it
And spills the upper boulders in the sun,
And makes gaps even two can pass abreast.
The work of hunters is another thing: 5
I have come after them and made repair
Where they have left not one stone on a stone,
But they would have the rabbit out of hiding,
To please the yelping dogs. The gaps I mean,
No one has seen them made or heard them made, 10
But at spring mending-time we find them there.
I let my neighbor know beyond the hill;
And on a day we meet to walk the line
And set the wall between us once again.
We keep the wall between us as we go. 15
To each the boulders that have fallen to each.
And some are loaves and some so nearly balls
We have to use a spell to make them balance:
"Stay where you are until our backs are turned!"
We wear our fingers rough with handling them. 20
Oh, just another kind of outdoor game,
One on a side. It comes to little more:
There where it is we do not need the wall:
He is all pine and I am apple orchard.
My apple trees will never get across 25
And eat the cones under his pines, I tell him.
He only says, "Good fences make good neighbors."
Spring is the mischief in me, and I wonder
If I could put a notion in his head:
"*Why* do they make good neighbors? Isn't it 30
Where there are cows? But here there are no cows.
Before I built a wall I'd ask to know
What I was walling in or walling out,
And to whom I was like to give offense.
Something there is that doesn't love a wall, 35
That wants it down." I could say "Elves" to him,
But it's not elves exactly, and I'd rather
He said it for himself. I see him there,

> Bringing a stone grasped firmly by the top
> In each hand, like an old-stone savage armed. 40
> He moves in darkness as it seems to me,
> Not of woods only and the shade of trees.
> He will not go behind his father's saying,
> And he likes having thought of it so well
> He says again, "Good fences make good neighbors." 45
>
> *Robert Frost* (1874–1963)

QUESTIONS

1. Does Frost use either end rhyme or internal rhyme in this poem?
2. Does the poem have a regular meter? If so, what is it?
3. Based on what you have learned from the two previous questions, explain which verse form Frost is using: *free verse, blank verse,* or *villanelle*?
4. It has often been said that Frost's poetry captures the rhythms of colloquial speech. Is this true of "Mending Wall"? Why or why not?
5. To what extent does Frost use alliteration, assonance, and other aural effects? For what purpose?
6. In several lines, words are repeated. Which of them are attributed to the speaker and which to his neighbor? What differences in outlook are emphasized by these repetitions?
7. What does the poem reveal about human relationships and communications? In what ways do the formal structures contribute to the development of these themes?

SESTINA

> September rain falls on the house.
> In the failing light, the old grandmother
> sits in the kitchen with the child
> beside the Little Marvel Stove,
> reading the jokes from the almanac, 5
> laughing and talking to hide her tears.
>
> She thinks that her equinoctial tears
> and the rain that beats on the roof of the house
> were both foretold by the almanac,
> but only known to a grandmother. 10
> The iron kettle sings on the stove.
> She cuts some bread and says to the child,

It's time for tea now; but the child
is watching the teakettle's small hard tears
dance like mad on the hot black stove,
the way the rain must dance on the house.
Tidying up, the old grandmother
hangs up the clever almanac

on its string. Bird-like, the almanac
hovers half open above the child,
hovers above the old grandmother
and her teacup full of dark brown tears.
She shivers and says she thinks the house
feels chilly, and puts more wood in the stove.

It was to be, says the Marvel Stove.
I know what I know, says the almanac.
With crayons the child draws a rigid house
and a winding pathway. Then the child
puts in a man with buttons like tears
and shows it proudly to the grandmother.

But secretly, while the grandmother
busies herself about the stove,
the little moons fall down like tears
from between the pages of the almanac
into the flower bed the child
has carefully placed in the front of the house.

Time to plant tears, says the almanac.
The grandmother sings to the marvellous stove
and the child draws another inscrutable house.

Elizabeth Bishop (b. 1911)

QUESTIONS

1. The sestina has an elaborate set of conventions. Read the poem carefully and describe them. Then check your findings against the forms chart.
2. Is this verse form needlessly complicated? Does Elizabeth Bishop manage to make it functional, a fit vehicle for her theme, or is "Sestina" a trivial exercise?
3. What is the theme of the poem? How do the repetitions and variations reflect it? What is the significance of the child's drawing? How is it related to the grandmother's behavior?
4. Certain transformations take place in the course of the poem. What are they? Does the poem remind you of anything from Mother Goose? From the Bible?

PETER QUINCE[1] AT THE CLAVIER

I

Just as my fingers on these keys
Make music, so the selfsame sounds
On my spirit make a music, too.

Music is feeling, then, not sound;
And thus it is that what I feel, 5
Here in this room, desiring you,

Thinking of your blue-shadowed silk,
Is music. It is like the strain
Waked in the elders by Susanna.

Of a green evening, clear and warm, 10
She bathed in her still garden, while
The red-eyed elders watching, felt

The basses of their beings throb
In witching chords, and their thin blood
Pulse pizzicati of Hosanna. 15

II

In the green water, clear and warm,
Susanna lay.
She searched
The touch of springs,
And found 20
Concealed imaginings.
She sighed,
For so much melody.

Upon the bank, she stood
In the cool 25
Of spent emotions.
She felt, among the leaves,
The dew
Of old devotions.

She walked upon the grass, 30
Still quavering.
The winds were like her maids,
On timid feet,
Fetching her woven scarves,
Yet wavering. 35

---

[1] The name of a character in one of Shakespeare's comedies, *A Midsummer Night's Dream*.

A breath upon her hand
Muted the night.
She turned—
A cymbal crashed,
And roaring horns. 40

III

Soon, with a noise like tambourines,
Came her attendant Byzantines.

They wondered why Susanna cried
Against the elders by her side;

And as they whispered, the refrain 45
Was like a willow swept by rain.

Anon, their lamps' uplifted flame
Revealed Susanna and her shame.

And then, the simpering Byzantines
Fled, with a noise like tambourines. 50

IV

Beauty is momentary in the mind—
The fitful tracing of a portal;
But in the flesh it is immortal.
The body dies; the body's beauty lives.
So evenings die, in their green going, 55
A wave, interminably flowing.
So gardens die, their meek breath scenting
The cowl of winter, done repenting.
So maidens die, to the auroral
Celebration of a maiden's choral. 60
Susanna's music touched the bawdy strings
Of those white elders; but, escaping,
Left only Death's ironic scraping.
Now, in its immortality, it plays
On the clear viol of her memory, 65
And makes a constant sacrament of praise.

Wallace Stevens (1879–1955)

QUESTIONS

1. How would you describe the form of this poem?
2. Why does Stevens divide the poem into five parts? Do the divisions correspond to changes of thought or changes of mood or both?

3. Locate parts of the poem that deal with sensuous pleasure. Do sound patterns enhance the pleasure described? How? What are the devices of sound used often by Stevens?

4. Does Stevens establish any kind of consistent rhyme scheme? Does he use slant rhyme? End-stopped lines? To what effect?

5. What is the basic meter in each part? Why is it appropriate? Do form and meter reinforce the theme? What is the theme of the poem?

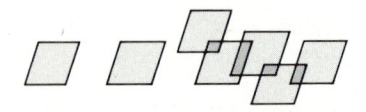

POEMS FOR FURTHER STUDY 2

WE REAL COOL
The Pool Players.
Seven at the Golden Shovel.

We real cool. We
Left school. We

Lurk late. We
Strike straight. We

Sing sin. We 5
Thin gin. We

Jazz June. We
Die soon.

Gwendolyn Brooks (b. 1917)

SONG: DRINK TO ME ONLY WITH THINE EYES

Drink to me only with thine eyes
    And I will pledge with mine;
Or leave a kiss but in the cup
    And I'll not look for wine.
The thirst that from the soul doth rise 5
    Doth ask a drink divine,
But might I of Jove's nectar sup
    I would not change for thine.

    I sent thee late a rosy wreath,
        Not so much honoring thee   10
    As giving it a hope that there
        It could not withered be.
    But thou thereon didst only breathe
        And sent'st it back to me—
    Since when, it grows and smells, I swear,   15
        Not of itself but thee.
            Ben Jonson (1573–1637)

SINCE THERE'S NO HELP

Since there's no help, come let us kiss and part.
Nay, I have done, you get no more of me,
And I am glad, yea glad with all my heart
That thus so cleanly I myself can free.
Shake hands forever, cancel all our vows,   5
And when we meet at any time again,
Be it not seen in either of our brows
That we one jot of former love retain.
Now at the last gasp of Love's latest breath,
When, his pulse failing, Passion speechless lies,   10
When Faith is kneeling by his bed of death,
And Innocence is closing up his eyes,
Now, if thou wouldst, when all have given him over,
From death to life thou mightst him yet recover.
            Michael Drayton (1563–1631)

ANTHEM FOR DOOMED YOUTH

What passing-bells for these who die as cattle?
    Only the monstrous anger of the guns.
    Only the stuttering rifles' rapid rattle
Can patter out their hasty orisons.
No mockeries now for them; no prayers nor bells,   5
    Nor any voice of mourning save the choirs,—
The shrill, demented choirs of wailing shells;
    And bugles calling for them from sad shires.

What candles may be held to speed them all?
    Not in the hands of boys, but in their eyes   10
Shall shine the holy glimmers of good-byes.
    The pallor of girls' brows shall be their pall;
Their flowers the tenderness of patient minds,
And each slow dusk a drawing-down of blinds.
            Wilfred Owen (1893–1918)

O SWEET SPONTANEOUS

O sweet spontaneous
earth how often have
the
doting

      fingers of
prurient philosophers pinched
and
poked
thee
, has the naughty thumb
of science prodded
thy

    beauty   . how
often have religions taken
thee upon their scraggy knees
squeezing and

buffeting thee that thou mightest conceive
gods
    (but
true

to the incomparable
couch of death thy
rhythmic
lover

    thou answerest

  them only with
        spring)

      E. E. Cummings (1894–1962)

DO NOT GO GENTLE INTO THAT GOOD NIGHT

Do not go gentle into that good night,
Old age should burn and rave at close of day;
Rage, rage against the dying of the light.

Though wise men at their end know dark is right,
Because their words had forked no lightning they
Do not go gentle into that good night.

Good men, the last wave by, crying how bright
Their frail deeds might have danced in a green bay,
Rage, rage against the dying of the light.

Wild men who caught and sang the sun in flight,   10
And learn, too late, they grieved it on its way,
Do not go gentle into that good night.

Grave men, near death, who see with blinding sight
Blind eyes could blaze like meteors and be gay,
Rage, rage against the dying of the light.   15

And you, my father, there on the sad height,
Curse, bless, me now with your fierce tears, I pray.
Do not go gentle into that good night.
Rage, rage against the dying of the light.

Dylan Thomas (1914–1953)

PART TWO

STUDENTS AND TEACHERS

YOU UNDERSTAND THE REQUIREMENTS

We are
sorry to have to
regret to
tell you
sorry sorry
regret sorry that you have
failed

your hair should have been
piled up higher

you have failed to
pass failed
your sorry
regret your
final hair comprehensive
exam satisfactorily
you understand the requirements

you understand we are
sorry final

and didn't look as professional
as desirable
or sorry dignified
and have little enough
sympathy for 16th century
sorry english anglicanism
we don't know doctoral
competency what to think and
regret you will sorry not
be able to stay
or finish

final regret your disappointment
the unsuccessfully completed best
wishes for the future
it has been a
regret sorry the requirements
the university policy

please don't call us.

Lyn Lifshin (b. 1942)

THE SCHOLARS

Bald heads forgetful of their sins,
Old, learned, respectable bald heads
Edit and annotate the lines
That young men, tossing on their beds,
Rhymed out in love's despair
To flatter beauty's ignorant ear.

All shuffle there; all cough in ink;
All wear the carpet with their shoes;
All think what other people think;
All know the man their neighbour knows.
Lord, what would they say
Did their Catullus walk that way?

William Butler Yeats (1865–1939)

THEME FOR ENGLISH B

The instructor said,

> *Go home and write*
> *a page tonight.*
> *And let that page come out of you—*
> *Then, it will be true.*

I wonder if it's that simple?
I am twenty-two, colored, born in Winston-Salem.
I went to school there, then Durham, then here
to this college on the hill above Harlem.
I am the only colored student in my class.
The steps from the hill lead down into Harlem,
through a park, then I cross St. Nicholas,
Eighth Avenue, Seventh, and I come to the Y,
the Harlem Branch Y, where I take the elevator
up to my room, sit down, and write this page:

It's not easy to know what is true for you or me
at twenty-two, my age. But I guess I'm what
I feel and see and hear, Harlem, I hear you:
hear you, hear me—we two—you, me, talk on this page.
(I hear New York, too.) Me—who?

Well, I like to eat, sleep, drink, and be in love.
I like to work, read, learn, and understand life.
I like a pipe for a Christmas present,
or records—Bessie, bop, or Bach.
I guess being colored doesn't make me *not* like

the same things other folks like who are other races.
So will my page be colored that I write?
Being me, it will not be white.
But it will be
a part of you, instructor. 30
You are white—
yet a part of me, as I am a part of you.
That's American.
Sometimes perhaps you don't want to be a part of me.
Nor do I often want to be a part of you. 35
But we are, that's true!
As I learn from you,
I guess you learn from me—
although you're older—and white—
and somewhat more free. 40

This is my page for English B.

Langston Hughes (1902–1967)

ZIMMER'S HEAD THUDDING AGAINST THE BLACKBOARD

At the blackboard I had missed
Five number problems in a row,
And was about to foul a sixth,
When the old, exasperated nun
Began to pound my head against 5
My six mistakes. When I cried,
She threw me back into my seat,
Where I hid my head and swore
That very day I'd be a poet,
And curse her yellow teeth with this. 10

Paul Zimmer (b. 1934)

TO MY STUDENTS
For John Logan

On these warm and humid summer nights
the echoes of your words swarm and buzz
around my brain. You are the mosquitoes
in the soft, strained light outside
my screened but opened window. Some of you, 5
the more ingenious perhaps, make your way
in. The others are no doubt victims

of a spider or the rain. Fascinated and
afraid, I watch you alighting gently
on my wrist: there among the scattered
hair as large as life, you probe for
blood beneath a tender spot of flesh.

How delicate your bodies and fragile
your frames fashioned somewhere in
the humid pulse of this warm night.
And how quickly, with almost invisible
wings, still damp, you circle toward
the light, and in birth blindness seek
the blood that some legend says is poison.
I pity you, although your small annoying
bodies are sometimes a relief from
the mounting monotony of memory.

    A. Poulin, Jr. (b. 1938)

A TEACHER
"And gladly wolde he lerne, and gladly teche."

He hated them all one by one but wanted to show them
What was Important and Vital and by God if
They thought they'd never have use for it he was
Sorry as hell for them, that's all, with their genteel
Mercantile Main Street Babbitt
Bourgeois-barbaric faces, they were beyond
Saving, clearly, quite out of reach, and so he
G-rrr
Got up every morning and
G-rrr
Ate his breakfast and
G-rrr
Lumbered off to his eight o'clock
Gladly to teach.

    Reed Whittemore (b. 1919)

ODE ON A DISTANT PROSPECT OF ETON COLLEGE

Ye distant spires, ye antique towers,
That crown the wat'ry glade,
Where grateful Science still adores
Her Henry's holy Shade;
And ye, that from the stately brow

Of Windsor's heights th' expanse below
Of grove, of lawn, of mead survey,
Whose turf, whose shade, whose flowers among
Wanders the hoary Thames along
His silver-winding way.   10

    Ah happy hills, ah pleasing shade,
Ah fields beloved in vain,
Where once my careless childhood strayed,
A stranger yet to pain!
I feel the gales that from ye blow   15
A momentary bliss bestow,
As waving fresh their gladsome wing,
My weary soul they seem to soothe,
And, redolent of joy and youth,
To breathe a second spring.   20

    Say, Father Thames, for thou hast seen
Full many a sprightly race
Disporting on thy margent green
The paths of pleasure trace,
Who foremost now delight to cleave   25
With pliant arm thy glassy wave?
The captive linnet which enthrall?
What idle progeny succeed
To chase the rolling circle's speed,
Or urge the flying ball?   30

    While some on earnest business bent
Their murmuring labors ply
'Gainst graver hours, that bring constraint
To sweeten liberty:
Some bold adventurers disdain   35
The limits of their little reign,
And unknown regions dare descry;
Still as they run they look behind,
They hear a voice in every wind
And snatch a fearful joy.   40

    Gay hope is theirs by fancy fed,
Less pleasing when possessed;
The tear forgot as soon as shed,
The sunshine of the breast;
Theirs buxom health of rosy hue,   45
Wild wit, invention ever new,
And lively cheer of vigor born;
The thoughtless day, the easy night,

The spirits pure, the slumbers light,
That fly th' approach of morn. 50

    Alas, regardless of their doom,
The little victims play!
No sense have they of ills to come,
Nor care beyond today:
Yet see how, all around 'em, wait 55
The Ministers of human fate
And black Misfortune's baleful train!
Ah, show them where in ambush stand
To seize their prey the murtherous band!
Ah, tell them, they are men! 60

    These shall the fury Passions tear,
The vultures of the mind:
Disdainful Anger, pallid Fear,
And Shame that skulks behind;
Or pining Love shall waste their youth, 65
Or Jealousy with rankling tooth,
That inly gnaws the secret heart,
And Envy wan, and faded Care,
Grim-visaged comfortless Despair,
And Sorrow's piercing dart. 70

    Ambition this shall tempt to rise,
Then whirl the wretch from high,
To bitter Scorn a sacrifice,
And grinning Infamy.
The stings of Falsehood those shall try, 75
And hard Unkindness' altered eye,
That mocks the tear it forced to flow;
And keen Remorse with blood defiled,
And moody Madness laughing wild
Amid severest woe. 80

    Lo, in the vale of years beneath
A grisly troop are seen,
The painful family of Death,
More hideous than their queen:
This racks the joints, this fires the veins. 85
That every laboring sinew strains,
Those in the deeper vitals rage;
Lo, Poverty, to fill the band,
That numbs the soul with icy hand,
And slow-consuming Age. 90

    To each his sufferings; all are men,
Condemned alike to groan:

The tender for another's pain,
Th' unfeeling for his own.
Yet, ah, why should they know their fate?   95
Since sorrow never comes too late,
And happiness too swiftly flies.
Thought would destroy their paradise.
No more: where ignorance is bliss,
'Tis folly to be wise.   100

        Thomas Gray (1716–1771)

❖ SPORTS AND GAMES ❖

FIRST PRACTICE

After the doctor checked to see
we weren't ruptured,
the man with the short cigar took us
under the grade school,
where we went in case of attack   5
or storm, and said
he was Clifford Hill, he was
a man who believed dogs
ate dogs, he had once killed
for his country, and if   10
there were any girls present
for them to leave now.
                  No one
left. OK, he said, he said I take
that to mean you are hungry   15
men who hate to lose as much
as I do. OK. Then
he made two lines of us
facing each other,
and across the way, he said,   20
is the man you hate most
in the world,
and if we are to win
that title I want to see how.
But I don't want to see   25
any marks when you're dressed,
he said. He said, *Now*.

        Gary Gildner (b. 1938)

TENNIS

Service is joy, to see or swing. Allow
All tumult to subside. Then tensest winds
Buffet, brace, viol and sweeping bow.
Courts are for love and volley. No one minds
The cruel ellipse of service and return,
Dancing white galliardes at tape or net
Till point, on the wire's tip, or the long burn-
ing arc to nethercourt marks game and set.
Purpose apart, perched like an umpire, dozes,
Dreams golden balls whirring through indigo.
Clay blurs the whitewash but day still encloses
The albinos, bonded in their flick and flow.
Playing in musicked gravity, the pair
Score liquid Euclids in foolscaps of air.

Margaret Avison (b. 1918)

SKIERS

With the motion of angels, out of
Snow-spume and swirl of gold mist, they
Emerge to the positive sun. At
That great height, small on that whiteness,
With the color of birds or of angels,
They swoop, sway, descend, and descending,
Cry their bright bird-cries, pure
In the sweet desolation of distance.
They slowly enlarge to our eyes. Now

On the flat where the whiteness is
Trodden and mud-streaked, not birds now,
Nor angels even, they stand. They

Are awkward, not yet well adjusted
To this world, new and strange, of Time and
Contingency, who now are only
Human. They smile. The human

Face has its own beauty.

Robert Penn Warren (b. 1905)

YOUNG WRESTLERS

The beautiful boys curve and writhe,
gone inward behind their contorted masks.
The blind hands reach;

the legs hook, lock, lever
the gleaming bodies into hold,
out of hold. Escape. Riding time.
"Sink a half!" and the arm snakes
rapid with love around the neck.

One is left who will cry somewhere.
For the other, the air bends
in to him, hot with voices.
The walls reappear, the colors.
He is one body again,
lonely with joy.
Many sweet dreams will be based
on that ferocious touch.

Grace Butcher (b. 1934)

RUNNING

Bleachers are empty.
Cries from a night-hawk.
It makes dark unpredictable lines.
It dives close—
The wings pant, their joints creak.
I feel the cold draft on my skin.

Finally stop.
Walk in the weak red light.
Stand in a good coat of sweat.
Clouds stretch like impossible layers of fat.
A rabbit zigzags through the fresh mow, a white scut
Lost in the brush.

A panic of drying grass in the nose
I turn home, jog up the hill
And the track lies below me—
That grave green mouth, those hard black lips.

Peter Makuck (b. 1940)

TO SATCH*

Sometimes I feel like I will never stop
Just go forever
Till one fine morning
I'll reach up and grab me a handful of stars
And swing out my long lean leg

And whip three hot strikes burning down the heavens
And look over at God and say
How about that!

Samuel Allen (b. 1917)

* Satchel Paige had a long and distinguished career as a baseball pitcher in the American Negro League and—after integration—in the major leagues.

SURFERS AT SANTA CRUZ

They have come by carloads
with Styrofoam surfboards
in the black wetsuits
of the affluent sixties,
the young Americans   5

kneeling paddle with their palms
and stand through the breakers
One World Polynesians
lying offshore
as if they were fishing for the village.   10

They are waiting for the ninth wave
when each lone boy falling downhill
ahead of the cresting hundreds of yards
balancing communicates
with the ocean on the Way   15

how beautiful they are
their youth and human skill
and communion with the nature of things,
how ugly they are
already sleek with narrow eyes.   20

Paul Goodman (1911–1972)

❖ **YOUTH AND AGE** ❖

**SONNET 2: WHEN FORTY WINTERS SHALL
BESIEGE THY BROW**

When forty winters shall besiege thy brow
And dig deep trenches in thy beauty's field,
Thy youth's proud livery, so gazed on now,
Will be a tattered weed of small worth held:

Then being asked where all thy beauty lies,
Where all the treasure of thy lusty days,
To say within thine own deep-sunken eyes
Were an all-eating shame and thriftless praise.
How much more praise deserved thy beauty's use
If thou couldst answer, 'This fair child of mine
Shall sum my count and make my old excuse,'
Proving his beauty by succession thine.
    This were to be new made when thou art old
    And see thy blood warm when thou feel'st it cold.

William Shakespeare (1564–1616)

AMONG SCHOOL CHILDREN

I

I WALK through the long schoolroom questioning;
A kind old nun in a white hood replies;
The children learn to cipher and to sing,
To study reading-books and histories,
To cut and sew, be neat in everything
In the best modern way—the children's eyes
In momentary wonder stare upon
A sixty-year-old smiling public man.

II

I dream of a Ledaean body, bent
Above a sinking fire, a tale that she
Told of a harsh reproof, or trivial event
That changed some childish day to tragedy—
Told, and it seemed that our two natures blent
Into a sphere from youthful sympathy,
Or else, to alter Plato's parable,
Into the yolk and white of the one shell.

III

And thinking of that fit of grief or rage
I look upon one child or t'other there
And wonder if she stood so at that age—
For even daughters of the swan can share
Something of every paddler's heritage—
And had that colour upon cheek or hair,
And thereupon my heart is driven wild:
She stands before me as a living child.

IV

Her present image floats into the mind—
Did Quattrocento finger fashion it

Hollow of cheek as though it drank the wind
And took a mess of shadows for its meat?
And I though never of Ledaean kind
Had pretty plumage once—enough of that, 30
Better to smile on all that smile, and show
There is a comfortable kind of old scarecrow.

V

What youthful mother, a shape upon her lap
Honey of generation had betrayed,
And that must sleep, shriek, struggle to escape 35
As recollection or the drug decide,
Would think her son, did she but see that shape
With sixty or more winters on its head,
A compensation for the pang of his birth,
Or the uncertainty of his setting forth? 40

VI

Plato thought nature but a spume that plays
Upon a ghostly paradigm of things;
Solider Aristotle played the taws
Upon the bottom of a king of kings;
World-famous golden-thighed Pythagoras 45
Fingered upon a fiddle-stick or strings
What a star sang and careless Muses heard:
Old clothes upon old sticks to scare a bird.

VII

Both nuns and mothers worship images,
But those the candles light are not as those 50
That animate a mother's reveries,
But keep a marble or a bronze repose.
And yet they too break hearts—O Presences
That passion, piety or affection knows,
And that all heavenly glory symbolise— 55
O self-born mockers of man's enterprise;

VIII

Labour is blossoming or dancing where
The body is not bruised to pleasure soul,
Nor beauty born out of its own despair,
Nor blear-eyed wisdom out of midnight oil. 60
O chestnut-tree, great-rooted blossomer,
Are you the leaf, the blossom or the bole?
O body swayed to music, O brightening glance,
How can we know the dancer from the dance?

William Butler Yeats (1865–1939)

THE BALL POEM

What is the boy now, who has lost his ball,
What, what is he to do? I saw it go
Merrily bouncing, down the street, and then
Merrily over—there it is in the water!
No use to say 'O there are other balls':
An ultimate shaking grief fixes the boy
As he stands rigid, trembling, staring down
All his young days into the harbour where
His ball went. I would not intrude on him,
A dime, another ball, is worthless. Now
He senses first responsibility
In a world of possessions. People will take balls,
Balls will be lost always, little boy,
And no one buys a ball back. Money is external.
He is learning, well behind his desperate eyes,
The epistemology of loss, how to stand up
Knowing what every man must one day know
And most know many days, how to stand up
And gradually light returns to the street,
A whistle blows, the ball is out of sight,
Soon part of me will explore the deep and dark
Floor of the harbour . . I am everywhere,
I suffer and move, my mind and my heart move
With all that move me, under the water
Or whistling, I am not a little boy.

John Berryman (1914–1972)

MY PAPA'S WALTZ

The whiskey on your breath
Could make a small boy dizzy;
But I hung on like death:
Such waltzing was not easy.

We romped until the pans
Slid from the kitchen shelf;
My mother's countenance
Could not unfrown itself.

The hand that held my wrist
Was battered on one knuckle;
At every step you missed
My right ear scraped a buckle.

You beat time on my head
With a palm caked hard by dirt,
Then waltzed me off to bed   15
Still clinging to your shirt.

   Theodore Roethke (1908–1963)

DADDY

You do not do, you do not do
Any more, black shoe
In which I have lived like a foot
For thirty years, poor and white,
Barely daring to breathe or Achoo.   5

Daddy, I have had to kill you.
You died before I had time——
Marble-heavy, a bag full of God,
Ghastly statue with one grey toe
Big as a Frisco seal   10

And a head in the freakish Atlantic
Where it pours bean green over blue
In the waters off beautiful Nauset.
I used to pray to recover you.
Ach, du.   15

In the German tongue, in the Polish town
Scraped flat by the roller
Of wars, wars, wars.
But the name of the town is common.
My Polack friend   20

Says there are a dozen or two.
So I never could tell where you
Put your foot, your root,
I never could talk to you.
The tongue stuck in my jaw.   25

It stuck in a barb wire snare.
Ich, ich, ich, ich,
I could hardly speak.
I thought every German was you.
And the language obscene   30

An engine, an engine
Chuffing me off like a Jew.
A Jew to Dachau, Auschwitz, Belsen.

I began to talk like a Jew.
I think I may well be a Jew.

The snows of the Tyrol, the clear beer of Vienna
Are not very pure or true.
With my gypsy ancestress and my weird luck
And my Taroc pack and my Taroc pack
I may be a bit of a Jew.

I have always been scared of *you*,
With your Luftwaffe, your gobbledygoo.
And your neat moustache
And your Aryan eye, bright blue.
Panzer-man, panzer-man, O You——

Not God but a swastika
So black no sky could squeak through.
Every woman adores a Fascist,
The boot in the face, the brute
Brute heart of a brute like you.

You stand at the blackboard, daddy,
In the picture I have of you,
A cleft in your chin instead of your foot
But no less a devil for that, no not
Any less the black man who
Bit my pretty red heart in two.
I was ten when they buried you.
At twenty I tried to die
And get back, back, back to you.
I thought even the bones would do.

But they pulled me out of the sack,
And they stuck me together with glue.
And then I knew what to do.
I made a model of you,
A man in black with a Meinkampf look

And a love of the rack and the screw.
And I said I do, I do.
So daddy, I'm finally through.
The black telephone's off at the root,
The voices just can't worm through.

If I've killed one man, I've killed two——
The vampire who said he was you
And drank my blood for a year,
Seven years, if you want to know.
Daddy, you can lie back now.

There's a stake in your fat black heart
And the villagers never liked you.
They are dancing and stamping on you.
They always *knew* it was you.
Daddy, daddy, you bastard, I'm through. 80

    Sylvia Plath (1932–1963)

THOSE WINTER SUNDAYS

Sundays too my father got up early
and put his clothes on in the blueblack cold,
then with cracked hands that ached
from labor in the weekday weather made
banked fires blaze. No one ever thanked him. 5

I'd wake and hear the cold splintering, breaking.
When the rooms were warm, he'd call,
and slowly I would rise and dress,
fearing the chronic angers of that house,

Speaking indifferently to him, 10
who had driven out the cold
and polished my good shoes as well.
What did I know, what did I know
of love's austere and lonely offices?

    Robert Hayden (1923–1980)

PARENTS

What it must be like to be an angel
or a squirrel, we can imagine sooner.

The last time we go to bed good,
they are there, lying about darkness.

They dandle us once too often, 5
these friends who become our enemies.

Suddenly one day, their juniors
are as old as we yearn to be.

They get wrinkles where it is better
smooth, odd coughs, and smells. 10

It is grotesque how they go on
loving us, we go on loving them.

The effrontery, barely imaginable,
of having caused us. And of how.

Their lives: surely
we can do better than that.

This goes on for a long time. Everything
they do is wrong, and the worst thing,

they all do it, is to die,
taking with them the last explanation,

how we came out of the wet sea
or wherever they got us from,

taking the last link
of that chain with them.

Father, mother, we cry, wrinkling,
to our uncomprehending children and grandchildren.

William Meredith (b. 1919)

❖❖ FAILURE TO COMMUNICATE ❖❖

RE ACCEPTING YOU

We are very pleased with your response
to our advertisement. The form
you found in which to couch your reply
is original and attractive.
It caught our attention immediately.
The fact that you did not wait,
but answered at once, is also
in your favor. This means
you are a decisive person,
and this is the type we are looking for.
So many people, these days,
are trapped in indecision.
We agree profoundly with everything
you have said. More than anything
we agree with the way you have said it.

You seem to have understood
that the person we need must be humorous.
That, we assure you, is a prime factor.
You have told us a great deal
about yourself, and the telling
was brief. This too is a virtue.
We like it. Lastly,

you appear not to have become bitter
from your experience. This
we find extraordinary.

At this point we would like to meet you.
You are invited to come here
for an evening we have arranged.
Everyone to whom we have written
favorable answers such as this one
will be here. You will come
at your own expense. The trip
will be worth the trouble. The party,
as long as it lasts, will be fun.
If things don't work out as you hope
you will not be reimbursed,
but you will be placed
on our mailing list.

Naomi Lazard (b. 19??)

DENIAL

When my devotions could not pierce
      Thy silent ears,
Then was my heart broken, as was my verse;
      My breast was full of fears
          And disorder.

My bent thoughts, like a brittle bow,
      Did fly asunder:
Each took his way; some would to pleasures go,
      Some to the wars and thunder
          Of alarms.

As good go anywhere, they say,
      As to benumb
Both knees and heart, in crying night and day,
      Come, come, my God, O come!
          But no hearing.

O that thou shouldst give dust a tongue
      To cry to thee,
And then not hear it crying! All day long
      My heart was in my knee,
          But no hearing.

Therefore my soul lay out of sight,
      Untuned, unstrung:

My feeble spirit, unable to look right,
    Like a nipped blossom, hung
        Discontented.

O cheer and tune my heartless breast,
    Defer no time;
That so thy favors granting my request,
    They and my mind may chime,
        And mend my rhyme.

    George Herbert (1593–1633)

TRYING TO TALK WITH A MAN

Out in this desert we are testing bombs,

that's why we came here.

Sometimes I feel an underground river
forcing its way between deformed cliffs
an acute angle of understanding
moving itself like a locus of the sun
into this condemned scenery.

What we've had to give up to get here—
whole LP collections, films we starred in
playing in the neighborhoods, bakery windows
full of dry, chocolate-filled Jewish cookies,
the language of love-letters, of suicide notes,
afternoons on the riverbank
pretending to be children

Coming out to this desert
we meant to change the face of
driving among dull green succulents
walking at noon in the ghost town
surrounded by a silence

that sounds like the silence of the place
except that it came with us
and is familiar
and everything we were saying until now
was an effort to blot it out—
Coming out here we are up against it

Out here I feel more helpless
with you than without you
You mention the danger

and list the equipment
we talk of people caring for each other 30
in emergencies—laceration, thirst—
but you look at me like an emergency

Your dry heat feels like power
your eyes are stars of a different magnitude
they reflect lights that spell out: EXIT 35
when you get up and pace the floor

talking of the danger
as if it were not ourselves
as if we were testing anything else.

Adrienne Rich (b. 1929)

LUNCHTIME

None said anything startling from the rest;
each held her coffee cup in her own way,
and one twanged, another whined and a third
shot out her phrases like a rear exhaust;
yet each stood for the same things: 5
the clothes in their conversation,
the food they ate and the men they could not
catch up with. They were not saying more
than could be said in a crowd, they made this
their unity, as the thinking of one person; 10
and getting up to go, lunch over
by the clock, each pulled out her own chair
from underneath her.

David Ignatow (b. 1914)

BALLAD OF A THIN MAN

You walk into the room
With your pencil in your hand
You see somebody naked
And you say, "Who is that man?"
You try so hard 5
But you don't understand
Just what you'll say
When you get home

Because something is happening here
But you don't know what it is 10
Do you, Mister Jones?

You raise up your head
And you ask, "Is this where it is?"
And somebody points to you and says
"It's his"
And you say, "What's mine?"
And somebody else says, "Where what is?"
And you say, "Oh my God
Am I here all alone?"

Because something is happening here
But you don't know what it is
Do you, Mister Jones?

You hand in your ticket
And you go watch the geek
Who immediately walks up to you
When he hears you speak
And says, "How does it feel
To be such a freak?"
And you say, "Impossible"
As he hands you a bone

Because something is happening here
But you don't know what it is
Do you, Mister Jones?

You have many contacts
Among the lumberjacks
To get you facts
When someone attacks your imagination
But nobody has any respect
Anyway they already expect you
To just give a check
To tax-deductible charity organizations

You've been with the professors
And they've all liked your looks
With great lawyers you have
Discussed lepers and crooks
You've been through all of
F. Scott Fitzgerald's books
You're very well read
It's well known

Because something is happening here
But you don't know what it is
Do you, Mister Jones?

Well, the sword swallower, he comes up to you
And then he kneels
He crosses himself   55
And then he clicks his high heels
And without further notice
He asks you how it feels
And he says, "Here is your throat back
Thanks for the loan"   60

Because something is happening here
But you don't know what it is
Do you, Mister Jones?

Now you see this one-eyed midget
Shouting the word "NOW"   65
And you say, "For what reason?"
And he says, "How?"
And you say, "What does this mean?"
And he screams back, "You're a cow
Give me some milk   70
Or else go home"

Because something is happening here
But you don't know what it is
Do you, Mister Jones?

Well, you walk into the room   75
Like a camel and then you frown
You put your eyes in your pocket
And your nose on the ground
There ought to be a law
Against you comin' around   80
You should be made
To wear earphones

Because something is happening here
But you don't know what it is
Do you, Mister Jones?   85

Bob Dylan (b. 1941)

WHEN IN ROME

Marrie dear
the box is full . . .
take
whatever you like
to eat . . .   5

```
        (an egg
     or soup
     . . . there ain't no meat.)
there's endive there
and
cottage cheese . . .
        (whew! if I had some
     black-eyed peas . . . )
there's sardines
on the shelves
and such . . .
but
don't
get my anchovies . . .
they cost
too much!
        (me get the
     anchovies indeed!
     what she think, she got—
     a bird to feed?)
there's plenty in there
to fill you up . . .
        (yes'm. just the
     sight's
     enough!
     Hope I lives till I get
     home
     I'm tired of eatin'
     what they eats in Rome . . . )
```

Mari Evans

FABLE OF THE MERMAID AND THE DRUNKS

All these fellows were there inside
when she entered, utterly naked.
They had been drinking, and began to spit at her.
Recently come from the river, she understood nothing.
She was a mermaid who had lost her way.
The taunts flowed over her glistening flesh.
Obscenities drenched her golden breasts.
A stranger to tears, she did not weep.

A stranger to clothes, she did not dress.
They pocked her with cigarette ends and with burnt corks,   10
and rolled on the tavern floor in raucous laughter.
She did not speak, since speech was unknown to her.
Her eyes were the colour of faraway love,
her arms were matching topazes.
Her lips moved soundlessly in coral light,   15
and ultimately, she left by that door.
Hardly had she entered the river than she was cleansed,
gleaming once more like a white stone in the rain;
and without a backward look, she swam once more,
swam towards nothingness, swam to her dying.   20

    Pablo Neruda (1904–1973)   (*trans. by Alastair Reid*)

❖ LOVE, SEX, AND FRIENDSHIP ❖

WESTERN WIND

Western wind, when will thou blow,
The small rain down can rain?
Christ! if my love were in my arms,
And I in my bed again!

    Anonymous (ca. 1500)

THEY FLEE FROM ME

They flee from me that sometime did me seek,
   With naked foot stalking in my chamber.
I have seen them gentle, tame, and meek
   That now are wild and do not remember
   That sometime they put themself in danger   5
To take bread at my hand; and now they range,
Busily seeking with a continual change.

Thanked be fortune, it hath been otherwise
   Twenty times better; but once in special,
In thin array, after a pleasant guise,   10
   When her loose gown from her shoulders did fall,
   And she me caught in her arms long and small,
Therewith all sweetly did me kiss,
And softly said, "Dear heart, how like you this?"

It was no dream: I lay broad waking.
    But all is turned thorough my gentleness
Into a strange fashion of forsaking;
    And I have leave to go of her goodness,
    And she also to use newfangleness.
But since that I so kindly am served,
I would fain know what she hath deserved.

          Sir Thomas Wyatt (1503–1542)

TO THE VIRGINS, TO MAKE MUCH OF TIME

Gather ye rosebuds while ye may,
    Old time is still a-flying;
And this same flower that smiles today
    Tomorrow will be dying.

The glorious lamp of heaven, the sun,
    The higher he's a-getting,
The sooner will his race be run,
    And nearer he's to setting.

That age is best which is the first,
    When youth and blood are warmer;
But being spent, the worse and worst
    Times still succeed the former.

Then be not coy, but use your time,
    And, while ye may, go marry;
For having lost but once your prime,
    You may forever tarry.

          Robert Herrick (1591–1674)

A LATE AUBADE

You could be sitting now in a carrel
Turning some liver-spotted page,
Or rising in an elevator-cage
Toward Ladies' Apparel.

You could be planting a raucous bed
Of salvia, in rubber gloves,
Or lunching through a screed of someone's loves
With pitying head,

Or making some unhappy setter
Heel, or listening to a bleak
Lecture on Schoenberg's serial technique.
Isn't this better?

Think of all the time you are not
Wasting, and would not care to waste,
Such things, thank God, not being to your taste. 15
Think what a lot

Of time, by woman's reckoning,
You've saved, and so may spend on this,
You who had rather lie in bed and kiss
Than anything. 20

It's almost noon, you say? If so,
Time flies, and I need not rehearse
The rosebuds-theme of centuries of verse.
If you *must* go,

Wait for a while, then slip downstairs 25
And bring us up some chilled white wine,
And some blue cheese, and crackers, and some fine
Ruddy-skinned pears.

Richard Wilbur (b. 1921)

SONNET 57: BEING YOUR SLAVE, WHAT SHOULD I DO BUT TEND

Being your slave, what should I do but tend
Upon the hours and times of your desire?
I have no precious time at all to spend
Nor services to do, till you require.
Nor dare I chide the world-without-end hour 5
Whilst I, my sovereign, watch the clock for you,
Nor think the bitterness of absence sour
When you have bid your servant once adieu.
Nor dare I question with my jealous thought
Where you may be, or your affairs suppose, 10
But, like a sad slave, stay and think of nought
Save where you are how happy you make those.
    So true a fool is love that in your will,
    Though you do anything, he thinks no ill.

William Shakespeare (1564–1616)

PASSER MORTUUS EST

Death devours all lovely things:
    Lesbia with her sparrow
Shares the darkness,—presently
    Every bed is narrow.

Unremembered as old rain
    Dries the sheer libation;
And the little petulant hand
    Is an annotation.

After all, my erstwhile dear,
    My no longer cherished,
Need we say it was not love,
    Just because it perished?

Edna St. Vincent Millay (1892–1950)

SEDUCTION

one day
you gonna walk in this house
and i'm gonna have on a long African
gown
you'll sit down and say "The Black . . ."
and i'm gonna take one arm out
then you—not noticing me at all—will say "What about
this brother . . ."
and i'm going to be slipping it over my head
and you'll rapp on about "The revolution . . ."
while i rest your hand against my stomach
you'll go on—as you always do—saying
"I just can't dig . . ."
while i'm moving your hand up and down
and i'll be taking your dashiki off
then you'll say "What we really need . . ."
and i'll be licking your arm
and "The way I see it we ought to . . ."
and unbuckling your pants
"And what about the situation . . ."
and taking your shorts off
then you'll notice
your state of undress
and knowing you you'll just say
"Nikki,
isn't this counterrevolutionary . . . ?"

                Nikki Giovanni (b. 1943)

A VALEDICTION FORBIDDING MOURNING

As virtuous men pass mildly away,
    And whisper to their souls to go,

Whilst some of their sad friends do say,
    The breath goes now, and some say, No:

So let us melt, and make no noise,
    No tear-floods, nor sigh-tempests move;
'Twere profanation of our joys
    To tell the laity our love.

Moving of the earth brings harms and fears,
    Men reckon what it did and meant;
But trepidation of the spheres,
    Though greater far, is innocent.

Dull sublunary lovers' love
    (Whose soul is sense) cannot admit
Absence, because it doth remove
    Those things which elemented it.

But we, by a love so much refined
    That ourselves know not what it is,
Inter-assurèd of the mind,
    Care less, eyes, lips, and hands to miss.

Our two souls, therefore, which are one,
    Though I must go, endure not yet
A breach, but an expansion,
    Like gold to airy thinness beat.

If they be two, they are two so
    As stiff twin compasses are two:
Thy soul, the fixed foot, makes no show
    To move, but doth if the other do.

And though it in the center sit,
    Yet when the other far doth roam,
It leans and harkens after it,
    And grows erect as that comes home.

Such wilt thou be to me, who must,
    Like the other foot, obliquely run;
Thy firmness makes my circle just,
    And makes me end where I begun.

        John Donne (1572–1631)

A SENSE OF PLACE

COMPOSED UPON WESTMINSTER BRIDGE
September 3, 1802

Earth has not anything to show more fair:
Dull would he be of soul who could pass by
A sight so touching in its majesty:
This City now doth, like a garment, wear
The beauty of the morning; silent, bare,
Ships, towers, domes, theatres, and temples lie
Open unto the fields, and to the sky;
All bright and glittering in the smokeless air.
Never did sun more beautifully steep
In his first splendour, valley, rock, or hill;
Ne'er saw I, never felt, a calm so deep!
The river glideth at his own sweet will:
Dear God! the very houses seem asleep;
And all that mighty heart is lying still!

William Wordsworth (1770–1850)

THE GARDEN

How vainly men themselves amaze
To win the palm, the oak, or bays,
And their incessant labors see
Crowned from some single herb, or tree,
Whose short and narrow-vergéd shade
Does prudently their toils upbraid;
While all flowers and all trees do close
To weave the garlands of repose!

Fair Quiet, have I found thee here,
And Innocence, thy sister dear?
Mistaken long, I sought you then
In busy companies of men.
Your sacred plants, if here below,
Only among the plants will grow;
Society is all but rude
To this delicious solitude.

No white nor red was ever seen
So amorous as this lovely green.
Fond lovers, cruel as their flame,
Cut in these trees their mistress' name:

Little, alas, they know or heed
How far these beauties hers exceed!
Fair trees, wheresoe'er your barks I wound,
No name shall but your own be found.

    When we have run our passion's heat,   25
Love hither makes his best retreat.
The gods, that mortal beauty chase,
Still in a tree did end their race;
Apollo hunted Daphne so,
Only that she might laurel grow;   30
And Pan did after Syrinx speed,
Not as a nymph, but for a reed.

    What wondrous life is this I lead!
Ripe apples drop about my head;
The luscious clusters of the vine   35
Upon my mouth do crush their wine;
The nectarine and curious peach
Into my hands themselves do reach;
Stumbling on melons, as I pass,
Ensnared with flowers, I fall on grass.   40

    Meanwhile the mind, from pleasure less,
Withdraws into its happiness;
The mind, that ocean where each kind
Does straight its own resemblance find;
Yet it creates, transcending these,   45
Far other worlds and other seas,
Annihilating all that's made
To a green thought in a green shade.

    Here at the fountain's sliding foot,
Or at some fruit tree's mossy root,   50
Casting the body's vest aside,
My soul into the boughs does glide;
There, like a bird, it sits and sings,
Then whets and combs its silver wings,
And, till prepared for longer flight,   55
Waves in its plumes the various light.

    Such was that happy garden-state,
While man there walked, without a mate:
After a place so pure and sweet,
What other help could yet be meet!   60
But 'twas beyond a mortal's share
To wander solitary there:

Two paradises 'twere in one
To live in paradise alone.

     How well the skillful gardener drew 65
Of flowers and herbs this dial new,
Where, from above, the milder sun
Does through a fragrant zodiac run;
And, as it works, the industrious bee
Computes its time as well as we! 70
How could such sweet and wholesome hours
Be reckoned but with herbs and flowers?

     Andrew Marvell (1621–1678)

NIKKI-ROSA

childhood remembrances are always a drag
if you're Black
you always remember things like living in Woodlawn
with no inside toilet
and if you become famous or something 5
they never talk about how happy you were to have
your mother
all to yourself and
how good the water felt when you got your bath
from one of those 10
big tubs that folk in chicago barbecue in
and somehow when you talk about home
it never gets across how much you
understood their feelings
as the whole family attended meetings about Hollydale 15
and even though you remember
your biographers never understand
your father's pain as he sells his stock
and another dream goes
And though you're poor it isn't poverty that 20
concerns you
and though they fought a lot
it isn't your father's drinking that makes any difference
but only that everybody is together and you
and your sister have happy birthdays and very good 25
Christmasses
and I really hope no white person ever has cause
to write about me
because they never understand
Black love is Black wealth and they'll 30

probably talk about my hard childhood
and never understand that
all the while I was quite happy

> *Nikki Giovanni* (b. 1943)

TO BROOKLYN BRIDGE

How many dawns, chill from his rippling rest
The seagull's wings shall dip and pivot him,
Shedding white rings of tumult, building high
Over the chained bay waters Liberty—

Then, with inviolate curve, forsake our eyes 5
As apparitional as sails that cross
Some page of figures to be filed away;
—Till elevators drop us from our day . . .

I think of cinemas, panoramic sleights
With multitudes bent toward some flashing scene 10
Never disclosed, but hastened to again,
Foretold to other eyes on the same screen;

And Thee, across the harbor, silver-paced
As though the sun took step of thee, yet left
Some motion ever unspent in thy stride,— 15
Implicitly thy freedom staying thee!

Out of some subway scuttle, cell or loft
A bedlamite speeds to thy parapets,
Tilting there momently, shrill shirt ballooning,
A jest falls from the speechless caravan. 20

Down Wall, from girder into street noon leaks,
A rip-tooth of the sky's acetylene;
All afternoon the cloud-flown derricks turn . . .
Thy cables breathe the North Atlantic still.

And obscure as that heaven of the Jews, 25
Thy guerdon . . . Accolade thou dost bestow
Of anonymity time cannot raise:
Vibrant reprieve and pardon thou dost show.

O harp and altar, of the fury fused,
(How could mere toil align thy choiring strings!) 30
Terrific threshold of the prophet's pledge,
Prayer of pariah, and the lover's cry,—

Again the traffic lights that skim thy swift
Unfractioned idiom, immaculate sigh of stars,

Beading thy path—condense eternity: 35
And we have seen night lifted in thine arms.

Under thy shadow by the piers I waited;
Only in darkness is thy shadow clear.
The City's fiery parcels all undone,
Already snow submerges an iron year . . . 40

O Sleepless as the river under thee,
Vaulting the sea, the prairies' dreaming sod,
Unto us lowliest sometime sweep, descend
And of the curveship lend a myth to God.

Hart Crane (1899–1933)

LYING IN A HAMMOCK AT WILLIAM DUFFY'S FARM IN PINE ISLAND, MINNESOTA

Over my head, I see the bronze butterfly,
Asleep on the black trunk,
Blowing like a leaf in green shadow.
Down the ravine behind the empty house,
The cowbells follow one another 5
Into the distances of the afternoon.
To my right,
In a field of sunlight between two pines,
The droppings of last year's horses
Blaze up into golden stones. 10
I lean back, as the evening darkens and comes on.
A chicken hawk floats over, looking for home.
I have wasted my life.

James Wright (1927–1980)

SUBDIVIDER

I smell the dust of stones in sunlight,
and the dust under them,
and the dust under my eyes
and running in my palms,
and crickets buried deep under tar, 5
the dust of their tiny hoofs,
and the ashes of orchards.

This desert is new.
Some bones are still pink;
little eyes drift in the wind 10
of our many machines.

At times I have seen an embroidery of nerves
scrawled in the rocks,
or garlands of fur drying
on a lattice of ribs.
So many have died recently;
so many are still dying.

The bulldozers work ten hours a day
though the hearts of birds are very small.
My hand against my face, even at dawn,
smells like a grave.

        Adrien Stoutenburg (b. 1916)

THE MOUTH OF THE HUDSON
(*For Esther Brooks*)

A single man stands like a bird-watcher,
and scuffles the pepper and salt snow
from a discarded, gray
Westinghouse Electric cable drum.
He cannot discover America by counting
the chains of condemned freight-trains
from thirty states. They jolt and jar
and junk in the siding below him.
He has trouble with his balance.
His eyes drop,
and he drifts with the wild ice
ticking seaward down the Hudson,
like the blank sides of a jig-saw puzzle.

The ice ticks seaward like a clock.
A Negro toasts
wheat-seeds over the coke-fumes
of a punctured barrel.
Chemical air
sweeps in from New Jersey,
and smells of coffee.

Across the river,
ledges of suburban factories tan
in the sulphur-yellow sun
of the unforgivable landscape.

        Robert Lowell (1917–1978)

DEATH

BALLAD OF BIRMINGHAM
(On the bombing of a church in Birmingham, Alabama, 1963)

"Mother dear, may I go downtown
Instead of out to play,
And march the streets of Birmingham
In a Freedom March today?"

"No, baby, no, you may not go, 5
For the dogs are fierce and wild,
And clubs and hoses, guns and jails
Aren't good for a little child."

"But, mother, I won't be alone.
Other children will go with me, 10
And march the streets of Birmingham
To make our country free."

"No, baby, no, you may not go,
For I fear those guns will fire.
But you may go to church instead 15
And sing in the children's choir."

She has combed and brushed her night-dark hair,
And bathed rose petal sweet,
And drawn white gloves on her small brown hands,
And white shoes on her feet. 20

The mother smiled to know her child
Was in the sacred place,
But that smile was the last smile
To come upon her face.

For when she heard the explosion, 25
Her eyes grew wet and wild.
She raced through the streets of Birmingham
Calling for her child.

She clawed through bits of glass and brick,
Then lifted out a shoe. 30
"O, here's the shoe my baby wore,
But, baby, where are you?"

Dudley Randall (b. 1914)

THE FURY OF AERIAL BOMBARDMENT

You would think the fury of aerial bombardment
Would rouse God to relent; the infinite spaces
Are still silent. He looks on shock-pried faces.
History, even, does not know what is meant.

You would feel that after so many centuries   5
God would give man to repent; yet he can kill
As Cain could, but with multitudinous will,
No farther advanced than in his ancient furies.

Was man made stupid to see his own stupidity?
Is God by definition indifferent, beyond us all?   10
Is the eternal truth man's fighting soul
Wherein the Beast ravens in its own avidity?

Of Van Wettering I speak, and Averill,
Names on a list, whose faces I do not recall
But they are gone to early death, who late in school   15
Distinguished the belt feed lever from the belt holding pawl.

Richard Eberhart (b. 1904)

A NOCTURNAL UPON ST. LUCY'S DAY; BEING THE SHORTEST DAY

'Tis the year's midnight, and it is the day's,
Lucy's, who scarce seven hours herself unmasks;
    The sun is spent, and now his flasks
    Send forth light squibs, no constant rays;
        The world's whole sap is sunk;   5
The general balm the hydroptic earth hath drunk,
Whither, as to the bed's-feet, life is shrunk,
Dead and interred; yet all these seem to laugh,
Compared with me, who am their epitaph.

Study me then, you who shall lovers be   10
At the next world, that is, at the next Spring:
    For I am every dead thing,
    In whom love wrought new alchemy.
        For his art did express
A quintessence even from nothingness;   15
From dull privations, and lean emptiness,
He ruin'd me, and I am re-begot
Of absence, darkness, death: things which are not.

All others, from all things, draw all that's good,
Life, soul, form, spirit, whence they being have;   20

    I, by Love's limbeck, am the grave
      Of all that's nothing. Oft a flood
          Have we two wept, and so
Drowned the whole world, us two; oft did we grow
To be two Chaoses, when we did show   25
Care to aught else; and often absences
Withdrew our souls, and made us carcasses.

But I am by her death (which word wrongs her)
Of the first nothing the Elixir grown;
    Were I a man, that I were one   30
      I needs must know; I should prefer,
          If I were any beast,
Some ends, some means; yea plants, yea stones, detest,
And love; all, all, some properties invest;
If I an ordinary nothing were,   35
As shadow, a light and body must be here.

But I am none; nor will my Sun renew.
You lovers, for whose sake the lesser sun
    At this time to the Goat is run
      To fetch new lust and give it you,   40
          Enjoy your summer all;
Since she enjoys her long night's festival,
Let me prepare towards her, and let me call
This hour her Vigil, and her Eve, since this
Both the year's and the day's deep midnight is.   45

        John Donne (1572–1631)

LADY LAZARUS

I have done it again.
One year in every ten
I manage it—

A sort of walking miracle, my skin
Bright as a Nazi lampshade,   5
My right foot

A paperweight,
My face a featureless, fine
Jew linen.

Peel off the napkin   10
O my enemy.
Do I terrify?—

The nose, the eye pits, the full set of teeth?
The sour breath
Will vanish in a day.

Soon, soon the flesh
The grave cave ate will be
At home on me

And I a smiling woman.
I am only thirty.
And like the cat I have nine times to die.

This is Number Three.
What a trash
To annihilate each decade.

What a million filaments.
The peanut-crunching crowd
Shoves in to see

Them unwrap me hand and foot—
The big strip tease.
Gentleman, ladies,

These are my hands,
My knees.
I may be skin and bone,

Nevertheless, I am the same, identical woman.
The first time it happened I was ten.
It was an accident.

The second time I meant
To last it out and not come back at all.
I rocked shut

As a seashell.
They had to call and call
And pick the worms off me like sticky pearls.

Dying
Is an art, like everything else.
I do it exceptionally well.

I do it so it feels like hell.
I do it so it feels real.
I guess you could say I've a call.

It's easy enough to do it in a cell.
It's easy enough to do it and stay put.
It's the theatrical

Comeback in broad day
To the same place, the same face, the same brute
Amused shout:

"A miracle!"   55
That knocks me out.
There is a charge

For the eyeing of my scars, there is a charge
For the hearing of my heart—
It really goes.   60

And there is a charge, a very large charge,
For a word or a touch
Or a bit of blood

Or a piece of my hair or my clothes.
So, so, Herr Doktor.   65
So, Herr Enemy.

I am your opus,
I am your valuable,
The pure gold baby

That melts to a shriek.   70
I turn and burn.
Do not think I underestimate your great concern.

Ash, ash—
You poke and stir.
Flesh, bone, there is nothing there—   75

A cake of soap,
A wedding ring,
A gold filling.

Herr God, Herr Lucifer,
Beware   80
Beware.

Out of the ash
I rise with my red hair
And I eat men like air.

Sylvia Plath (1932–1963)

ON MY FIRST DAUGHTER

Here lies, to each her parents' ruth,
Mary, the daughter of their youth;
Yet all heaven's gifts being heaven's due,

It makes the father less to rue.
At six months' end she parted hence 5
With safety of her innocence;
Whose soul heaven's queen, whose name she bears,
In comfort of her mother's tears,
Hath placed amongst her virgin-train:
Where, while that severed doth remain, 10
This grave partakes the fleshly birth,
Which cover lightly, gentle earth!

Ben Jonson (1573–1637)

WITH RUE MY HEART IS LADEN

With rue my heart is laden
    For golden friends I had,
For many a rose-lipt maiden
    And many a lightfoot lad.

By brooks too broad for leaping 5
    The lightfoot boys are laid;
The rose-lipt girls are sleeping
    In fields where roses fade.

A. E. Housman (1859–1936)

I HEARD A FLY BUZZ

I heard a Fly buzz—when I died—
The Stillness in the Room
Was like the Stillness in the Air—
Between the Heaves of Storm—

The Eyes around—had wrung them dry— 5
And Breaths were gathering firm
For that last Onset—when the King
Be witnessed—in the Room—

I willed my Keepsakes—Signed away
What portion of me be 10
Assignable—and then it was
There interposed a Fly—

With Blue—uncertain stumbling Buzz—
Between the light—and me—
And then the Windows failed—and then 15
I could not see to see—

Emily Dickinson (1830–1886)

PERSPECTIVES ON RELIGION

CHURCH GOING

Once I am sure there's nothing going on
I step inside, letting the door thud shut.
Another church: matting, seats, and stone,
And little books, sprawlings of flowers, cut
For Sunday, brownish now; some brass and stuff
Up at the holy end; the small neat organ;
And a tense, musty, unignorable silence,
Brewed God knows how long. Hatless, I take off
My cycle-clips in awkward reverence,

Move forward, run my hand around the font.
From where I stand, the roof looks almost new—
Cleaned, or restored? Someone would know: I don't.
Mounting the lectern, I peruse a few
Hectoring large-scale verses, and pronounce
'Here endeth' much more loudly than I'd meant.
The echoes snigger briefly. Back at the door
I sign the book, donate an Irish sixpence,
Reflect the place was not worth stopping for.

Yet stop I did: in fact I often do,
And always end much at a loss like this,
Wondering what to look for; wondering, too,
When churches fall completely out of use
What we shall turn them into, if we shall keep
A few cathedrals chronically on show,
Their parchment, plate and pyx in locked cases,
And let the rest rent-free to rain and sheep.
Shall we avoid them as unlucky places?

Or, after dark, will dubious women come
To make their children touch a particular stone;
Pick simples for a cancer; or on some
Advised night see walking a dead one?
Power of some sort or other will go on
In games, in riddles, seemingly at random;
But superstition, like belief, must die,
And what remains when disbelief has gone?
Grass, weedy pavement, brambles, buttress, sky,

A shape less recognisable each week,
A purpose more obscure. I wonder who

Will be the last, the very last, to seek
This place for what it was; one of the crew
That tap and jot and know what rood-lofts were?
Some ruin-bibber, randy for antique,
Or Christmas-addict, counting on a whiff
Of gown-and-bands and organ-pipes and myrrh?
Or will he be my representative,

Bored, uninformed, knowing the ghostly silt
Dispersed, yet tending to this cross of ground
Through suburb scrub because it held unspilt
So long and equably what since is found
Only in separation—marriage, and birth,
And death, and thoughts of these—for whom was built
This special shell? For, though I've no idea
What this accoutred frowsty barn is worth,
It pleases me to stand in silence here;

A serious house on serious earth it is,
In whose blent air all our compulsions meet,
Are recognised, and robed as destinies.
And that much never can be obsolete,
Since someone will forever be surprising
A hunger in himself to be more serious,
And gravitating with it to this ground,
Which, he once heard, was proper to grow wise in,
If only that so many dead lie round.

Philip Larkin (b. 1922)

A HYMN TO GOD THE FATHER

Wilt thou forgive that sin where I begun,
    Which is my sin, though it were done before?
Wilt thou forgive those sins through which I run,
    And do them still: though still I do deplore?
        When thou hast done, thou hast not done,
            For I have more.

Wilt thou forgive that sin by which I won
    Others to sin? and made my sin their door?
Wilt thou forgive that sin which I did shun
    A year, or two, but wallow'd in, a score?
        When thou hast done, thou hast not done,
            For I have more.

I have a sin of fear, that when I have spun
    My last thread, I shall perish on the shore;

Swear by thy self, that at my death thy Sun
Shall shine as it shines now, and heretofore;
    And, having done that, thou hast done,
        I have no more.
           John Donne (1572–1631)

THE JESUS INFECTION

Jesus is with me
on the Blue Grass Parkway going eastbound
He is with me
on the old Harrodsburg Road coming home
I am listening
to country gospel music
in the borrowed Subaru
The gas pedal
and the words
leap to the music
O throw out the lifeline!
Someone is drifting away.

Flags fly up in my mind
without my knowing
where they've been lying furled
and I am happy
living in the sunlight
where Jesus is near.
A man is driving his polled Herefords
across the gleamings of a cornfield
while I am bound for the kingdom of the free.
At the little trestle bridge that has no railing
I see that I won't have to cross Jordan alone.

Signposts every mile exhort me
to Get Right With God
and I move over.
There's a neon message blazing
at the crossroad
catty-corner to the Burger Queen:
Ye Come With Me.
Is it well with my soul, Jesus?
It sounds so easy
to be happy after the sunrise,
to be washed in the crimson flood.

Now I am tailgating
and I read a bumper sticker

on a Ford truck full of Poland Chinas.
It says: Honk If You Know Jesus
and I do it.
My sound blats out for miles
behind the pigsqueal
and it's catching in the front end,
in the axle,
in the universal joint,
this rich contagion.

We are going down the valley on a hairpin turn,
the swine and me, we're breakneck in
we're leaning on
the everlasting arms.

Maxine Kumin (b. 1925)

REDEMPTION

Having been tenant long to a rich lord,
    not thriving, I resolved to be bold,
    And make a suit unto him, to afford
A new small-rented lease and cancel the old.
In heaven at his manor I him sought;
    They told me there that he was lately gone
    About some land, which he had dearly bought
Long since on earth, to take possession.
I straight returned, and knowing his great birth,
    Sought him accordingly in great resorts:
    In cities, theaters, gardens, parks, and courts;
At length I heard a ragged noise and mirth
    Of thieves and murderers; there I him espied,
    Who straight, *Your suit is granted*, said, and died.

George Herbert (1593–1633)

THE WORLD

I saw Eternity the other night,
Like a great Ring of pure and endless light,
    All calm as it was bright;
And round beneath it, Time in hours, days, years,
    Driven by the spheres,
Like a vast shadow moved, in which the world
    And all her train were hurled.
The doting lover in his quaintest strain
    Did there complain;

Near him, his lute, his fancy, and his flights, 10
    Wit's sour delights,
With gloves and knots, the silly snares of pleasure,
    Yet his dear treasure,
All scattered lay, while he his eyes did pore
    Upon a flower. 15

The darksome statesman, hung with weights and woe,
Like a thick midnight-fog, moved there so slow,
    He did not stay nor go;
Condemning thoughts, like sad eclipses, scowl
    Upon his soul, 20
And clouds of crying witnesses without
    Pursued him with one shout.
Yet digged the mole, and lest his ways be found,
    Worked under ground,
Where he did clutch his prey; but one did see 25
    That policy:
Churches and altars fed him; perjuries
    Were gnats and flies;
It rained about him blood and tears; but he
    Drank them as free. 30

The fearful miser on a heap of rust
Sat pining all his life there, did scarce trust
    His own hands with the dust,
Yet would not place one piece above, but lives
    In fear of thieves. 35
Thousands there were as frantic as himself,
    And hugged each one his pelf;
The downright epicure placed heaven in sense
    And scorned pretense;
While others, slipped into a wide excess, 40
    Said little less;
The weaker sort, slight, trivial wares enslave,
    Who think them brave;
And poor, despisèd Truth sat counting by
    Their victory. 45

Yet some, who all this while did weep and sing,
And sing and weep, soared up into the Ring;
    But most would use no wing.
O fools (said I) thus to prefer dark night
    Before true light! 50
To live in grots and caves, and hate the day
    Because it shows the way,

The way which from this dead and dark abode
    Leads up to God,
A way where you might tread the sun and be 55
    More bright than he.
But as I did their madness so discuss,
    One whispered thus:
"This Ring the Bridegroom did for none provide,
    But for His bride." 60

Henry Vaughan (1622–1695)

GOD'S GRANDEUR

The world is charged with the grandeur of God.
    It will flame out, like shining from shook foil;
    It gathers to a greatness, like the ooze of oil
Crushed. Why do men then now not reck his rod?
Generations have trod, have trod, have trod; 5
    And all is seared with trade; bleared, smeared with toil;
    And wears man's smudge and shares man's smell: the soil
Is bare now, nor can foot feel, being shod.

And for all this, nature is never spent;
    There lives the dearest freshness deep down things; 10
And though the last lights off the black West went
    Oh, morning, at the brown brink eastward, springs—
Because the Holy Ghost over the bent
    World broods with warm breast and with ah! bright wings.

Gerard Manley Hopkins (1844–1889)

❖ POETRY AND OTHER ARTS ❖

IN MY CRAFT OR SULLEN ART

In my craft or sullen art
Exercised in the still night
When only the moon rages
And the lovers lie abed
With all their griefs in their arms, 5
I labour by singing light
Not for ambition or bread
Or the strut and trade of charms
On the ivory stages

But for the common wages
Of their most secret heart.

Not for the proud man apart
From the raging moon I write
On these spindrift pages
Nor for the towering dead
With their nightingales and psalms
But for the lovers, their arms
Round the griefs of the ages,
Who pay no praise or wages
Nor heed my craft or art.

 Dylan Thomas (1914–1953)

CONSTANTLY RISKING ABSURDITY

  Constantly risking absurdity
       and death
   whenever he performs
      above the heads
         of his audience
 the poet like an acrobat
    climbs on rime
      to a high wire of his own making
and balancing on eyebeams
      above a sea of faces
  paces his way
    to the other side of day
 performing entrechats
    and sleight-of-foot tricks
and other high theatrics
    and all without mistaking
  any thing
    for what it may not be

 For he's the super realist
     who must perforce perceive
  taut truth
    before the taking of each stance or step
 in his supposed advance
    toward that still higher perch
where Beauty stands and waits
     with gravity
       to start her death-defying leap

And he
> a little charleychaplin man
>> who may or may not catch
> her fair eternal form
>> spreadeagled in the empty air
> of existence

Lawrence Ferlinghetti (b. 1919)

ODE ON A GRECIAN URN

Thou still unravished bride of quietness,
> Thou foster-child of silence and slow time,
Sylvan historian, who canst thus express
> A flowery tale more sweetly than our rhyme:
What leaf-fringed legend haunts about thy shape
> Of deities or mortals, or of both,
>> In Tempe or the dales of Arcady?
> What men or gods are these? What maidens loth?
What mad pursuit? What struggle to escape?
> What pipes and timbrels? What wild ecstasy?

Heard melodies are sweet, but those unheard
> Are sweeter; therefore, ye soft pipes, play on;
Not to the sensual ear, but, more endeared,
> Pipe to the spirit ditties of no tone:
Fair youth, beneath the trees, thou canst not leave
> Thy song, nor ever can those trees be bare;
>> Bold Lover, never, never canst thou kiss,
Though winning near the goal—yet, do not grieve;
> She cannot fade, though thou hast not thy bliss,
>> For ever wilt thou love, and she be fair!

Ah, happy, happy boughs! that cannot shed
> Your leaves, nor ever bid the Spring adieu;
And, happy melodist, unwearied,
> For ever piping songs for ever new;
More happy love! more happy, happy love!
> For ever warm and still to be enjoyed,
>> For ever panting and for ever young;
All breathing human passion far above,
> That leaves a heart high-sorrowful and cloyed,
>> A burning forehead, and a parching tongue.

Who are these coming to the sacrifice?
> To what green altar, O mysterious priest,
Lead'st thou that heifer lowing at the skies,
> And all her silken flanks with garlands drest?

What little town by river or sea shore, 35
    Or mountain-built with peaceful citadel,
        Is emptied of its folks, this pious morn?
        And, little town, thy streets for evermore
    Will silent be; and not a soul to tell
        Why thou art desolate, can e'er return. 40

O Attic shape! Fair attitude! with brede
    Of marble men and maidens overwrought,
With forest branches and the trodden weed;
    Thou, silent form, dost tease us out of thought
As doth eternity: Cold Pastoral! 45
    When old age shall this generation waste,
        Thou shalt remain, in midst of other woe
    Than ours, a friend to man, to whom thou say'st,
Beauty is truth, truth beauty,—that is all
        Ye know on earth, and all ye need to know. 50

            John Keats (1795–1821)

MUSEÉ DES BEAUX ARTS

About suffering they were never wrong,
The Old Masters: how well they understood
Its human position; how it takes place
While someone else is eating or opening a window or just walking
    dully along;
How, when the aged are reverently, passionately waiting 5
For the miraculous birth, there always must be
Children who did not specially want it to happen, skating
On a pond at the edge of the wood:
They never forgot
That even the dreadful martyrdom must run its course 10
Anyhow in a corner, some untidy spot
Where the dogs go on with their doggy life and the torturer's horse
Scratches its innocent behind on a tree.

In Brueghel's *Icarus*, for instance: how everything turns away
Quite leisurely from the disaster; the ploughman may 15
Have heard the splash, the forsaken cry,
But for him it was not an important failure; the sun shone
As it had to on the white legs disappearing into the green
Water; and the expensive delicate ship that must have seen
Something amazing, a boy falling out of the sky, 20
Had somewhere to get to and sailed calmly on.

            W. H. Auden (1907–1973)

LANDSCAPE WITH THE FALL OF ICARUS

According to Brueghel
when Icarus fell
it was spring

a farmer was ploughing
his field
the whole pageantry

of the year was
awake tingling
near

the edge of the sea
concerned
with itself

sweating in the sun
that melted
the wings' wax

unsignificantly
off the coast
there was

a splash quite unnoticed
this was
Icarus drowning

William Carlos Williams (1883–1963)

THE KNIGHT, DEATH, AND THE DEVIL

Cowhorn-crowned, shockheaded, cornshuck-bearded,
Death is a scarecrow—his death's-head a teetotum
That tilts up toward man confidentially
But trimmed with adders; ringlet-maned, rope-bridled,
The mare he rides crops herbs beside a skull.
He holds up, warning, the crossed cones of time:
Here, narrowing into now, the Past and Future
Are quicksand.   A hoofed pikeman trots behind.
His pike's claw-hammer mocks—in duplicate, inverted—
The pocked, ribbed, soaring crescent of his horn.
A scapegoat aged into a steer; boar-snouted;
His great limp ears stuck sidelong out in air;
A dewlap bunched at his breast; a ram's-horn wound

Beneath each ear; a spur licked up and out
From the hide of his forehead; bat-winged, but in bone;
His eye a ring inside a ring inside a ring
That leers up, joyless, vile, in meek obscenity—
This is the devil. Flesh to flesh, he bleats
The herd back to the pit of being.

In fluted mail; upon his lance the bush
Of that old fox; a sheep-dog bounding at his stirrup,
In its eyes the cast of faithfulness (our help,
Our foolish help); his dun war-horse pacing
Beneath in strength, in ceremonious magnificence;
His castle—some man's castle—set on every crag:
So, companioned so, the knight moves through this world.
The fiend moos in amity, Death mouths, reminding:
He listens in assurance, has no glance
To spare for them, but looks past steadily
At—at—
    a man's look completes itself.

The death of his own flesh, set up outside him;
The flesh of his own soul, set up outside him—
Death and the devil, what are these to him?
His being accuses him—and yet his face is firm
In resolution, in absolute persistence;
The folds of smiling do for steadiness;
The face is its own fate—*a man does what he must*—
And the body underneath it says: *I am.*

          Randall Jarrell (1914–1965)

PART THREE

OLD AND MIDDLE ENGLISH

THE SEAFARER

A song I sing   of my sea-adventure,
The strain of peril,   the stress of toil,
Which oft I endured   in anguish of spirit
Through weary hours   of aching woe.
My bark was swept   by the breaking seas;   5
Bitter the watch   from the bow by night
As my ship drove on   within sound of the rocks.
My feet were numb   with the nipping cold,
Hunger sapped   a sea-weary spirit,
And care weighed heavy   upon my heart.   10
   Little the landlubber,   safe on shore,
Knows what I've suffered   in icy seas
Wretched and worn   by the winter storms,
Hung with icicles,   stung by hail,
Lonely and friendless   and far from home.   15
In my ears no sound   but the roar of the sea,
The icy combers,   the cry of the swan;
In place of the mead-hall   and laughter of men
My only singing   the sea-mew's call,
The scream of the gannet,   the shriek of the gull; 20
Through the wail of the wild gale   beating the bluffs
The piercing cry   of the ice-coated petrel,
The storm-drenched eagle's echoing scream.
In all my wretchedness,   weary and lone,
I had no comfort   of comrade or kin.   25
   Little indeed can he credit,   whose town-life
Pleasantly passes   in feasting and joy,
Sheltered from peril,   what weary pain
Often I've suffered   in foreign seas.
Night shades darkened   with driving snow   30
From the freezing north,   and the bonds of frost
Firm-locked the land,   while falling hail,
Coldest of kernels,   encrusted earth.
   Yet still, even now,   my spirit within me
Drives me seaward   to sail the deep,   35
To ride the long swell   of the salt sea-wave.
Never a day   but my heart's desire
Would launch me forth   on the long sea-path,
Fain of far harbors   and foreign shores.
Yet lives no man   so lordly of mood,   40

So eager in giving,   so ardent in youth,
So bold in his deeds,   or so dear to his lord,
Who is free from dread   in his far sea-travel,
Or fear of God's purpose   and plan for his fate.
The beat of the harp,   and bestowal of treasure,   45
The love of woman,   and worldly hope,
Nor other interest   can hold his heart
Save only the sweep   of the surging billows;
His heart is haunted   by love of the sea.
    Trees are budding   and towns are fair,   50
Meadows kindle   and all life quickens,
All things hasten   the eager-hearted,
Who joyeth therein,   to journey afar,
Turning seaward   to distant shores.
The cuckoo stirs him   with plaintive call,   55
The herald of summer,   with mournful song,
Foretelling the sorrow   that stabs the heart.
Who liveth in luxury,   little he knows
What woe men endure   in exile's doom.
    Yet still, even now,   my desire outreaches,   60
My spirit soars   over tracts of sea,
O'er the home of the whale,   and the world's expanse.
Eager, desirous,   the lone sprite returneth;
It cries in my ears   and it urges my heart
To the path of the whale   and the plunging sea.   65

                Anonymous (date unknown)
                (*trans. by Charles W. Kennedy*)

WILD SWAN

My attire is noiseless   when I tread the earth,
Rest in its dwellings   or ride its waters.
At times my pinions   and the lofty air
Lift me high   o'er the homes of men,
And the strength of the clouds   carries me far   5
High over the folk.   My feathers gay
Sound and make music,   singing shrill,
When no longer I linger   by field or flood,
But soar in air,   a wandering spirit.

                Anonymous (date unknown)
                (*trans. by Charles W. Kennedy*)

DEOR'S LAMENT

Weland knew fully   affliction and woe,
Hero unflinching   enduring distress;
Had for companionship   heart-break and longing,
Wintry exile   and anguish of soul,
When Nithhad bound him,   the better man,   5
Grimly constrained him   with sinewy bonds.
That evil ended.   So also may this!
  Nor was brother's death   to Beadohild
A sorrow as deep   as her own sad plight,
When she knew the weight   of the child in her womb,   10
But little could know   what her lot might be.
That evil ended.   So also may this!
  Many have heard   of the rape of Hild,
Of her father's affection   and infinite love,
Whose nights were sleepless   with sorrow and grief.   15
That evil ended.   So also may this!
  For thirty winters   Theodoric held,
As many have known,   the Mæring's stronghold.
That evil ended.   So also may this!
  We have heard of Eormanric's   wolf-like ways,   20
Widely ruling   the realm of the Goths;
Grim was his menace,   and many a man,
Weighted with sorrow   and presage of woe,
Wished that the end   of his kingdom were come.
That evil ended.   So also may this!   25
  He who knows sorrow,   despoiled of joys,
Sits heavy of mood;   to his heart it seemeth
His measure of misery   meeteth no end.
Yet well may he think   how oft in this world
The wise Lord varies   His ways to men,   30
Granting wealth and honor   to many an eorl,
To others awarding   a burden of woe.
  And so I can sing   of my own sad plight
Who long stood high   as the Heodenings' bard,
Deor my name,   dear to my lord.   35
Mild was my service   for many a winter,
Kindly my king   till Heorrenda came
Skillful in song   and usurping the land-right
Which once my gracious lord   granted to me.
That evil ended.   So also may this!   40

Anonymous (date unknown)
(*trans. by Charles W. Kennedy*)

I HAVE A GENTLE COCK

I have a gentle cock, croweth me the day;
He doth me risen early my matins for to say.

I have a gentle cock, comen he is of great;
His comb is of red corral, his tail is of jet.

I have a gentle cock, comen he is of kind; 5
His comb is of red corral, his tail is of Inde.

His legges be of azure, so gentle and so small,
His spurs are of silver-white up to the wortwale.

His eyen are of crystal, locked all in amber,
And every night he percheth him in my lady's chamber. 10

Anonymous (fifteenth century) (modernized)

CHAUCER'S WORDES UNTO ADAM, HIS OWNE SCRIVEYN

Adam scriveyn, if ever it thee bifalle
Boece or Troylus for to wryten newe,
Under thy long lokkes thou most have the scalle,
But after my makyng thou wryte more trewe:
So ofte a-day I mot thy werk renewe, 5
It to correct and eek to rubbe and scrape;
And al is through thy negligence and rape.

Geoffrey Chaucer (ca. 1343–1400)

THE COMPLAINT OF CHAUCER TO HIS PURSE

To yow, my purse, and to noon other wight
Complayne I, for ye be my lady dere!
I am so sory now that ye been lyght;
For certes, but ye make me hevy chere,
Me were as leef be layd upon my bere; 5
For which unto your mercy thus I crye:
Beth hevy ageyn, or elles moot I dye!

Now voucheth sauf this day, or yt be nyght,
That I of yow the blisful soun may here,
Or see your colour lyk the sonne bryght, 10
That of yelownesse hadde never pere.
Ye be my lyf, ye be myn hertes steerer,
Quene of comfort and of good companye:
Beth hevy ageyn, or elles moot I dye!

Now purse, that ben to me my lyves lyght 15
And saveour, as doun in this world here,
Out of this toune helpe me thurgh your myght,
Syn that ye wole nat ben my tresorere;
For I am shave as nye as any frere;
But yet I pray unto your curtesye: 20
Beth hevy agen, or elles moot I dye!

   Lenvoy de Chaucer
O conquerour of Brutes Albyon,
Which that by lyne and free eleccion
Been verray kyng, this song to yow I sende;
And ye that mowen alle oure harmes amende, 25
Have mynde upon my supplicacion!

   Geoffrey Chaucer (ca. 1343–1400)

RENAISSANCE

PSALM 91

He that dwelleth in the secret place of the most High
Shall abide under the shadow of the Almighty.
I will say of the Lord, He is my refuge and my fortress;
My God; in him will I trust.
Surely he shall deliver thee from the snare of the fowler, 5
And from the noisome pestilence.
He shall cover thee with his feathers,
And under his wings shalt thou trust:
His truth shall be thy shield and buckler.
Thou shalt not be afraid for the terror by night; 10
Nor for the arrow that flieth by day;
Nor for the pestilence that walketh in darkness;
Nor for the destruction that wasteth at noonday.
A thousand shall fall at thy side,
And ten thousand at thy right hand; 15
But it shall not come nigh thee.
Only with thine eyes shalt thou behold
And see the reward of the wicked.
Because thou hast made the Lord, which is my refuge,
Even the most High, thy habitation; 20
There shall no evil befall thee,
Neither shall any plague come nigh thy dwelling.

For he shall give his angels charge over thee,
To keep thee in all thy ways.
They shall bear thee up in their hands,
Lest thou dash thy foot against a stone.
Thou shalt tread upon the lion and adder:
The young lion and the dragon shalt thou trample under feet.
Because he hath set his love upon me, therefore will I deliver him:
I will set him on high, because he hath known my name.
He shall call upon me, and I will answer him:
I will be with him in trouble;
I will deliver him, and honour him.
With long life will I satisfy him,
And show him my salvation.

Authorized (King James) Version (1611)

THERE IS A GARDEN IN HER FACE

There is a garden in her face,
Where roses and white lilies grow.
A heavenly paradise is that place,
Wherein all pleasant fruits do flow.
There cherries grow, which none may buy
Till "Cherry ripe!" themselves do cry.

Those cherries fairly do enclose
Of orient pearl a double row,
Which when her lovely laughter shows,
They look like rosebuds filled with snow.
Yet them nor peer nor prince can buy,
Till "Cherry ripe!" themselves do cry.

Her eyes like angels watch them still;
Her brows like bended bows do stand,
Threatening with piercing frowns to kill
All that attempt with eye or hand
Those sacred cherries to come nigh,
Till "Cherry ripe!" themselves do cry.

Thomas Campion (1567–1620)

A SONG

Ask me no more where Jove bestows,
When June is past, the fading rose;
For in your beauty's orient deep
These flowers, as in their causes, sleep.

Ask me no more whither doth stray
The golden atoms of the day;
For in pure love heaven did prepare
Those powders to enrich your hair.

Ask me no more whither doth haste
The nightingale when May is past;
For in your sweet dividing throat
She winters, and keeps warm her note.

Ask me no more where those stars light
That downwards fall in dead of night;
For in your eyes they sit, and there
Fixèd become, as in their sphere.

Ask me no more if east or west
The phœnix builds her spicy nest;
For unto you at last she flies
And in your fragrant bosom dies.

Thomas Carew (1594–1640)

ON OUR LORD CRUCIFIED, NAKED AND BLOODY

They have left Thee naked, Lord. O that they had!
   This garment, too, I would they had denied.
   Thee with Thyself they have too richly clad,
Opening the purple wardrobe of Thy side.
   O never could there garment be too good
   For Thee to wear, but this, of Thine own blood!

Richard Crashaw (1613–1649)

THE DREAM

Dear love, for nothing less than thee
Would I have broke this happy dream;
   It was a theme
For reason, much too strong for fantasy,
Therefore thou wak'dst me wisely; yet
My dream thou brok'st not, but continued'st it,
Thou art so truth, that thoughts of thee suffice
To make dreams truths, and fables histories;
Enter these arms, for since thou thought'st it best
Not to dream all my dream, let's act the rest.

As lightning, or a taper's light,
Thine eyes, and not thy noise, waked me;
   Yet I thought thee

(For thou lovest truth) an angel, at first sight,
But when I saw thou sawest my heart, 15
And knew'st my thoughts, beyond an angel's art,
When thou knew'st what I dreamt, when thou knew'st when
Excess of joy would wake me, and cam'st then,
I must confess, it could not choose but be
Profane to think thee anything but thee. 20

Coming and staying showed thee, thee,
But rising makes me doubt that now
    Thou art not thou.
That love is weak where fear's as strong as he;
'Tis not all spirit, pure and brave, 25
If mixture it of *fear, shame, honor* have.
Perchance, as torches which must ready be,
Men light and put out, so thou deal'st with me;
Thou cam'st to kindle, goest to come; then I
Will dream that hope again, but else would die. 30

John Donne (1572–1631)

FAREWELL TO LOVE

    Whilst yet to prove,
I thought there was some deity in love;
    So did I reverence, and gave
Worship, as atheists at their dying hour
Call what they cannot name, an unknown power; 5
    As ignorantly did I crave:
        Thus when
Things not yet known are coveted by men,
    Our desires give them fashion, and so
As they wax lesser, fall, as they size, grow. 10

    But, from late fair
His Highness sitting in a golden chair
    Is not less cared for after three days
By children, than the thing which lovers so
Blindly admire and with such worship woo; 15
    Being had, enjoying it decays:
        And thence,
What before pleased them all, takes but one sense,
    And that so lamely as it leaves behind
A kind of sorrowing dullness to the mind. 20

    Why cannot we,
As well as cocks and lions, jocund be
    After such pleasures? Unless wise

Nature decreed (since each such act, they say,
Diminisheth the length of life a day)
    This, as she would man should despise
        The sport,
Because that other curse of being short,
    And only for a minute made to be,
Eagers desire, to raise posterity.

    Since so, my mind
Shall not desire what no man else can find;
    I'll no more dote and run
To pursue things which had endamaged me.
And when I come where moving beauties be,
    As men do when the summer's sun
        Grows great,
Though I admire their greatness, shun their heat;
    Each place can afford shadows. If all fail,
'Tis but applying wormseed to the tail.

        John Donne (1572–1631)

SONG: GO AND CATCH A FALLING STAR

Go and catch a falling star,
    Get with child a mandrake root,
Tell me where all past years are,
    Or who cleft the Devil's foot,
Teach me to hear mermaids singing,
Or to keep off envy's stinging,
        And find
        What wind
Serves to advance an honest mind.

If thou beest born to strange sights,
    Things invisible to see,
Ride ten thousand days and nights,
    Till age snow white hairs on thee.
Thou, when thou return'st, wilt tell me
All strange wonders that befell thee,
        And swear
        No where
Lives a woman true and fair.

If thou find'st one, let me know:
    Such a pilgrimage were sweet.
Yet do not; I would not go,
    Though at next door we might meet.

Though she were true when you met her,
And last till you write your letter,
      Yet she 25
      Will be
False, ere I come, to two or three.

John Donne (1572–1631)

HOW MANY PALTRY, FOOLISH, PAINTED THINGS

How many paltry, foolish, painted things
That now in coaches trouble every street
Shall be forgotten, whom no poet sings,
Ere they be well wrapped in their winding-sheet!
Where I to thee eternity shall give 5
When nothing else remaineth of these days,
And queens hereafter shall be glad to live
Upon the alms of thy superfluous praise.
Virgins and matrons reading these my rhymes
Shall be so much delighted with thy story 10
That they shall grieve they lived not in these times,
To have seen thee, their sex's only glory.
    So shalt thou fly above the vulgar throng,
    Still to survive in my immortal song.

Michael Drayton (1563–1631)

THE ALTAR

A broken altar, Lord, Thy servant rears,
Made of a heart and cemented with tears;
  Whose parts are as Thy hand did frame;
  No workman's tool hath touched the same.
      A   heart   alone 5
      Is such a stone,
      As nothing but
      Thy power doth cut.
      Wherefore each part
      Of my hard heart 10
      Meets in this frame
      To praise Thy name,
  That if I chance to hold my peace,
  These stones to praise Thee may not cease.
Oh, let Thy blessed sacrifice be mine, 15
And sanctify this altar to be Thine.

George Herbert (1593–1633)

VANITY (I)

    The fleet astronomer can bore
And thread the spheres with his quick-piercing mind.
He views their stations, walks from door to door,
    Surveys as if he had designed
To make a purchase there; he sees their dances,
        And knoweth long before
Both their full-eyed aspects and secret glances.

    The nimble diver with his side
Cuts through the working waves, that he may fetch
His dearly-earnéd pearl, which God did hide
    On purpose from the venturous wretch,
That he might save his life, and also hers
        Who with excessive pride
Her own destruction and his danger wears.

    The subtle chymic can divest
And strip the creature naked, till he find
The callow principles within their nest.
    There he imparts to them his mind,
Admitted to their bed-chamber, before
        They appear trim and dressed
To ordinary suitors at the door.

    What hath not man sought out and found
But his dear God? who yet His glorious law
Embosoms in us, mellowing the ground
    With showers and frosts, with love and awe,
So that we need not say, "Where's this command?"
        Poor man, thou searchest round
To find out death, but missest life at hand.

        George Herbert (1593–1633)

DELIGHT IN DISORDER

A sweet disorder in the dress
Kindles in clothes a wantonness.
A lawn about the shoulders thrown
Into a fine distraction,
An erring lace which here and there
Enthralls the crimson stomacher,
A cuff neglectful, and thereby
Ribbons to flow confusedly,
A winning wave (deserving note)
In the tempestuous petticoat,

A careless shoestring in whose tie
I see a wild civility,
Do more bewitch me than when art
Is too precise in every part.

  Robert Herrick (1591–1674)

UPON PRUE, HIS MAID

In this little urn is laid
Prudence Baldwin, once my maid,
From whose happy spark here let
Spring the purple violet.

  Robert Herrick (1591–1674)

THE VINE

I dreamed this mortal part of mine
Was metamorphosed to a vine
Which, crawling one and every way,
Enthralled my dainty Lucia.
Methought her long small legs and thighs 5
I with my tendrils did surprise;
Her belly, buttocks, and her waist
By my soft nervelets were embraced;
About her head I writhing hung,
And with rich clusters, hid among 10
The leaves, her temples I behung,
So that my Lucia seemed to me
Young Bacchus ravished by his tree.
My curls about her neck did crawl,
And arms and hands they did enthrall, 15
So that she could not freely stir,
All parts there made one prisoner.
But when I crept with leaves to hide
Those parts which maids keep unespied,
Such fleeting pleasures there I took 20
That with the fancy I awook,
And found (Ah me!) this flesh of mine
More like a stock than like a vine.

  Robert Herrick (1591–1674)

COMPLAINT OF A LOVER REBUKED

Love that doth reign and live within my thought,
And built his seat within my captive breast,
Clad in the arms wherein with me he fought,
Oft in my face he doth his banner rest.
But she that taught me love and suffer pain, 5
My doubtful hope and eke my hot desire
With shamefast look to shadow and refrain,
Her smiling grace converteth straight to ire.
And coward Love then to the heart apace
Taketh his flight, where he doth lurk and plain 10
His purpose lost, and dare not show his face.
For my lord's guilt thus faultless bide I pain.
    Yet from my lord shall not my foot remove:
    Sweet is the death that taketh end by love.

    Henry Howard, Earl of Surrey (ca. 1517–1547)

SONG: COME, MY CELIA

Come, my Celia, let us prove,
While we may, the sports of love.
Time will not be ours forever;
He at length our good will sever.
Spend not then his gifts in vain: 5
Suns that set may rise again;
But if once we lose this light,
'Tis with us perpetual night.
Why should we defer our joys?
Fame and rumor are but toys. 10
Cannot we delude the eyes
Of a few poor household spies?
Or his easier ears beguile,
So removéd by our wile?
'Tis no sin love's fruit to steal, 15
But the sweet theft to reveal;
To be taken, to be seen,
These have crimes accounted been.

    Ben Jonson (1572–1637)

STILL TO BE NEAT

Still to be neat, still to be dressed,
As you were going to a feast;
Still to be powdered, still perfumed;

Lady, it is to be presumed,
Though art's hid causes are not found,
All is not sweet, all is not sound.

Give me a look, give me a face
That makes simplicity a grace;
Robes loosely flowing, hair as free;
Such sweet neglect more taketh me
Then all the adulteries of art:
They strike mine eyes, but not my heart.

   Ben Jonson (1572–1637)

LA BELLA BONA ROBA

I cannot tell who loves the skeleton
Of a poor marmoset, nought but bone, bone.
Give me a nakedness with her clothes on.

Such whose white satin upper coat of skin,
Cut upon velvet rich incarnadin,
Has yet a body (and of flesh) within.

Sure it is meant good husbandry in men
Who do incorporate with airy lean,
T' repair their sides and get their rib again.

Hard hap unto that huntsman that decrees
Fat joys for all his sweat, whenas he sees,
After his 'say, nought but his keeper's fees.

Then Love, I beg, when next thou tak'st thy bow,
Thy angry shafts, and dost heart-chasing go,
Pass rascal deer, strike me the largest doe.

   Richard Lovelace (1618–1658)

TO LUCASTA, GOING TO THE WARS

Tell me not, sweet, I am unkind
That from the nunnery
Of thy chaste breast and quiet mind,
To war and arms I fly.

True, a new mistress now I chase,
The first foe in the field;
And with a stronger faith embrace
A sword, a horse, a shield.

Yet this inconstancy is such
As you too shall adore;
I could not love thee, dear, so much,
Loved I not honor more.

    Richard Lovelace (1618–1658)

THE PASSIONATE SHEPHERD TO HIS LOVE

Come live with me and be my love,
And we will all the pleasures prove
That valleys, groves, hills, and fields,
Woods, or steepy mountain yields.

And we will sit upon the rocks,
Seeing the shepherds feed their flocks
By shallow rivers to whose falls
Melodious birds sing madrigals.

And I will make thee beds of roses
And a thousand fragrant posies,
A cap of flowers and a kirtle
Embroidered all with leaves of myrtle;

A gown made of the finest wool
Which from our pretty lambs we pull;
Fair linèd slippers for the cold,
With buckles of the purest gold;

A belt of straw and ivy buds,
With coral clasps and amber studs.
And if these pleasures may thee move,
Come live with me and be my love.

The shepherd swains shall dance and sing
For thy delight each May morning.
If these delights thy mind may move,
Then live with me and be my love.

    Christopher Marlowe (1564–1593)

THE DEFINITION OF LOVE

My love is of a birth as rare
As 'tis, for object, strange and high;
It was begotten by Despair
Upon Impossibility.

Magnanimous Despair alone
Could show me so divine a thing,
Where feeble Hope could ne'er have flown,
But vainly flapped its tinsel wing.

And yet I quickly might arrive
Where my extended soul is fixed;
But Fate does iron wedges drive
And always crowds itself betwixt.

For Fate with jealous eyes does see
Two perfect loves, nor lets them close;
Their union would her ruin be
And her tyrannic power depose.

And therefore her decrees of steel
Us as the distant poles have placed
(Though Love's whole world on us doth wheel),
Not by themselves to be embraced;

Unless the giddy heaven fall
And earth some new convulsion tear,
And, us to join, the world should all
Be cramped into a planisphere.

As lines, so loves, oblique may well
Themselves in every angle greet;
But ours, so truly parallel,
Though infinite, can never meet.

Therefore the love which us doth bind,
But Fate so enviously debars,
Is the conjunction of the mind
And opposition of the stars.

Andrew Marvell (1621–1678)

THE PICTURE OF LITTLE T.C. IN A PROSPECT OF FLOWERS

See with what simplicity
This nymph begins her golden days!
In the green grass she loves to lie,
And there with her fair aspect tames
The wilder flowers, and gives them names;
But only with the roses plays,
    And them does tell
What color best becomes them, and what smell.

Who can foretell for what high cause
This darling of the gods was born? 10
Yet this is she whose chaster laws
The wanton Love shall one day fear,
And, under her command severe,
See his bow broke and ensigns torn.
    Happy who can 15
Appease this virtuous enemy of man!

O then let me in time compound
And parley with those conquering eyes
Ere they have tried their force to wound;
Ere with their glancing wheels they drive 20
In triumph over hearts that strive,
And them that yield but more despise:
    Let me be laid
Where I may see thy glories from some shade.

Meantime, whilst every verdant thing 25
Itself does at thy beauty charm,
Reform the errors of the spring:
Make that the tulips may have share
Of sweetness, seeing they are fair;
And roses of their thorns disarm; 30
    But most procure
That violets may a longer age endure.

But, O young beauty of the woods,
Whom nature courts with fruits and flowers,
Gather the flowers, but spare the buds, 35
Lest Flora, angry at thy crime
To kill her infants in their prime,
Do quickly make the example yours;
    And ere we see,
Nip in the blossom all our hopes and thee. 40

    Andrew Marvell (1621–1678)

HOW SOON HATH TIME

How soon hath Time, the subtle thief of youth,
    Stol'n on his wing my three and twentieth year!
    My hasting days fly on with full career,
    But my late spring no bud or blossom show'th.

Perhaps my semblance might deceive the truth, 5
    That I to manhood am arrived so near,

    And inward ripeness doth much less appear,
    That some more timely-happy spirits endu'th.
Yet be it less or more, or soon or slow,
    It shall be still in strictest measure even   10
    To that same lot, however mean or high,
Toward which Time leads me, and the will of Heaven;
    All is, if I have grace to use it so,
    As ever in my great Taskmaster's eye.

                John Milton (1608–1674)

WHEN I CONSIDER HOW MY LIGHT IS SPENT

When I consider how my light is spent
    Ere half my days in this dark world and wide,
    And that one talent which is death to hide
    Lodged with me useless, though my soul more bent
To serve therewith my Maker, and present   5
    My true account, lest He returning chide.
    "Doth God exact day-labor, light denied?"
    I fondly° ask. But Patience, to prevent   °foolishly
That murmur, soon replies, "God doth not need
    Either man's work or his own gifts; who best   10
    Bear His mild yoke, they serve Him best. His state
Is kingly: thousands at His bidding speed
    And post° o'er land and ocean without rest: °travel with haste
    They also serve who only stand and wait."

                John Milton (1608–1674)

THE NYMPH'S REPLY TO THE SHEPHERD

If all the world and love were young,
And truth in every shepherd's tongue,
These pretty pleasures might me move
To live with thee and be thy love.

Time drives the flocks from field to fold   5
When rivers rage and rocks grow cold,
And Philomel becometh dumb;
The rest complains of cares to come.

The flowers do fade, and wanton fields
To wayward winter reckoning yields;   10
A honey tongue, a heart of gall,
Is fancy's spring but sorrow's fall.

Thy gowns, thy shoes, thy beds of roses,
Thy cap, thy kirtle, and thy posies
Soon break, soon wither, soon forgotten,   15
In folly ripe, in reason rotten.

Thy belt of straw and ivy buds,
Thy coral clasps and amber studs,
All these in me no means can move
To come to thee and be thy love.   20

But could youth last and love still breed,
Had joys no date, nor age no need,
Then these delights my mind might move
To live with thee and be thy love.

    Sir Walter Raleigh (ca. 1552–1618)

SONNET 18: SHALL I COMPARE THEE TO A SUMMER'S DAY

Shall I compare thee to a summer's day?
Thou art more lovely and more temperate.
Rough winds do shake the darling buds of May,
And summer's lease hath all too short a date;
Sometime too hot the eye of heaven shines,   5
And often is his gold complexion dimmed;
And every fair from fair sometimes declines,
By chance, or nature's changing course, untrimmed.
But thy eternal summer shall not fade
Nor lose possession of that fair thou owest,   10
Nor shall Death brag thou wand'rest in his shade
When in eternal lines to time thou growest.
    So long as men can breathe or eyes can see,
    So long lives this, and this gives life to thee.

    William Shakespeare (1564–1616)

SONNET 29: WHEN IN DISGRACE WITH FORTUNE AND MEN'S EYES

When in disgrace with Fortune and men's eyes
I all alone beweep my outcast state
And trouble deaf heaven with my bootless cries
And look upon myself and curse my fate,
Wishing me like to one more rich in hope,   5
Featured like him, like him with friends possessed,
Desiring this man's art and that man's scope,
With what I most enjoy contented least;

Yet in these thoughts myself almost despising,
Haply I think on thee, and then my state,
Like to the lark at break of day arising
From sullen earth, sings hymns at heaven's gate;
    For thy sweet love remembered such wealth brings
    That then I scorn to change my state with kings.

William Shakespeare (1564–1616)

SONNET 33: FULL MANY A GLORIOUS MORNING HAVE I SEEN

Full many a glorious morning have I seen
Flatter the mountain tops with sovereign eye,
Kissing with golden face the meadows green,
Gilding pale streams with heavenly alchemy;
Anon permit the basest clouds to ride
With ugly rack on his celestial face,
And from the forlorn world his visage hide,
Stealing unseen to west with this disgrace.
Even so my sun one early morn did shine
With all-triumphant splendor on my brow;
But, out alack, he was but one hour mine:
The region cloud hath masked him from me now.
    Yet him for this my love no whit disdaineth;
    Suns of the world may stain when heaven's sun staineth.

William Shakespeare (1564–1616)

SONNET 129: TH' EXPENSE OF SPIRIT IN A WASTE OF SHAME

Th' expense of spirit in a waste of shame
Is lust in action; and, till action, lust
Is perjured, murd'rous, bloody, full of blame,
Savage, extreme, rude, cruel, not to trust;
Enjoyed no sooner but despisèd straight;
Past reason hunted, and no sooner had,
Past reason hated as a swallowed bait
On purpose laid to make the taker mad—
Mad in pursuit, and in possession so;
Had, having, and in quest to have, extreme;
A bliss in proof, and proved, a very woe;
Before, a joy proposed; behind, a dream.
    All this the world well knows, yet none knows well
    To shun the heaven that leads men to this hell.

William Shakespeare (1564–1616)

SONNET 146: POOR SOUL, THE CENTER OF MY SINFUL EARTH

Poor soul, the center of my sinful earth,
[Fooled by] these rebel pow'rs that thee array,
Why dost thou pine within and suffer dearth,
Painting thy outward walls so costly gay?
Why so large cost, having so short a lease,　　　　　　　　5
Dost thou upon thy fading mansion spend?
Shall worms, inheritors of this excess,
Eat up thy charge? Is this thy body's end?
Then, soul, live thou upon thy servant's loss,
And let that pine to aggravate thy store.　　　　　　　　10
Buy terms divine in selling hours of dross;
Within be fed, without be rich no more:
    So shalt thou feed on Death, that feeds on men;
    And Death once dead, there's no more dying then.

William Shakespeare (1564–1616)

LEAVE ME, O LOVE

Leave me, O love, which reachest but to dust,
And thou, my mind, aspire to higher things.
Grow rich in that which never taketh rust:
Whatever fades but fading pleasure brings.
Draw in thy beams, and humble all thy might　　　　　　　5
To that sweet yoke where lasting freedoms be,
Which breaks the clouds and opens forth the light
That doth both shine and give us sight to see.
O take fast hold: let that light be thy guide
In this small course which birth draws out to death,　　　10
And think how evil becometh him to slide
Who seeketh heaven and comes of heavenly breath.
Then farewell, world! thy uttermost I see!
Eternal Love, maintain thy life in me.

Sir Philip Sidney (1554–1586)

LOVING IN TRUTH

Loving in truth, and fain in verse my love to show,
That she, dear she, might take some pleasure of my pain,
Pleasure might cause her read, reading might make her know,
Knowledge might pity win, and pity grace obtain,
I sought fit words to paint the blackest face of woe:　　　5

Studying inventions fine, her wits to entertain,
Oft turning others' leaves, to see if thence would flow
Some fresh and fruitful showers upon my sunburned brain.
But words came halting forth, wanting Invention's stay;
Invention, Nature's child, fled stepdame Study's blows;   10
And others' feet still seemed but strangers in my way.
Thus, great with child to speak and helpless in my throes,
Biting my truant pen, beating myself for spite:
"Fool," said my Muse to me, "look in thy heart, and write."

Sir Philip Sidney (1554–1586)

THE BURNING BABE

As I in hoary winter's night stood shivering in the snow,
Surprised I was with sudden heat which made my heart to glow;
And lifting up a fearful eye to view what fire was near,
A pretty babe all burning bright did in the air appear,
Who, scorchèd with exceeding heat such floods of tears did shed,   5
As though his floods should quench his flames with what his tears
    were fed.
"Alas!" quoth he, "but newly born in fiery heats I fry,
Yet none approach to warm their hearts or feel my fire but I.
My faultless breast the furnace is, the fuel wounding thorns;
Love is the fire and sighs the smoke, the ashes shame and scorns;   10
The fuel Justice layeth on, and Mercy blows the coals;
The metal in this furnace wrought are men's defilèd souls;
For which, as now on fire I am, to work them to their good,
So will I melt into a bath, to wash them in my blood."
With this he vanished out of sight, and swiftly shrunk away,   15
And straight I callèd unto mind that it was Christmas Day.

Robert Southwell (ca. 1561–1595)

LIKE AS A HUNTSMAN

Like as a huntsman, after weary chase,
Seeing the game from him escaped away,
Sits down to rest him in some shady place,
With panting hounds beguiléd of their prey:
So after long pursuit and vain assay,   5
When I all weary had the chase forsook,
The gentle deer returned the self-same way,
Thinking to quench her thirst at the next brook.
There she, beholding me with milder look,
Sought not to fly, but fearless still did bide: 10

Till I in hand her yet half trembling took
And with her own good will her firmly tied.
Strange thing, me seemed, to see a beast so wild,
So goodly won, with her own will beguiled.

   Edmund Spenser (ca. 1552–1599)

ONE DAY I WROTE HER NAME UPON THE STRAND

One day I wrote her name upon the strand,
But came the waves and washéd it away:
Again I wrote it with a second hand,
But came the tide and made my pains his prey.
"Vain man," said she, "that dost in vain assay,   5
A mortal thing so to immortalize,
But I myself shall like to this decay,
And eke my name be wiped out likewise."
"Not so!" quod I. "Let baser things devise
To die in dust, but you shall live by fame: 10
My verse your virtues rare shall eternize
And in the heavens write your glorious name:
  Where whenas death shall all the world subdue,
  Our love shall live, and later life renew."

   Edmund Spenser (ca. 1552–1599)

OUT UPON IT!

Out upon it! I have loved
  Three whole days together,
And am like to love three more,
  If it prove fair weather.

Time shall molt away his wings,   5
  Ere he shall discover
In the whole wide world again
  Such a constant lover.

But the spite on 't is, no praise
  Is due at all to me: 10
Love with me had made no stays
  Had it any been but she.

Had it any been but she
  And that very face,
There had been at least ere this   15
  A dozen dozen in her place.

 Sir John Suckling (1609–1642)

SONG

    Go, lovely rose!
Tell her that wastes her time and me
    That now she knows,
When I resemble her to thee,
How sweet and fair she seems to be.

    Tell her that's young
And shuns to have her graces spied,
    That hadst thou sprung
In deserts where no men abide
Thou must have uncommended died.

    Small is the worth
Of beauty from the light retired;
    Bid her come forth,
Suffer herself to be desired,
And not blush so to be admired.

    Then die! that she
The common fate of all things rare
    May read in thee;
How small a part of time they share
That are so wondrous sweet and fair!

    Edmund Waller (1606–1687)

WHOSO LIST TO HUNT

Whoso list to hunt, I know where is an hind,
    But as for me, alas, I may no more:
    The vain travail hath wearied me so sore,
    I am of them that farthest cometh behind.
Yet may I by no means my wearied mind
    Draw from the Deer, but as she fleeth afore.
Fainting I follow. I leave off therefore,
    Since in a net I seek to hold the wind.
Who list her hunt (I put him out of doubt)
    As well as I may spend his time in vain.
    And graven with diamonds in letters plain,
There is written her fair neck round about,
    "*Noli me tangere,* for Caesar's I am,
    And wild for to hold, though I seem tame."

    Sir Thomas Wyatt (1503–1545)

RESTORATION AND EIGHTEENTH CENTURY

ODE TO THE SPACIOUS FIRMAMENT

The spacious firmament on high,
With all the blue ethereal sky
And spangled heavens, a shining frame,
Their great Original proclaim.
The unwearied sun from day to day   5
Does his Creator's power display,
And publishes to every land
The work of an Almighty hand.

Soon, as the evening shades prevail,
The moon takes up the wondrous tale   10
And nightly to the listening earth
Repeats the story of her birth;
Whilst all the stars that round her burn
And all the planets in their turn
Confirm the tidings as they roll   15
And spread the truth from pole to pole.

What though in solemn silence, all
Move round this dark terrestrial ball?
What though nor real voice nor sound
Amidst their radiant orbs be found?   20
In Reason's ear they all rejoice,
And utter forth a glorious voice,
Forever singing as they shine:
"The hand that made us is divine!"

Joseph Addison (1672–1719)

ODE TO EVENING

If aught of oaten stop or pastoral song
May hope, chaste Eve, to soothe thy modest ear,
    Like thy own solemn springs,
    Thy springs and dying gales,

O nymph reserved, while now the bright-haired sun   5
Sits in yon western tent, whose cloudy skirts,
    With brede ethereal wove,
    O'erhang his wavy bed—

Now air is hushed, save where the weak-eyed bat,
With short shrill shriek, flits by on leathern wing; 10
    Or where the beetle winds
    His small but sullen horn,

As oft he rises 'midst the twilight path
Against the pilgrim borne in heedless hum—
    Now teach me, maid composed, 15
    To breathe some softened strain,

Whose numbers, stealing through thy darkening vale,
May not unseemly with its stillness suit,
    As musing slow, I hail
    Thy genial loved return! 20

For when thy folding-star arising shows
His paly circlet, at his warning lamp
    The fragrant Hours, and elves
    Who slept in flowers the day,

And many a nymph who wreathes her brows with sedge 25
And sheds the freshening dew, and, lovelier still,
    The pensive Pleasures sweet
    Prepare thy shadowy car.

Then lead, calm vot'ress, where some sheety lake
Cheers the lone heath, or some time-hallowed pile 30
    Or upland fallows gray
    Reflect its last cool gleam.

But when chill blustering winds or driving rain
Forbid my willing feet, be mine the hut
    That from the mountain's side 35
    Views wilds, and swelling floods,

And hamlets brown, and dim-discovered spires,
And hears their simple bell, and marks o'er all
    Thy dewy fingers draw
    The gradual dusky veil. 40

While Spring shall pour his showers, as oft he wont,
And bathe thy breathing tresses, meekest Eve;
    While Summer loves to sport
    Beneath thy lingering light;

While sallow Autumn fills thy lap with leaves; 45
Or Winter, yelling through the troublous air,
    Affrights thy shrinking train,
    And rudely rends thy robes;

So long, sure-found beneath the sylvan shed,
Shall Fancy, Friendship, Science, rose-lipped Health, 50
    Thy gentlest influence own,
    And hymn thy favorite name!

               William Collins (1721–1759)

TO THE MEMORY OF MR. OLDHAM

Farewell, too little and too lately known,
Whom I began to think and call my own;
For sure our Souls were near allied, and thine
Cast in the same Poetic mould with mine,
One common Note on either Lyre did strike, 5
And Knaves and Fools we both abhorred alike:
To the same Goal did both our Studies drive,
The last set out the soonest did arrive.
Thus Nisus fell upon the slippery place,
While his young Friend performed and won the Race. 10
O early ripe! to thy abundant store
What could advancing Age have added more?
It might (what Nature never gives the young)
Have taught the numbers of thy native Tongue.
But Satyr needs not those, and Wit will shine 15
Through the harsh cadence of a rugged line.
A noble Error, and but seldom made,
When Poets are by too much force betrayed.
Thy generous fruits, though gathered ere their prime
Still showed a quickness; and maturing time 20
But mellows what we write to the dull sweets of Rime.
Once more, hail and farewell; farewell thou young,
But ah too short, Marcellus of our Tongue;
Thy Brows with Ivy, and with Laurels bound;
But Fate and gloomy Night encompass thee around. 25

               John Dryden (1631–1700)

AN ELEGY ON THE DEATH OF A MAD DOG

Good people all, of ev'ry sort,
    Give ear unto my song;
And if you find it wondrous short,
    It cannot hold you long.

In Isling town there was a man, 5
    Of whom the world might say,

That still a godly race he ran,
    Whene'er he went to pray.

A kind and gentle heart he had,
    To comfort friends and foes;   10
The naked ev'ry day he clad,
    When he put on his clothes.

And in that town a dog was found,
    As many dogs there be,
Both mongrel, puppy, whelp and hound,   15
    And curs of low degree.

This dog and man at first were friends;
    But when a pique began,
The dog, to gain some private ends,
    Went mad and bit the man.   20

Around from all the neighb'ring streets,
    The wond'ring neighbours ran,
And swore the dog had lost his wits,
    To bite so good a man.

The wound it seem'd both sore and sad,   25
    To ev'ry Christian eye;
And while they swore the dog was mad,
    They swore the man would die.

But soon a wonder came to light,
    That show'd the rogues they lied;   30
The man recover'd of the bite,
    The dog it was that died.

        Oliver Goldsmith (1730–1774)

WHEN LOVELY WOMAN STOOPS TO FOLLY

When lovely woman stoops to folly
    And finds too late that men betray,
What charm can soothe her melancholy,
    What art can wash her guilt away?

The only art her guilt to cover,   5
    To hide her shame from every eye,
To give repentance to her lover,
    And wring his bosom—is to die.

        Oliver Goldsmith (1730–1774)

ODE

*On the Death of a Favorite Cat,
Drowned in a Tub of Goldfishes*

'Twas on a lofty vase's side,
Where China's gayest art had dyed
    The azure flowers that blow;
Demurest of the tabby kind,
The pensive Selima, reclined,
    Gazed on the lake below.

Her conscious tail her joy declared;
The fair round face, the snowy beard,
    The velvet of her paws,
Her coat that with the tortoise vies,
Her ears of jet, and emerald eyes,
    She saw—and purred applause.

Still had she gazed; but 'midst the tide
Two angel forms were seen to glide,
    The genii of the stream:
Their scaly armor's Tyrian hue
Through richest purple to the view
    Betrayed a golden gleam.

The hapless nymph with wonder saw:
A whisker first and then a claw
    (With many an ardent wish)
She stretched in vain to reach the prize.
What female heart can gold despise?
    What cat's averse to fish?

Presumptuous maid! with looks intent
Again she stretched, again she bent,
    Nor knew the gulf between.
(Malignant Fate sat by and smiled)
The slippery verge her feet beguiled,
    She tumbled headlong in.

Eight times emerging from the flood
She mewed to every watery god,
    Some speedy aid to send.
No dolphin came, no Nereid stirred;
Nor cruel Tom, nor Susan heard;
    A favorite has no friend!

From hence, ye beauties, undeceived,
Know: one false step is ne'er retrieved;
    And be with caution bold.

Not all that tempts your wandering eyes
And heedless hearts is lawful prize;
    Nor all that glisters, gold.

        Thomas Gray (1716–1771)

ODE ON SOLITUDE

Happy the man whose wish and care
    A few paternal acres bound,
Content to breathe his native air
    In his own ground,

Whose herds with milk, whose fields with bread,
    Whose flocks supply him with attire,
Whose trees in summer yield him shade,
    In winter fire.

Blest, who can unconcernedly find
    Hours, days, and years slide soft away,
In health of body, peace of mind,
    Quiet by day,

Sound sleep by night; study and ease,
    Together mixed; sweet recreation;
And innocence, which most does please
    With meditation.

Thus let me live, unseen, unknown;
    Thus unlamented let me die,
Steal from the world, and not a stone
    Tell where I lie.

        Alexander Pope (1688–1744)

A DESCRIPTION OF A CITY SHOWER

    Careful observers may foretell the hour
(By sure prognostics) when to dread a shower:
While rain depends, the pensive cat gives o'er
Her frolics and pursues her tail no more.
Returning home at night, you'll find the sink
Strike your offended sense with double stink.
If you be wise, then go not far to dine;
You'll spend in coach hire more than save in wine.
A coming shower your shooting corns presage,
Old aches throb, your hollow tooth will rage.
Sauntering in coffeehouse is Dulman seen;

He damns the climate and complains of spleen.
      Meanwhile the South, rising with dabbled wings,
A sable cloud athwart the welkin flings,
That swilled more liquor than it could contain,   15
And, like a drunkard, gives it up again.
Brisk Susan whips her linen from the rope,
While the first drizzling shower is borne aslope:
Such is that sprinkling which some careless quean
Flirts on you from her mop, but not so clean: 20
You fly; invoke the gods; then, turning, stop
To rail; she, singing, still whirls on her mop.
Not yet the dust had shunned the unequal strife
But, aided by the wind, fought still for life,
And wafted with its foe by violent gust,   25
'Twas doubtful which was rain and which was dust.
Ah! where must needy poet seek for aid,
When dust and rain at once his coat invade?
Sole coat, where dust cemented by the rain
Erects the nap, and leaves a mingled stain.   30
      Now in contiguous drops the flood comes down,
Threatening with deluge this devoted town.
To shops in crowds the daggled females fly,
Pretend to cheapen goods, but nothing buy.
The Templar spruce, while every spout's abroach,   35
Stays till 'tis fair, yet seems to call a coach.
The tucked-up sempstress walks with hasty strides,
While streams run down her oiled umbrella's sides.
Here various kinds, by various fortunes led,
Commence acquaintance underneath a shed.   40
Triumphant Tories and desponding Whigs
Forget their feuds and join to save their wigs.
Boxed in a chair, the beau impatient sits,
While spouts run clattering o'er the roof by fits,
And ever and anon with frightful din   45
The leather sounds; he trembles from within.
So when Troy chairmen bore the wooden steed,
Pregnant with Greeks impatient to be freed
(Those bully Greeks, who, as the moderns do,
Instead of paying chairmen, run them through),   50
Laocoön struck the outside with his spear,
And each imprisoned hero quaked for fear.
      Now from all parts the swelling kennels flow
And bear their trophies with them as they go:
Filth of all hues and odors seem to tell   55

What street they sailed from, by their sight and smell.
They, as each torrent drives with rapid force,
From Smithfield or St. Pulchre's shape their course,
And in huge confluence joined at Snow Hill ridge,
Fall from the conduit prone to Holborn Bridge. 60
Sweepings from butchers' stalls, dung, guts, and blood,
Drowned puppies, stinking sprats, all drenched in mud,
Dead cats, and turnip tops, come tumbling down the flood.

Jonathan Swift (1667–1745)

A DESCRIPTION OF THE MORNING

Now hardly here and there a Hackney-Coach
Appearing, showed the Ruddy Morn's Approach.
Now Betty from her Master's Bed had flown,
And softly stole to discompose her own.
The Slipshod Prentice from his Master's Door, 5
Had par'd the Dirt, and Sprinkled round the Floor.
Now Moll had whirled her Mop with dext'rous Airs,
Prepared to Scrub the Entry and the Stairs.
The Youth with Broomy Stumps began to trace
The Kennel-Edge, where Wheels had worn the Place. 10
The Smallcoal-Man was heard with Cadence deep,
'Till drowned in Shriller Notes of Chimney-Sweep.
Duns at his Lordship's Gate began to meet,
And Brickdust Moll had Screamed through half a Street.
The Turnkey now his Flock returning sees, 15
Duly let out a Nights to Steal for Fees.
The watchful Bailiffs take their silent Stands,
And School-Boys lag with Satchels in their Hands.

Jonathan Swift (1667–1745)

THE DAY OF JUDGEMENT

With a Whirl of Thought oppressed,
I sink from Reverie to Rest.
An horrid Vision seized my Head,
I saw the Graves give up their Dead.
Jove, armed with Terrors, burst the Skies, 5
And Thunder roars and Light'ning flies!
Amazed, confused, its Fate unknown,
The World stands trembling at his Throne.
While each pale Sinner hangs his Head,
Jove, nodding, shook the Heavens, and said, 10
"Offending Race of Human Kind,

By Nature, Reason, Learning, blind;
You who through Frailty stepped aside,
And you who never fell—through Pride;
You who in different Sects have shammed,   15
And come to see each other damned;
 (So some Folks told you, but they knew
No more of Jove's Designs than you)
The World's mad Business now is o'er,
And I resent these Pranks no more.   20
I to such Blockheads set my Wit!
I damn such Fools!—Go, go, you're bit."

    Jonathan Swift (1667–1745)

❖ ROMANTIC AND VICTORIAN ❖

THE GARDEN OF LOVE

I went to the Garden of Love,
And saw what I never had seen;
A Chapel was built in the midst,
Where I used to play on the green.

And the gates of this Chapel were shut,   5
And 'Thou shalt not' writ over the door;
So I turned to the Garden of Love
That so many sweet flowers bore;

And I saw it was filled with graves,
And tomb-stones where flowers should be;   10
And Priests in black gowns were walking their rounds,
And binding with briars my joys and desires.

    William Blake (1757–1827)

THE LITTLE BLACK BOY

My mother bore me in the southern wild,
And I am black, but O! my soul is white;
White as an angel is the English child,
But I am black, as if bereaved of light.

My mother taught me underneath a tree,   5
And sitting down before the heat of day,
She took me on her lap and kissèd me,
And pointing to the east, began to say:

"Look on the rising sun: there God does live,
And gives his light, and gives his heat away;
And flowers and trees and beasts and men receive
Comfort in morning, joy in the noonday.

"And we are put on earth a little space,
That we may learn to bear the beams of love;
And these black bodies and this sunburnt face
Is but a cloud, and like a shady grove.

"For when our souls have learned the heat to bear,
The cloud will vanish; we shall hear his voice,
Saying: 'Come out from the grove, my love and care,
And round my golden tent like lambs rejoice.'"

Thus did my mother say, and kissèd me;
And thus I say to little English boy:
When I from black and he from white cloud free,
And round the tent of God like lambs we joy,

I'll shade him from the heat, till he can bear
To lean in joy upon our Father's knee;
And then I'll stand and stroke his silver hair,
And be like him, and he will then love me.

William Blake (1757–1827)

SONG: HOW SWEET I ROAMED

How sweet I roamed from field to field,
    And tasted all the summer's pride,
'Till I the prince of love beheld,
    Who in the sunny beams did glide!

He shewed me lilies for my hair,
    And blushing roses for my brow;
He led me through his gardens fair,
    Where all his golden pleasures grow.

With sweet May dews my wings were wet,
    And Phoebus fired my vocal rage;
He caught me in his silken net,
    And shut me in his golden cage.

He loves to sit and hear me sing,
    Then, laughing, sports and plays with me;
Then stretches out my golden wing,
    And mocks my loss of liberty.

William Blake (1757–1827)

PROMETHEUS

Titan! to whose immortal eyes
    The sufferings of mortality,
    Seen in their sad reality,
Were not as things that gods despise;
What was thy pity's recompense?
A silent suffering, and intense;
The rock, the vulture, and the chain,
All that the proud can feel of pain,
The agony they do not show,
The suffocating sense of woe,
    Which speaks but in its loneliness,
And then is jealous lest the sky
Should have a listener, nor will sigh
    Until its voice is echoless.

Titan! to thee the strife was given
    Between the suffering and the will,
    Which torture where they cannot kill;
And the inexorable Heaven,
And the deaf tyranny of Fate,
The ruling principle of Hate,
Which for its pleasure doth create
The things it may annihilate,
Refused thee even the boon to die:
The wretched gift eternity
Was thine—and thou hast borne it well.
All that the Thunderer wrung from thee
Was but the menace which flung back
On him the torments of thy rack;
The fate thou didst so well foresee,
But would not to appease him tell;
And in thy Silence was his Sentence,
And in his Soul a vain repentance,
And evil dread so ill dissembled,
That in his hand the lightnings trembled.

Thy Godlike crime was to be kind,
    To render with thy precepts less
    The sum of human wretchedness,
And strengthen Man with his own mind;
But baffled as thou wert from high,
Still in thy patient energy,
In the endurance, and repulse
    Of thine impenetrable Spirit,

Which Earth and Heaven could not convulse,
    A mighty lesson we inherit:
Thou art a symbol and a sign
    To Mortals of their fate and force;
Like thee, Man is in part divine,
    A troubled stream from a pure source;
And Man in portions can foresee
His own funereal destiny;
His wretchedness, and his resistance,
And his sad unallied existence:
To which his Spirit may oppose
Itself—and equal to all woes,
    And a firm will, and a deep sense,
Which even in torture can descry
    Its own concenter'd recompense,
Triumphant where it dares defy,
And making Death a Victory.

    George Gordon, Lord Byron (1788–1824)

SHE WALKS IN BEAUTY

She walks in beauty, like the night
    Of cloudless climes and starry skies;
And all that's best of dark and bright
    Meet in her aspect and her eyes:
Thus mellowed to that tender light
    Which heaven to gaudy day denies.

One shade the more, one ray the less,
    Had half impaired the nameless grace
Which waves in every raven tress,
    Or softly lightens o'er her face;
Where thoughts serenely sweet express
    How pure, how dear their dwelling-place.

And on that cheek, and o'er that brow,
    So soft, so calm, yet eloquent,
The smiles that win, the tints that glow,
    But tell of days in goodness spent,
A mind at peace with all below,
    A heart whose love is innocent!

    George Gordon, Lord Byron (1788–1824)

KUBLA KHAN

In Xanadu did Kubla Khan
A stately pleasure-dome decree:
Where Alph, the sacred river, ran
Through caverns measureless to man
    Down to a sunless sea. 5
So twice five miles of fertile ground
With walls and towers were girdled round:
And there were gardens bright with sinuous rills,
Where blossomed many an incense-bearing tree;
And here were forests ancient as the hills, 10
Enfolding sunny spots of greenery.

But oh! that deep romantic chasm which slanted
Down the green hill athwart a cedarn cover!
A savage place! as holy and enchanted
As e'er beneath a waning moon was haunted 15
By woman wailing for her demon-lover!
And from this chasm, with ceaseless turmoil seething,
As if this earth in fast thick pants were breathing,
A mighty fountain momently was forced:
Amid whose swift half-intermitted burst 20
Huge fragments vaulted like rebounding hail
Or chaffy grain beneath the thresher's flail:
And 'mid these dancing rocks at once and ever
It flung up momently the sacred river.
Five miles meandering with a mazy motion 25
Through wood and dale the sacred river ran,
Then reached the caverns measureless to man,
And sank in tumult to a lifeless ocean:
And 'mid this tumult Kubla heard from far
Ancestral voices prophesying war! 30
    The shadow of the dome of pleasure
    Floated midway on the waves;
    Where was heard the mingled measure
    From the fountain and the caves.
It was a miracle of rare device, 35
A sunny pleasure-dome with caves of ice!

    A damsel with a dulcimer
    In a vision once I saw:
    It was an Abyssinian maid,
    And on her dulcimer she played, 40
    Singing of Mount Abora.
    Could I revive within me

>   Her symphony and song,
>   To such a deep delight 'twould win me
> That with music loud and long 45
> I would build that dome in air,
> That sunny dome! those caves of ice!
> And all who heard should see them there,
> And all should cry, Beware! Beware! 50
> His flashing eyes, his floating hair!
> Weave a circle round him thrice,
> And close your eyes with holy dread,
> For he on honey-dew hath fed,
> And drunk the milk of Paradise.

>   *Samuel Taylor Coleridge* (1772–1834)

THE BUSTLE IN A HOUSE

The Bustle in a House
The Morning after Death
Is solemnest of industries
Enacted upon Earth—

The Sweeping up the Heart 5
And putting Love away
We shall not want to use again
Until Eternity.

                Emily Dickinson (1830–1886)

I DIED FOR BEAUTY

I died for Beauty—but was scarce
Adjusted in the Tomb
When One who died for Truth, was lain
In an adjoining Room—

He questioned softly "Why I failed"? 5
"For Beauty," I replied—
"And I—for Truth—Themself are One—
We Brethren, are," He said—

And so, as Kinsmen, met a Night—
We talked between the Rooms— 10
Until the Moss had reached our lips—
And covered up—our names—

                Emily Dickinson (1830–1886)

THE LAST NIGHT THAT SHE LIVED

The last Night that She lived
It was a Common Night
Except the Dying—this to Us
Made Nature different

We noticed smallest things—
Things overlooked before
By this great light upon our Minds
Italicized—as 'twere.

As We went out and in
Between Her final Room
And Rooms where Those to be alive
Tomorrow were, a Blame

That Others could exist
While She must finish quite
A Jealousy for Her arose
So nearly infinite—

We waited while She passed—
It was a narrow time—
Too jostled were Our Souls to speak
At length the notice came.

She mentioned, and forgot—
Then lightly as a Reed
Bent to the Water, struggled scarce—
Consented, and was dead—

And We—We placed the Hair—
And drew the Head erect—
And then an awful leisure was
Belief to regulate—

Emily Dickinson (1830–1886)

BRIGHT STAR, WOULD I WERE STEADFAST AS THOU ART

Bright star, would I were steadfast as thou art—
    Not in lone splendor hung aloft the night,
And watching, with eternal lids apart,
    Like nature's patient, sleepless Eremite
The moving waters at their priest-like task
    Of pure ablution round earth's human shores,

Or gazing on the new soft-fallen mask
    Of snow upon the mountains and the moors—
No—yet still steadfast, still unchangeable,
    Pillowed upon my fair love's ripening breast,
To feel for ever its soft fall and swell,
    Awake for ever in a sweet unrest,
Still, still to hear her tender-taken breath,
And so live ever—or else swoon to death.

John Keats (1795–1821)

ODE TO A NIGHTINGALE

I

My heart aches, and a drowsy numbness pains
    My sense, as though of hemlock I had drunk,
Or emptied some dull opiate to the drains
    One minute past, and Lethe-wards had sunk:
'Tis not through envy of thy happy lot,
    But being too happy in thine happiness—
        That thou, light-winged Dryad of the trees,
           In some melodious plot
Of beechen green, and shadows numberless,
    Singest of summer in full-throated ease.

II

O for a draught of vintage! that hath been
    Cooled a long age in the deep-delved earth,
Tasting of Flora and the country green,
    Dance, and Provençal song, and sunburnt mirth!
O for a beaker full of the warm South,
    Full of the true, the blushful Hippocrene,
        With beaded bubbles winking at the brim,
           And purple-stained mouth;
That I might drink, and leave the world unseen,
    And with thee fade away into the forest dim:

III

Fade far away, dissolve, and quite forget
    What thou among the leaves hast never known,
The weariness, the fever, and the fret
    Here, where men sit and hear each other groan;
Where palsy shakes a few, sad, last grey hairs,
    Where youth grows pale, and specter-thin, and dies;
        Where but to think is to be full of sorrow
           And leaden-eyed despairs,

Where Beauty cannot keep her lustrous eyes,
    Or new Love pine at them beyond to-morrow.   30

IV

Away! away! for I will fly to thee,
    Not charioted by Bacchus and his pards,
But on the viewless wings of Poesy,
    Though the dull brain perplexes and retards:
Already with thee! tender is the night,   35
    And haply the Queen-Moon is on her throne,
        Clustered around by all her starry Fays;
           But here there is no light,
Save what from heaven is with the breezes blown
        Through verdurous glooms and winding mossy ways.   40

V

I cannot see what flowers are at my feet,
    Nor what soft incense hangs upon the boughs,
But, in embalmed darkness, guess each sweet
    Wherewith the seasonable month endows
The grass, the thicket, and the fruit tree wild;   45
    White hawthorn, and the pastoral eglantine;
        Fast fading violets covered up in leaves;
           And mid-May's eldest child,
The coming musk rose, full of dewy wine,
        The murmurous haunt of flies on summer eves.   50

VI

Darkling I listen; and, for many a time
    I have been half in love with easeful Death,
Called him soft names in many a mused rhyme,
    To take into the air my quiet breath;
Now more than ever seems it rich to die,   55
    To cease upon the midnight with no pain,
        While thou art pouring forth thy soul abroad
           In such an ecstasy!
    Still wouldst thou sing, and I have ears in vain—
        To thy high requiem become a sod.   60

VII

Thou wast not born for death, immortal Bird!
    No hungry generations tread thee down;
The voice I hear this passing night was heard
    In ancient days by emperor and clown:

Perhaps the self-same song that found a path 65
    Through the sad heart of Ruth, when, sick for home,
        She stood in tears amid the alien corn;
           The same that oft-times hath
    Charmed magic casements, opening on the foam
        Of perilous seas, in faery lands forlorn. 70

        VIII

Forlorn! the very word is like a bell
    To toll me back from thee to my sole self!
Adieu! the fancy cannot cheat so well
    As she is famed to do, deceiving elf.
Adieu! adieu! thy plaintive anthem fades 75
    Past the near meadows, over the still stream,
        Up the hillside; and now 'tis buried deep
           In the next valley glades:
Was it a vision, or a waking dream?
    Fled is that music:—Do I wake or sleep? 80

        John Keats (1795–1821)

ENGLAND IN 1819

An old, mad, blind, despised, and dying king;
Princes, the dregs of their dull race, who flow
Through public scorn—mud from a muddy spring;
Rulers who neither see, nor feel, nor know,
But leech-like to their fainting country cling, 5
Till they drop, blind in blood, without a blow;
A people starved and stabbed in the untilled field;
An army, which liberticide and prey
Makes as a two-edged sword to all who wield—
Golden and sanguine laws which tempt and slay— 10
Religion Christless, Godless—a book sealed;
A Senate—Time's worst statute unrepealed,—
Are graves, from which a glorious Phantom may
Burst, to illumine our tempestuous day.

      Percy Bysshe Shelley (1792–1822)

CAVALRY CROSSING A FORD

A line in long array where they wind betwixt green islands,
They take a serpentine course, their arms flash in the sun—hark to the
  musical clank,

Behold the silvery river, in it the splashing horses loitering stop to drink,
Behold the brown-faced men, each group, each person a picture, the negligent rest on the saddles,
Some emerge on the opposite bank, others are just entering the ford—while, 5
Scarlet and blue and snowy white,
The guidon flags flutter gayly in the wind.

       Walt Whitman (1819–1892)

A NOISELESS PATIENT SPIDER

A noiseless patient spider,
I mark'd where on a little promontory it stood isolated,
Mark'd how to explore the vacant vast surrounding,
It launch'd forth filament, filament, filament, out of itself,
Ever unreeling them, ever tirelessly speeding them. 5

And you O my soul where you stand,
Surrounded, detached, in measureless oceans of space,
Ceaselessly musing, venturing, throwing, seeking the spheres to connect them,
Till the bridge you will need be form'd, till the ductile anchor hold,
Till the gossamer thread you fling catch somewhere, O my soul. 10

       Walt Whitman (1819–1892)

IT IS A BEAUTEOUS EVENING, CALM AND FREE

It is a beauteous evening, calm and free,
The holy time is quiet as a Nun
Breathless with adoration; the broad sun
Is sinking down in its tranquility;
The gentleness of heaven broods o'er the Sea: 5
Listen! the mighty Being is awake,
And doth with his eternal motion make
A sound like thunder—everlastingly.
Dear Child! dear Girl! that walkest with me here,
If thou appear untouched by solemn thought, 10
Thy nature is not therefore less divine:
Thou liest in Abraham's bosom all the year,
And worship'st at the Temple's inner shrine,
God being with thee when we know it not.

   William Wordsworth (1770–1850)

THE WORLD IS TOO MUCH WITH US

The world is too much with us; late and soon,
Getting and spending, we lay waste our powers;
Little we see in Nature that is ours;
We have given our hearts away, a sordid boon!
This Sea that bares her bosom to the moon,
The winds that will be howling at all hours,
And are up-gathered now like sleeping flowers,
For this, for everything, we are out of tune;
It moves us not.   Great God! I'd rather be
A Pagan suckled in a creed outworn;
So might I, standing on this pleasant lea,
Have glimpses that would make me less forlorn;
Have sight of Proteus rising from the sea;
Or hear old Triton blow his wreathéd horn.

William Wordsworth (1770–1850)

REQUIESCAT

Strew on her roses, roses,
    And never a spray of yew!
In quiet she reposes;
    Ah, would that I did too!

Her mirth the world required;
    She bathed it in smiles of glee
But her heart was tired, tired,
    And now they let her be.

Her life was turning, turning,
    In mazes of heat and sound.
But for peace her soul was yearning,
    And now peace laps her round.

Her cabined, ample spirit,
    It fluttered and failed for breath.
Tonight it doth inherit
    The vasty hall of death.

Matthew Arnold (1822–1888)

SOLILOQUY OF THE SPANISH CLOISTER

Gr-r-r—there go, my heart's abhorrence!
    Water your damned flower-pots, do!
If hate killed men, Brother Lawrence,
    God's blood, would not mine kill you!

What? your myrtle-bush wants trimming?
    Oh, that rose has prior claims—
Needs its leaden vase filled brimming?
    Hell dry you up with its flames!

At the meal we sit together.
    Salve tibi! I must hear
Wise talk of the kind of weather,
    Sort of season, time of year:
Not a plenteous cork-crop; scarcely
    Dare we hope oak-galls, I doubt;
What's the Latin name for "parsley"?
    What's the Greek name for Swine's Snout?

Whew! We'll have our platter burnished,
    Laid with care on our own shelf!
With a fire-new spoon we're furnished,
    And a goblet for ourself,
Rinsed like something sacrificial
    Ere 'tis fit to touch our chaps—
Marked with L. for our initial!
    (He-he! There his lily snaps!)

Saint, forsooth! While brown Dolores
    Squats outside the Convent bank
With Sanchicha, telling stories,
    Steeping tresses in the tank,
Blue-black, lustrous, thick like horsehairs,
    —Can't I see his dead eye glow,
Bright as 'twere a Barbary corsair's?
    (That is, if he'd let it show!)

When he finishes refection,
    Knife and fork he never lays
Cross-wise, to my recollection,
    As do I, in Jesu's praise.
I the Trinity illustrate,
    Drinking watered orange-pulp—
In three sips the Arian frustrate;
    While he drains his at one gulp.

Oh, those melons! if he's able
    We're to have a feast! so nice!
One goes to the Abbot's table,
    All of us get each a slice.
How go on your flowers? None double?
    Not one fruit-sort can you spy?

Strange!—And I, too, at such trouble,
    Keep them close-nipped on the sly!

There's a great text in Galatians,
    Once you trip on it, entails
Twenty-nine distinct damnations,
    One sure, if another fails;
If I trip him just a-dying,
    Sure of heaven as sure can be,
Spin him round and send him flying
    Off to hell, a Manichee?

Or, my scrofulous French novel
    On grey paper with blunt type!
Simply glance at it, you grovel
    Hand and foot in Belial's gripe;
If I double down its pages
    At the woeful sixteenth print,
When he gathers his greengages,
    Ope a sieve and slip it in't?

Or, there's Satan!—one might venture
    Pledge one's soul to him, yet leave
Such a flaw in the indenture
    As he'd miss till, past retrieve,
Blasted lay that rose-acacia
    We're so proud of! *Hy, Zy, Hine.* . . .
'St, there's Vespers! *Plena gratiâ,*
    Ave, Virgo! Gr-r-r—you swine!

    Robert Browning (1812–1889)

THE DARKLING THRUSH

I leant upon a coppice gate
    When Frost was spectre-gray,
And Winter's dregs made desolate
    The weakening eye of day.
The tangled bine-stems scored the sky
    Like strings of broken lyres,
And all mankind that haunted nigh
    Had sought their household fires.

The land's sharp features seemed to be
    The Century's corpse outleant,
His crypt the cloudy canopy,
    The wind his death-lament.

The ancient pulse of germ and birth
    Was shrunken hard and dry,
And every spirit upon earth   15
    Seemed fervourless as I.

At once a voice arose among
    The bleak twigs overhead
In a full-hearted evensong
    Of joy illimited;   20
An aged thrush, frail, gaunt, and small,
    In blast-beruffled plume,
Had chosen thus to fling his soul
    Upon the growing gloom.

So little cause for carolings   25
    Of such ecstatic sound
Was written on terrestrial things
    Afar or nigh around,
That I could think there trembled through
    His happy good night air   30
Some blessed Hope, whereof he knew
    And I was unaware.

                Thomas Hardy (1840–1928)

HAP

If but some vengeful god would call to me
From up the sky, and laugh: "Thou suffering thing,
Know that thy sorrow is my ecstasy,
That thy love's loss is my hate's profiting!"

Then would I bear it, clench myself, and die,   5
Steeled by the sense of ire unmerited;
Half-eased in that a Powerfuller than I
Had willed and meted me the tears I shed.

But not so.   How arrives it joy lies slain,
And why unblooms the best hope ever sown?   10
—Crass Casualty obstructs the sun and rain,
And dicing Time for gladness casts a moan. . . .
These purblind Doomsters had as readily strown
Blisses about my pilgrimage as pain.

                Thomas Hardy (1840–1928)

CARRION COMFORT

Not, I'll not, carrion comfort, Despair, not feast on thee;
Not untwist—slack they may be—these last strands of man
In me ór, most weary, cry *I can no more*. I can;
Can something, hope, wish day come, not choose not to be.
But ah, but O thou terrible, why wouldst thou rude on me
Thy wring-world right foot rock? lay a lionlimb against me? scan
With darksome devouring eyes my bruisèd bones? and fan,
O in turns of tempest, me heaped there; me frantic to avoid thee and flee?

    Why? That my chaff might fly, my grain lie, sheer and clear.
Nay in all that toil, that coil, since (seems) I kissed the rod,
Hand rather, my heart lo! lapped strength, stole joy, would laugh, chéer.
Cheer whom though? the hero whose heaven-handling flung me, fóot tród
Me? or me that fought him? O which one? is it each one? That night, that year
Of now done darkness I wretch lay wrestling with (my God!) my God.

Gerard Manley Hopkins (1844–1889)

THE WINDHOVER:
To Christ our Lord

I caught this morning morning's minion, king-
    dom of daylight's dauphin, dapple-dawn-drawn Falcon, in his riding
    Of the rolling level underneath him steady air, and striding
High there, how he rung upon the rein of a wimpling wing
In his ecstasy! then off, off forth on swing,
    As a skate's heel sweeps smooth on a bow-bend: the hurl and gliding
    Rebuffed the big wind. My heart in hiding
Stirred for a bird,—the achieve of, the mastery of the thing!

Brute beauty and valour and act, oh, air, pride, plume here
    Buckle! AND the fire that breaks from thee then, a billion
Times told lovelier, more dangerous, O my chevalier!

    No wonder of it: shéer plód makes plough down sillion
Shine, and blue-bleak embers, ah my dear,
    Fall, gall themselves, and gash gold-vermilion.

Gerard Manley Hopkins (1844–1889)

INTO MY HEART AN AIR THAT KILLS

Into my heart an air that kills
    From yon far country blows:
What are those blue remembered hills,
    What spires, what farms are those?

That is the land of lost content,
    I see it shining plain,
The happy highways where I went
    And cannot come again.

      A. E. Housman (1859–1936)

ON MOONLIT HEATH AND LONESOME BANK

On moonlit heath and lonesome bank
    The sheep beside me graze;
And yon the gallows used to clank
    Fast by the four cross ways.

A careless shepherd once would keep
    The flocks by moonlight there,
And high amongst the glimmering sheep
    The dead man stood on air.

They hang us now in Shrewsbury jail:
    The whistles blow forlorn,
And trains all night groan on the rail
    To men that die at morn.

There sleeps in Shrewsbury jail to-night,
    Or wakes, as may betide,
A better lad, if things went right,
    Than most that sleep outside.

And naked to the hangman's noose
    The morning clocks will ring
A neck God made for other use
    Than strangling in a string.

And sharp the link of life will snap,
    And dead on air will stand
Heels that held up as straight a chap
    As treads upon the land.

So here I'll watch the night and wait
    To see the morning shine,
When he will hear the stroke of eight
    And not the stroke of nine;

And wish my friend as sound a sleep
    As lads' I did not know,
That shepherded the moonlit sheep
    A hundred years ago.

      A. E. Housman (1859–1936)

TERENCE, THIS IS STUPID STUFF

'Terence, this is stupid stuff:
You eat your victuals fast enough;
There can't be much amiss, 'tis clear,
To see the rate you drink your beer.
But oh, good Lord, the verse you make, 5
It gives a chap the belly-ache.
The cow, the old cow, she is dead;
It sleeps well, the horned head:
We poor lads, 'tis our turn now
To hear such tunes as killed the cow. 10
Pretty friendship 'tis to rhyme
Your friends to death before their time
Moping melancholy mad:
Come, pipe a tune to dance to, lad.'

Why, if 'tis dancing you would be, 15
There's brisker pipes than poetry.
Say, for what were hop-yards meant,
Or why was Burton built on Trent?
Oh many a peer of England brews
Livelier liquor than the Muse, 20
And malt does more than Milton can
To justify God's ways to man.
Ale, man, ale's the stuff to drink
For fellows whom it hurts to think:
Look into the pewter pot 25
To see the world as the world's not.
And faith, 'tis pleasant till 'tis past:
The mischief is that 'twill not last.
Oh I have been to Ludlow fair
And left my necktie God knows where, 30
And carried half-way home, or near,
Pints and quarts of Ludlow beer:
Then the world seemed none so bad,
And I myself a sterling lad;
And down in lovely muck I've lain, 35
Happy till I woke again.
Then I saw the morning sky:
Heigho, the tale was all a lie;
The world, it was the old world yet,
I was I, my things were wet, 40
And nothing now remained to do
But begin the game anew.

  Therefore, since the world has still
Much good, but much less good than ill,
And while the sun and moon endure   45
Luck's a chance, but trouble's sure,
I'd face it as a wise man would,
And train for ill and not for good.
'Tis true, the stuff I bring for sale
Is not so brisk a brew as ale: 50
Out of a stem that scored the hand
I wrung it in a weary land.
But take it: if the smack is sour,
The better for the embittered hour;
It should do good to heart and head   55
When your soul is in my soul's stead;
And I will friend you, if I may,
In the dark and cloudy day.

  There was a king reigned in the East:
There, when kings will sit to feast,   60
They get their fill before they think
With poisoned meat and poisoned drink.
He gathered all that springs to birth
From the many-venomed earth;
First a little, thence to more,   65
He sampled all her killing store;
And easy, smiling, seasoned sound,
Sate the king when healths went round.
They put arsenic in his meat
And stared aghast to watch him eat;   70
They poured strychnine in his cup
And shook to see him drink it up:
They shook, they stared as white's their shirt:
Them it was their poison hurt.
—I tell the tale that I heard told.   75
Mithridates, he died old.

     A. E. Housman (1859–1936)

IN AN ARTIST'S STUDIO

One face looks out from all his canvases,
  One selfsame figure sits or walks or leans:
  We found her hidden just behind those screens;
That mirror gave back all her loveliness.

A queen in opal or in ruby dress,
    A nameless girl in freshest summer-greens,
    A saint, an angel—every canvas means
The same one meaning, neither more nor less.
He feeds upon her face by day and night,
    And she with true kind eyes looks back on him,
Fair as the moon and joyful as the light:
    Not wan with waiting, not with sorrow dim;
Not as she is, but was when hope shone bright;
    Not as she is, but as she fills his dream.

        Christina Rossetti (1830–1894)

BARREN SPRING

Once more the changed year's turning wheel returns:
And as a girl sails balanced in the wind,
And now before and now again behind,
Stoops as it swoops, with cheek that laughs and burns—
So Spring comes merry toward me here, but earns
No answering smile from me, whose life is twined
With the dead boughs that winter still must bind
And whom today the Spring no more concerns.
Behold, this crocus is a withering flame;
This snowdrop, snow; this apple-blossom's part
To breed the fruit that breeds the serpent's art.
Nay, for these Spring-flowers, turn thy face from them,
Nor stay till on the year's last lily-stem
The white cup shrivels round the golden heart.

        Dante Gabriel Rossetti (1828–1888)

BREAK, BREAK, BREAK

Break, break, break,
    On thy cold gray stones, O Sea!
And I would that my tongue could utter
    The thoughts that arise in me.

O well for the fisherman's boy,
    That he shouts with his sister at play!
O well for the sailor lad,
    That he sings in his boat on the bay!

And the stately ships go on
    To their haven under the hill;
But O for the touch of a vanished hand,
    And the sound of a voice that is still!

Break, break, break,
> At the foot of thy crags, O Sea!
But the tender grace of a day that is dead 15
> Will never come back to me.

> *Alfred, Lord Tennyson* (1809–1892)

THE EAGLE

He clasps the crag with crooked hands;
Close to the sun in lonely lands,
Ringed with the azure world, he stands.

The wrinkled sea beneath him crawls;
He watches from his mountain walls, 5
And like a thunderbolt he falls.

> *Alfred, Lord Tennyson* (1809–1892)

❖ MODERN AND CONTEMPORARY ❖

THE CITY LIMITS

When you consider the radiance, that it does not withhold
itself but pours its abundance without selection into every
nook and cranny not overhung or hidden; when you consider

that birds' bones make no awful noise against the light but
lie low in the light as in a high testimony; when you consider 5
the radiance, that it will look into the guiltiest

swervings of the weaving heart and bear itself upon them,
not flinching into disguise or darkening; when you consider
the abundance of such resource as illuminates the glow-blue

bodies and gold-skeined wings of flies swarming the dumped 10
guts of a natural slaughter or the coil of shit and in no
way winces from its storms of generosity; when you consider

that air or vacuum, snow or shale, squid or wolf, rose or lichen,
each is accepted into as much light as it will take, then
the heart moves roomier, the man stands and looks about, the 15

leaf does not increase itself above the grass, and the dark
work of the deepest cells is of a tune with May bushes
and fear lit by the breadth of such calmly turns to praise.

> *A. R. Ammons* (b. 1926)

SO I SAID I AM EZRA

So I said I am Ezra
and the wind whipped my throat
gaming for the sounds of my voice
    I listened to the wind
go over my head and up into the night
Turning to the sea I said
    I am Ezra
but there were no echoes from the waves
The words were swallowed up
    in the voice of the surf
or leaping over swells
lost themselves oceanward
    Over the bleached and broken fields
I moved my feet and turning from the wind
    that ripped sheets of sand
    from the beach and threw them
    like seamists across the dunes
swayed as if the wind were taking me away
and said
    I am Ezra
As a word too much repeated
falls out of being
so I Ezra went out into the night
like a drift of sand
and splashed among the windy oats
that clutch the dunes
of unremembered seas

    A. R. Ammons (b. 1926)

WINTER SCENE

There is now not a single
leaf on the cherry tree:

except when the jay
plummets in, lights, and,

in pure clarity, squalls:
then every branch

quivers and
breaks out in blue leaves.

  A. R. Ammons (b. 1926)

MY EROTIC DOUBLE

He says he doesn't feel like working today.
It's just as well. Here in the shade
Behind the house, protected from street noises,
One can go over all kinds of old feeling,
Throw some away, keep others.
      The wordplay
Between us gets very intense when there are
Fewer feelings around to confuse things.
Another go-round? No, but the last things
You always find to say are charming, and rescue me
Before the night does. We are afloat
On our dreams as on a barge made of ice,
Shot through with questions and fissures of starlight
That keep us awake, thinking about the dreams
As they are happening. Some occurrence. You said it.

I said it but I can hide it. But I choose not to.
Thank you. You are a very pleasant person.
Thank you. You are too.
   John Ashbery (b. 1927)

LULLABY

Lay your sleeping head, my love,
Human on my faithless arm;
Time and fevers burn away
Individual beauty from
Thoughtful children, and the grave
Proves the child ephemeral:
But in my arms till break of day
Let the living creature lie,
Mortal, guilty, but to me
The entirely beautiful.

Soul and body have no bounds:
To lovers as they lie upon
Her tolerant enchanted slope
In their ordinary swoon,
Grave the vision Venus sends
Of supernatural sympathy,
Universal love and hope;
While an abstract insight wakes
Among the glaciers and the rocks
The hermit's carnal ecstasy.

Certainty, fidelity
On the stroke of midnight pass
Like vibrations of a bell
And fashionable madmen raise
Their pedantic boring cry: 25
Every farthing of the cost,
All the dreaded cards foretell,
Shall be paid, but from this night
Not a whisper, not a thought,
Not a kiss nor look be lost. 30

Beauty, midnight, vision dies:
Let the winds of dawn that blow
Softly round your dreaming head
Such a day of welcome show
Eye and knocking heart may bless, 35
Find our mortal world enough;
Noons of dryness find you fed
By the involuntary powers,
Nights of insult let you pass
Watched by every human love. 40

   W. H. Auden (1907–1973)

EPITAPH ON A TYRANT

Perfection, of a kind, was what he was after,
And the poetry he invented was easy to understand;
He knew human folly like the back of his hand,
And was greatly interested in armies and fleets;
When he laughed, respectable senators burst with laughter, 5
And when he cried the little children died in the streets.

   W. H. Auden (1907–1973)

THE LOVE FEAST

In an upper room at midnight
See us gathered on behalf
Of love according to the gospel
Of the radio-phonograph.

Lou is telling Anne what Molly 5
Said to Mark behind her back;
Jack likes Jill who worships George
Who has the hots for Jack.

Catechumens make their entrance;
Steep enthusiastic eyes 10

Flicker after tits and baskets;
Someone vomits; someone cries.

Willy cannot bear his father,
Lilian is afraid of kids;
The Love that rules the sun and stars 15
Permits what He forbids.

Adrian's pleasure-loving dachshund
In a sinner's lap lies curled;
Drunken absent-minded fingers
Pat a sinless world. 20

Who is Jenny lying to
In her call, Collect, to Rome?
The Love that made her out of nothing
Tells me to go home.

But that Miss Number in the corner 25
Playing hard to get. . . .
I am sorry I'm not sorry . . .
Make me chaste, Lord, but not yet.

   W. H. Auden (1907–1973)

PREFACE TO A TWENTY VOLUME SUICIDE NOTE

Lately, I've become accustomed to the way
The ground opens up and envelopes me
Each time I go out to walk the dog.
Or the broad edged silly music the wind
Makes when I run for a bus . . . 5

Things have come to that.

And now, each night I count the stars,
And each night I get the same number.
And when they will not come to be counted,
I count the holes they leave. 10

Nobody sings anymore.

And then last night, I tiptoed up
To my daughter's room and heard her
Talking to someone, and when I opened
The door, there was no one there . . . 15
Only she on her knees, peeking into

Her own clasped hands.

   Imamu Amiri Baraka (b. 1934)
   (LeRoi Jones)

A PROFESSOR'S SONG

(. . rabid or dog-dull.) Let me tell you how
The Eighteenth Century couplet ended. Now
Tell me. Troll me the sources of that Song—
Assigned last week—by Blake. Come, come along,
Gentlemen. (Fidget and huddle, do. Squint soon.)
I want to end these fellows all by noon.

'That deep romantic chasm'—an early use;
The word is from the French, by our abuse
Fished out a bit. (Red all your eyes. O when?)
'A poet is a man speaking to men':
But I am then a poet, am I not?—
Ha ha. The radiator, please. Well, what?

Alive now—no—Blake would have written prose,
But movement following movement crisply flows,
So much the better, better the much so,
As burbleth Mozart. Twelve. The class can go.
Until I meet you, then, in Upper Hell
Convulsed, foaming immortal blood: farewell.

John Berryman (1914–1972)

THE ARMADILLO
for Robert Lowell

This is the time of year
when almost every night
the frail, illegal fire balloons appear.
Climbing the mountain height,

rising toward a saint
still honored in these parts,
the paper chambers flush and fill with light
that comes and goes, like hearts.

Once up against the sky it's hard
to tell them from the stars—
planets, that is—the tinted ones:
Venus going down, or Mars,

or the pale green one. With a wind,
they flare and falter, wobble and toss;
but if it's still they steer between
the kite sticks of the Southern Cross,

receding, dwindling, solemnly
and steadily forsaking us,
or, in the downdraft from a peak,
suddenly turning dangerous.   20

Last night another big one fell.
It splattered like an egg of fire
against the cliff behind the house.
The flame ran down. We saw the pair

of owls who nest there flying up   25
and up, their whirling black-and-white
stained bright pink underneath, until
they shrieked up out of sight.

The ancient owls' nest must have burned.
Hastily, all alone,   30
a glistening armadillo left the scene,
rose-flecked, head down, tail down,

and then a baby rabbit jumped out,
short-eared, to our surprise.
So soft!—a handful of intangible ash   35
with fixed, ignited eyes.

Too pretty, dreamlike mimicry!
O falling fire and piercing cry
and panic, and a weak mailed fist
clenched ignorant against the sky!   40

   Elizabeth Bishop (1911–1980)

DRIVING TO TOWN LATE TO MAIL A LETTER

It is a cold and snowy night. The main street is deserted.
The only things moving are swirls of snow.
As I lift the mailbox door, I feel its cold iron.
There is a privacy I love in this snowy night.
Driving around, I will waste more time.   5

   Robert Bly (b. 1926)

("THOUSANDS—KILLED IN ACTION")

You need the untranslatable ice to watch.
You need to loiter a little among the vague
Hushes, the clever evasions of the vagueness
Above the healthy energy of decay.

You need the untranslatable ice to watch, 5
The purple and black to smell.

Before your horror can be sweet.
Or proper.
Before your grief is other than discreet.

The intellectual damn 10
Will nurse your half-hurt. Quickly you are well.

But weary. How you yawn, have yet to see
Why nothing exhausts you like this sympathy.

Gwendolyn Brooks (b. 1917)

MEN MARRY WHAT THEY NEED. I MARRY YOU

Men marry what they need. I marry you,
morning by morning, day by day, night by night,
and every marriage makes this marriage new.

In the broken name of heaven, in the light
that shatters granite, by the spitting shore, 5
in air that leaps and wobbles like a kite,

I marry you from time and a great door
is shut and stays shut against wind, sea, stone,
sunburst, and heavenfall. And home once more

inside our walls of skin and struts of bone, 10
man-woman, woman-man, and each the other,
I marry you by all dark and all dawn

and learn to let time spend. Why should I bother
the flies about me? Let them buzz and do.
Men marry their queen, their daughter, or their mother 15

by names they prove, but that thin buzz whines through
when reason falls to reasons, cause is true.
Men marry what they need. I marry you.

John Ciardi (b. 1916)

I SAW A MAN PURSUING THE HORIZON

I saw a man pursuing the horizon;
Round and round they sped.
I was disturbed at this;
I accosted the man.

"It is futile," I said,
"You can never—"

"You lie," he cried,
And ran on.

  Stephen Crane (1871–1900)

THE WAYFARER

The wayfarer
Perceiving the pathway to truth
Was struck with astonishment.
It was thickly grown with weeds.
"Ha," he said,
"I see that none has passed here
In a long time."
Later he saw that each weed
Was a singular knife.
"Well," he mumbled at last,
"Doubtless there are other roads."

  Stephen Crane (1871–1900)

THE WINDOW

Position is where you
put it, where it is,
did you, for example, that

large tank there, silvered,
with the white church along-
side, lift

all that, to what
purpose? How
heavy the slow

world is with
everything put
in place. Some

man walks by, a
car beside him on
the dropped

road, a leaf of
yellow color is
going to

fall. It
all drops into
place. My

face is heavy
with the sight. I can
feel my eye breaking.

Robert Creeley (b. 1926)

"NEXT TO OF COURSE GOD AMERICA I"

"next to of course god america i
love you land of the pilgrims' and so forth oh
say can you see by the dawn's early my
country 'tis of centuries come and go
and are no more what of it we should worry
in every language even deafanddumb
thy sons acclaim your glorious name by gorry
by jingo by gee by gosh by gum
why talk of beauty what could be more beautiful than these heroic happy dead
who rushed like lions to the roaring slaughter
they did not stop to think they died instead
then shall the voice of liberty be mute?"

He spoke. And drank rapidly a glass of water

E. E. Cummings (1894–1962)

SHE BEING BRAND

she being Brand

-new;and you
know consequently a
little stiff i was
careful of her and (having

thoroughly oiled the universal
joint tested my gas felt of
her radiator made sure her springs were O.

K.)i went right to it flooded-the-carburetor cranked her

up,slipped the
clutch (and then somehow got into reverse she
kicked what
the hell) next
minute i was back in neutral tried and

again slo-wly;bare,ly nudg.   ing (my   15
lev-er Right-
oh and her gears being in
A 1 shape passed
from low through
second-in-to-high like   20
greased lightning, just as we turned the corner of Divinity

avenue i touched the accelerator and give

her the juice,good

                    (it

was the first ride and believe i we was   25
happy to see how nice she acted right up to
the last minute coming back down by the Public
Gardens i slammed on
the

internalexpanding   30
&
externalcontracting
brakes Bothatonce and

brought allofher tremB
-ling   35

to a:dead.

stand—
;Still)

                E. E. Cummings (1894–1962)

WHEN SERPENTS BARGAIN FOR THE RIGHT TO SQUIRM

when serpents bargain for the right to squirm
and the sun strikes to gain a living wage—
when thorns regard their roses with alarm
and rainbows are insured against old age

when every thrush may sing no new moon in   5
if all screech-owls have not okayed his voice
—and any wave signs on the dotted line
or else an ocean is compelled to close

when the oak begs permission of the birch
to make an acorn—valleys accuse their   10

mountains of having altitude—and march
denounces april as a saboteur

then we'll believe in that incredible
unanimal mankind (and not until)

E. E. Cummings (1894–1962)

ADULTERY

We have all been in rooms
We cannot die in, and they are odd places, and sad.
Often Indians are standing eagle-armed on hills

In the sunrise   open wide to the Great Spirit
Or gliding in canoes   or cattle are browsing on the walls   5
Far away   gazing down with the eyes of our children

Not far away   or there are men driving
The last railspike, which has turned
Gold in their hands. Gigantic forepleasure lives

Among such scenes, and we are alone with it   10
At last. There is always some weeping
Between us   and someone is always checking

A wrist watch by the bed to see how much
Longer we have left. Nothing can come
Of this   nothing can come   15

Of us: of me with my grim techniques
Or you who have sealed your womb
With a ring of convulsive rubber:

Although we come together,
Nothing will come of us. But we would not give   20
It up, for death is beaten

By praying Indians   by distant cows   historical
Hammers   by hazardous meetings that bridge
A continent. One could never die here

Never die   never die   25
While crying. My lover, my dear one
I will see you next week

When I'm in town. I will call you
If I can. Please get hold of   please don't
Oh God, Please don't any more I can't bear . . . Listen: 30

We have done it again   we are
Still living. Sit up and smile,
God bless you. Guilt is magical.

James Dickey (b. 1923)

CHERRYLOG ROAD

Off Highway 106
At Cherrylog Road I entered
The '34 Ford without wheels,
Smothered in kudzu,
With a seat pulled out to run   5
Corn whiskey down from the hills,

And then from the other side
Crept into an Essex
With a rumble seat of red leather
And then out again, aboard   10
A blue Chevrolet, releasing
The rust from its other color,

Reared up on three building blocks.
None had the same body heat;
I changed with them inward, toward   15
The weedy heart of the junkyard,
For I knew that Doris Holbrook
Would escape from her father at noon

And would come from the farm
To seek parts owned by the sun   20
Among the abandoned chassis,
Sitting in each in turn
As I did, leaning forward
As in a wild stock-car race

In the parking lot of the dead.   25
Time after time, I climbed in
And out the other side, like
An envoy or movie star
Met at the station by crickets.
A radiator cap raised its head,   30

Become a real toad or a kingsnake
As I neared the hub of the yard,
Passing through many states,
Many lives, to reach
Some grandmother's long Pierce-Arrow   35
Sending platters of blindness forth

From its nickel hubcaps
And spilling its tender upholstery
On sleepy roaches,
The glass panel in between
Lady and colored driver
Not all the way broken out,

The back-seat phone
Still on its hook.
I got in as though to exclaim,
"Let us go to the orphan asylum,
John; I have some old toys
For children who say their prayers."

I popped with sweat as I thought
I heard Doris Holbrook scrape
Like a mouse in the southern-state sun
That was eating the paint in blisters
From a hundred car tops and hoods.
She was tapping like code,

Loosening the screws,
Carrying off headlights,
Sparkplugs, bumpers,
Cracked mirrors and gear-knobs,
Getting ready, already,
To go back with something to show

Other than her lips' new trembling
I would hold to me soon, soon,
Where I sat in the ripped back seat
Talking over the interphone,
Praying for Doris Holbrook
To come from her father's farm

And to get back there
With no trace of me on her face
To be seen by her red-haired father
Who would change, in the squalling barn,
Her back's pale skin with a strop,
Then lay for me

In a bootlegger's roasting car
With a string-triggered 12-gauge shotgun
To blast the breath from the air.
Not cut by the jagged windshields,
Through the acres of wrecks she came
With a wrench in her hand,

Through dust where the blacksnake dies
Of boredom, and the beetle knows
The compost has no more life.
Someone outside would have seen
The oldest car's door inexplicably
Close from within:

I held her and held her and held her,
Convoyed at terrific speed
By the stalled, dreaming traffic around us,
So the blacksnake, stiff
With inaction, curved back
Into life, and hunted the mouse

With deadly overexcitement,
The beetles reclaimed their field
As we clung, glued together,
With the hooks of the seat springs
Working through to catch us red-handed
Amidst the gray breathless batting

That burst from the seat at our backs.
We left by separate doors
Into the changed, other bodies
Of cars, she down Cherrylog Road
And I to my motorcycle
Parked like the soul of the junkyard

Restored, a bicycle fleshed
With power, and tore off
Up Highway 106, continually
Drunk on the wind in my mouth,
Wringing the handlebar for speed,
Wild to be wreckage forever.

James Dickey (b. 1923)

WE WEAR THE MASK

We wear the mask that grins and lies,
It hides our cheeks and shades our eyes,—
This debt we pay to human guile;
With torn and bleeding hearts we smile,
And mouth with myriad subtleties.

Why should the world be overwise,
In counting all our tears and sighs?
Nay, let them only see us, while
    We wear the mask.

We smile, but, O great Christ, our cries
To thee from tortured souls arise.
We sing, but oh the clay is vile
Beneath our feet, and long the mile;
But let the world dream otherwise,
    We wear the mask!

    Paul Laurence Dunbar (1872–1906)

POETRY, A NATURAL THING

    Neither our vices nor our virtues
further the poem. "They came up
    and died
just like they do every year
    on the rocks."

    The poem
feeds upon thought, feeling, impulse,
    to breed   itself,
a spiritual urgency at the dark ladders leaping.

This beauty is an inner persistence
    toward the source
striving against (within) down-rushet of the river,
    a call we heard and answer
in the lateness of the world
    primordial bellowings
from which the youngest world might spring,

salmon not in the well where the
    hazelnut falls
but at the falls battling, inarticulate,
    blindly making it.

This is one picture apt for the mind.

A second: a moose painted by Stubbs,
where last year's extravagant antlers
    lie on the ground.
The forlorn moosey-faced poem wears
    new antler-buds,
    the same,

"a little heavy, a little contrived,"
his only beauty to be
    all moose.

    Robert Duncan (b. 1919)

THE GROUNDHOG

In June, amid the golden fields,
I saw a groundhog lying dead.
Dead lay he; my senses shook,
And my mind outshot our naked frailty.
There lowly in the vigorous summer 5
His form began its senseless change,
And made my senses waver dim
Seeing nature ferocious in him.
Inspecting close his maggots' might
And seething cauldron of his being, 10
Half with loathing, half with a strange love,
I poked him with an angry stick.
The fever arose, became a flame
And Vigour circumscribed the skies,
Immense energy in the sun, 15
And through my frame a sunless trembling.
My stick had done nor good nor harm.
Then stood I silent in the day
Watching the object, as before;
And kept my reverence for knowledge 20
Trying for control, to be still,
To quell the passion of the blood;
Until I had bent down on my knees
Praying for joy in the sight of decay.
And so I left; and I returned 25
In Autumn strict of eye, to see
The sap gone out of the groundhog,
But the bony sodden hulk remained.

Richard Eberhart (b. 1904)

THE HORSE CHESTNUT TREE

Boys in sporadic but tenacious droves
Come with sticks, as certainly as Autumn,
To assault the great horse chestnut tree.

There is a law governs their lawlessness.
Desire is in them for a shining amulet 5
And the best are those that are highest up.

They will not pick them easily from the ground.
With shrill arms they fling to the higher branches,
To hurry the work of nature for their pleasure.

I have seen them trooping down the street
Their pockets stuffed with chestnuts shucked, unshucked. 10
It is only evening keeps them from their wish.

Sometimes I run out in a kind of rage
To chase the boys away: I catch an arm,
Maybe, and laugh to think of being the lawgiver. 15

I was once such a young sprout myself
And fingered in my pocket the prize and trophy.
But still I moralize upon the day

And see that we, outlaws on God's property,
Fling out imagination beyond the skies, 20
Wishing a tangible good from the unknown.

And likewise death will drive us from the scene
With the great flowering world unbroken yet,
Which we held in idea, a little handful.

Richard Eberhart (b. 1904)

THE LOVE SONG OF J. ALFRED PRUFROCK

S'io credesse che mia risposta fosse
A persona che mai tornasse al mondo,
Questa fiamma staria senza piu scosse.
Ma perciocche giammai di questo fondo
Non torno vivo alcun, s'i'odo il vero,
Senza tema d'infamia ti rispondo.*

Let us go then, you and I,
When the evening is spread out against the sky
Like a patient etherised upon a table;
Let us go, through certain half-deserted streets,
The muttering retreats 5
Of restless nights in one-night cheap hotels
And sawdust restaurants with oyster-shells:
Streets that follow like a tedious argument
Of insidious intent
To lead you to an overwhelming question . . . 10
Oh, do not ask, "What is it?"
Let us go and make our visit.

    In the room the women come and go
Talking of Michelangelo.

---

* This epigraph, drawn from Dante's *Inferno*, is spoken by Guido da Montefeltroo, who had been consigned to one of the circles of Hell for being a false counselor. In this passage, he says that if he thought his words were being addressed to someone able to return to the world of the living, the flame that consumes him would cease to move, but since no one has ever returned alive, he believes that he can speak "without fear of infamy."

    The yellow fog that rubs its back upon the window-panes,
The yellow smoke that rubs its muzzle on the window-panes
Licked its tongue into the corners of the evening,
Lingered upon the pools that stand in drains,
Let fall upon its back the soot that falls from chimneys,
Slipped by the terrace, made a sudden leap,
And seeing that it was a soft October night,
Curled once about the house, and fell asleep.

    And indeed there will be time
For the yellow smoke that slides along the street,
Rubbing its back upon the window-panes;
There will be time, there will be time
To prepare a face to meet the faces that you meet;
There will be time to murder and create,
And time for all the works and days of hands
That lift and drop a question on your plate;
Time for you and time for me,
And time yet for a hundred indecisions,
And for a hundred visions and revisions,
Before the taking of a toast and tea.

    In the room the women come and go
Talking of Michelangelo.

    And indeed there will be time
To wonder, "Do I dare?" and, "Do I dare?"
Time to turn back and descend the stair,
With a bald spot in the middle of my hair—
[They will say: "How his hair is growing thin!"]
My morning coat, my collar mounting firmly to the chin,
My necktie rich and modest, but asserted by a simple pin—
[They will say: "But how his arms and legs are thin!"]
Do I dare
Disturb the universe?
In a minute there is time
For decisions and revisions which a minute will reverse.

    For I have known them all already, known them all:—
Have known the evenings, mornings, afternoons,
I have measured out my life with coffee spoons;
I know the voices dying with a dying fall
Beneath the music from a farther room.
    So how should I presume?

    And I have known the eyes already, known them all—
The eyes that fix you in a formulated phrase,
And when I am formulated, sprawling on a pin,

When I am pinned and wriggling on the wall,
Then how should I begin
To spit out all the butt-ends of my days and ways? 60
    And how should I presume?

    And I have known the arms already, known them all—
Arms that are braceleted and white and bare
[But in the lamplight, downed with light brown hair!]
Is it perfume from a dress 65
That makes me so digress?
Arms that lie along a table, or wrap about a shawl.
    And should I then presume?
    And how should I begin?

         .   .   .   .   .

Shall I say, I have gone at dusk through narrow streets 70
And watched the smoke that rises from the pipes
Of lonely men in shirt-sleeves, leaning out of windows? . . .

    I should have been a pair of ragged claws
Scuttling across the floors of silent seas.

         .   .   .   .   .

And the afternoon, the evening, sleeps so peacefully! 75
Smoothed by long fingers,
Asleep . . . tired . . . or it malingers,
Stretched on the floor, here beside you and me.
Should I, after tea and cakes and ices,
Have the strength to force the moment to its crisis? 80
But though I have wept and fasted, wept and prayed,
Though I have seen my head [grown slightly bald] brought in
    upon a platter,
I am no prophet—and here's no great matter;
I have seen the moment of my greatness flicker,
And I have seen the eternal Footman hold my coat, and snicker, 85
And in short, I was afraid.

    And would it have been worth it, after all,
After the cups, the marmalade, the tea,
Among the porcelain, among some talk of you and me,
Would it have been worth while, 90
To have bitten off the matter with a smile,
To have squeezed the universe into a ball
To roll it toward some overwhelming question,
To say: "I am Lazarus, come from the dead,
Come back to tell you all, I shall tell you all"— 95
If one, settling a pillow by her head,

    Should say: "That is not what I meant at all.
    That is not it, at all."

    And would it have been worth it, after all,
Would it have been worth while,
After the sunsets and the dooryards and the sprinkled streets,
After the novels, after the teacups, after the skirts that trail along
   the floor—
And this, and so much more?—
It is impossible to say just what I mean!
But as if a magic lantern threw the nerves in patterns on a screen:
Would it have been worth while
If one, settling a pillow or throwing off a shawl,
And turning toward the window, should say:
    "That is not it at all,
    That is not what I meant, at all."

        . . . . .

No! I am not Prince Hamlet, nor was meant to be;
Am an attendant lord, one that will do
To swell a progress, start a scene or two,
Advise the prince; no doubt, an easy tool,
Deferential, glad to be of use,
Politic, cautious, and meticulous;
Full of high sentence, but a bit obtuse;
At times, indeed, almost ridiculous—
Almost, at times, the Fool.

    I grow old . . . I grow old . . .
I shall wear the bottoms of my trousers rolled.

    Shall I part my hair behind? Do I dare to eat a peach?
I shall wear white flannel trousers, and walk upon the beach.
I have heard the mermaids singing, each to each.

    I do not think that they will sing to me.

    I have seen them riding seaward on the waves
Combing the white hair of the waves blown back
When the wind blows the water white and black.

    We have lingered in the chambers of the sea
By sea-girls wreathed with seaweed red and brown
Till human voices wake us, and we drown.

                        T. S. Eliot (1888–1965)

NEITHER OUT FAR NOR IN DEEP

The people along the sand
All turn and look one way.
They turn their back on the land.
They look at the sea all day.

As long as it takes to pass
A ship keeps raising its hull;
The wetter ground like glass
Reflects a standing gull.

The land may vary more;
But wherever the truth may be—
The water comes ashore,
And the people look at the sea.

They cannot look out far.
They cannot look in deep.
But when was that ever a bar
To any watch they keep?

Robert Frost (1874–1963)

THE ROAD NOT TAKEN

Two roads diverged in a yellow wood,
And sorry I could not travel both
And be one traveler, long I stood
And looked down one as far as I could
To where it bent in the undergrowth;

Then took the other, as just as fair,
And having perhaps the better claim,
Because it was grassy and wanted wear;
Though as for that, the passing there
Had worn them really about the same,

And both that morning equally lay
In leaves no step had trodden black.
Oh, I kept the first for another day!
Yet knowing how way leads on to way,
I doubted if I should ever come back.

I shall be telling this with a sigh
Somewhere ages and ages hence:
Two roads diverged in a wood, and I—
I took the one less traveled by,
And that has made all the difference.

Robert Frost (1874–1963)

A SUPERMARKET IN CALIFORNIA

What thoughts I have of you tonight, Walt Whitman, for I walked down the sidestreets under the trees with a headache self-conscious looking at the full moon.

In my hungry fatigue, and shopping for images, I went into the neon fruit supermarket, dreaming of your enumerations!

What peaches and what penumbras! Whole families shopping at night! Aisles full of husbands! Wives in the avocados, babies in the tomatoes!—and you, Garcia Lorca, what were you doing down by the watermelons?

I saw you, Walt Whitman, childless, lonely old grubber, poking among the meats in the refrigerator and eyeing the grocery boys.

I heard you asking questions of each: Who killed the pork chops? What price bananas? Are you my Angel?

I wandered in and out of the brilliant stacks of cans following you, and followed in my imagination by the store detective.

We strode down the open corridors together in our solitary fancy tasting artichokes, possessing every frozen delicacy, and never passing the cashier.

Where are we going, Walt Whitman? The doors close in an hour. Which way does your beard point tonight?

(I touch your book and dream of our odyssey in the supermarket and feel absurd.)

Will we walk all night through solitary streets? The trees add shade to shade, lights out in the houses, we'll both be lonely.

Will we stroll dreaming of the lost America of love past blue automobiles in driveways, home to our silent cottage?

Ah, dear father, graybeard, lonely old courage-teacher, what America did you have when Charon quit poling his ferry and you got out on a smoking bank and stood watching the boat disappear on the black waters of Lethe?

Allen Ginsberg (b. 1926)

ON HEARING "THE GIRL WITH THE FLAXEN HAIR"

He has a girl who has flaxen hair
My woman has hair of gray
I have a woman who wakes up at dawn
His girl can sleep through the day

His girl has hands soothed with perfumes sweet
She has lips soft and pink
My woman's lips burn in midday sun
My woman's hands—black like ink

He can make music to please his girl
Night comes I'm tired and beat
He can make notes, make her heart beat fast
Night comes I want off my feet

Maybe if I don't pick cotton so fast
Maybe I'd sing pretty too
Sing to my woman with hair of gray
Croon softly, Baby it's you

   Nikki Giovanni (b. 1943)

"MORE LIGHT! MORE LIGHT!"
for Heinrich Blücher and Hannah Arendt

Composed in the Tower before his execution
These moving verses, and being brought at that time
Painfully to the stake, submitted, declaring thus:
"I implore my God to witness that I have made no crime."

Nor was he forsaken of courage, but the death was horrible,
The sack of gunpowder failing to ignite.
His legs were blistered sticks on which the black sap
Bubbled and burst as he howled for the Kindly Light.

And that was but one, and by no means one of the worst;
Permitted at least his pitiful dignity;
And such as were by made prayers in the name of Christ,
That shall judge all men, for his soul's tranquillity.

We move now to outside a German wood.
Three men are there commanded to dig a hole
In which the two Jews are ordered to lie down
And be buried alive by the third, who is a Pole.

Not light from the shrine at Weimar beyond the hill
Nor light from heaven appeared. But he did refuse.
A Lüger settled back deeply in its glove.
He was ordered to change places with the Jews.

Much casual death had drained away their souls.
The thick dirt mounted toward the quivering chin.
When only the head was exposed the order came
To dig him out again and to get back in.

No light, no light in the blue Polish eye.
When he finished a riding boot packed down the earth.
The Lüger hovered lightly in its glove.
He was shot in the belly and in three hours bled to death.

No prayers or incense rose up in those hours
Which grew to be years, and every day came mute
Ghosts from the ovens, sifting through crisp air,
And settled upon his eyes in a black soot.

Anthony Hecht (b. 1923)

WODWO

What am I? Nosing here, turning leaves over
Following a faint stain on the air to the river's edge
I enter water. What am I to split
The glassy grain of water looking upward I see the bed
Of the river above me upside down very clear
What am I doing here in mid-air? Why do I find
this frog so interesting as I inspect its most secret
interior and make it my own? Do these weeds
know me and name me to each other have they
seen me before, do I fit in their world? I seem
separate from the ground and not rooted but dropped
out of nothing casually I've no threads
fastening me to anything I can go anywhere
I seem to have been given the freedom
of this place what am I then? And picking
bits of bark off this rotten stump gives me
no pleasure and it's no use so why do I do it
me and doing that have coincided very queerly
But what shall I be called am I the first
have I an owner what shape am I what
shape am I am I huge if I go
to the end on this way past these trees and past these trees
till I get tired that's touching one wall of me
for the moment if I sit still how everything
stops to watch me I suppose I am the exact centre
but there's all this what is it roots
roots roots roots and here's the water
again very queer but I'll go on looking

Ted Hughes (b. 1930)

MISSOULA SOFTBALL TOURNAMENT

This summer, most friends out of town
and no wind playing flash and dazzle
in the cottonwoods, music of the Clark Fork stale,
I've gone back to the old ways of defeat,
the softball field, familiar dust and thud,   5
pitcher winging drops and rises, and wives,
the beautiful wives in the stands, basic, used,
screeching runners home, infants unattended
in the dirt. A long triple sails into right center.
Two men on. Shouts from dugout: go, Ron, go.   10
Life is better run from. Distance to the fence,
both foul lines and dead center, is displayed.

I try to steal the tricky manager's signs.
Is hit-and-run the pulling of the ear?
The ump gives pitchers too much low inside.   15
Injustice? Fraud? Ancient problems focus
in the heat. Bad hop on routine grounder.
Close play missed by the team you want to win.
Players from the first game, high on beer,
ride players in the field. Their laughter   20
falls short of the wall. Under lights, the moths
are momentary stars, and wives, the beautiful wives
in the stands now take the interest they once feigned,
oh, long ago, their marriage just begun, years
of helping husbands feel important just begun,   25
the scrimping, the anger brought home evenings
from degrading jobs. This poem goes out to them.
Is steal-of-home the touching of the heart?
Last pitch. A soft fly. A can of corn
the players say. Routine, like mornings,   30
like the week. They shake hands on the mound.
Nice grab on that shot to left. Good game. Good game.
Dust rotates in their headlight beams.
The wives, the beautiful wives are with their men.

Richard Hugo (b. 1923)

A CAMP IN THE PRUSSIAN FOREST

I walk beside the prisoners to the road.
Load on puffed load,
Their corpses, stacked like sodden wood,
Lie barred or galled with blood

By the charred warehouse. No one comes today 5
In the old way
To knock the fillings from their teeth;
The dark, coned, common wreath

Is plaited for their grave—a kind of grief.
The living leaf 10
Clings to the planted profitable
Pine if it is able;

The boughs sigh, mile on green, calm, breathing mile,
From this dead file
The planners ruled for them. . . . One year 15
They sent a million here:

Here men were drunk like water, burnt like wood.
The fat of good
And evil, the breast's star of hope
Were rendered into soap. 20

I paint the star I sawed from yellow pine—
And plant the sign
In soil that does not yet refuse
Its usual Jews

Their first asylum. But the white, dwarfed star— 25
This dead white star—
Hides nothing, pays for nothing; smoke
Fouls it, a yellow joke,

The needles of the wreath are chalked with ash,
A filmy trash 30
Litters the black woods with the death
Of men; and one last breath

Curls from the monstrous chimney. . . . I laugh aloud
Again and again;
The star laughs from its rotting shroud 35
Of flesh. O star of men!

Randall Jarrell (1914–1965)

NUDE DESCENDING A STAIRCASE

Toe upon toe, a snowing flesh,
A gold of lemon, root and rind,
She sifts in sunlight down the stairs
With nothing on. Nor on her mind.

We spy beneath the banister
A constant thresh of thigh on thigh—
Her lips imprint the swinging air
That parts to let her parts go by.

One-woman waterfall, she wears
Her slow descent like a long cape
And pausing, on the final stair
Collects her motions into shape.

   X. J. Kennedy (b. 1929)

PERMANENTLY

One day the Nouns were clustered in the street.
An Adjective walked by, with her dark beauty.
The Nouns were struck, moved, changed.
The next day a Verb drove up, and created the Sentence.

Each Sentence says one thing—for example, "Although it was a dark
 rainy day when the Adjective walked by, I shall remember the pure
 and sweet expression on her face until the day I perish from the green,
 effective earth."
Or, "Will you please close the window, Andrew?"
Or, for example, "Thank you, the pink pot of flowers on the window
 sill has changed color recently to a light yellow, due to the heat from
 the boiler factory which exists nearby."

In the springtime the Sentences and the Nouns lay silently on the grass.
A lonely Conjunction here and there would call, "And! But!"
But the Adjective did not emerge.

As the adjective is lost in the sentence,
So I am lost in your eyes, ears, nose, and throat—
You have enchanted me with a single kiss
Which can never be undone
Until the destruction of language.

   Kenneth Koch (b. 1925)

CARELESS LOVE

Who have been lonely once
Are comforted by their guns.
Affectionately they speak
To the dark beauty, whose cheek
Beside their own cheek glows.
They are calmed by such repose,

Such power held in hand;
Their young bones understand
The shudder in that frame.
Without nation, without name, 10
They give the load of love,
And it's returned, to prove
How much the husband heart
Can hold of it: for what
This nymphomaniac enjoys 15
Inexhaustibly is boys.

  Stanley Kunitz (b. 1905)

THE ACHE OF MARRIAGE

The ache of marriage:

thigh and tongue, beloved,
are heavy with it,
it throbs in the teeth

We look for communion 5
and are turned away, beloved,
each and each

It is leviathan and we
in its belly
looking for joy, some joy 10
not to be known outside it

two by two in the ark of
the ache of it.

  Denise Levertov (b. 1923)

LOSING TRACK

Long after you have swung back
away from me
I think you are still with me:

you come in close to the shore
on the tide 5
and nudge me awake the way

a boat adrift nudges the pier:
am I a pier
half-in half-out of the water?

and in the pleasure of that communion
I lose track,
the moon I watch goes down, the

tide swings you away before
I know I'm
alone again long since,

mud sucking at gray and black
timbers of me,
a light growth of green dreams drying.

   Denise Levertov (b. 1923)

ANIMALS ARE PASSING FROM OUR LIVES

It's wonderful how I jog
on four honed-down ivory toes
my massive buttocks slipping
like oiled parts with each light step.

I'm to market. I can smell
the sour, grooved block, I can smell
the blade that opens the hole
and the pudgy white fingers

that shake out the intestines
like a hankie. In my dreams
the snouts drool on the marble,
suffering children, suffering flies,

suffering the consumers
who won't meet their steady eyes
for fear they could see. The boy
who drives me along believes

that any moment I'll fall
on my side and drum my toes
like a typewriter or squeal
and shit like a new housewife

discovering television,
or that I'll turn like a beast
cleverly to hook his teeth
with my teeth. No. Not this pig.

   Philip Levine (b. 1928)

MEMORIES OF WEST STREET AND LEPKE

Only teaching on Tuesdays, book-worming
in pajamas fresh from the washer each morning,
I hog a whole house on Boston's
"hardly passionate Marlborough Street,"
where even the man
scavenging filth in the back alley trash cans,
has two children, a beach wagon, a helpmate,
and is a "young Republican."
I have a nine months' daughter,
young enough to be my granddaughter.
Like the sun she rises in her flame-flamingo infants' wear.

These are the tranquillized *Fifties,*
and I am forty. Ought I to regret my seedtime?
I was a fire-breathing Catholic C. O.,
and made my manic statement,
telling off the state and president, and then
sat waiting sentence in the bull pen
beside a Negro boy with curlicues
of marijuana in his hair.

Given a year,
I walked on the roof of the West Street Jail, a short
enclosure like my school soccer court,
and saw the Hudson River once a day
through sooty clothesline entanglements
and bleaching khaki tenements.
Strolling, I yammered metaphysics with Abramowitz,
a jaundice-yellow ("it's really tan")
and fly-weight pacifist,
so vegetarian,
he wore rope shoes and preferred fallen fruit.
He tried to convert Bioff and Brown,
the Hollywood pimps, to his diet.
Hairy, muscular, suburban,
wearing chocolate double-breasted suits,
they blew their tops and beat him black and blue.

I was so out of things, I'd never heard
of the Jehovah's Witnesses.
"Are you a C. O.?" I asked a fellow jailbird.
"No," he answered, "I'm a J.W."
He taught me the "hospital tuck,"
and pointed out the T shirted back
of *Murder Incorporated's* Czar Lepke,

there piling towels on a rack,
or dawdling off to his little segregated cell full
of things forbidden the common man:
a portable radio, a dresser, two toy American
flags tied together with a ribbon of Easter palm.
Flabby, bald, lobotomized,
he drifted in a sheepish calm,
where no agonizing reappraisal
jarred his concentration on the electric chair—
hanging like an oasis in his air
of lost connections. . . .

Robert Lowell (1917–1978)

SKUNK HOUR
[*for Elizabeth Bishop*]

Nautilus Island's hermit
heiress still lives through winter in her Spartan cottage;
her sheep still graze above the sea.
Her son's a bishop. Her farmer
is first selectman in our village;
she's in her dotage.

Thirsting for
the hierarchic privacy
of Queen Victoria's century,
she buys up all
the eyesores facing her shore,
and lets them fall.

The season's ill—
we've lost our summer millionaire,
who seemed to leap from an L. L. Bean
catalogue. His nine-knot yawl
was auctioned off to lobstermen.
A red fox stain covers Blue Hill.

And now our fairy
decorator brightens his shop for fall;
his fishnet's filled with orange cork,
orange, his cobbler's bench and awl;
there is no money in his work,
he'd rather marry.

One dark night,
my Tudor Ford climbed the hill's skull;
I watched for love-cars. Lights turned down,

they lay together, hull to hull,
where the graveyard shelves on the town. . . .
My mind's not right.

A car radio bleats,
"Love, O careless Love. . . ." I hear
my ill-spirit sob in each blood cell,
as if my hand were at its throat. . . .
I myself am hell;
nobody's here—

only skunks, that search
in the moonlight for a bite to eat.
They march on their soles up Main Street:
white stripes, moonstruck eyes' red fire
under the chalk-dry and spar spire
of the Trinitarian Church.

I stand on top
of our back steps and breathe the rich air—
a mother skunk with her column of kittens swills the garbage
    pail.
She jabs her wedge-head in a cup
of sour cream, drops her ostrich tail,
and will not scare.

Robert Lowell (1917–1978)

YOU, ANDREW MARVELL

And here face down beneath the sun
And here upon earth's noonward height
To feel the always coming on
The always rising of the night:

To feel creep up the curving east
The earthy chill of dusk and slow
Upon those under lands the vast
And ever climbing shadow grow

And strange at Ecbatan the trees
Take leaf by leaf the evening strange
The flooding dark about their knees
The mountains over Persia change

And now at Kermanshah the gate
Dark empty and the withered grass
And through the twilight now the late
Few travelers in the westward pass

And Baghdad darken and the bridge
Across the silent river gone
And through Arabia the edge
Of evening widen and steal on   20

And deepen on Palmyra's street
The wheel rut in the ruined stone
And Lebanon fade out and Crete
High through the clouds and overblown

And over Sicily the air   25
Still flashing with the landward gulls
And loom and slowly disappear
The sails above the shadowy hulls

And Spain go under and the shore
Of Africa the gilded sand   30
And evening vanish and no more
The low pale light across that land

Nor now the long light on the sea:

And here face downward in the sun
To feel how swift how secretly   35
The shadow of the night comes on . . .

      Archibald Macleish (b. 1892)

WINTER VERSE FOR HIS SISTER

Moonlight washes the west side of the house
As clean as bone, it carpets like a lawn
The stubbled field tilting eastward
Where there is no sign yet of dawn.
The moon is an angel with a bright light sent   5
To surprise me once before I die
With the real aspect of things.
It holds the light steady and makes no comment.

Practicing for death I have lately gone
To that other house   10
Where our parents did most of their dying,
Embracing and not embracing their conditions.
Our father built bookcases and little by little stopped reading,
Our mother cooked proud meals for common mouths.
Kindly, they raised two children. We raked their leaves   15
And cut their grass, we ate and drank with them.
Reconciliation was our long work, not all of it joyful.

Now outside my own house at a cold hour
I watch the noncommittal angel lower
The steady lantern that's worn these clapboards thin   20
In a wash of moonlight, while men slept within,
Accepting and not accepting their conditions,
And the fingers of trees plied a deep carpet of decay
On the gravel web underneath the field,
And the field tilting always toward day.   25

William Meredith (b. 1919)

LISTENERS AT THE BREATHING PLACE
For John Maloney

*"The seal hunters sometimes call themselves
listeners at the breathing places."*
—From Eskimo Prints, *by James Houston*

The air says what it means, regardless of what
we want it to say. It holds our breath. Conundrums
tumble like seals. We listen. We catch one,
if we are lucky, the way a camera catches the gallop
of horses, their legs in positions we would never imagine.   5

Van Gogh knew. There is something to be said
for the word's inadequacies, the swirls of light
and movement which will always escape, astound us.
Rain on water, a lover's turning to go. Those places
breathe too, saying: "Be brave, believe in us."   10

In the end, we will lay down our words and embrace
the air that shapes them here, just as, at the peak
of loving, a cry shakes the candle's aureola in a room
too small for all this, and the body for now needs
to be held, to be held back, from that blinding other.   15

Gary Miranda (b. 1938)

THE GOOSE FISH

On the long shore, lit by the moon
To show them properly alone,
Two lovers suddenly embraced
So that their shadows were as one.
The ordinary night was graced   5
For them by the swift tide of blood
That silently they took at flood,
And for a little time they prized
    Themselves emparadised.

Then, as if shaken by stage-fright
Beneath the hard moon's bony light,
They stood together on the sand
Embarrassed in each other's sight
But still conspiring hand in hand,
Until they saw, there underfoot,
As though the world had found them out,
The goose fish turning up, though dead,
    His hugely grinning head.

There in the china light he lay,
Most ancient and corrupt and grey.
They hesitated at his smile,
Wondering what it seemed to say
To lovers who a little while
Before had thought to understand,
By violence upon the sand,
The only way that could be known
    To make a world their own.

It was a wide and moony grin
Together peaceful and obscene;
They knew not what he would express,
So finished a comedian
He might mean failure or success,
But took it for an emblem of
Their sudden, new and guilty love
To be observed by, when they kissed,
    That rigid optimist.

So he became their patriarch,
Dreadfully mild in the half-dark.
His throat that the sand seemed to choke,
His picket teeth, these left their mark
But never did explain the joke
That so amused him, lying there
While the moon went down to disappear
Along the still and tilted track
    That bears the zodiac.

        Howard Nemerov (b. 1920)

YOU ARE ODYSSEUS

You are Odysseus
returning home each evening
tentative, a little angry.

And I who thought to be
one of the Sirens (cast up
on strewn sheets
at dawn)
hide my song
under my tongue—
merely Penelope after all.
Meanwhile the old wars
go on, their dim music
can be heard even at night.
You leave each morning,
soon our son will follow.
Only my weaving is real.

      Linda Pastan (b. 1932)

THE APPLICANT

First, are you our sort of a person?
Do you wear
A glass eye, false teeth or a crutch,
A brace or a hook,
Rubber breasts or a rubber crotch,

Stitches to show something's missing? No, no? Then
How can we give you a thing?
Stop crying.
Open your hand.
Empty? Empty. Here is a hand

To fill it and willing
To bring teacups and roll away headaches
And do whatever you tell it.
Will you marry it?
It is guaranteed

To thumb shut your eyes at the end
And dissolve of sorrow.
We make a new stock from the salt.
I notice you are stark naked.
How about this suit—

Black and stiff, but not a bad fit.
Will you marry it?
It is waterproof, shatterproof, proof
Against fire and bombs through the roof.
Believe me, they'll bury you in it.

Now your head, excuse me, is empty.
I have the ticket for that.
Come here, sweetie, out of the closet.
Well, what do you think of *that?*
Naked as paper to start 30

But in twenty-five years she'll be silver,
In fifty, gold.
A living doll, everywhere you look.
It can sew, it can cook,
It can talk, talk, talk. 35

It works, there is nothing wrong with it.
You have a hole, it's a poultice.
You have an eye, it's an image.
My boy, it's your last resort.
Will you marry it, marry it, marry it. 40

Sylvia Plath (1932–1963)

MIRROR

I am silver and exact. I have no preconceptions.
Whatever I see I swallow immediately
Just as it is, unmisted by love or dislike.
I am not cruel, only truthful—
The eye of a little god, four-cornered. 5
Most of the time I meditate on the opposite wall.
It is pink, with speckles. I have looked at it so long
I think it is a part of my heart. But it flickers.
Faces and darkness separate us over and over.

Now I am a lake. A woman bends over me, 10
Searching my reaches for what she really is.
Then she turns to those liars, the candles or the moon.
I see her back, and reflect it faithfully.
She rewards me with tears and an agitation of hands.
I am important to her. She comes and goes. 15
Each morning it is her face that replaces the darkness.
In me she has drowned a young girl, and in me an old woman
Rises toward her day after day, like a terrible fish.

Sylvia Plath (1932–1963)

MORNING SONG

Love set you going like a fat gold watch.
The midwife slapped your footsoles, and your bald cry
Took its place among the elements.

Our voices echo, magnifying your arrival. New statue.
In a drafty museum, your nakedness
Shadows our safety. We stand round blankly as walls.

I'm no more your mother
Than the cloud that distils a mirror to reflect its own slow
Effacement at the wind's hand.

All night your moth-breath
Flickers among the flat pink roses. I wake to listen:
A far sea moves in my ear.

One cry, and I stumble from bed, cow-heavy and floral
In my Victorian nightgown.
Your mouth opens clean as a cat's. The window square

Whitens and swallows its dull stars. And now you try
Your handful of notes;
The clear vowels rise like balloons.

Sylvia Plath (1932–1963)

THE BATH TUB

As a bathtub lined with white porcelain,
When the hot water gives out or goes tepid,
So is the slow cooling of our chivalrous passion,
O my much praised but-not-altogether-satisfactory lady.

Ezra Pound (1885–1972)

IN A STATION OF THE METRO

The apparition of these faces in the crowd;
Petals on a wet, black bough.

Ezra Pound (1885–1972)

THE ROOFWALKER
—for Denise Levertov

Over the half-finished houses
night comes. The builders
stand on the roof. It is
quiet after the hammers,
the pulleys hang slack.
Giants, the roofwalkers,
on a listing deck, the wave
of darkness about to break

on their heads. The sky
is a torn sail where figures 10
pass magnified, shadows
on a burning deck.

I feel like them up there:
exposed, larger than life,
and due to break my neck. 15

Was it worth while to lay—
with infinite exertion—
a roof I can't live under?
—All those blueprints,
closings of gaps, 20
measurings, calculations?
A life I didn't choose
chose me: even
my tools are the wrong ones
for what I have to do. 25
I'm naked, ignorant,
a naked man fleeing
across the roofs
who could with a shade of difference
be sitting in the lamplight 30
against the cream wallpaper
reading—not with indifference—
about a naked man
fleeing across the roofs.

Adrienne Rich (b. 1929)

MR. FLOOD'S PARTY

Old Eben Flood, climbing alone one night
Over the hill between the town below
And the forsaken upland hermitage
That held as much as he should ever know
On earth again of home, paused warily. 5
The road was his with not a native near;
And Eben, having leisure, said aloud,
For no man else in Tilbury Town to hear:

"Well, Mr. Flood, we have the harvest moon
Again, and we may not have many more; 10
The bird is on the wing, the poet says,
And you and I have said it here before.
Drink to the bird." He raised up to the light
The jug that he had gone so far to fill,

And answered huskily: "Well, Mr. Flood,
Since you propose it, I believe I will."

Alone, as if enduring to the end
A valiant armor of scarred hopes outworn,
He stood there in the middle of the road
Like Roland's ghost winding a silent horn.
Below him, in the town among the trees,
Where friends of other days had honored him,
A phantom salutation of the dead
Rang thinly till old Eben's eyes were dim.

Then, as a mother lays her sleeping child
Down tenderly, fearing it may awake,
He set the jug down slowly at his feet
With trembling care, knowing that most things break;
And only when assured that on firm earth
It stood, as the uncertain lives of men
Assuredly did not, he paced away,
And with his hand extended paused again:

"Well, Mr. Flood, we have not met like this
In a long time; and many a change has come
To both of us, I fear, since last it was
We had a drop together. Welcome home!"
Convivially returning with himself,
Again he raised the jug up to the light;
And with an acquiescent quaver said:
"Well, Mr. Flood, if you insist, I might.

"Only a very little, Mr. Flood—
For auld lang syne. No more, sir; that will do."
So, for the time, apparently it did,
And Eben evidently thought so too;
For soon amid the silver loneliness
Of night he lifted up his voice and sang,
Secure, with only two moons listening,
Until the whole harmonious landscape rang—

"For auld lang syne." The weary throat gave out,
The last word wavered, and the song was done.
He raised again the jug regretfully
And shook his head, and was again alone.
There was not much that was ahead of him,
And there was nothing in the town below—
Where strangers would have shut the many doors
That many friends had opened long ago.

Edwin Arlington Robinson (1869–1935)

DOLOR

I have known the inexorable sadness of pencils,
Neat in their boxes, dolor of pad and paper-weight,
All the misery of manilla folders and mucilage,
Desolation in immaculate public places,
Lonely reception room, lavatory, switchboard, 5
The unalterable pathos of basin and pitcher,
Ritual of multigraph, paper-clip, comma,
Endless duplication of lives and objects.
And I have seen dust from the walls of institutions,
Finer than flour, alive, more dangerous than silica, 10
Sift, almost invisible, through long afternoons of tedium,
Dropping a fine film on nails and delicate eyebrows,
Glazing the pale hair, the duplicate grey standard faces.

Theodore Roethke (1908–1963)

I KNEW A WOMAN

I knew a woman, lovely in her bones,
When small birds sighed, she would sigh back at them;
Ah, when she moved, she moved more ways than one:
The shapes a bright container can contain!
Of her choice virtues only gods should speak, 5
Or English poets who grew up on Greek
(I'd have them sing in chorus, cheek to cheek).

How well her wishes went! She stroked my chin,
She taught me Turn, and Counter-turn, and Stand;
She taught me Touch, that undulant white skin; 10
I nibbled meekly from her proffered hand;
She was the sickle; I, poor I, the rake,
Coming behind her for her pretty sake
(But what prodigious mowing we did make).

Love likes a gander, and adores a goose: 15
Her full lips pursed, the errant note to seize;
She played it quick, she played it light and loose;
My eyes, they dazzled at her flowing knees;
Her several parts could keep a pure repose,
Or one hip quiver with a mobile nose 20
(She moved in circles, and those circles moved).

Let seed be grass, and grass turn into hay:
I'm martyr to a motion not my own;

What's freedom for? To know eternity.
I swear she cast a shadow white as stone. 25
But who would count eternity in days?
These old bones live to learn her wanton ways:
(I measure time by how a body sways).

    Theodore Roethke (1908–1963)

SONG FOR A LADY

On the day of breasts and small hips
the window pocked with bad rain,
rain coming on like a minister,
we coupled, so sane and insane.
We lay like spoons while the sinister 5
rain dropped like flies on our lips
and our glad eyes and our small hips.

"The room is so cold with rain," you said
and you, feminine you, with your flower
said novenas to my ankles and elbows. 10
You are a national product and power.
Oh my swan, my drudge, my dear wooly rose,
even a notary would notarize our bed
as you knead me and I rise like bread.

    Anne Sexton (1928–1974)

US

I was wrapped in black
fur and white fur and
you undid me and then
you placed me in gold light
and then you crowned me, 5
while snow fell outside
the door in diagonal darts.
While a ten-inch snow
came down like stars
in small calcium fragments, 10
we were in our own bodies
(that room that will bury us)
and you were in my body
(that room that will outlive us)
and at first I rubbed your 15
feet dry with a towel

because I was your slave
and then you called me princess.
Princess!

Oh then
I stood up in my gold skin
and I beat down the psalms
and I beat down the clothes
and you undid the bridle
and you undid the reins
and I undid the buttons,
the bones, the confusions,
the New England postcards,
the January ten o'clock night,
and we rose up like wheat,
acre after acre of gold,
and we harvested,
we harvested.

    Anne Sexton (1928–1974)

THE MAN WHO MARRIED MAGDALENE

The man who married Magdalene
Had not forgiven her.
God might pardon every sin . . .
Love is no pardoner.

Her hands were hollow, pale and blue,
Her mouth like watered wine.
He watched to see if she were true
And waited for a sign.

It was old harlotry, he guessed,
That drained her strength away,
So gladly for the dark she dressed,
So sadly for the day.

Their quarrels made her dull and weak
And soon a man might fit
A penny in the hollow cheek
And never notice it.

At last, as they exhausted slept,
Death granted the divorce,
And nakedly the woman leapt
Upon that narrow horse.

But when he woke and woke alone
He wept and would deny
The loose behavior of the bone
And the immodest thigh.

Louis Simpson (b. 1923)

DR. JOSEPH GOEBBELS
—1 May, 1945; 1800 hours.

(The day after Hitler's death, Goebbels and his wife climbed the steps into the garden where both committed suicide.)

Say goodbye to the help, the ranks
Of Stalin-bait. Give too much thanks
To Naumann—Magda's lover: we
Thank him for *all* his loyalty.
Schwaegermann; Rach. After a while 5
Turn back to them with a sad smile:
We'll save them trouble—no one cares
Just now to carry us upstairs.

Turn away; check your manicure;
Pull on your gloves. Take time; make sure 10
The hat brim curves though the hat's straight.
Give her your arm. Let the fools wait;
They act like they've someplace to go.
Take the stairs, now. Self-control. Slow.
A slight limp; just enough to see. 15
Pass on, and infect history.

The rest is silence. Left like sperm
In a stranger's gut, waiting its term,
Each thought, each step lies; the roots spread.
They'll believe in us when we're dead. 20
When we took "Red Berlin" we found
We always worked best underground.
So; the vile body turns to spirit
That speaks soundlessly. They'll hear it.

W. D. Snodgrass (b. 1926)

OLD APPLE TREES

Like battered old mill hands, they stand in the orchard—
Like drunk legionnaires, heaving themselves up,
Lurching to attention. Not one of them wobbles
The same way as another. Uniforms won't fit them—

All those cramps, humps, bulges. Here, a limb's gone;
There, rain and corruption have eaten the whole core.
They've all grown too tall, too thick, or too something.
Like men bent too long over desks, engines, benches,
Or bent under mail sacks, under loss.
They've seen too much history and bad weather, grown
Around rocks, into high winds, diseases, grown
Too long to be willful, too long to be changed.

Oh, I could replant, bulldoze the lot,
Get nursery stock, all the latest ornamentals,
Make the whole place look like a suburb,
Each limb sleek as a teenybopper's—pink
To the very crotch—each trunk smoothed, ideal
As the fantasy life of an adman.
We might just own the Arboreal Muscle Beach,
Each tree disguised as its neighbor. Or each disguised
As if not its neighbor—each doing its own thing
Like executives' children.

                Oh, at least I could prune.
At least I should trim the dead wood; fill holes
Where the rain collects and decay starts. Well, I should;
I should. There's a red squirrel nests here someplace.
I live in the hope of hearing one saw-whet owl.
Then, too, they're right about spring. These gnarled, rough boughs
Run riot. This whole orchard's an orgy. Bees hum
Through these branches like lascivious intentions. The white
Petals drift down, sift across the ground; this air's so rich
No man should come here except on a working pass;
No man should leave here without going to confession.
All fall, apples nearly crack the boughs;
They hang here red as candles in the
White oncoming snow.

Tonight we'll drive down to the bad part of town
To the New Hungarian Bar or the Klub Polski,
To the Old Hellas where we'll eat the new spring lamb;
Drink good mavrodaphne, say, at the Laikon Bar,
Send drinks to the dancers, those meat cutters and laborers
Who move in their native dances, the archaic forms.
Maybe we'll still find our old crone selling chestnuts,
Whose toothless gums can spit out fifteen languages,
Who turns, there, late at night, in the center of the floor,
Her ancient dry hips wheeling their slow, slow tsamikos;
We'll stomp under the tables, whistle, we'll all hiss

Till even the belly dancer leaves, disgraced.
We'll drive back, lushed and vacant, in the first dawn;
Out of the light gray mists may rise our flowering 50
Orchard, the rough trunks holding their formations
Like elders of Colonus, the old men of Thebes
Tossing their white hair, almost whispering,

> Soon, each one of us will be taken
> By dark powers under this ground 55
> That drove us here, that warped us.
> Not one of us got it his own way.
> Nothing like any one of us
> Will be seen again, forever.
> Each of us held some noble shape in mind. 60
> It seemed better that we kept alive.

W. D. Snodgrass (b. 1926)

BESS

Ours are the streets where Bess first met her
cancer. She went to work every day past the
secure houses. At her job in the library
she arranged better and better flowers, and when
students asked for books her hand went out 5
to help. In the last year of her life
she had to keep her friends from knowing
how happy they were. She listened while they
complained about food or work or the weather.
And the great national events danced 10
their grotesque, fake importance. Always

Pain moved where she moved. She walked
ahead; it came. She hid; it found her.
No one ever served another so truly;
no enemy ever meant so strong a hate. 15
It was almost as if there was no room
left for her on earth. But she remembered
where joy used to live. She straightened its flowers;
she did not weep when she passed its houses;
and when finally she pulled into a tiny corner 20
and slipped from pain, her hand opened
again, and the streets opened, and she wished all well.

William Stafford (b. 1914)

TRAVELING THROUGH THE DARK

Traveling through the dark I found a deer
dead on the edge of the Wilson River road.
It is usually best to roll them into the canyon:
that road is narrow; to swerve might make more dead.

By glow of the tail-light I stumbled back of the car   5
and stood by the heap, a doe, a recent killing;
she had stiffened already, almost cold.
I dragged her off; she was large in the belly.

My fingers touching her side brought me the reason—
her side was warm; her fawn lay there waiting,   10
alive, still, never to be born.
Beside that mountain road I hesitated.

The car aimed ahead its lowered parking lights;
under the hood purred the steady engine.
I stood in the glare of the warm exhaust turning red;   15
around our group I could hear the wilderness listen.

I thought hard for us all—my only swerving—,
then pushed her over the edge into the river.

William Stafford (b. 1914)

ANECDOTE OF THE JAR

I placed a jar in Tennessee,
And round it was, upon a hill.
It made the slovenly wilderness
Surround that hill.

The wilderness rose up to it,   5
And sprawled around, no longer wild.
The jar was round upon the ground
And tall and of a port in air.

It took dominion everywhere.
The jar was gray and bare.   10
It did not give of bird or bush,
Like nothing else in Tennessee.

Wallace Stevens (1879–1955)

THE EMPEROR OF ICE-CREAM

Call the roller of big cigars,
The muscular one, and bid him whip

In kitchen cups concupiscent curds.
Let the wenches dawdle in such dress
As they are used to wear, and let the boys
Bring flowers in last month's newspapers.
Let be be finale of seem.
The only emperor is the emperor of ice-cream.

Take from the dresser of deal.
Lacking the three glass knobs, that sheet
On which she embroidered fantails once
And spread it so as to cover her face.
If her horny feet protrude, they come
To show how cold she is, and dumb.
Let the lamp affix its beam.
The only emperor is the emperor of ice-cream.

Wallace Stevens (1879–1955)

AND DEATH SHALL HAVE NO DOMINION

And death shall have no dominion.
Dead men naked they shall be one
With the man in the wind and the west moon;
When their bones are picked clean and the clean bones gone,
They shall have stars at elbow and foot;
Though they go mad they shall be sane,
Though they sink through the sea they shall rise again;
Though lovers be lost love shall not;
And death shall have no dominion.

And death shall have no dominion.
Under the windings of the sea
They lying long shall not die windily;
Twisting on racks when sinews give way,
Strapped to a wheel, yet they shall not break;
Faith in their hands shall snap in two,
And the unicorn evils run them through;
Split all ends up they shan't crack;
And death shall have no dominion.

And death shall have no dominion.
No more may gulls cry at their ears
Or waves break loud on the seashores;
Where blew a flower may a flower no more
Lift its head to the blows of the rain;
Though they be mad and dead as nails,

Heads of the characters hammer through daisies;　　　　25
Break in the sun till the sun breaks down,
And death shall have no dominion.

　　　　　　　Dylan Thomas (1914–1953)

THE FORCE THAT THROUGH THE GREEN FUSE DRIVES THE FLOWER

The force that through the green fuse drives the flower
Drives my green age; that blasts the roots of trees
Is my destroyer.
And I am dumb to tell the crooked rose
My youth is bent by the same wintry fever.　　　　5

The force that drives the water through the rocks
Drives my red blood; that dries the mouthing streams
Turns mine to wax.
And I am dumb to mouth unto my veins
How at the mountain spring the same mouth sucks.　　　　10

The hand that whirls the water in the pool
Stirs the quicksand; that ropes the blowing wind
Hauls my shroud sail.
And I am dumb to tell the hanging man
How of my clay is made the hangman's lime.　　　　15

The lips of time leech to the fountain head;
Love drips and gathers, but the fallen blood
Shall calm her sores.
And I am dumb to tell a weather's wind
How time has ticked a heaven round the stars.　　　　20

And I am dumb to tell the lover's tomb
How at my sheet goes the same crooked worm.

　　　　　　　Dylan Thomas (1914–1953)

UNEASY RIDER

Falling in love with a mustache
is like saying
you can fall in love with
the way a man polishes his shoes
　　which,　　　　5
　　of course,
　　is one of the things that turns on
　　my tuned-up engine

those trim buckled boots

(I feel like an advertisement
for men's fashions
when I think of your ankles)

Yeats was hung up with a girl's beautiful face

and I find myself

a bad moralist,

a failing aesthetician,

a sad poet,

wanting to touch your arms and feel the muscles
that make a man's body have so much substance,
that makes a woman
lean and yearn in that direction
that makes her melt/ she is a rainy day
in your presence
the pool of wax under a burning candle
the foam from a waterfall

You are more beautiful than any Harley-Davidson
She is the rain,
waits in it for you,
finds blood spotting her legs
from the long ride.

Diane Wakoski (b. 1937)

THE LINE OF AN AMERICAN POET

That American poet's future
Was bright because he began
With the know-how of Ford and Chrysler
And the faith of American Can.

He fathomed success's secret
And stuck to his P's & Q's
And urged himself over and over
To produce and produce and produce.

His very first models were cleverly
Built. The market boomed.
Some of the world's most critical
Consumers looked and consumed.

Lines off his line came smoother
And smoother as more and more
Know-how blew in the window
And verses rolled out the door

Until everyone in the market
Knew that his new works were sure
To be just what the country had need of:
Poems uniform, safe and pure.

      Reed Whittemore (b. 1919)

COTTAGE STREET, 1953

Framed in her phoenix fire-screen, Edna Ward
Bends to the tray of Canton, pouring tea
For frightened Mrs. Plath; then, turning toward
The pale, slumped daughter, and my wife, and me,

Asks if we would prefer it weak or strong.
Will we have milk or lemon, she enquires?
The visit seems already strained and long.
Each in his turn, we tell her our desires.

It is my office to exemplify
The published poet in his happiness,
Thus cheering Sylvia, who has wished to die;
But half-ashamed, and impotent to bless,

I am a stupid life-guard who has found,
Swept to his shallows by the tide, a girl
Who, far from shore, has been immensely drowned,
And stares through water now with eyes of pearl.

How large is her refusal; and how slight
The genteel chat whereby we recommend
Life, of a summer afternoon, despite
The brewing dusk which hints that it may end.

And Edna Ward shall die in fifteen years,
After her eight-and-eighty summers of
Such grace and courage as permit no tears,
The thin hand reaching out, the last word *love*,

Outliving Sylvia who, condemned to live,
Shall study for a decade, as she must,
To state at last her brilliant negative
In poems free and helpless and unjust.

      Richard Wilbur (b. 1921)

LOVE CALLS US TO THE THINGS OF THIS WORLD

    The eyes open to a cry of pulleys,
And spirited from sleep, the astounded soul
Hangs for a moment bodiless and simple
As false dawn.
             Outside the open window
The morning air is all awash with angels.

    Some are in bed-sheets, some are in blouses,
Some are in smocks: but truly there they are.
Now they are rising together in calm swells
Of halcyon feeling, filling whatever they wear
With the deep joy of their impersonal breathing;

    Now they are flying in place, conveying
The terrible speed of their omnipresence, moving
And staying like white water; and now of a sudden
They swoon down into so rapt a quiet
That nobody seems to be there.
               The soul shrinks

    From all that it is about to remember,
From the punctual rape of every blessèd day,
And cries,
        "Oh, let there be nothing on earth but laundry,
Nothing but rosy hands in the rising steam
And clear dances done in the sight of heaven."

    Yet, as the sun acknowledges
With a warm look the world's hunks and colors,
The soul descends once more in bitter love
To accept the waking body, saying now
In a changed voice as the man yawns and rises,

    "Bring them down from their ruddy gallows;
Let there be clean linen for the backs of thieves;
Let lovers go fresh and sweet to be undone,
And the heaviest nuns walk in a pure floating
Of dark habits,
          keeping their difficult balance."

                    Richard Wilbur (b. 1921)

PIAZZA DI SPAGNA, EARLY MORNING

          I can't forget
How she stood at the top of that long marble stair
    Amazed, and then with a sleepy pirouette
Went dancing slowly down to the fountain-quieted square;

       Nothing upon her face 5
But some impersonal loneliness,—not then a girl,
    But as it were a reverie of the place,
        A called-for falling glide and whirl;

    As when a leaf, petal, or thin chip
Is drawn to the falls of a pool and, circling a moment above it, 10
        Rides on over the lip—
    Perfectly beautiful, perfectly ignorant of it.

                 Richard Wilbur (b. 1921)

NANTUCKET

Flowers through the window
lavender and yellow

changed by white curtains—
Smell of cleanliness—

Sunshine of late afternoon— 5
On the glass tray

a glass pitcher, the tumbler
turned down, by which

a key is lying—And the
immaculate white bed 10

    William Carlos Williams
       (1883–1963)

THE YACHTS

contend in a sea which the land partly encloses
shielding them from the too heavy blows
of an ungoverned ocean which when it chooses

tortures the biggest hulls, the best man knows
to pit against its beatings, and sinks them pitilessly. 5
Mothlike in mists, scintillant in the minute

brilliance of cloudless days, with broad bellying sails
they glide to the wind tossing green water
from their sharp prows while over them the crew crawls

ant like, solicitously grooming them, releasing, 10
making fast as they turn, lean far over and having
caught the wind again, side by side, head for the mark.

In a well guarded arena of open water surrounded by
lesser and greater craft which, sycophant, lumbering
and flittering follow them, they appear youthful, rare

as the light of a happy eye, live with the grace
of all that in the mind is feckless, free and
naturally to be desired. Now the sea which holds them

is moody, lapping their glossy sides, as if feeling
for some slightest flaw but fails completely.
Today no race. Then the wind comes again. The yachts

move, jockeying for a start, the signal is set and they
are off. Now the waves strike at them but they are too
well made, they slip through, though they take in canvas.

Arms with hands grasping seek to clutch at the prows.
Bodies thrown recklessly in the way are cut aside.
It is a sea of faces about them in agony, in despair

until the horror of the race dawns staggering the mind,
the whole sea become an entanglement of watery bodies
lost to the world bearing what they cannot hold. Broken,

beaten, desolate, reaching from the dead to be taken up
they cry out, failing, failing! their cries rising
in waves still as the skillful yachts pass over.

William Carlos Williams (1883–1963)

A BLESSING

Just off the highway to Rochester, Minnesota,
Twilight bounds softly forth on the grass.
And the eyes of those two Indian ponies
Darken with kindness.
They have come gladly out of the willows
To welcome my friend and me.
We step over the barbed wire into the pasture
Where they have been grazing all day, alone.
They ripple tensely, they can hardly contain their happiness
That we have come.
They bow shyly as wet swans. They love each other.
There is no loneliness like theirs.
At home once more,
They begin munching the young tufts of spring in the darkness.
I would like to hold the slenderer one in my arms,
For she has walked over to me
And nuzzled my left hand.

She is black and white,
Her mane falls wild on her forehead,
And the light breeze moves me to caress her long ear 20
That is delicate as the skin over a girl's wrist.
Suddenly I realize
That if I stepped out of my body I would break
Into blossom.

James Wright (1927–1980)

BETWEEN THE WORLD AND ME

And one morning while in the woods I stumbled suddenly upon the thing,
Stumbled upon it in a grassy clearing guarded by scaly oaks and elms.
And the sooty details of the scene rose, thrusting themselves between the world and me . . .

There was a design of white bones slumbering forgottenly upon a cushion of ashes.
There was a charred stump of a sapling pointing a blunt finger accusingly at the sky. 5
There were torn tree limbs, tiny veins of burnt leaves, and a scorched coil of greasy hemp;
A vacant shoe, an empty tie, a ripped shirt, a lonely hat, and a pair of trousers stiff with black blood.
And upon the trampled grass were buttons, dead matches, butt-ends of cigars and cigarettes, peanut shells, a drained gin-flask, and a whore's lipstick;
Scattered traces of tar, restless arrays of feathers, and the lingering smell of gasoline.
And through the morning air the sun poured yellow surprise into the eye sockets of a stony skull . . . 10
And while I stood my mind was frozen with a cold pity for the life that was gone.
The ground gripped my feet and my heart was circled by icy walls of fear—
The sun died in the sky; a night wind muttered in the grass and fumbled the leaves in the trees; the woods poured forth the hungry yelping of hounds; the darkness screamed with thirsty voices; and the witnesses rose and lived:
The dry bones stirred, rattled, lifted, melting themselves into my bones.
The gray ashes formed flesh firm and black, entering into my flesh. 15
The gin-flask passed from mouth to mouth; cigars and cigarettes glowed, the whore smeared the lipstick red upon her lips,

And a thousand faces swirled around me, clamoring that my life be
    burned . . .

And then they had me, stripped me, battering my teeth into my throat
    till I swallowed my own blood.
My voice was drowned in the roar of their voices, and my black wet
    body slipped and rolled in their hands as they bound me to the
    sapling.
And my skin clung to the bubbling hot tar, falling from me in limp
    patches.   20
And the down and quills of the white feathers sank into my raw flesh,
    and I moaned in my agony.
Then my blood was cooled mercifully, cooled by a baptism of gasoline.
And in a blaze of red I leaped to the sky as pain rose like water, boiling
    my limbs.
Panting, begging I clutched child-like, clutched to the hot sides of death.
Now I am dry bones and my face a stony skull staring in yellow surprise
    at the sun . . .   25

Richard Wright (1908–1960)

SAILING TO BYZANTIUM

I

That is no country for old men. The young
In one another's arms, birds in the trees
—Those dying generations—at their song,
The salmon-falls, the mackerel-crowded seas,
Fish, flesh, or fowl, commend all summer long   5
Whatever is begotten, born, and dies.
Caught in that sensual music all neglect
Monuments of unageing intellect.

II

An aged man is but a paltry thing,
A tattered coat upon a stick, unless   10
Soul clap its hands and sing, and louder sing
For every tatter in its mortal dress,
Nor is there singing school but studying
Monuments of its own magnificence;
And therefore I have sailed the seas and come   15
To the holy city of Byzantium.

III

O sages standing in God's holy fire
As in the gold mosaic of a wall,
Come from the holy fire, perne in a gyre,

And be the singing-masters of my soul.
Consume my heart away; sick with desire
And fastened to a dying animal
It knows not what it is; and gather me
Into the artifice of eternity.

                    IV
Once out of nature, I shall never take
My bodily form from any natural thing,
But such a form as Grecian goldsmiths make
Of hammered gold and gold enamelling
To keep a drowsy Emperor awake;
Or set upon a golden bough to sing
To lords and ladies of Byzantium
Of what is past, or passing, or to come.

           William Butler Yeats (1865–1939)

THE SECOND COMING

Turning and turning in the widening gyre
The falcon cannot hear the falconer;
Things fall apart; the centre cannot hold;
Mere anarchy is loosed upon the world,
The blood-dimmed tide is loosed, and everywhere
The ceremony of innocence is drowned;
The best lack all conviction, while the worst
Are full of passionate intensity.

Surely some revelation is at hand;
Surely the Second Coming is at hand.
The Second Coming! Hardly are those words out
When a vast image out of *Spiritus Mundi*
Troubles my sight: somewhere in sands of the desert
A shape with lion body and the head of a man,
A gaze blank and pitiless as the sun,
Is moving its slow thighs, while all about it
Reel shadows of the indignant desert birds.
The darkness drops again; but now I know
That twenty centuries of stony sleep
Were vexed to nightmare by a rocking cradle,
And what rough beast, its hour come round at last,
Slouches towards Bethlehem to be born?

           William Butler Yeats (1865–1939)

THE WILD SWANS AT COOLE

The trees are in their autumn beauty,
The woodland paths are dry,
Under the October twilight the water
Mirrors a still sky;
Upon the brimming water among the stones   5
Are nine-and-fifty swans.

The nineteenth autumn has come upon me
Since I first made my count;
I saw, before I had well finished,
All suddenly mount   10
And scatter wheeling in great broken rings
Upon their clamorous wings.

I have looked upon those brilliant creatures,
And now my heart is sore.
All's changed since I, hearing at twilight,   15
The first time on this shore,
The bell-beat of their wings above my head,
Trod with a lighter tread.

Unwearied still, lover by lover,
They paddle in the cold   20
Companionable streams or climb the air;
Their hearts have not grown old;
Passion or conquest, wander where they will,
Attend upon them still.

But now they drift on the still water,   25
Mysterious, beautiful;
Among what rushes will they build,
By what lake's edge or pool
Delight men's eyes when I awake some day
To find they have flown away?   30

William Butler Yeats (1865–1939)

GLOSSARY

The following list of poetic terms is intended as a convenient reference guide. Much fuller, in-context discussions of the great majority of these terms can be found in the text, on the pages indicated at the end of each glossary definition.

Abstract Language: Any language that employs general concepts rather than specific concrete images and therefore appeals to the mind without including an appeal to the senses. Its terms are intangible rather than image-producing, general rather than particular. It is the opposite of concrete language. p. 126.

Accentual Meter: Meter in which only the number of accented syllables is counted, without consideration of the total number of syllables. p. 215.

Accentual-Syllabic Meter: The regular meter in English poetry, based on both the placement of the accent and the number of syllables in a line. p. 215.

Alexandrine: A one-line poetic form, in iambic hexameter, in which the rhyme scheme is dependent on the form with which it is combined. p. 234.

Allegory: A narrative with a consistent second level of meaning that is more important than the literal level. p. 202.

Alliteration: The repetition of an initial consonant sound in two or more stressed syllables close to one another, p. 210.

Allusion: A reference (often very slight) to a person, place, literary work, historical event, or anything else that lies outside the immediate context of the poem. p. 77.

Ambiguity: The capacity of words to generate thought in several directions at once and to suggest multiple meanings, several of which may be appropriate in the given context of a poem. p. 11.

Anapest/Anapestic Foot: A metrical foot that consists of two unstressed syllables followed by one stressed syllable (e.g., ŭndĕrneáth). A poem consisting primarily of such feet is written in anapestic meter. p. 215.

Archetypal Symbol: See *Symbol*.

Assonance: The repetition of vowel sounds in two or more stressed syllables close to each other. p. 210.

Audience: The "you" of the poem (stated or implied) to whom the persona speaks. p. 24.

Ballad: A narrative poem, originally a part of oral folk tradition. The term is often used, however, to designate a literary work written in imitation of a folk ballad. Such works are usually referred to as "literary ballads." pp. 233–234.

GLOSSARY

Ballad Stanza: See Forms Chart, pp. 233–234.

Blank Verse: Unrhymed iambic pentameter. p. 235.

Cacophony: A harsh, strident, discordant combination of sounds. p. 212.

Caesura: The breath-pause within a line, made necessary by punctuation, word meaning, or syntax. p. 222.

Closure: A final statement which snaps the poem shut, giving finality to the issue, and to which the poem has been building up from the start. p. 52.

Conceit: An exaggerated comparison, simile, or metaphor. Petrarchan conceits tend to compare the tangible with the tangible and to become conventional (I am a hunter; my love is a doe). Metaphysical conceits often compare the physical with the spiritual, require intellectual analysis, and are used as the basis for "far-fetched" arguments. (You and I together are a phoenix).

Concrete Language: Any language which employs specific concrete images and therefore appeals not only to the mind but also to the senses of seeing, hearing, feeling, smelling, tasting. It is the opposite of abstract language.

Connotations: The associations and implications surrounding a word, suggesting meanings beyond its denotation, or dictionary definition. p. 77.

Consonance: Any kind of consonant repetition, regardless of whether the corresponding sounds occur in stressed or unstressed syllables, at the beginnings of words or within them, or before and/or after different vowel sounds. p. 210.

Context: The frame of reference for the poem, to which all the details contribute and by which all the details are colored. p. 10.

Conventional Symbol: See *Symbol,* as well as p. 189.

Couplet: See Forms Chart, pp. 233, 234.

Dactyl/Dactylic Foot: A metrical foot containing a stressed syllable followed by an unstressed syllable (e.g., súmmărў). Dactylic meter is meter that contains a predominance of dactylic feet. p. 215.

Denotation: The explicit meaning, or dictionary definition, of a word or phrase. p. 77.

Dimeter: A poetic line consisting of two feet. p. 216.

Dramatic Irony: See *Irony.*

Dramatic Monologue: A speech occasioned by a dramatic situation and delivered by an individualized character to an implied or identifiable listener within the poem. p. 24.

Elegy: A poem that is a lament for the deceased. p. 187.

End Rhyme: See *Rhyme.*

English, or Shakespearean, sonnet: A fourteen line, iambic pentameter poem, divided into three quatrains and one couplet, with a rhyme scheme of abab cdcd efef gg.

Enjambment: The continuation of phrasing and meaning beyond the end of one line and into the next. The result of enjambment is a run-on line. p. 231.

Eulogy: A poem that offers praise for the deceased. p. 187.

Euphony: A smooth, melodic blend of harmonious sounds. p. 212.

Extended Figure: A metaphor or other figure of speech developed through a number of lines or a whole poem. p. 156.

Field of Domain: The area of human activity with which a figure of speech associates a literal subject. A cluster of different images often relates to a single field of domain.

Figurative Language: See *Figure of speech*.

Figure of Speech: An individual, isolatable utterance that, by comparing two subjects not literally comparable, means something other than precisely what it says. Included in this category are simile, metaphor, hyperbole, metonymy, synecdoche, and other devices. A closely related term is *figurative language,* which may be used to describe either a particular figure of speech, a cluster of figures, or—more generally—a poetic style. p. 148.

Foot (Metrical Foot): The smallest unit containing the basic rhythm of a poem; a group of syllables which form a metrical pattern through a combination of stressed and unstressed syllables—e.g., iamb (˘/), trochee (/˘), anapest (˘˘/), dactyl (/˘˘), and the substitute feet spondee (//) and pyrrhic (˘˘). p. 215.

Formal Patterns: See *Structure*.

Free Verse: A form of verse that does not obey the rules of conventional meter; it lacks regularity in rhythm pattern and line length, reflecting instead natural speech rhythms. pp. 221, 235.

Grounds for Comparison: The basis on which a comparison is made, the ways a literal and a figurative subject are said to be alike. p. 150.

Heptameter: A poetic line consisting of seven feet. p. 216.

Hexameter: A poetic line consisting of six feet. p. 216.

Hyperbole: See *Overstatement*.

Iamb/Iambic Foot: The most common metrical unit in English poetry; an unstressed syllable followed by a stressed syllable (e.g., ăfláme). Iambic meter is meter with a predominance of iambic feet. p. 215.

Image: A word or group of words that stimulates one or more of the physical senses by calling up concrete word pictures, smells, sounds, etc. pp. 60, 125.

Implied Metaphor: A figure of speech that implies that a literal subject is identical to a figurative subject by using characteristics of the figurative to describe the literal—e.g., "time flies" (time = bird). p. 156.

Incongruity: A disparity or discrepancy that results from the juxtaposition of conflicting objects, incidents, tones, or other elements in a poem. p. 102.

Internal Rhyme: See *Rhyme*.

Irony: A form of incongruity that creates a sense of disparity or discrepancy between seemingly incompatible things in order to suggest something other than (often the opposite of) what the literal words state. Irony takes a number of different forms: *dramatic irony,* which is based on the discrepancy between a character's limited perceptions or assumptions and the fuller knowledge of the audience or reader; *situational irony,* which results when there is a reversal of expected events or circumstances; *verbal irony,* a mode of speech or writing in which the usual or expected meanings of words are in some way modified or reversed. When verbal irony is emphatic, biting, and unmistakable, it is called *sarcasm.* pp. 109–113.

Limerick: See Forms Chart, pp. 234, 237.

Metaphor: A figure of speech that claims two unlike things are identical (literal subject = figurative subject). pp. 151, 153.

Meter: The strict repetitive pattern of stressed and unstressed syllables (rhythm) found in many poems. p. 215.

Metonymy: A figure of speech that substitutes something associated with the literal subject for that subject. p. 158.

Monometer: A poetic line containing one metrical foot. p. 216.

Monosyllabic Foot: A poetic line consisting of one foot. p. 216.

Myth: A sacred story accepted as truth by a large segment of a culture; a literary invention which attempts to explain the origin of something in the manner of a myth. p. 198.

Octameter: A line containing eight metrical feet. p. 216.

Octave: See Forms Chart, pp. 225, 234.

Ode: A long, serious, meditative work written in an elevated, formal style. Originating with the Greek poet Pindar, this form has been used by a great many later poets, especially by English poets of the seventeenth and eighteenth centuries. p. 240.

Onomatopoeia: The use of words that sound like what they mean (e.g., buzz).

Open Form: Seemingly unstructured but actually disciplined form. p. 231.

Overstatement (Hyperbole): A form of incongruity that uses an exaggeration of the truth (in content or emotion) to achieve impact. p. 109.

Oxymoron: A type of incongruity in which two successive words seemingly contradict one another (e.g., wise fool). See also *Paradox*.

Paradox: A statement or situation that appears to be self-contradictory but on closer analysis proves to be true. p. 107.

Paraphrase: The restatement of a passage as accurately as possible in one's own words. p. 11.

Parody: The conscious imitation of the style, language, or ideas of another author or work with the intent of ridiculing or mocking the original. p. 103.

Pentameter: A line containing five metrical feet. p. 216.

Persona: The "I" of the poem, the speaker, the literary creation whose voice is heard in the poem. p. 18.

Personal Symbol: See *Symbol*.

Personification: A comparison in which a thing, an abstraction, or an animal is endowed with human characteristics. p. 157.

Petrarchan, or Italian, Sonnet: A sonnet form consisting of fourteen iambic pentameter lines divided into an octave rhymed *abba* and a sestet rhymed cdcdcd or cdcdee. p. 225.

Pun: A play on words requiring the reader or listener to perceive a discrepancy between two or more meanings in the same word. p. 103.

Quatrain: See Forms Chart, pp. 223, 234.

Refrain: A group of words or a line repeated at intervals in a poem, especially in a song.

Rhyme: The similarity of sound produced by two or more vowel clusters and following consonants (e.g., fast/past). *True* or *perfect rhyme* requires an identical sound in the final stressed vowel and following consonants with different consonant sounds preceding the vowel, as in the previous example. *Identical rhymes* have the same preceding consonant (e.g., fast/fast). *Slant rhyme, off-rhyme,* or *near rhyme* allows for similarity rather than exactness of the repeated sound (e.g., tough/bough). *End rhyme* occurs at the ends of lines; *internal rhyme* includes sounds from the middle of a line as well as from the end. Rhyme between final stressed syllables is called *masculine rhyme*; rhyme that extends over two or more syllables and ends on unstressed syllables is called *feminine rhyme*. *Rhyme scheme* is the arrangement of rhymes in a unit (e.g., abba). p. 210.

Rhythm: The alternation of stressed and unstressed syllables. A strict repetitive pattern is called meter. The basic kinds of rhythm in English poetry are iambic (˘/), trochaic (/˘), anapestic (˘˘/), and dactylic (/˘˘). Occasionally, a spondaic (//) or pyrrhic foot (˘˘) will substitute for the basic foot. pp. 214–217.

Run-on Line: See *Enjambment*.

Sarcasm: See *Irony*.

Satire: A literary form or technique used to expose human frailties and bring about reform by holding up to ridicule the customs, values, or institutions of society. p. 112.

Scansion: The analysis of meter in a poem by using stress marks, dividing lines into feet, and noting the rhythm pattern and rhyme (if any). p. 217.

Sestet: See Forms Chart, pp. 225, 234.

Simile: A figure of speech that expresses the likeness between two logically unlike things by means of an explicit connective such as "like," "as," "as if," "than," or "seems." p. 150.

Situation: The physical setting, time of the action, social and historical context, and circumstances (including events that have occurred before the opening of the poem) that influence the thought and action of a work. p. 26.

Situational Irony: See *Irony*.

Slant Rhyme (Off-Rhyme): See *Rhyme*.

Sonnet: See Forms Chart, p. 235.

Spondee: A metrical foot consisting of two stressed syllables (//), as in "rún hárd." p. 216.

Stanza/Stanza Form: Most basically, a group of lines set off typographically as a unit. Stanzaic form is a precise pattern (meter, number of lines, rhyme scheme) which is repeated in each stanza of the poem. p. 223.

Stress (Accent): The emphasis given to one syllable in relation to another. The noun *récŏrd* is distinguished from the verb *rĕcórd* by stressing the first syllable and leaving the second unstressed. In this book, *stress* and *accent* are used interchangeably. The alternation of stressed and unstressed syllables creates rhythm and meter. p. 214.

Structure: The organizational patterns on which a poem is built and by which the poet controls the matter of the poem and the reaction of the reader. In this book, the kinds of organization that depend on the meaning of words and that develop ideas are called *thematic structures* (e.g., narrative, description, analysis, argument, syntax, image pattern); those that depend on the form (physical properties) of words are called *formal patterns* (e.g., line length, stanza division, sound patterns, metrics, verse forms). p. 49.

Symbol: A reference to a concrete image, object, character, pattern, or action which, by virtue of the mental associations it evokes, suggests meanings in addition to and often more significant than its literal meaning. On the basis of their origin and appeal, symbols may be classified as *archetypal symbols,* which, because they derive from longstanding recognition of the commonalities of human experience, have enduring and universal meaning; *conventional symbols,* which have a shared traditional meaning for a particular culture, nation, or group; and *personal symbols,* which, rather than being commonly recognized, are unique to a given poem or poet. p. 181.

Synecdoche: A figure of speech in which a part of something is used for the whole, the whole is used for a part, or a material is used for the object made from the material. p. 159.

Tenor: The literal subject of a figure of speech, especially of a metaphor; the thing with which the figurative subject (vehicle) is equated. p. 150.

Tercet: See Forms Chart, pp. 223, 234.

Terza Rima: See Forms Chart, p. 235.

Tetrameter: A line containing four metrical feet. p. 216.

Thematic Structure: See *Structure*.

Theme: The central idea, description, or mood a poem develops concerning its subject(s). p. 12.

Tone: The author's attitude toward the subject matter, the speaker, and/or the audience of a work. p. 78.

Trimeter: A line containing three metrical feet. p. 216.

Triplet: See Forms Chart, pp. 223, 234.

Trochee/Trochaic Foot: A metrical foot containing a stressed syllable followed by an unstressed syllable (e.g., sómethĭng). Trochaic meter is meter that contains a predominance of trochaic feet. p. 215.

Turn: The shift in tone, theme, or imagery that marks the separation between burden and release, question and answer, problem and solution, etc. in a poem—especially a sonnet. p. 225.

Understatement: Language in a poem that says less than the situation seems to call for as a way of calling attention to it. p. 109.

Vehicle: The figurative subject of a figure of speech, especially of a metaphor; the thing the literal subject (tenor) is being compared to. p. 150.

Verbal Irony: See *Irony*.

Verse Form: Any structural unit—a stanza, a part of a stanza or poem, or a complete poem—that has been used repeatedly by a number of writers or is so closely associated with a particular poem that the two are synonymous. pp. 223–235.

Villanelle: See Forms Chart, p. 235.

INDEX OF FIRST LINES

About suffering they were never wrong, 301
A broken altar, Lord, Thy servant rears, 316
According to Brueghel, 302
'A cold coming we had of it, 199
ADAM scriveyn, if ever it thee bifalle, 310
A dying firelight slides along the quirt, 26
After great pain, a formal feeling comes —, 16
After the doctor checked to see, 259
A guest at Thanksgiving said And you've got, 204
Ah Sun-flower! weary of time, 203
A line in long array where they wind betwixt green islands, 348
All these fellows were there inside, 275
An ant on the tablecloth, 176
And death shall have no dominion, 407
And here face down beneath the sun, 391
And one morning while in the woods I stumbled suddenly upon the thing, 414
A noiseless patient spider, 349
An old, mad, blind, despised, and dying king, 348
A pretty young thing from St. Paul, 236
As a bathtub lined with white porcelain, 397
As a sloop with a sweep of immaculate wing on her delicate spine, 115
As I in hoary winter's night stood shivering in the snow, 328
A single man stands like a bird-watcher, 286
As I was walking all alane, 88
Ask me no more when Jove bestows, 312
A song I sing of my sea-adventure, 307
As virtuous men pass mildly away, 279
A sweet disorder in the dress, 317
At the blackboard I had missed, 255

BALD heads forgetful of their sins, 254
Batter my heart, three-personed God, for you, 45

Before, 45
Being your slave, what should I do but tend, 278
Below the thunders of the upper deep, 139
Bent double, like old beggars under sacks, 129
biscuits with honey running down into the deep crevices, 166
Bleachers are empty, 261
Boys in sporadic but tenacious droves, 375
Break, break, break, 358
Bright star, would I were steadfast as thou art—, 345
Busy old fool, unruly sun, 35

Call the roller of big cigars, 406
Careful observers may foretell the hour, 336
childhood remembrances are always a drag, 283
Coax it, clutch it, kick it, 75
Come live with me and be my love, 321
Come, my Celia, let us prove, 319
Composed in the Tower before his execution, 382
Constantly risking absurdity, 299
Cowhorn-crowned, shockheaded, cornhusk-bearded, 302

Dear love, for nothing less than thee, 313
Death devours all lovely things:, 278
Do not go gentle into that good night, 248
Do not weep, maiden, for war is kind, 123
Drinking hot saké, 127
Drink to me only with thine eyes, 246

Earth has not anything to show more fair:, 281

Falling in love with a mustache, 408
Farewell, too little and too lately known, 333

427

INDEX OF FIRST LINES

Far far from gusty waves these children's faces, 92
Fearful of beauty, I always went, 53
First, are you our sort of a person?, 395
Flowers through the window, 412
For God's sake hold your tongue, and let me love, 169
Framed in her phoenix fire-screen, Edna Ward, 410
From my mother's sleep I fell into the State, 20
Full deep green, 72
Full many a glorious morning have I seen, 326

Gaily bedight, 183
Gather ye rosebuds while ye may, 277
Go and catch a falling star, 315
God moves in a mysterious way, 79
Go, lovely rose!, 330
Good people all, of ev'ry sort, 333
Good people all, with one accord, 89
Gr-r-r—there go, my heart's abhorrence!, 350

Had we but world enough, and time, 56
Happy the man whose wish and care, 336
He clasps the crag with crooked hands, 359
He has a girl who has flaxen hair, 381
He hated them all one by one but wanted to show them, 256
Here lies, to each her parents' ruth, 291
He that dwelleth in the secret place of the most High, 311
He was born in Alabama, 96
He was found by the Bureau of Statistics to be, 33
He would slump to his knees, now that his agonies, 137
High on his stockroom ladder like a dunce, 119
How careful was I, when I took my way, 37
How many dawns, chill from his rippling rest, 284
How soon hath Time, the subtle thief of youth, 322
How sweet I roamed from field to field, 340
How vainly men themselves amaze, 281

I am silver and exact. I have no preconceptions, 396
I cannot tell who loves the skeleton, 320
I can't forget, 411
I caught this morning morning's minion, king-, 354
I chopped down the house that you had been saving to live in next summer, 104
I died for Beauty—but was scarce, 344
I dreamed this mortal part of mine, 318
If all the world and love were young, 324
If aught of oaten stop or pastoral song, 331
If but some vengeful god would call to me, 353
I found a dimpled spider fat and white, 83
I have a gentle cock, croweth me the day, 310
I have been one acquainted with the night, 10
I have done it again, 289
I have eaten, 47
I have known the inexorable sadness of pencils, 400
I heard a Fly buzz—when I died—, 292
I knew a woman, lovely in her bones, 400
I leant upon a coppice gate, 352
I learned the truth at seventeen, 17
I'm a riddle in nine syllables, 151
I met a traveller from an antique land, 114
In an upper room at midnight, 362
In his sea-lit, 14
In June, amid the golden fields, 375
Ink runs from the corners of my mouth, 3
In my craft or sullen art, 298
In this little urn is laid, 318
Into my heart an air that kills, 354
In Xanadu did Kubla Khan, 343
I placed a jar in Tennessee, 406
I remember the neckcurls, limp and damp as tendrils, 91
I saw a man pursuing the horizon, 366
I saw Eternity the other night, 296
I saw in Louisiana a live-oak growing, 206
I shall begin by learning to throw, 110
I sit in the top of the wood, my eyes closed, 31

INDEX OF FIRST LINES

I smell the dust of stones in sunlight, 285
I struck the board and cried, "No more!, 118
I taste a liquor never brewed—, 176
It dropped so low—in my Regard—, 147
It is a beauteous evening, calm and free, 349
It is a cold and snowy night. The main street is deserted, 365
It little profits that an idle king, 172
I traveled on, seeing the hill, where lay, 201
It's wonderful how I jog, 388
I wake to sleep, and take my waking slow, 227
I walk beside the prisoners to the road, 384
I WALK through the long schoolroom questioning, 263
I was wrapped in black, 401
I went out to the hazel wood, 213
I went to the Garden of Love, 122, 339
I wish I could teach you how ugly, 194

Jesus is with me, 295
Just as my fingers on these keys, 244
Just off the highway to Rochester, Minnesota, 413

Lately, I've become accustomed to the way, 363
Lay your sleeping head, my love, 361
Leave me, O love, which reachest but to dust, 327
Legs!, 100
Let the boy try along this bayonet-blade, 123
Let us go then, you and I, 376
Like as a huntsman, after weary chase, 328
Like as the waves make towards the pebbled shore, 224
Like battered old mill hands, they stand in the orchard—, 403
Long after you have swung back, 387
Long long ago when the world was a wild place, 41
Lord, who createdst man in wealth and store, 70
Love bade me welcome, yet my soul drew back, 175

"Love seeketh not itself to please, 82
Love set you going like a fat gold watch, 396
Love that doth reign and live within my thought, 319
Loving in truth, and fain in verse my love to show, 327

Márgarét, are you grieving, 209
Marrie dear, 274
Me imperturbe, standing at ease in Nature, 236
Men marry what they need. I marry you, 366
middle | aged, 72
Moonlight washes the west side of the house, 392
"Mother dear, may I go downtown, 287
Much have I traveled in the realms of gold, 237
My attire is noiseless when I tread the earth, 308
My clumsiest dead, whose hands shipwreck vases, 120
My heart aches, and a drowsy numbness pains, 346
My love is of a birth as rare, 321
My mistress' eyes are nothing like the sun, 165
My mother bore me in the southern wild, 339

Nautilus Island's hermit, 390
Neither our vices nor our virtues, 374
"next to of course god america i, 368
None said anything starting from the rest, 272
Nothing is plumb, level or square:, 73
NOT, I'll not, carrion comfort, Despair, not feast on thee, 354
Now as at all times I can see in the mind's eye, 198
Now as I was young and easy under the apple boughs, 94
Now as the train bears west, 128
Now hardly here and there a Hackney-Coach, 338

Observe how he negotiates his way, 155
Off Highway 106, 371
Ofttimes, for diversion, the men of the crew, 202

Old Eben Flood, climbing alone one night, 398
On a withered branch, 125
Once I am sure there's nothing going on, 293
Once more the changed year's turning wheel returns:, 358
Once over water, to you borne brightly, 219
Once riding in old Baltimore, 15
one day, 279
One day I wrote her name upon the strand, 329
One day the Nouns were clustered in the street, 386
One face looks out from all his canvasses, 357
One must have a mind of winter, 206
Only teaching on Tuesdays, book-worming, 389
On moonlit heath and lonesome bank, 355
On the day of breasts and small hips, 401
On the long shore, lit by the moon, 393
On these warm and humid summer nights, 255
O Rose, thou art sick!, 208
O sweet spontaneous, 248
OTHERS because you did not keep, 141
Ours are the streets where Bess first met her, 405
Out in this desert we are testing bombs, 271
Out upon it! I have loved, 329
Over my head, I see the bronze butterfly, 285
Over the half-finished houses, 397
O wild West Wind, thou breath of Autumn's being, 238

Pearl Avenue runs past the high-school lot, 164
Perfection, of a kind, was what he was after, 362
Pity would be no more, 143
Poor soul, the center of my sinful earth, 327
Position is where you, 367
Prayer: the church's banquet, angels' age, 71

(. . rabid or dog-dull.) Let me tell you how, 364
Razors pain you, 5

Say goodbye to the help, the ranks, 403
Season of mists and mellow fruitfulness, 140
September rain falls on the house, 242
Service is joy, to see or swing. Allow, 260
Shall I compare thee to a summer's day?, 325
she being Brand, 368
She dwelt among the untrodden ways, 108
She had thought the studio would keep itself, 64
She is all there, 167
She walks in beauty, like the night, 342
Shiny record albums scattered over, 142
Since brass, nor stone, nor earth, nor boundless sea, 37
Since I am coming to that holy room, 207
Since there's no help, come let us kiss and part, 247
Snow falling and night falling fast, oh, fast, 197
Softly, in the dusk, a woman is singing to me, 136
So I said I am Ezra, 360
Some say the world will end in fire, 69
Something there is that doesn't love a wall, 241
Sometimes I feel like I will never stop, 261
so much depends, 138
So there stood Matthew Arnold and this girl, 40
Spring is like a perhaps hand, 28
Stand still, and I will read to thee, 66
Still to be neat, still to be dressed, 319
Strange fits of passion have I known, 178
Strapped down, 42
Strew on her roses, roses, 350
Success is counted sweetest, 116
sun breaks over the eucalyptus, 61
Sundays too my father got up early, 268

Tell me not, sweet, I am unkind, 320
'Terence, this is stupid stuff:, 356
That American poet's future, 409
That is no country for old men. The young, 415
That night when joy began, 65
That's my last Duchess painted on the wall, 22
That time of year thou mayst in me behold, 68
The ache of marriage:, 387

INDEX OF FIRST LINES

The air says what it means, regardless of what, 393
The apparition of these faces in the crowd, 397
The beautiful boys curve and writhe, 260
The broken pillar of the wing jags from the clotted shoulder, 32
The Bustle in a House, 344
The buzz saw snarled and rattled in the yard, 121
The eyes open to a cry of pulleys, 411
The fleet astronomer can bore, 317
The force that through the green fuse drives the flower, 408
The great cracked shadow of the Sierra Nevada, 70
The hand that signed the paper felled a city, 158
The heavy bear who goes with me, 205
The instructor said, 254
The king sits in Dumferling toune, 50
The last Night that She lived, 345
The Lord feeds some of His prisoners better than others, 80
The man who married Magdalene, 402
The pennycandystore beyond the El, 230
The people along the sand, 380
There is a cop who is both prowler and father, 44
There is a garden in her face, 312
There is now not a single, 360
There was such speed in her little body, 121
There were three ravens set on a tree, 87
The sea is calm tonight, 38
The Soul selects her own Society—, 235
The spacious firmament on high, 331
The time you won your town the race, 186
The trees are in their autumn beauty, 417
The tusks that clashed in mighty brawls, 102
The water began to fall quite quietly, 361
The wayfarer, 367
The whiskey on your breath, 265
The winter evening settles down, 145
THE world is charged with the grandeur of God, 298
The world is too much with us; late and soon, 350
Th' expense of spirit in a waste of shame, 326

The yachts, 412
"They called it Annandale—and I was there, 25
They flee from me that sometime did me seek, 276
They have come by carloads, 262
They have left Thee naked, Lord. O that they had!, 313
They that have power to hurt and will do none, 117
This is the time of year, 364
This morning something, 162
This summer, most friends out of town, 384
Though love repine, and reason chafe, 125
Thou still unravished bride of quietness, 300
Thumb, loose tooth of a horse, 174
'Tis the year's midnight, and it is the day's, 288
Titan! to whose immortal eyes, 341
To-day we have naming of parts. Yesterday, 34
Toe upon toe, a snowing flesh, 385
To Mercy, Pity, Peace, and Love, 142
Too tight, it is running over, 190
To this much-tossed Ulysses, never done, 171
To what purpose, April, do you return again?, 95
To yow, my purse, and to noon other wight, 310
Traveling through the dark I found a deer, 406
Turning and turning in the widening gyre, 416
'Twas on a lofty vase's side, 335
Two roads diverged in a yellow wood, 380
Tyger! Tyger! burning bright, 99

Vandergast to his neighbors—, 97

We are, 253
We are very pleased with your response, 269
We have all been in rooms, 370
Weland knew fully   affliction and woe, 309
We real cool. We, 246
Western wind, when will thou blow, 276
We wear the mask that grins and lies, 373

What am I? Nosing here, turning leaves over, 383
What happens to a dream deferred?, 149
What I like most is when, 43
What is the boy now, who has lost his ball, 265
What it must be like to be an angel, 268
What passing-bells for these who die as cattle?, 247
What thoughts I have of you tonight, Walt Whitman, for, 381
Whenas in silks my Julia goes, 71
When forty winters shall besiege thy brow, 262
When getting my nose in a book, 93
When I, 161
When I consider how my light is spent, 324
When I go away from you, 139
When in disgrace with Fortune and men's eyes, 325
When I was one-and-twenty, 15
When lovely woman stoops to folly, 334
When Love with unconfinèd wings, 106
When my devotions could not pierce, 270
when serpents bargain for the right to squirm, 369
When you consider the radiance, that it does not withhold, 359
When you drive on the freeway, cars follow you, 86
Whilst yet to prove, 314
Who have been lonely once, 386
Whose woods these are I think I know, 73
Whoso list to hunt, I know where is an hind, 330
Why so pale and wan, fond lover?, 99
Wilt thou forgive that sin where I begin, 294
With a Whirl of Thought oppressed, 338
With rue my heart is laden, 292
With the motion of angels, out of, 260

Ye distant spires, yet antique towers, 256
You are Odysseus, 394
You are tired, 132
You could be sitting now in a carrel, 277
You do not do, you do not do, 266
You need the untranslatable ice to watch, 365
Your smiling, or the hope, the thought of it, 174
You walk into the room, 272
You were no mere slip of a grille, 115
You would think the fury of aerial bombardment, 288

INDEX OF AUTHORS AND TITLES

Ache of Marriage, The, 387
Acquainted with the Night, 10
Addison, Joseph
   Ode to the Spacious Firmament, 331
Adultery, 370
After great pain, a formal feeling comes, 16
Ah Sun-flower, 203
Alas, Poor Buick, 115
Albatross, The (translation), 202
Allen, Samuel
   To Satch, 261
Altar, The, 316
Ammons, A. R.
   City Limits, The, 359
   So I said I am Ezra, 360
   Winter Scene, 360
Among School Children, 263
And death shall have no dominion, 407
Anecdote of the Jar, 106
Animals Are Passing From Our Lives, 388
Anonymous
   A pretty young thing from St. Paul, 236
   Deor's Lament (translation), 309
   I Have a Gentle Cock, 310
   Seafarer, The (translation), 307
   Sir Patrick Spence, 50
   Three Ravens, The, 87
   Twa Corbies, The, 88
   Western Wind, 276
   Wild Swan (translation), 308
Anthem for Doomed Youth, 247
Applicant, The, 395
Armadillo, The, 364
Arms and the Boy, 123
Arnold, Matthew
   Dover Beach, 38
   Requiescat, 350
Ashbery, John
   Shower, The, 361
As You Leave Me, 142
At Seventeen, 17

Auden, W. H.
   Epitaph on a Tyrant, 362
   Love Feast, The, 362
   Lullaby, 361
   Musée des Beaux Arts, 301
   That night when joy began, 65
   Unknown Citizen, The, 33
Avison, Margaret
   Tennis, 260

Baker, Donald
   Formal Application, 110
Ballad of a Thin Man, 272
Ballad of Birmingham, 287
Ball Poem, The, 265
Baraka, Imamu Amiri (LeRoi Jones)
   Preface to a Twenty Volume Suicide Note, 363
Barren Spring, 358
Bashō, Matsuo
   On a withered branch (translation), 125
Bath Tub, The, 397
Batter my heart, three-personed God, 45
Baudelaire, Charles
   Albatross, The (translation), 202
Bedtime Story, 41
Bella Bona Roba, La, 320
Bells for John Whiteside's Daughter, 121
Berry, D. C.
   On Reading Poems to a Senior Class at South High, 45
Berryman, John
   Ball Poem, The, 265
   Professor's Song, A, 364
Bess, 405
Bestiary for the Fingers of My Right Hand, 174
Between the World and Me, 414
Bishop, Elizabeth
   Armadillo, The, 364
   Sestina, 242

433

Blake, William
   Ah Sun-flower, 203
   Clod and the Pebble, The, 82
   Divine Image, The, 142
   Garden of Love, The, 122, 339
   Human Abstract, The, 143
   Little Black Boy, The, 339
   Sick Rose, The, 208
   Song: How Sweet I Roamed, 340
   Tyger, The, 99
Blessing, A, 413
Bly, Robert
   Driving to Town Late to Mail a Letter, 365
Break, break, break, 358
Bright star, would I were steadfast as thou art, 345
Brooks, Gwendolyn
   Of De Witt Williams on His Way to Lincoln Cemetery, 96
   ("Thousands—Killed in Action"), 365
   We Real Cool, 246
Browne, Michael Dennis
   Paranoia, 86
Browning, Robert, 23, 24
   My Last Duchess, 22
   Soliloquy of the Spanish Cloister, 350
Buick, 115
Burning Babe, The, 328
Bustle in a House, The, 344
Butcher, Grace
   On Driving Behind a School Bus for Mentally Retarded Children, 72
   Young Wrestlers, 260
Byron, George Gordon, Lord
   Prometheus, 341
   She Walks in Beauty, 342

Camp in the Prussian Forest, A, 384
Campion, Thomas
   There Is a Garden in Her face, 312
Canonization, The, 169
Careless Love, 386
Carew, Thomas
   Song, A, 312
Carrion Comfort, 354
Cavalry Crossing a Ford, 348
Chaucer, Geoffrey
   Chaucer's Wordes unto Adam, His Owne Scriveyn, 310
   Complaint of Chaucer to His Purse, The, 310
Cherrylog Road, 371
Church Going, 293

Ciardi, John
   On Flunking a Nice Boy out of School, 194
   Men marry what they need. I marry you, 366
City Limits, The, 359
Clod and the Pebble, The, 82
Coleridge, Samuel Taylor
   Kubla Khan, 343
Collar, The, 118
Collins, William
   Ode to Evening, 331
Complaint of a Lover Rebuked, 319
Complaint of Chaucer to His Purse, The, 310
Composed upon Westminster Bridge, 281
Constantly risking absurdity, 299
Cottage Street, 1953, 410
Cowper, William
   Light Shining out of Darkness, 79
Crane, Hart
   To Brooklyn Bridge, 284
Crane, Stephen
   I saw a man pursuing the horizon, 366
   War is Kind, 123
   Wayfarer, The, 367
Crashaw, Richard
   On Our Lord Crucified, Naked and Bloody, 313
Creature, The, 162
Creeley, Robert
   Window, The, 367
Crimes of Passion: The Slasher, 43
Cullen, Countee
   Incident, 15
Cummings, E. E.
   "next to of course god america i," 368
   O sweet spontaneous, 248
   she being Brand, 368
   Spring is like a perhaps hand, 28
   when serpents bargain for the right to squirm, 369

Daddy, 266
Darkling Thrush, The, 352
Day of Judgement, The, 338
Death of the Ball Turret Gunner, The, 20
Deep-Sworn Vow, A, 141
Definition of Love, The, 321
Delight in Disorder, 317
Denial, 270

INDEX OF AUTHORS AND TITLES

Deor's Lament (translation), 309
Departmental, 176
Description of a City Shower, A, 336
Description of the Morning, A, 338
Desert Places, 197
Design, 83
Dickey, James
    Adultery, 370
    Cherrylog Road, 371
    Fence Wire, 190
Dickinson, Emily
    After great pain, a formal feeling comes, 16
    Bustle in a House, The, 344
    I Died for Beauty, 344
    I Heard a Fly Buzz, 292
    I Taste a Liquor Never Brewed, 176
    It Dropped So Low—In My Regard, 147
    Soul selects her own Society, The, 235
    Success Is Counted Sweetest, 116
    The last Night that She lived, 345
Divine Image, The, 142
Dr. Joseph Goebbels, 403
Dolor, 400
Donne, John
    Batter my heart, three-personed God, 45
    Canonization, The, 169
    Dream, The, 313
    Farewell to Love, 314
    Hymn to God My God, in My Sickness, 207
    Hymn to God the Father, A, 294
    Lecture upon the Shadow, A, 66
    Nocturnal upon St Lucy's Day, A, 288
    Song: Go and catch a falling star, 315
    Sun Rising, The, 35
    Valediction Forbidding Mourning, A, 279
Do not go gentle into that good night, 248
Double Play, The, 14
Dover Beach, 38
Dover Bitch, The, 40
Drayton, Michael
    How Many Paltry, Foolish, Painted Things, 316
    Since There's No Help, 247
Dream, The, 313
Dream Deferred, 149
Drinking Hot Saké, 127
Driving to Town Late to Mail a Letter, 365

Dryden, John
    To the Memory of Mr. Oldham, 333
Dugan, Alan
    Love Song: I and Thou, 73
Dulce et Decorum Est, 129
Dunbar, Paul Lawrence
    We Wear the Mask, 373
Duncan, Robert
    Poetry, a Natural Thing, 374
Dylan, Bob
    Ballad of a Thin Man, 272

Eagle, The, 359
Easter Wings, 67
Eating Poetry, 3
Eberhart, Richard
    Fury of Aerial Bombardment, The, 288
    Groundhog, The, 375
    Horse Chestnut Tree, The, 375
Eldorado, 183
Elegy for Jane, 91
Elegy on That Glory of Her Sex, Mrs. Mary Blaize, An, 89
Elegy on the Death of a Mad Dog, An, 333
Elementary School Classroom in a Slum, An, 92
Eliot, T. S.
    Journey of the Magi, 199
    Love Song of J. Alfred Prufrock, The, 376
    Preludes, 145
Ellis, Ron
    Alas, Poor Buick, 115
Emerson, Ralph Waldo
    Sacrifice, 125
Emperor of Ice-Cream, The, 406
Enamel Girl, The, 53
End of the Weekend, The, 26
England in 1819, 348
Epitaph on a Tyrant, 362
Evans, Mari
    When in Rome, 274
Ex-Basketball Player, 164

Fable of the Mermaid and the Drunks, 275
Farewell to Love, 314
Faring, The, 219
Fence Wire, 190
Ferlinghetti, Lawrence

INDEX OF AUTHORS AND TITLES

Constantly risking absurdity, 299
Pennycandystore beyond the El, The, 230
Fern Hill, 94
Figure, 137
Fire and Ice, 69
First Practice, 259
Fish, The, 144
Force that through the green fuse drives the flower, The, 408
Formal Application, 110
For My Lover, Returning to His Wife, 167
40—Love, 72
Fury of Aerial Bombardment, The, 288
Francis, Robert
   Swimmer, 155
Fraser, Kathleen
   Poem in Which My Legs Are Accepted, 100
Frost, Robert
   Acquainted with the Night, 10
   Departmental, 176
   Desert Places, 197
   Design, 83
   Fire and Ice, 69
   Mending Wall, 241
   Neither Out Far Nor In Deep, 380
   "Out, Out—," 121
   Road Not Taken, The, 380
   Stopping by Woods on a Snowy Evening, 73

Gambling in Stateline, Nevada, 70
Garden, The, 281
Garden of Love, The, 122, 339
Gildner, Gary
   First Practice, 259
Ginsberg, Allen
   Supermarket in California, A, 381
Giovanni, Nikki
   Nikki-Rosa, 283
   On Hearing "The Girl with the Flaxen Hair", 381
   Seduction, 279
God's Grandeur, 298
Goldsmith, Oliver
   Elegy on That Glory of Her Sex, Mrs. Mary Blaize, An, 89
   Elegy on the Death of a Mad Dog, An, 333
   When lovely woman stoops to folly, 334
Goodman, Paul

Surfers at Santa Cruz, 262
Goose Fish, The, 393
Graves, Robert
   Ulysses, 171
Gray, Thomas
   Ode, 335
   Ode on a Distant Prospect of Eton College, 256
Green Water Tower, 204
Groundhog, The, 375
Guiterman, Arthur
   On the Vanity of Earthly Greatness, 102

Hand That Signed the Paper, The, 158
Hap, 353
Hardy, Thomas
   Darkling Thrush, The, 352
   Hap, 353
Hawk Roosting, 31
Hayden, Robert
   Figure, 137
   Those Winter Sundays, 268
Hazo, Samuel
   My Roosevelt Coupé, 75
Heavy Bear Who Goes with Me, The, 205
Hecht, Anthony
   Dover Bitch, The, 40
   End of the Weekend, The, 26
   "More Light! More Light!", 382
Herbert, George
   Altar, The, 316
   Collar, The, 118
   Denial, 270
   Easter Wings, 67
   Love (III), 175
   Pilgrimage, The, 201
   Prayer (I), 71
   Vanity (I), 317
Herrick, Robert
   Delight in Disorder, 317
   To the Virgins, To Make Much of Time, 277
   Upon Julia's Clothes, 71
   Upon Prue, His Maid, 318
   Vine, The, 318
Holy Bible, Authorized (King James) Version
   Psalm 91, 311
Hopkins, Gerard Manley
   Carrion Comfort, 354
   God's Grandeur, 298
   Spring and Fall: to a young child, 209

INDEX OF AUTHORS AND TITLES

Windhover, The: To Christ our Lord, 354
Horse Chestnut Tree, The, 375
Housman, A. E.
   Into my heart an air that kills, 354
   On moonlit heath and lonesome bank, 355
   Terence, this is stupid stuff, 356
   To an Athlete Dying Young, 186
   When I was one-and-twenty, 15
   With rue my heart is laden, 292
How Annandale Went Out, 25
Howard, Henry, Earl of Surrey
   Complaint of a Lover Rebuked, 319
How many paltry, foolish, painted things, 316
How Soon Hath Time, 322
Hughes, Langston
   Dream Deferred, 149
   Theme for English B, 254
Hughes, Ted
   Hawk Roosting, 31
   Wodwo, 383
Hugo, Richard
   Missoula Softball Tournament, 384
Human Abstract, The, 143
Hurt Hawks, 32
Hymn to God My God, in My Sickness, 207
Hymn to God the Father, A, 294

Ian, Janis, 18–20
   At Seventeen, 17
I Died for Beauty, 344
Ignatow, David
   Lunchtime, 272
I Have a Gentle Cock, 310
I Heard a Fly Buzz, 292
I Knew a Woman, 400
In an Artist's Studio, 357
In a Station of the Metro, 397
Incident, 15
In my craft or sullen art, 298
Into my heart an air that kills, 354
I saw a man pursuing the horizon, 366
I saw in Louisiana a live-oak growing, 206
I taste a liquor never brewed, 176
It dropped so low—In my regard, 147
It is a beauteous evening, calm and free, 349

Jarrell, Randall, 20, 21
   Camp in the Prussian Forest, A, 384
   Death of the Ball Turret Gunner, The, 20
   Knight, Death, and the Devil, The, 302
Jeffers, Robinson
   Hurt Hawks, 32
Jesus Infection, The, 295
Jones, Leroi, *see* Baraka, Imamu Amiri
Jonson, Ben
   On My First Daughter, 291
   Song: Come, my Celia, 319
   Song: Drink to me only with thine eyes, 246
   Still To Be Neat, 319
Journey of the Magi, 199

Keats, John
   Bright star, would I were steadfast as thou art, 345
   Ode on a Grecian Urn, 300
   Ode to a Nightingale, 346
   On First Looking into Chapman's Homer, 237
   To Autumn, 140
Kennedy, X. J.
   Nude Descending a Staircase, 385
Knight, Death, and the Devil, The, 302
Knight, Etheridge
   As You Leave Me, 142
Koch, Kenneth
   Permanently, 386
   Variations on a Theme by William Carlos Williams, 104
Kraken, The, 139
Kubla Khan, 343
Kumin, Maxine
   Jesus Infection, The, 295
Kunitz, Stanley
   Careless Love, 386

Lady Lazarus, 289
Landscape with the Fall of Icarus, 302
Larkin, Philip
   Church Going, 293
   Study of Reading Habits, A, 93
Last Night that She lived, The, 345
Late Aubade, A, 277
Lawrence, D. H.
   Piano, 136
Lazard, Naomi
   Re Accepting You, 269
Leave Me, O Love, 327
Lecture upon the Shadow, A, 66

INDEX OF AUTHORS AND TITLES

Levertov, Denise
    Ache of Marriage, The, 387
    Losing Track, 387
Levine, Philip
    Animals Are Passing From Our Lives, 388
Lifshin, Lyn
    You Understand the Requirements, 253
Light Shining out of Darkness, 79
Like as a Huntsman, 328
Line of an American Poet, The, 409
Listeners at the Breathing Place, 393
Little Black Boy, The, 339
Living in Sin, 64
Losing Track, 387
Love (III), 175
Love Calls Us to the Things of This World, 411
Love Feast, The, 362
Lovelace, Richard
    Bella Bona Roba, La, 320
    To Althea from Prison, 106
    To Lucasta, Going to the Wars, 320
Love Poem, 120
Love Song: I and Thou, 73
Love Song of J. Alfred Prufrock, The, 376
Loving in Truth, 327
Lowell, Amy
    Taxi, The, 139
Lowell, Robert
    Memories of West Street and Lepke, 389
    Mouth of the Hudson, The, 286
    Skunk Hour, 390
Lullaby, 361
Lunchtime, 272
Lux, Thomas
    Midnight Tennis Match, The, 132
Lying in a Hammock at William Duffy's Farm in Pine Island, Minnesota, 285

MacBeth, George
    Bedtime Story, 41
McGough, Roger
    40—Love, 72
Macleish, Archibald
    You, Andrew Marvell, 391
Magi, The, 198
Makuck, Peter
    Running, 261

Man who married Magdalene, The, 402
Marin-An, 61
Marlow, Christopher
    Passionate Shepherd to His Love, The, 321
Marvell, Andrew
    Definition of Love, The, 321
    Garden, The, 281
    Picture of Little T.C. in a Prospect of Flowers, The, 322
    To His Coy Mistress, 56
Me Imperturbe, 236
Memories of West Street and Lepke, 389
Mending Wall, 241
Men marry what they need. I marry you, 366
Meredith, William
    Parents, 268
    Winter Verse for His Sister, 392
Merwin, W. S.
    Green Water Tower, 204
Metaphors, 151
Midnight Tennis Match, The, 132
Millay, Edna St. Vincent
    Passer Mortuus Est, 278
    Spring, 95
Milton, John
    How Soon Hath Time, 322
    When I consider how my light is spent, 324
Miranda, Gary
    Listeners at the Breathing Place, 393
Mirror, 396
Missoula Softball Tournament, 384
Mr. Flood's Party, 398
Moore, Marianne
    Fish, The, 144
"More Light! More Light!", 382
Morning Song, 396
Mouth of the Hudson, The, 286
Musée des Beaux Arts, 301
My Last Duchess, 22
My Papa's Waltz, 265
My Roosevelt Coupé, 75

Naming of Parts, 34
Nantucket, 412
Neither Out Far Nor In Deep, 380
Nemerov, Howard
    Goose Fish, The, 393
Neruda, Pablo
    Fable of the Mermaid and the Drunks, 275

INDEX OF AUTHORS AND TITLES

"next to of course god america i", 368
Night Journey, 128
Nikki-Rosa, 283
Nims, John Frederick
   Love Poem, 120
Nocturnal upon St Lucy's Day, A, 288
Noiseless patient spider, A, 349
Notes from the Delivery Room, 42
Nude Descending a Staircase, 385
Nymph's Reply to the Shepherd, The, 324

Ode, 335
Ode on a Distant Prospect of Eton College, 256
Ode on a Grecian Urn, 300
Ode on Solitude, 336
Ode to the Spacious Firmament, 331
Ode to a Nightingale, 346
Ode to Evening, 331
Ode to the West Wind, 238
Of De Witt Williams on His Way to Lincoln Cemetery, 96
Old Apple Trees, 403
On a withered branch (translation), 125
On Driving Behind a School Bus for Mentally Retarded Children, 72
One day I wrote her name upon the strand, 329
On First Looking into Chapman's Homer, 237
On Flunking a Nice Boy out of School, 194
On Hearing "The Girl with the Flaxen Hair", 381
On moonlit heath and lonesome bank, 355
On My First Daughter, 291
On Our Lord Crucified, Naked and Bloody, 313
On Reading Poems to a Senior Class at South High, 45
On the Vanity of Earthly Greatness, 102
O sweet spontaneous, 248
"Out, Out—", 121
Out Upon It!, 329
Overweight Poem, 166
Owen, Alfred
   Anthem for Doomed Youth, 247
   Arms and the Boy, 123
   Dulce et Decorum Est, 129
Ozymandias, 114

Paranoia, 86
Parents, 268
Parker, Dorothy
   Résumé, 5
Passer Mortuus Est, 278
Passionate Shepherd to His Love, The, 321
Pastan, Linda
   Notes from the Delivery Room, 42
   You are Odysseus, 394
Pennycandystore beyond the El, The, 230
Permanently, 386
Peter Quince at the Clavier, 244
Piano, 136
Piazza di Spagna, Early Morning, 411
Picture of Little T.C. in a Prospect of Flowers, The, 322
Pilgrimage, The, 201
Plath, Sylvia
   Applicant, The, 395
   Daddy, 266
   Lady Lazarus, 289
   Metaphors, 151
   Mirror, 396
   Morning Song, 396
Playboy, 119
Poe, Edgar Allan
   Eldorado, 183
Poem in Which My Legs Are Accepted, 100
Poetry, a Natural Thing, 374
Pope, Alexander
   Ode on Solitude, 336
Poulin, A., Jr.
   To My Students, 255
Pound, Ezra
   Bath Tub, The, 397
   In a Station of the Metro, 397
Prayer (I), 71
Preface to a Twenty Volume Suicide Note, 363
Preludes, 145
Pretty young thing from St. Paul, A, 236
Professor's Song, A, 364
Prometheus, 341
Psalm, 80
Psalm 91, 311

Raleigh, Sir Walter
   Nymph's Reply to the Shepherd, The, 324
Randall, Dudley

INDEX OF AUTHORS AND TITLES

Ballad of Birmingham, 287
Ransom, John Crowe
    Bells for John Whiteside's Daughter, 121
Rape, 44
Re Accepting You, 269
Red Wheelbarrow, The, 138
Reed, Henry
    Naming of Parts, 34
Requiescat, 350
Résumé, 5
Rich, Adrienne
    Living in Sin, 64
    Rape, 44
    Roofwalker, The, 397
    Trying to Talk with a Man, 271
Road Not Taken, The, 380
Robinson, Edwin Arlington
    How Annandale Went Out, 25
    Mr. Flood's Party, 398
Roethke, Theodore
    Dolor, 400
    Elegy for Jane, 91
    I Knew a Woman, 400
    My Papa's Waltz, 265
    Night Journey, 128
    Waking, The, 227
Roofwalker, The, 397
Rossetti, Christina
    In an Artist's Studio, 357
Rossetti, Dante Gabriel
    Barren Spring, 358
Running, 261

Sacrifice, 125
Sailing to Byzantium, 415
Scholars, The, 254
Schwartz, Delmore
    Heavy Bear Who Goes with Me, The, 205
Seafarer, The (translation), 307
Second Coming, The, 416
Seduction, 279
Sestina, 242
Sexton, Anne
    For My Lover, Returning to His Wife, 167
    Song for a Lady, 401
    Us, 401
Shakespeare, William
    Sonnet 2: When forty winters shall besiege thy brow, 262
    Sonnet 18: Shall I compare thee to a summer's day, 325
    Sonnet 29: When in disgrace with Fortune and men's eyes, 325
    Sonnet 33: Full many a glorious morning have I seen, 326
    Sonnet 48: How careful was I, when I took my way, 37
    Sonnett 57: Being your slave, what should I do but tend, 278
    Sonnet 60: Like as the waves make towards the pebbled shore, 224
    Sonnet 65: Since brass, nor stone, nor earth, nor boundless sea, 37
    Sonnet 73: That time of year thou mayst in me behold, 68
    Sonnet 94: They that have power to hurt and will do none, 117
    Sonnet 129: Th' expense of spirit in a waste of shame, 326
    Sonnet 130: My mistress' eyes are nothing like the sun, 165
    Sonnet 146: Poo! soul, the center of my sinful earth, 327
Shapiro, Karl
    Buick, 115
she being Brand, 368
She dwelt among the untrodden ways, 108
Shelley, Percy Bysshe
    England in 1819, 348
    Ode to the West Wind, 238
    Ozymandias, 114
She Walks in Beauty, 342
Shower, The, 361
Sick Rose, The, 208
Sidney, Sir Philip
    Leave Me, O Love, 327
    Loving in Truth, 327
Simic, Charles
    Bestiary for the Fingers of My Right Hand, 174
Simile for Her Smile, 174
Simpson, Louis
    Man who married Magdalene, The, 402
    Vandergast and the Girl, 97
Since There's No Help, 247
Sir Patrick Spense, 50
Skiers, 260
Skunk Hour, 390
Snodgrass, W. D.
    Dr. Joseph Goebbels, 403
    Old Apple Trees, 403
Snow Man, The, 206
Snyder, Gary
    Drinking Hot Saké, 127

INDEX OF AUTHORS AND TITLES 441

Marin-An, 61
So I said I am Ezra, 360
Soliloquy of the Spanish Cloister, 350
Song, 330
Song, A, 312
Song: Come, my Celia, 319
Song: Drink to me only with thine eyes, 246
Song for a Lady, 401
Song: Go and catch a falling star, 315
Song: How Sweet I Roamed, 340
Song of Wandering Aengus, The, 213
Song: Why So Pale and Wan?, 99
Sonnet 2: When forty winters shall besiege thy brow, 262
Sonnet 18: Shall I compare thee to a summer's day, 325
Sonnet 29: When in disgrace with Fortune and men's eyes, 325
Sonnet 33: Full many a glorious morning have I seen, 326
Sonnet 48: How careful was I when I took my way, 37
Sonnet 57: Being your slave, what should I do but tend, 278
Sonnet 60: Like as the waves make towards the pebbled shore, 224
Sonnet 65: Since brass, nor stone, nor earth, nor boundless sea, 37
Sonnet 73: That time of year thou mayst in me behold, 68
Sonnet 94: They that have power to hurt and will do none, 117
Sonnet 129: Th' expense of spirit in a waste of shame, 326
Sonnet 130: My mistress' eyes are nothing like the sun, 165
Sonnet 146: Poor soul, the center of my sinful earth, 327
Soto, Gary
    Creature, The, 162
Soul selects her own Society, The, 235
Southwell, Robert
    Burning Babe, The, 328
Spender, Stephen
    Elementary Schol Classroom in a Slum, An, 92
Spenser, Edmund
    Like as a Huntsman, 328
    One day I wrote her name upon the strand, 329
Spring, 95
Spring and Fall: to a young child, 209
Spring is like a perhaps hand, 28
Stafford, William

Bess, 405
    Traveling Through the Dark, 406
Stevens, Wallace
    Anecdote of the Jar, 406
    Emperor of Ice-Cream, The, 406
    Peter Quince at the Clavier, 244
    Snow Man, The, 206
Still To Be Neat, 319
Stokes, Terry
    Crimes of Passion: The Slasher, 43
Stopping by Woods on a Snowy Evening, 73
Stoutenburg, Adrien
    Subdivider, 285
Strand, Mark
    Eating Poetry, 3
Strange Fits of Passion, 178
Study of Reading Habits, A, 93
Subdivider, 285
Success Is Counted Sweetest, 116
Suckling, Sir John
    Out Upon It!, 329
    Song: Why So Pale and Wan?, 99
Sun Rising, The, 35
Supermarket in California, A, 381
Surfers at Santa Cruz, 262
Swenson, May
    Watch, The, 161
Swift, Jonathan
    Day of Judgement, The, 338
    Description of a City Shower, A, 336
    Description of the Morning, A, 338
Swimmer, 155

Taggard, Genevieve
    Enamel Girl, The, 53
Taxi, The, 139
Teacher, A, 256
Tennis, 260
Tennyson, Alfred, Lord
    Break, break, break, 358
    Eagle, The, 359
    Kraken, The, 139
    Ulysses, 172
Terence, this is stupid stuff, 356
That night when joy began, 65
Theme for English B, 254
There Is a Garden in Her Face, 312
They Flee from Me, 276
This Is Just to Say, 47
Thomas, Dylan
    And death shall have no dominion, 407
    Do not go gentle into that good night, 248

INDEX OF AUTHORS AND TITLES

Fern Hill, 94
Force that through the green fuse drive the flower, The, 408
Hand That Signed the Paper, The, 158
In my craft or sullen art, 298
Those Winter Sundays, 268
"Thousands—Killed in Action", 365
Three Ravens, The, 87
To Althea from Prison, 106
To an Athlete Dying Young, 186
To Autumn, 140
To Brooklyn Bridge, 284
To His Coy Mistress, 56
To My Students, 255
To Lucasta, Going to the Wars, 320
To Satch, 261
To the Memory of Mr. Oldham, 333
To the Virgins, To Make Much of Time, 277
Traveling Through the Dark, 406
Trying to Talk with a Man, 271
Twa Corbies, The, 88
Tyger, The, 99

Ulysses (Graves), 171
Ulysses (Tennyson), 172
Uneasy Rider, 408
Unknown Citizen, The, 33
Updike, John
    Ex-Basketball Player, 164
Upon Julia's Clothes, 71
Upon Prue, His Maid, 318
Us, 401

Valediction Forbidding Mourning, A, 279
Vandergast and the Girl, 97
Vanity (I), 317
Variations on a Theme by William Carlos Williams, 104
Vaughan, Henry
    World, The, 296
Vine, The, 318

Waking, The, 227
Wakoski, Diane
    Overweight Poem, 166
    Uneasy Rider, 408
Wallace, Robert
    Double Play, The, 14
Waller, Edmund
    Song, 330

War is Kind, 123
Warren, Robert Penn
    Faring, The, 219
    Skiers, 260
Watch, The, 161
Wayfarer, The, 367
We Real Cool, 246
We Wear the Mask, 373
Western Wind, 276
When I consider how my light is spent, 324
When in Rome, 274
When I was one-and-twenty, 15
When lovely woman stoops to folly, 334
when serpents bargain for the right to squirm, 369
Whitman, Walt
    Cavalry Crossing a Ford, 348
    I saw in Louisiana a live-oak growing, 206
    Me Imperturbe, 236
    Noiseless patient spider, A, 349
Whittemore, Reed
    Line of an American Poet, The, 409
    Psalm, 80
    Teacher, A, 256
Whoso List to Hunt, 330
Wilbur, Richard
    Cottage Street, 1953, 410
    Late Aubade, A, 277
    Love Calls Us to the Things of This World, 411
    Piazza di Spagna, Early Morning, 411
    Playboy, 119
    Simile for Her Smile, A, 174
Wild Swan (translation), 308
Wild Swans at Coole, The, 417
Willams, William Carlos
    Landscape with the Fall of Icarus, 302
    Nantucket, 412
    Red Wheelbarrow, The, 138
    This Is Just to Say, 47
    Yachts, The, 412
Windhover, The: To Christ our Lord, 354
Window, The, 367
Winter Scene, 360
Winter Verse for His Sister, 392
With rue my heart is laden, 292
Wodwo, 383
Wordsworth, William
    Composed upon Westminster Bridge, 281

INDEX OF AUTHORS AND TITLES

It is a beauteous evening, calm and free, 349
She dwelt among the untrodden ways, 108
Stronge Fits of Passion, 178
World Is Too Much with Us, The, 350
World, The, 296
World Is Too Much with Us, The, 350
Wright, James
   Blessing, A, 413
   Gambling in Stateline, Nevada, 70
   Lying in a Hammock at William Duffy's Farm in Pine Island, Minnesota, 285
Wright, Richard
   Between the World and Me, 414
Wyatt, Sir Thomas
   They Flee from Me, 276
   Whoso List to Hunt, 330

Yachts, The, 412
Yeats, William Butler
   Among School Children, 263
   Deep-Sworn Vow, A, 141
   Magi, The, 198
   Sailing to Byzantium, 415
   Scholars, The, 254
   Second Coming, The, 416
   Song of Wandering Aengus, The, 213
   Wild Swans at Coole, The, 417
You, Andrew Marvell, 391
You are Odysseus, 394
Young Wrestlers, 260
You Understand the Requirements, 253

Zimmer, Paul
   Zimmer's Head Thudding Against the Blackboard, 255
Zimmer's Head Thudding Against the Blackboard, 255

PERMISSIONS AND ACKNOWLEDGMENTS

p. 3, "Eating Poetry." From *Reasons For Moving* by Mark Strand. Copyright © 1966 Mark Strand. From *The Late Hour* by Mark Strand. Originally appeared in *The New Yorker*. Copyright © 1978 Mark Strand. All reprinted by permission of Atheneum Publishers.

p. 5, "Résumé." Reprinted by permission of Viking Penguin Inc.: "Résumé" from *The Portable Dorothy Parker*. Copyright 1926, renewed 1954 by Dorothy Parker.

p. 10, "Acquainted with the Night." From *The Poetry of Robert Frost* edited by Edward Connery Lathem. Copyright 1916, 1923, 1928, 1930, 1939, © 1969 by Holt, Rinehart and Winston. Copyright 1936, 1944, 1951, © 1956, 1958 by Robert Frost. Copyright © 1967 by Lesley Frost Ballantine. Reprinted by permission of Holt, Rinehart and Winston, Publishers.

p. 14, "The Double Play." Copyright © 1960 by Robert Wallace.

p. 15, "When I was One-and-Twenty." From "A Shropshire Lad"—Authorised Edition—from *The Collected Poems of A. E. Housman*. Copyright 1939, 1940, © 1965 by Holt, Rinehart and Winston. Copyright © 1967, 1968 by Robert E. Symons. Reprinted by permission of Holt, Rinehart and Winston, Publishers. Permission granted by The Society of Authors Ltd. as the literary representative of the Estate of A. E. Housman, and Jonathan Cape Ltd., publishers of A. E. Housman's *Collected Poems*.

p. 15, "Incident." From *On These I Stand* by Contee Cullen. Copyright 1925 by Harper and Row, Publishers, Inc.; renewed 1953 by Ida M. Cullen. Reprinted by permission of Harper & Row, Publishers, Inc.

p. 16, "After Great Pain, A Formal Feeling Comes." From *The Complete Poems of Emily Dickinson*, edited by Thomas H. Johnson. Copyright 1929 by Martha Dickinson Bianchi; Copyright © 1957, 1960 by Mary L. Hampson.

p. 17, "At Seventeen." Reprinted by permission of Mine Music Ltd. Copyright © 1974 Mine Music Ltd.

p. 20, "The Death of the Ball Turret Gunner." Reprinted by permission of Farrar, Straus and Giroux, Inc. From *The Complete Poems* by Randall Jarrell. Copyright 1945 by Partisan Review. Copyright renewed © 1972 by Mrs. Randall Jarrell.

p. 25, "How Annandale Went Out." From *The Town by the River*, by Edwin Arlington Robinson. Copyright 1910 by Charles Scribner's Sons; copyright renewed. Reprinted with the permission of the publishers.

p. 26, "The End of the Weekend." From *The Hard Hours*, by Anthony Hecht. Copyright © 1967 by Anthony E. Hecht. Reprinted with the permission of Atheneum Publishers.

p. 28, "Spring is Like a Perhaps Hand." Selections are reprinted from *Tulips & Chimneys* by E. E. Cummings by permission of Liveright Publishing Corporation. Copyright 1923, 1925, and renewed 1951, 1953 by E. E. Cummings. Copyright © 1973, 1976 by Nancy T. Andrews. Copyright © 1973, 1976 by George James Firmage.

p. 31, "Hawk Roosting." From *Selected Poems* by Ted Hughes. Copyright © 1959 by Ted Hughes. Reprinted by permission of Harper & Row, Publishers, Inc. Reprinted by permission of Faber and Faber Ltd. from *Lupercal* by Ted Hughes.

p. 32, "Hurt Hawks." Copyright 1928 and renewed 1956 by Robinson Jeffers. Reprinted from *Selected Poems*, by Robinson Jeffers, by permission of Random House, Inc.

p. 33, "The Unknown Citizen." Reprinted by permission of Faber and Faber Ltd. from *Collected Shorter Poems 1927–1957* by W. H. Auden. Copyright 1940 and renewed 1968 by W. H. Auden. Reprinted from

W. H. Auden: Collected Poems, by W. H. Auden, edited by Edward Mendelson, by permission of Random House, Inc.

p. 34, "Naming of Parts." By Henry Reed from *A Map of Verona,* published by Jonathan Cape Ltd. Permission granted by the publisher.

p. 40, "The Dover Bitch." From *The Hard Hours,* by Anthony Hecht. Copyright © 1967 by Anthony E. Hecht. Reprinted with the permission of Atheneum Publishers.

p. 41, "Bedtime Story." From *Collected Poems, 1958–1970,* by George MacBeth. Copyright © 1971 by George MacBeth. Reprinted with the permission of Atheneum Publishers.

p. 42, "Notes from the Delivery Room." From *A Perfect Circle of Sun* by Linda Pastan published by The Swallow Press, copyright 1971. Reprinted with the permission of the Ohio University Press, Athens. Canadian Rights granted by Linda Pastan.

p. 43, "Crimes of Passion: The Slasher." Copyright © 1973 by Terry Stokes. Reprinted from *Crimes of Passion,* by Terry Stokes, by permission of Alfred A. Knopf, Inc.

p. 44, "Rape." From *Poems, Selected and New 1950–1974,* by Adrienne Rich, by permission of W. W. Norton & Co. Inc. Copyright © 1975, 1973, 1971, 1969, 1966 by W. W. Norton & Company, Inc. Copyright © 1967, 1964, 1962, 1961, 1960, 1959, 1958, 1957, 1956, 1955, 1954, 1953, 1952, 1951 by Adrienne Rich.

p. 47, "This is Just to Say." From *Collected Earlier Poems of William Carlos Williams.* Copyright 1938 by New Directions Publishing Corporation. Reprinted by permission.

p. 53, "The Enamel Girl" from *Traveling Standing Still: Poems 1918–1928,* by Genevieve Taggard.

p. 61, "Marin-An." Gary Snyder, *The Back Country.* Copyright © 1968 by Gary Snyder.

p. 64, "Living in Sin." Reprinted from *Poems, Selected and New, 1950–1974,* by Adrienne Rich, by permission of W. W. Norton & Company, Inc. Copyright © 1975, 1973, 1971, 1969, 1966 by W. W. Norton & Company, Inc. Copyright © 1967, 1963, 1962, 1961, 1960, 1959, 1958, 1957, 1956, 1955, 1954, 1953, 1952, 1951 by Adrienne Rich.

p. 65, "That Night When Joy Began." Copyright 1937 and renewed 1965 by W. H. Auden. Reprinted from *W. H. Auden: Collected Poems,* by W. H. Auden, edited by Edward Mendelson, by permission of Random House, Inc. Reprinted by permission of Faber and Faber Ltd. from *Collected Shorter Poems 1927–1957* by W. H. Auden.

p. 69, "Fire and Ice." From *The Poetry of Robert Frost* edited by Edward Connery Lathem. Copyright 1916, 1923, 1928, 1930, 1939, © 1969 by Holt, Rinehart and Winston. Copyright 1936, 1944, 1951, © 1956 by Robert Frost. Copyright © 1967 by Lesley Frost Ballantine. Reprinted by permission of Holt, Rinehart and Winston, Publishers.

p. 70, "Gambling in Stateline, Nevada." Copyright © 1968 by James Wright. Reprinted from *Collected Poems* by permission of Wesleyan University Press.

p. 72, "40—Love." Copyright © 1971 by Roger McGough from *After the Merrymaking.* Reprinted by permission of Jonathan Cape Ltd.

p. 72, "On Driving Behind a School Bus for Mentally Retarded Children." From *Rumors of Ecstasy, Rumors of Death,* The Ashland Poetry Press, Third printing, 1977.

p. 73, "Love Song: I and Thou," from *Poems.* Copyright © 1961 by Alan Dugan.

p. 73, "Stopping By Woods on a Snowy Evening." From *The Poetry of Robert Frost,* edited by Edward Connery Lathem. Copyright 1916, 1923, 1928, 1930, 1939, © 1969 by Holt, Rinehart and Winston. Copyright 1936, 1944, 1951, © 1956, 1958 by Robert Frost. Copyright © 1967 by Lesley Frost Ballantine. Reprinted by permission of Holt, Rinehart and Winston, Publishers.

p. 75, "My Roosevelt Coupé." Reprinted from *Once for the Last Bandit* by Samuel Hazo by permission of the University of Pittsburgh Press. © 1972 by Samuel Hazo.

p. 80, "Psalm." From *The Mother's Breast and the Father's House* by Reed Whittemore. Reprinted by permission of Houghton Mifflin Company.

p. 83, "Design." From *The Poetry of Robert Frost* edited by Edward Connery Lathem. Copyright 1916, 1923, 1928, 1930, 1939, © 1969 by Holt, Rinehart and Winston. Copyright 1936, 1944, 1951, © 1956, 1958 by Robert Frost. Copyright © 1967 by Leslie Frost Ballantine. Reprinted by permission of Holt, Rinehart and Winston, Publishers.

PERMISSIONS AND ACKNOWLEDGMENTS

p. 86, "Paranoia." By Michael Dennis Brown, copyright © 1973 by Antaeus. Reprinted by permission.

p. 91, "Elegy for Jane." Copyright 1950 by Theodore Roethke; from the book *The Collected Poems of Theodore Roethke*. Reprinted by permission of Doubleday & Company, Inc.

p. 92, "An Elementary School Classroom in a Slum." Copyright 1942 and renewed 1979 by Stephen Spender. Reprinted from *Collected Poems, 1928–1953* by Stephen Spender, by permission of Random House, Inc. Reprinted by permission of Faber and Faber Ltd. from Collected Poems of Stephen Spender.

p. 93, "A Study of Reading Habits." Reprinted by permission of Faber & Faber Ltd from *The Whitsun Weddings* by Philip Larken.

p. 94, "Fern Hill." From *The Poems of Dylan Thomas*. Copyright 1939, 1943, 1946, by New Directions. Reprinted from *Collected Poems*, by permission of David Higham Associates Ltd.

p. 95, "Spring." From *Collected Poems*, Harper & Row. Copyright 1921, 1948 by Edna St. Vincent Millay.

p. 96, "of De Witt Williams on His way to Lincoln Cemetery." From *The World of Gwendolyn Brooks* by Gwendolyn Brooks, copyright 1945 by Gwendolyn Brooks Blakely.

p. 97, "Van der Gast and the Girl." From *Adventures of the Letter I* by Louis Simpson. Copyright © 1970 by Louis Simpson. Originally appeared in *The New Yorker* and reprinted by permission of Harper & Row, Publishers, Inc.

p. 100, "Poem in Which My Legs Are Accepted." From *The Young American Poets*, reprinted by permission of the author, Kathleen Fraser.

p. 102, "On the Vanity of Earthly Greatness." By Arthur Guiterman, from *Gaily The Troubadour*, reprinted by permission of Louise H. Schlove.

p. 104, "Variations on a Theme by William Carlos Williams." From *Thank You and Other Poems*, by permission of Kenneth Koch. Copyright © 1962 by Kenneth Koch.

p. 110, "Formal Application." From *Twelve Hawks and Other Poems* by Donald Baker. Reprinted by permission of the author.

p. 115, "Buick." Copyright 1942 and renewed 1970 by Karl Jay Shapiro. Reprinted from *Collected Poems, 1940–1978* by Karl Shapiro, by permission of Random House, Inc.

p. 115, "Alas, Poor Buick." By courtesy of the author, Ron Ellis. Reprinted with the permission of Monmouth College from *Monmouth Review*, Vol. I, no. 1 (Spring 1972).

p. 116, "Success is Counted Sweetest." Reprinted by permission of the publishers and the Trustees of Amherst College from *The Poems of Emily Dickinson*, edited by Thomas H. Johnson, Cambridge, Mass.: The Belknap Press of Harvard University Press, Copyright 1951 © 1955, 1979 by the President and Fellows of Harvard College.

p. 119, "Playboy." Copyright © 1968 by Richard Wilbur. Reprinted from his volume *Walking to Sleep* by permission of Harcourt Brace Jovanovich, Inc.

p. 120, "Love Poem." Copyright, 1947, by John Frederick Nims.

p. 121, "Bells for John Whiteside's Daughter." Copyright 1924 by Alfred A. Knopf, Inc. and renewed 1952 by John Crowe Ransom. Reprinted from *Selected Poems, Third Edition, Revised and Enlarged*, by John Crowe Ransom, by permission of Alfred A. Knopf, Inc.

p. 121, "Out, Out—" From *The Poetry of Robert Frost* edited by Edward Connery Lanthem. Copyright 1916, 1923, 1928, 1930, 1939, © 1969 by Holt, Rinehart and Winston. Copyright 1944, 1951, © 1956, 1958, by Robert Frost. Copyright © 1967 by Lesley Frost Ballantine. Reprinted by permission of Holt, Rinehart and Winston, Publishers.

p. 123, "Arms and the Boy." From *Collected Poems of Wilfred Owen*. Copyright © Chatto & Windus, Ltd. 1946, 1963.

p. 125, "On a Withered Branch." By Basho from *An Introduction to Haiku* translated by Harold G. Henderson. Copyright © 1958 by Harold G. Henderson. Reprinted by permission of Doubleday & Company, Inc.

p. 127, "Drinking Hot Saké." By Gary Snyder, *The Back Country*. Copyright © 1968 by Gary Snyder.

p. 128, "Night Journey." Copyright 1940 by Theodore Roethke, from the book *The Collected Poems of Theodore Roethke*. Reprinted by permission of Doubleday & Company, Inc.

PERMISSIONS AND ACKNOWLEDGMENTS

p. 129, "Dolce et Decorum Est." From *Collected Poems of Wilfred Owen*. Copyright © Chatto & Windus, Ltd., 1946, 1963. Reprinted by permission of the Owen Estate and Chatto & Windus Ltd.

p. 132, "The Midnight Tennis Match." Reprinted from *Memory's Handgrenade*, © 1972 by Thomas Lux, with permission of the author and Pym-Randall Press.

p. 136, "Piano." Copyright © 1964 by Angelo Ravagli and C. M. Weekley, Executors of The Estate of Frieda Lawrence Ravagli.

p. 137, "Figure." From *figure of time: number three*, The Counterpoise Series by Robert Hayden. Copyright © 1955 The Counterpoise Series number three. Reprinted by permission of the Estate of Robert Hayden.

p. 138, "The Red Wheelbarrow." From *Collected Earlier Poems of William Carlos Williams*. Copyright 1938 by New Directions Publishing Corporation. Reprinted by permission.

p. 139, "The Taxi." From *The Complete Poetical Works of Amy Lowell* by Amy Lowell. Copyright 1955 by Houghton Mifflin Company. Reprinted by permission of Houghton Mifflin Company.

p. 141, "A Deep Sworn Vow." Reprinted with permission of Macmillan Publishing Co., Inc. from *Collected Poems* by William Butler Yeats. Copyright 1919 by Macmillan Publishing Co., Inc., renewed 1947 by Bertha Georgie Yeats. Reprinted by permission of M. B. Yeats and Anne Yeats, and Macmillan London Ltd.

p. 142, "As You Leave Me." From *Poems from Prison* by Etheridge Knight. Reprinted with permission from Broadside/Crummell Press, Detroit, Michigan.

p. 144, "The Fish." Reprinted with permission of Macmillan Publishing Co., Inc. from *Collected Poems* by Marianne Moore. Copyright 1935 by Marianne Moore, renewed 1963 by Marianne Moore and T. S. Eliot.

p. 145, "Preludes." From *Collected Poems 1909–1962* by T. S. Eliot, copyright, 1936, by Harcourt Brace Jovanovich, Inc.: copyright © 1963, 1964 by T. S. Eliot. Reprinted by permission of the publisher. Reprinted by permission of Faber and Faber Ltd from *Collected Poems 1909–1962* by T. S. Eliot.

p. 147, "It Dropped So Low—In My Regard." From *Complete Poems of Emily Dickinson*, edited by Thomas H. Johnson. Copyright 1929 by Martha Dickinson Bianchi; Copyright © 1957, 1960 by Mary L. Hampson.

p. 149, "Dream Deferred." Copyright 1951 by Langston Hughes. Reprinted from *The Panther and the Lash*, by Langston Hughes, by permission of Alfred A. Knopf, Inc.

p. 151, "Metaphors." From *Ariel* by Sylvia Plath, Copyright © 1961 by Ted Hughes. From *Ariel* by Sylvia Plath published by Faber & Faber London, copyright Ted Hughes 1965.

p. 155, "Swimmer." Copyright © 1953 by Robert Francis. Reprinted from *The Orb Weaver* by permission of Wesleyan University Press.

p. 158, "The Hand that Signed the Paper." From *The Poems of Dylan Thomas*. Copyright 1939, 1943, 1946, by New Directions. Reprinted with permission from David Higham Associates Limited.

p. 161, "The Watch." From *New & Selected Things Taking Place* by May Swenson. Copyright © 1967 by May Swenson.

p. 162, "The Creature." Reprinted with permission of *The Nation*.

p. 164, "Ex-Basketball Player." From *The Carpentered Hen* by John Updike. Copyright © 1957 by John Updike. Originally appeared in *The New Yorker*.

p. 166, "Overweight Poem." Copyright © 1972 by Diane Wakoski from *Smudging*, published by Black Sparrow Press.

p. 167, "For My Lover, Returning to his Wife." From *Love Poems* by Anne Sexton. Copyright © 1967, 1968, 1969 by Anne Sexton. Reprinted by permission of Houghton Mifflin Company.

p. 171, "Ulysses." Reprinted by permission of Curtis Brown, Ltd. Copyright © 1933 by Robert Graves.

p. 174, "A Simile for Her Smile." From *Things of this World*. © 1956 by Richard Wilbur. Reprinted by permission of Harcourt Brace Jovanovich, Inc.

p. 174, "Bestiary for the Fingers of my Right Hand." Reprinted from *Dismantling The Silence* by Charles Simic by permission of the publisher, George Braziller, Inc. © 1971 by Charles Simic.

p. 176, "I Taste A Liquor Never Brewed." Reprinted by permission of the publishers

PERMISSIONS AND ACKNOWLEDGMENTS

and the Trustees of Amherst College from *The Poems of Emily Dickinson*, edited by Thomas H. Johnson, Cambridge, Mass.: The Belknap Press of Harvard University Press, Copyright 1951, © 1955, 1979 by the President and Fellows of Harvard College.

p. 176, "Departmental." From *The Poetry of Robert Frost* edited by Edward Connery Lathem. Copyright 1916, 1923, 1930, 1939, © 1969 by Holt, Rinehart and Winston. Copyright 1936, 1944, 1951, © 1956, 1958 by Robert Frost. Copyright © 1967 by Leslie Frost Ballantine. Reprinted by permission of Holt, Rinehart and Winston, Publishers.

p. 186, "To An Athlete Dying Young." From "A Shropshire Lad"—Authorised Edition—from *The Collected Poems of A. E. Housman*. Copyright 1939, 1940, © 1965 by Holt, Rinehart and Winston. Copyright © 1967, 1968 by Robert E. Symons. Reprinted by permission of Holt, Rinehart and Winston, Publishers. Permission granted by The Society of Authors as the literary representative of the Estate of A. E. Housman, and Jonathan Cape Ltd., publishers of A. E. Housman's *Collected Poems*.

p. 190, "Fence Wire." Copyright © 1966 by James Dickey. Reprinted by permission of Wesleyan University Press.

p. 194, "On Flunking a Nice Boy Out of School." Reprinted by permission of the author.

p. 196, "Desert Places." From *The Poetry of Robert Frost* edited by Edward Connery Lathem. Copyright 1916, 1923, 1928, 1930, 1939, © 1969 by Holt, Rinehart and Winston. Copyright 1936, 1944, 1951, © 1956, 1958 by Robert Frost, Copyright © 1967 by Lesley Frost Ballantine. Reprinted by permission of Holt, Rinehart and Winston, Publishers.

p. 198, "The Magi." From *Collected Poems by William Butler Yeats*. Copyright 1916 by Macmillan Publishing Co., Inc., renewed 1944 by Bertha Georgie Yeats. Reprinted with permission of M. B. Yeats and Anne Yeats, and Macmillan London Limited.

p. 199, "Journey of the Magi." From *Collected Poems 1909–1962* by T. S. Eliot, copyright, 1936, by Harcourt Brace Jovanovich, Inc.: copyright © 1963, 1964, by T. S. Eliot. Reprinted by permission of the publisher.

p. 202, "The Albatross." From *An Anthology of French Poetry from Nerval to Valery*, edited by Angel Flors.

p. 204, "Green Water Tower." Reprinted by permission; © 1977 *The New Yorker* Magazine, Inc.

p. 205, "The Heavy Bear Who Goes With Me." By Delmore Schwartz, *Selected Poems: Summer Knowledge*. Copyright 1938 by New Directions, © 1966 by Delmore Schwartz.

p. 206, "The Snow Man." Copyright 1923 and renewed 1951 by Wallace Stevens. Reprinted from *The Collected Poems of Wallace Stevens*, by Wallace Stevens, by permission of Alfred A. Knopf, Inc.

p. 213, "The Song of Wandering Aengus." From *Collected Poems*, by William Butler Yeats. Copyright 1906 by Macmillan Publishing Co., Inc., renewed 1934 by William Butler Yeats. Reprinted with permission of M. B. Yeats and Anne Yeats, and Macmillan London Limited.

p. 219, "The Faring." Copyright © 1974 by Robert Penn Warren.

p. 227, "The Waking." Copyright 1954 by Theodore Roethke from the book *The Collected Poems of Theodore Roethke*. Reprinted by permission of Doubleday & Company, Inc.

p. 230, "The Pennycandy store Beyond the El." By Lawrence Ferlinghetti, *A Coney Island of the Mind*. Copyright © 1958 by Lawrence Ferlinghetti.

p. 235, "The Soul Selects Her Own Society." Reprinted by permission of the publishers and the Trustees of Amherst College from *The Poems of Emily Dickinson*, edited by Thomas H. Johnson, Cambridge, Mass.: The Belknap Press of Harvard University Press, Copyright 1951, © 1955, 1979 by the President and Fellows of Harvard College.

p. 241, "Mending Wall." From *The Poetry of Robert Frost* edited by Edward Connery Lathem. Copyright 1916, 1923, 1928, 1930, 1939, © 1969 by Holt, Rinehart and Winston. Copyright 1936, 1944, 1951, © 1956, 1958 by Robert Frost. Copyright © 1967 by Lesley Frost Ballantine. Reprinted by permission of Holt, Rinehart and Winston, Publishers.

p. 242, "Westina." By Elizabeth Bishop, Copyright © 1956, 1957, 1969 by Elizabeth Bishop. Reprinted by permission of Farrar, Straus and Giroux, Inc.

p. 244, "Peter Quince At The Clavier." Copyright 1923 and renewed 1951 by Wallace Stevens. Reprinted from *The Col-

PERMISSIONS AND ACKNOWLEDGMENTS

lected *Poems of Wallace Stevens*, by Wallace Stevens, by permission of Alfred A. Knopf, Inc.

p. 246, "We Real Cool." From *The World of Gwendolyn Brooks* by Gwendolyn Brooks, copyright 1959 by Gwendolyn Brooks.

p. 247, "Anthem for Doomed Youth." From *Collected Poems of Wilfred Owen*. Copyright © Chatto & Windus, Ltd., 1946, 1963. Reprinted by permission of the Owen Estate and Chatto & Windus Ltd.

p. 248, "O sweet spontaneous." Reprinted from *Tulips & Chimneys* by E. E. Cummings by permission of Liveright Publishing Corporation. Copyright 1923, 1925, and renewed 1951, 1953 by E. E. Cummings. Copyright © 1973, 1976 by Nancy T. Andrews. Copyright © 1973, 1976 by George James Firmage.

p. 248, "Do Not Go Gentle Into That Good Night." From *The Poems of Dylan Thomas*. Copyright 1939, 1943, 1946, by New Directions. Reprinted with permission from David Higham Associates Ltd.

p. 252, "You Understand the Requirements." Copyright by Lyn Lifshin, 1973. From *Black Apples*, published by the Crossing Press, Trumansburg, New York, 14886.

p. 254, "The Scholars." From *Collected Poems*, by William Butler Yeats. Copyright 1919 by Macmillan Publishing Co., Inc., renewed 1947 by Bertha Georgie Yeats. Reprinted with permission of M. B. Yeats and Anne Yeats, and Macmillan London.

p. 254, "Theme for English B." Reprinted by permission of Harold Ober Associates Incorporated. Copyright © 1949, 1977 by Langston Hughes.

p. 255, "Zimmer's Head Thudding Against the Blackboard." © 1969 by Paul Zimmer. Published by October House.

p. 255, "To My Students." © 1972 by A. Poulin, Jr. Reprinted from *In Advent* with the permission of the author.

p. 256, "A Teacher." From *The Mother's Breast and the Father's House* by Reed Whittemore. Copyright © 1974 by Reed Whittemore. Reprinted by permission of Houghton Mifflin Company.

p. 259, "First Practice." From *First Practice* by Gary Gildner, copyright © 1969 by Gary Gildner.

p. 260, "Tennis." Copyright © by Margaret Avison and reprinted by her permission.

p. 260, "Skiers." Copyright © 1968 by Robert Penn Warren.

p. 260, "Young Wrestlers." From *Rumors of Ecstasy, Rumors of Death*, The Ashland Poetry Press, Third printing, 1977.

p. 261, "To Satch." Permission granted by Samuel Allen, the author.

p. 262, "Surfers at Santa Cruz." Copyright © 1966 by Paul Goodman. Reprinted from *Collected Poems*, by Paul Goodman, edited by Taylor Stoehr, by permission of Random House, Inc.

p. 263, "Among School Children." From *Collected Poems* by William Butler Yeats. Reprinted with permission of Macmillan Publishing Co., copyright 1928 by Macmillan Publishing Co., Inc., renewed 1956 by Georgie Yeats. Reprinted with the permission of M. B. Yeats and Anne Yeats, and Macmillan London Ltd.

p. 265, "The Ball Poem." From *Short Poems* by John Berryman. Copyright 1948 by John Berryman. Copyright renewed © 1976 by Kate Berryman. Reprinted by permission of Farrar, Straus and Giroux, Inc.

p. 265, "My Papa's Waltz." Copyright 1942 by Hearst Magazines, Inc., from the book *The Collected Poems of Theodore Roethke*. Reprinted by permission of Doubleday & Company, Inc.

p. 266, "Daddy." From *Ariel* by Sylvia Plath, copyright © 1963 by Ted Hughes. Reprinted by permission of Harper & Row, Publishers, Inc. Reprinted with permission from Faber & Faber of London.

p. 268, "Those Winter Sundays." Reprinted from *Angle of Ascent*, New and Selected Poems, by Robert Hayden, with the permission of Liveright Publishing Corporation, Copyright © 1975, 1972, 1970, 1966, by Robert Hayden.

p. 268, "Parents." Copyright © 1980 by William Meredith. Reprinted from *The Cheer*, by William Meredith, by permission of Alfred A. Knopf, Inc.

p. 269, "Re Accepting You." Copyright 1978 by Naomi Lazard. All rights reserved.

p. 271, "Trying to Talk with a Man." Reprinted from *Poems, Selected and New, 1950–1974*, by Adrienne Rich, by permission of W. W. Norton & Company, Inc.

PERMISSIONS AND ACKNOWLEDGMENTS

Copyright © 1975, 1973, 1971, 1969, 1966 by W. W. Norton & Company, Inc. Copyright © 1967, 1963, 1962, 1961, 1959, 1958, 1957, 1956, 1955, 1954, 1953, 1952, 1951 by Adrienne Rich.

p. 272, "Lunchtime." Copyright © 1955 by David Ignatow from *The Gentle Weight Lifter*. Reprinted from Selected Poems by permission of Wesleyan University Press.

p. 272, "Ballad of A Thin Man." © 1965 WARNER BROS. INC. All Rights Reserved. Used By Permission.

p. 274, "When In Rome." From *I Am A Black Woman*, published by William Morrow & Company, 1970, by permission of the author.

p. 275, "Fable of the Mermaid and the Drinks." From *Selected Poems* by Pablo Neruda. Translated by Alastair Reid. Edited by Nathaniel Tarn. Copyright © 1970 by Anthony Kerrigan, W. S. Merwin, Alastair Reid, and Nathaniel Tar. Copyright © 1972 by Dell Publishing Co., Inc. Reprinted by permission of Delacorte Press/Seymour Lawrence.

p. 277, "A Late Aubade." From *Things of This World*, © 1956 by Richard Wilbur. Reprinted by permission of Harcourt Brace Jovanovich, Inc.

p. 278, "Passer Mortuus Est." From *Collected Poems*, Harper & Row. Copyright 1921, 1948 by Edna St. Vincent Millay.

p. 279, "Seduction." From *Black Feeling, Black Talk, Black Judgement* by Nikki Giovanni. Copyright © 1968, 1970 by Nikki Giovanni. By permission of William Morrow & Company.

p. 283, "Nikki-Rosa." From *Black Feeling, Black Talk, Black Judgement* by Nikki Giovanni. Copyright © 1968, 1970 by Nikki Giovanni. By permission of William Morrow & Company.

p. 284, "To Brooklyn Bridge." Reprinted from *The Complete Poems and Selected Letters and Prose of Hart Crane*, edited by Brom Weber, with the permission of Liveright Publishing Corporation. Copyright 1933, © 1958, 1966 by Liveright Publishing Corporation.

p. 285, "Lying in a Hammock at William Duffy's Farm in Pine Island, Minnesota." Copyright © 1961 by James Wright. Reprinted from *Collected Poems* by permission of Wesleyan University Press.

p. 285, "Subdivider." From *Short History of the Fur Trade* by Adrien Stoutenburg. Copyright © 1968 by Adrien Stoutenburg. Reprinted by permission of Houghton Mifflin Company.

p. 287, "Ballad of Birmingham." From *Poem Counterpoem*, copyright © 1966 by Dudley Randall. Reprinted by permission of Dudley Randall.

p. 288, "The Fury of Aerial Bombardment." From *Collected Poems 1930–1976* by Richard Eberhart. Copyright © 1976 by Richard Eberhart. Reprinted by permission of Oxford University Press, Inc.

p. 289, "Lady Lazarus." From *Ariel* by Sylvia Plath, copyright © 1963 by Ted Hughes. Reprinted by permission of Harper & Row, Publishers, Inc. Permission granted by Faber and Faber of London.

p. 292, "With Rue My Heart is Laden." From "A Shropshire Lad"—Authorized Edition—from *The Collected Poems of A. E. Housman*. Copyright 1939, 1940, © 1965 by Holt, Rinehart and Winston. Copyright © 1967, 1968, by Robert E. Symons. Reprinted by permission of Holt, Rinehart and Winston, Publishers. With permission of The Society of Authors as the literary representative of the Estate of A. E. Housman, and Jonathan Cape Ltd., publishers of A. E. Housman's *Collected Poems*.

p. 292, "I Heard a Fly Buzz." Reprinted by permission of the publishers and the Trustees of Amherst College from *The Poems of Emily Dickinson*, edited by Thomas H. Johnson, Cambridge, Mass.: The Belknap Press of Harvard University Press, Copyright 1951, © 1955, 1979 by the President and Fellows of Harvard College.

p. 293, "Church Going." Reprinted from *The Less Deceived* by permission of The Marvel Press, England.

p. 295, "The Jesus Infection." From *House, Bridge, Fountain, Gate* by Dorothy Parker. Reprinted by permission of Viking Penguin Inc.

p. 298, "In my Craft or Sullen Art." From *The Poems of Dylan Thomas*. Copyright 1939, 1943, 1946, by New Directions. Reprinted with permission of David Higham Associates Limited.

p. 299, "Constantly Risking Absurdity." By Lawrence Ferlinghetti, *A Coney Is-*

land of the Mind. Copyright © 1958 by Lawrence Ferlinghetti.

p. 301, "Musée des Beaux Arts." Copyright 1940 and renewed 1968 by W. H. Auden. Reprinted by permission of Faber and Faber Ltd from *Collected Shorter Poems 1927–1957*, by W. H. Auden.

p. 302, "Landscape With the Fall of Icarus." From *Pictures from Brueghel and Other Poems* by William Carlos Williams. Copyright © 1962 by William Carlos Williams.

p. 302, "The Knight, Death, and the Devil." From the *Complete Poems* by Randall Jarrell. Reprinted by permission of Farrar, Straus and Giroux, Inc.

p. 307, "The Seafarer." From *An Anthology of Old English Poetry*, translated by Charles W. Kennedy. Copyright © 1960 by Oxford University Press, Inc. Reprinted by permission.

p. 309, "Wild Swan." From *An Anthology of Old English Poetry*, translated by Charles W. Kennedy. Copyright © 1960 by Oxford University Press, Inc. Reprinted by permission.

p. 309, "Deor's Lament." From *An Anthology of Old English Poetry*, translated by Charles W. Kennedy. Copyright © 1960 by Oxford University Press, Inc. Reprinted by permission.

p. 344, "The Bustle in a House." Reprinted by permission of the publishers and the Trustees of Amherst College from *The Poems of Emily Dickinson*, edited by Thomas H. Johnson, Cambridge, Mass.: The Belknap Press of Harvard University Press, Copyright 1951, © 1955, 1979 by the President and Fellows of Harvard College.

p. 344, "I Died for Beauty." Reprinted by permission of the publishers and the Trustees of Amherst College from *The Poems of Emily Dickinson*, edited by Thomas H. Johnson, Cambridge, Mass.: The Belknap Press of Harvard University Press, Copyright 1951, © 1955, 1979 by the President and Fellows of Harvard College.

p. 345, "The Last Night That She Lived." Reprinted by permission of the publishers and the Trustees of Amherst College from *The Poems of Emily Dickinson*, edited by Thomas H. Johnson, Cambridge, Mass.: The Belknap Press of Harvard University Press, Copyright 1951, © 1955, 1979 by the President and Fellows of Harvard College.

p. 354, "Into My Heart An Air That Kills." From "A Shropshire Lad"—Authorized Edition—from *The Collected Poems of A. E. Housman*. Copyright 1939, 1940, © 1965 by Holt, Rinehart and Winston. Copyright © 1967, 1968 by Robert E. Symons. Reprinted by permission of Holt, Rinehart and Winston, Publishers. Reprinted with permission of The Society of Authors as the literary representative of the Estate of A. E. Housman, and Jonathan Cape Ltd., publishers of A. E. Housman's Poems.

p. 355, "On Moonlit Heath and Lonesome Bank." same as above.

p. 356, "Terence, This is Stupid Stuff." same as above.

p 359, "The City Limits." Reprinted from *Collected Poems,* 1951–1971 by A. R. Ammons, with permission of W.W. Norton & Company, Inc. Copyright © 1972 by A. R. Ammons.

p. 360, "So I Said I am Ezra." Reprinted from *Collected Poems, 1951–1971* by A. R. Ammons, with permission of W. W. Norton & Company, Inc. Copyright © 1972 by A. R. Ammons.

p. 360, "Winter Scene." Reprinted from *Collected Poems, 1951–1971* by A. R. Ammons, with permission of W. W. Norton & Company, Inc. Copyright © 1972 by A. R. Ammons.

p. 361, "My Erotic Double" from *As We Know* by John Ashberry. Copyright © 1979 by John Ashberry. Reprinted by permission of Viking Penguin Inc.

p. 361, "Lullaby." Copyright 1940 and renewed 1968 by W. H. Auden. Reprinted by permission of Faber and Faber Ltd from *Collected Shorter Poems 1927–1957* by W. H. Auden.

p. 362, "Epitaph on a Tyrant." Copyright 1940 and renewed 1968 by W. H. Auden. Reprinted by permission of Faber and Faber Ltd. from *Collected Shorter Poems. 1927–1957* by W. H. Auden.

p. 362, "The Love Feast." Copyright 1951 by W. H. Auden.

p. 363, "Preface to a Twenty Volume Suicide Note." Copyright © 1961 by LeRoi Jones (Amiri Baraka). Used by permission of The Sterling Lord Agency.

PERMISSIONS AND ACKNOWLEDGMENTS 453

p. 364, "A Professor's Song." From *Short Poems* by John Berryman. Copyright 1948 by John Berryman. Copyright renewed © 1976 by Kate Berryman. Reprinted by permission of Farrar, Straus, and Giroux, Inc.

p 364, "The Armadillo." From *The Complete Poems* by Elizabeth Bishop. Copyright © 1956, 1957, 1969 by Elizabeth Bishop. Reprinted with permission of Farrar, Straus and Giroux, Inc.

p. 365, "Driving to Town Late to Mail a Letter." From *Silence in the Snowy Fields*. Wesleyan University Press, 1962 © 1962 by Robert Bly, reprinted with his permission.

p. 365, " 'thousands—killed in action'," from "Leaves from a Loose-leaf war diary." From *The World of Gwendolyn Brooks* by Gwendolyn Brooks. Copyright © 1949, reprinted by permission of Harper & Row, Publishers, Inc.

p. 366, "Men Marry What They Need. I Marry You." By John Ciardi, reprinted by permission of the author.

p. 367, "The Window." From *Words* by Robert Creeley. Copyright © 1967 by Robert Creeley. Reprinted with the permission of Charles Scribner's Sons.

p. 368, "Next to of course god america i." Reprinted from *IS5 Poems* by E. E. Cummings by permission of Liveright Publishing Corporation. Copyright 1926 by Horace Liveright. Copyright renewed 1953 by E. E. Cummings.

p. 368, "she being brand." Reprinted from *IS5 Poems* by E. E. Cummings, by permission of Liveright Publishing Corporation 1926 by Horace Liveright. Copyright renewed 1953 by E. E. Cummings.

p. 369, "when serpents bargain for the right to squirm." Copyright 1948 by E. E. Cummings. Reprinted from his volume *Complete Poems 1913–1962* by permission of Harcourt Brace Jovanovich, Inc.

p. 370, "Adultery." Copyright © 1966 by James Dickey. Reprinted by permission of Wesleyan University Press.

p. 371, "Cherrylog Road." Copyright © 1963 by James Dickey. Reprinted by permission of Wesleyan University Press. First appeared in *The New Yorker*.

p. 373, "We Wear the Mask." Reprinted by permission of Dodd, Mead & Company, Inc. from *The Complete Poems of Paul Laurence Dunbar*.

p. 374, "Poetry, A Natural Thing." By Robert Duncan, from *The Opening of the Field*. Copyright © 1960 by Robert Duncan.

p. 375, "The Groundhog." From *Collected Poems 1930–1976* by Richard Eberhart. Copyright © 1976 by Richard Eberhart. Reprinted by permission of Oxford University Press, Inc. Permission granted by Chatto & Windus Ltd.

p. 375, "The Horse Chestnut Tree." From *Collected Poems 1930–1976*, by Richard Eberhart. Copyright © 1976 by Richard Eberhart. Reprinted by permission of Oxford University Press, Inc. Permission granted by Chatto & Windus Ltd.

p. 376, "The Love Song of J. Alfred Prufrock." From *Collected Poems 1909–1962* by T. S. Eliot, copyright, 1936, by Harcourt Brace Jovanovich, Inc.; copyright © 1963, 1964 by T. S. Eliot. Reprinted by permission of the publisher. Reprinted by permission of Faber & Faber Ltd from *Collected Poems 1909–1962*.

p. 380, "Neither Out Far Nor in Deep." From *The Poetry of Robert Frost* edited by Edward Connery Lathem. Copyright 1916, 1923, 1928, 1930, 1939, © 1969 by Holt, Rinehart and Winston. Copyright 1936, 1944, 1951, © 1956, 1958 by Robert Frost. Copyright © 1967 by Lesley Frost Ballantine. Reprinted by permission of Holt, Rinehart and Winston.

p. 380, "The Road Not Taken." From *The Poetry of Robert Frost* edited by Edward Connery Lathem. Copyright 1916, 1923, 1928, 1930, 1939, © 1969 by Holt, Rinehart and Winston. Copyright 1936, 1944, 1951, © 1956, 1958 by Robert Frost. Copyright © 1967 by Lesley Frost Ballantine. Reprinted by permission of Holt, Rinehart and Winston, Publishers.

p. 381, "A Supermarket in California." Copyright 1956, 1959 by Allen Ginsberg. Reprinted by permission of City Lights Books.

p. 381, "On Hearing 'The Girl With the Flaxen Hair.'" From *Black Feeling, Black Talk, Black Judgement* by Nikki Giovanni. Copyright © 1968, 1970 by Nikki Giovanni. By permission of William Morrow & Company.

p. 382, "More Light More Light." From *The Hard Hours,* by Anthony Hecht.

Copyright © 1967 by Anthony E. Hecht. Reprinted with the permission of Atheneum Publishers.

p. 383, "Wodwo." From *Selected Poems* by Ted Hughes. Copyright 1962 by Ted Hughes. Reprinted by permission of Harper & Row, Publishers, Inc. Reprinted by permission of Faber and Faber Ltd. from *Wodwo* by Ted Hughes.

p. 384, "Missoula Softball Tournament." Reprinted from *The Lady in Kicking Horse Reservoir,* Poems by Richard Hugo, by permission of W. W. Norton & Company Inc. Copyright © 1973 by Richard Hugo.

p. 384, "A Camp in the Prussian Forest." From *The Complete Poems* by Randall Jarrell. Copyright 1946 by *The Nation.* Copyright renewed © 1973 by Mrs. Randall Jarrell. Reprinted by permission of Farrar, Straus and Giroux, Inc.

p. 385, "Nude Descending a Staircase." Copyright © 1960 by X. J. Kennedy from the book *Nude Descending A Staircase.* Reprinted by permission of Doubleday & Company, Inc.

p. 386, "Permanently." From *Thank You and Other Poems* by permission of Kenneth Koch. Copyright © 1962 by Kenneth Koch.

p. 386, "Careless Love." From *The Poems of Stanley Kunitz 1928–1978,* by Stanley Kunitz. Copyright 1930, 1944 by Stanley Kunitz; Copyright © renewed 1958, 1971 by Stanley Kunitz. By permission of Little, Brown and Company in association with the Atlantic Monthly Press.

p. 387, "The Ache of Marriage." By Denise Levertov, from *O Taste and See.* Copyright © 1963, 1964 by Denise Levertov.

p. 387, "Losing Track." By Denise Levertov, from *O Taste and See.* Copyright © 1963, 1964 by Denise Levertov. "Losing Track" was first published in *Poetry.*

p. 388, "Animals Are Passing From Our Lives." Copyright © 1968 by Philip Levine. Reprinted by permission of Wesleyan University Press.

p. 389, "Memories of West Street and Lepke." From *Life Studies* by Robert Lowell. Copyright © 1956, 1959 by Robert Lowell.

p. 390, "Skunk Hour." From *Life Studies* by Robert Lowell. Copyright © 1956, 1959 by Robert Lowell.

p. 391, "You Andrew Marvell." From *New and Collected Poems 1917–1976* by Archibald MacLeish. Copyright © 1976 by Archibald MacLeish. Reprinted by permission of Houghton Mifflin Company.

p. 392, "Winter Verse for His Sister." Copyright © 1967 by William Meredith. Reprinted from *Earth Walk: New and Selected Poems,* by William Meredith, by permission of Alfred A. Knopf, Inc.

p. 393, "Listeners at the Breathing Place." From *Poems, Listeners At the Breathing Place* by Gary Miranda, (copyright © 1978 by Princeton University Press), p. 18. Reprinted by permission of Princeton University Press.

p. 393, "The Goose Fish." From *The Collected Poems of Howard Nemerov.* The University of Chicago Press, 1977. Reprinted by permission of the author.

p. 394, "You Are Odysseus." Reprinted from *Aspects of Eve,* poems by Linda Pastan, with the permission of Liveright Publishing Corporation. Copyright © 1970, 1971, 1972, 1973, 1974, 1975, by Linda Pastan.

p. 395, "The Applicant." From *Ariel* by Sylvia Plath, Copyright 1963 by Ted Hughes. Permission granted by Faber & Faber of London, copyright by Ted Hughes 1965.

p. 396, "Mirror." From *Crossing the Water* by Sylvia Plath. Copyright © 1963 by Ted Hughes. Originally appeared in *The New Yorker.* With permission from Faber & Faber of London, copyright Ted Hughes 1971.

p. 396, "Morning Song." From *Ariel* by Sylvia Plath, copyright 1961 by Ted Hughes. With permission from Faber & Faber of London, copyright by Ted Hughes, 1965.

p. 397, "In a Station of the Metro." By Ezra Pound, from *Personae.* Copyright 1926 by Ezra Pound.

p. 397, "The Bath Tub." By Ezra Pound, from *Personae.* Copyright 1926 by Ezra Pound.

p. 397, "The Roofwalker." Reprinted from *Poems, Selected and New, 1950–1974,* by Adrienne Rich, by permission of W. W. Norton & Company, Inc. Copyright © 1975, 1973, 1971, 1969, 1966 by W. W. Norton & Company, Inc. Copyright © 1967, 1963, 1962, 1961, 1959, 1958, 1957,

PERMISSIONS AND ACKNOWLEDGMENTS

1956, 1955, 1954, 1953, 1952, 1951 by Adrienne Rich.

p. 398, "Mr. Flood's Party." Reprinted with permission of Macmillan Publishing Co., Inc. From *Collected Poems* by Edwin Arlington Robinson. Copyright 1921 by Edwin Arlington Robinson, renewed 1949 by Ruth Nivison.

p. 400, "Dolor." Copyright 1943 by Modern Poetry Association, Inc., from the book *The Collected Poems of Theodore Roethke*. Reprinted by permission of Doubleday & Company, Inc.

p. 400, "I Knew A Woman." Copyright 1954 by Theodore Roethke, from the book *The Collected Poems of Theodore Roethke*. Reprinted by permission of Doubleday & Company, Inc.

p. 401, "Song for a Lady." From *Love Poems* by Anne Sexton. Copyright © 1967, 1968, 1969 by Anne Sexton. Reprinted by permission of Houghton Mifflin Company.

p. 401, "Us." From *Love Poems* by Anne Sexton. Copyright © 1967, 1968, 1969 by Anne Sexton. Reprinted by permission of Houghton Mifflin Company.

p. 402, "The Man Who Married Magdalene." From *Poets of Today II: Good News of Death and Other Poems*. Copyright © 1955 by Louis Simpson. Reprinted with the permission of Charles Scribner's Sons.

p. 403, "Dr. Joseph Goebbels." © 1977 by W. D. Snodgrass. Reprinted from *The Fuherer Bunker: A Cycle of Poems in Progress* with the permission of BOA Editions.

p. 403, "Old Apple Trees." Reprinted by permission; © 1971 *The New Yorker* Magazine, Inc.

p. 405, "Bess." From *Stories that Could Be True*, by William Stafford. Copyright © 1966 by William Stafford. Reprinted by permission of Harper & Row, Publishers, Inc.

p. 406, "Traveling Through the Dark." From *Stories That Could Be True* by William Stafford, copyright © 1960 by William Stafford. Reprinted by permission of Harper & Row, Publishers, Inc.

p. 406, "Anecdote of the Jar." Copyright 1923 and renewed 1951 by Wallace Stevens. Reprinted from *The Collected Poems of Wallace Stevens*, by Wallace Stevens, by permission of Alfred A. Knopf, Inc.

p. 406, "The Emperor of Ice-Cream." Copyright 1923 and renewed 1951 by Wallace Stevens. Reprinted from *The Collected Poems of Wallace Stevens*, by Wallace Stevens, by permission of Alfred A. Knopf, Inc.

p. 407, "And Death Shall Have No Dominion." From *The Poems of Dylan Thomas*. Copyright 1939, 1943, 1946, by New Directions. With permission of David Higham Associates Limited, the Trustees for the copyright for the late Dylan Thomas.

p. 408, "The Force That Through the Green Fust Drives the Flower." From *The Poems of Dylan Thomas*. Copyright 1939, 1943, 1946 by New Directions. With permission of David Higham Associates Limited, the Trustees for the copyright for the late Dylan Thomas.

p. 408, "Uneasy Rider." © Diane Wakoski 1981.

p. 409, "The Line of an American Poet." From *The Mother's Breast and the Father's House* by Reed Whittemore. Copyright © 1974 by Reed Whittemore. Reprinted by permission of Houghton Mifflin Company.

p. 410, "Cottage Street, 1953." Copyright © 1972 by Richard Wilbur. Reprinted from his volume *The Mind-Reader* by permission of Harcourt Brace Jovanovich, Inc.

p. 411, "Love Calls Us to the Things of This World." From *Things of this World*, © 1956 by Richard Wilbur. Reprinted by permission of Harcourt Brace Jovanovich, Inc.

p. 411, "Piazza Di Spagna, Early Morning." From *Things of this World*, © 1956 by Richard Wilbur. Reprinted by permission of Harcourt Brace Jovanovich, Inc.

p. 412, "Nantucket." From *Collected Earlier Poems of William Carlos Williams*. Copyright 1938 by New Directions Publishing Corporation. Reprinted by permission.

p. 412, "The Yachts." From *Collected Earlier Poems by William Carlos Williams*. Copyright 1938 by New Directions Publishing Corporation. Reprinted by permission.

p. 413, "A Blessing." Copyright © 1961 by James Wright. Reprinted from *Collected*

456 PERMISSIONS AND ACKNOWLEDGMENTS

Poems by permission of Wesleyan University Press. "A Blessing" first appeared in *Poetry*.

p. 414, "Between the World and Me." From *White Man, Listen* by Richard Wright. Copyright © 1957 by Richard Wright. Reprinted by permission of Doubleday & Company, Inc.

p. 415, "Sailing to Byzantium." Reprinted with permission of Macmillan Publishing Co., Inc. from *Collected Poems* by William Butler Yeats. Copyright 1928 by Macmillan Publishing Co., Inc., renewed 1956 by Georgie Yeats. Reprinted with the permission of M. B. Yeats and Anne Yeats, and Macmillan London Limited.

p. 416, "The Second Coming." Reprinted with permission of Macmillan Publishing Co., Inc. from *Collected Poems* by William Butler Yeats. Copyright 1924 by Macmillan Publishing Co., Inc., renewed 1952 by Bertha Georgie Yeats. Reprinted with the permission of M. B. Yeats and Anne Yeats, and Macmillan London Limited.

p. 417, "The Wild Swans at Coole." Reprinted with permission of Macmillan Publishing Co., Inc. from *Collected Poems* by William Butler Yeats. Copyright 1919 by Macmillan Publishing Co., Inc., renewed 1947 by Bertha Georgie Yeats. Reprinted with the permission of M. B. Yeats and Anne Yeats, and Macmillan London Limited.

ABOUT THE AUTHORS

James W. Kirkland (Ph.D., University of Tennessee, 1969) is Associate Professor of English and Director of Freshman Composition at East Carolina University. An experienced teacher of literature, folklore, and composition, he has published articles on various subjects, co-edited the text *Fiction: The Narrative Art* (Prentice-Hall, 1977), and served as advisory editor and reviewer for *Tar River Poetry*.

F. David Sanders, Professor of English at East Carolina University, is Coordinator of the Honors Program and Director of Undergraduate Studies in English. He holds a Ph.D. from the University of North Carolina at Chapel Hill. A specialist in Shakespeare and early seventeenth-century poetry, he has taught at the University of Richmond and the College of William and Mary in addition to East Carolina University, and he served several years as Assistant to the Director of Bread Loaf School of English at Middlebury College. He has authored several articles and co-authored a non-fiction novel.